JOHN T. DUNLOP
HARVARD UNIVERSITY

Industrial Relations Systems

SOUTHERN ILLINOIS UNIVERSITY PRESS

Carbondale and Edwardsville

FEFFER & SIMONS, INC.

London and Amsterdam

Library of Congress Cataloging in Publication Data

Dunlop, John Thomas, 1914–
  Industrial relations systems.

  (Arcturus books; AB 141)
  Reprint of the ed. published by Holt, New York.
  Bibliography: p.
  Includes index.
  1. Industrial relations. I Title.
[HD6971.D85   1977]   331   77-24354
ISBN 0-8093-0850-9

INDUSTRIAL RELATIONS SYSTEMS was first published in 1958, and I am grateful to the Southern Illinois University Press and to Professor Albert A. Blum of Michigan State University for again making it available through this reprint. The stated purpose of the volume was to present "a general theory of industrial relations; to provide tools of analysis to interpret and to gain understanding of the widest possible range of industrial-relations facts and practices." (p. vii) One measure of the extent to which this objective has been approached is to examine some of the diverse studies, cited in the note below, which were written by others with explicit resort to this theoretical schema.[1] Reference should also be made to my own more recent writings designed to elaborate or to illustrate the central theoretical analysis.[2]

It is unfortunate that more international comparative work has not been done on an industry basis, along the lines of chapters 5 and 6 on bituminous-coal and building in this volume. The study of Vernon H. Jensen on longshoring in five ports[3] is a

[1] Three volumes are illustrative: James D. Morris, *Elites, Intellectuals and Consensus, A Study of the Social Question and the Industrial Relations System in Chile* (Ithaca, New York: New York State School of Industrial Relations, Cornell University, 1966); John M. Baitsell, *Airline Industrial Relations, Pilots and Flight Engineers* (Division of Research, Graduate School of Business Administration, Harvard University, Boston, 1966); Kenneth F. Walker, *Australian Industrial Relations Systems* (Cambridge, Mass.: Harvard University Press, 1970).

[2] See, "The Industrial Relations System in Construction," in *The Structure of Collective Bargaining, Problems and Perspectives*, Arnold R. Weber, Ed. (The Free Press of Glencoe, Inc., 1961, pp. 255–77); "Industrial Relations Systems at Work," in *Essays in Industrial Relations Theory*, Gerald G. Somers, Ed. (Ames, Iowa: The Iowa State University Press, 1969, pp. 25–38); "Political Systems and Industrial Relations," Second World Congress, International Industrial Relations Association, Geneva, September 1–4, 1970.

[3] *Hiring of Dock Workers* (Cambridge, Mass.: Harvard University Press, 1964).

notable exception as is the work in process by Frederic Meyers on the glass industry. Such investigations require a detailed knowledge of technological and market forces as well as a perception of the independent influences of national industrial relations factors on the rules of the work place. Comparative studies among countries at national levels tend to emphasize political and ideological considerations and fail to illuminate the interaction among workers and their organizations, managers, and governmental agencies at the work place and in an industry.

The theoretical analysis of industrial relations systems illuminates two groups of questions which are of increasing interest across countries: (1) To what extent is there a long-run tendency for convergence among different national industrial relations systems? Are industrial relations becoming more similar, or less similar, between the United States and England or Western Europe, or between Eastern and Western countries? Will developing countries take on the same industrial relations features as advanced countries? (2) Under what circumstances, and to what extent, can industrial relations institutions or practices be transferred from one country to another? What is the experience with multi-national firms? What can be expected to be the long-term effect of the Common Market on national industrial relations? The attempt to impose United States institutions on Japan and Germany under military government did not prove successful. Yet some colonial transplants have not been dislocated by national independence and have even flourished. The British experience with industrial relations reform following the Donovan Report and the 1970 elections may provide some further evidence on these complex questions.

The systematic pursuit of industrial relations experience with the aid of analytical tools which stress the coherence and interdependence among the participants within an environment in a system has high intellectual rewards and can also be rewarding to a reflective participant.

JOHN T. DUNLOP

Cambridge, Massachusetts
October 1970

Preface

IT HAS BEEN ONLY A CENTURY and a quarter since England first achieved a significant measure of industrial activity. The industrial process has since spread to the rest of the Western world; it was adopted by Japanese leaders and by Communist intellectuals dedicated to the elimination of backwardness from old Russia in their lifetimes. Since the end of World War II the grossly underdeveloped countries, including the regions emerging from colonial status, have everywhere embarked upon industrial-development programs. Our generation is certain to see the emergence of an industrial world, save for a few stagnant areas. Just as it is ordinarily said that by 1830 [1] England as a whole had crossed the divide to an industrial society, so in our times the world as a whole will have passed this frontier on an irreversible journey.

Every industrializing community, regardless of its political form, creates workers and managers. The status of these workers and managers and their interrelations come to be defined in greater or lesser detail. The national state cannot ignore these vital relations in industrial society, particularly when governments in the contemporary world are actively engaged in stimulating and directing developmental programs. Industrial societies necessarily create industrial relations, defined as the complex of interrelations among managers, workers, and agencies of government.

[1] T. S. Ashton, *The Industrial Revolution 1760–1830*, London, Oxford University Press, 1948.

v

As is often the case in human affairs, there were raw facts of industrial relations long before their study became a recognized field of study. While writings concerned with industrial relations go back to the beginning of the industrial process, a systematic and theoretical discipline of industrial relations is still to be established. The earliest scholarly writings concerned the history of the organizations of workers and managers and the role of government.[2] There subsequently developed a few comparative studies among countries which tended to be theoretical to a degree; the comparative method leads to questions regarding the reasons for the observed comparisons and contrasts. The spread of industrialization is providing a rapidly expanding body of facts about industrial relations. In addition to the industrial-relations experience of more developed countries, there is now available for stimulating comparisons and contrasts the emerging relations among workers, managers, and governments in such countries as India, Brazil, Spain, and Yugoslavia, to mention only a few.

While there is no disposition here to deprecate the gathering of facts of industrial relations, and many additional detailed studies are imperative, the field of industrial relations today may be described in the words of Julian Huxley: "Mountains of facts have been piled up on the plains of human ignorance. . . . The result is a glut of raw material. Great piles of facts are lying around unutilized, or utilized only in an occasional and partial manner."[3] Facts have outrun ideas. Integrating theory has lagged far behind expanding experience. The many worlds of industrial relations have been changing more rapidly than the ideas to interpret, to explain, and to relate them.

My present interest is in a level of generality greater than that achieved in studies of particular industries or countries. But it

[2] For an account of the development of writings in the United States, see Mark Perlman, *Labor Union Theories in America, Background and Development*, Evanston, Ill., Row, Peterson and Company, 1958.

[3] *New Bottles for New Wine*, London, Chatto and Windus, 1957, pp. 95–96.

is not nearly so broad as a general theory of all social action.[4] It is limited to the industrial-relations aspects of social action in industrial societies. This volume reflects the judgment that far too much of the writing concerned with industrial relations, particularly in the United States, which has the largest output measured in bulk, has lacked intellectual rigor and discipline. The need has been for theoretical structure and orientation. This judgment does not preclude more limited analytical interests, staying closer to a set of facts, as is characteristic of the high quality of some recent British writings. But a greater degree of generality of conception is to be preferred in the light of the expanding scope of industrial-relations experience.

1. The present volume presents a general theory of industrial relations; it seeks to provide tools of analysis to interpret and to gain understanding of the widest possible range of industrial-relations facts and practices. This is admittedly an ambitious and precarious undertaking. But the objective is made less difficult by a number of recent studies of industrial relations in particular enterprises and industries in single countries, by a growing number of intercountry comparisons, and by the various studies of industrial relations in the course of economic development in the larger project which has provided the opportunity for the present volume.

2. An objective of this study is to illustrate a type of research and inquiry which may well provide a basis for a number of further volumes of comparative studies of industrial relations among different countries and industries.

3. This writing constitutes, for the author, an attempt to make one world of direct experience in industrial relations and the realm of ideas. Direct participation in a few industries in a single country over a period of ten or fifteen years has constituted a wealth of experience in some sense, but it could have been only

[4] T. Parsons, R. F. Bales, and E. A. Shils, *Working Papers in the Theory of Action*, Glencoe, Ill., The Free Press, 1953.

an infinitesimal speck of the universe of industrial-relations experiences. The challenge is to relate this direct experience to those of others and to the rapidly expanding universe of industrial-relations facts and experience.

The generalized framework is designed to be applicable at once to three broad areas of industrial-relations experience: (1) industrial relations within an enterprise, industry, or other segment of a country and to comparisons among such sectors, (2) industrial relations within a country as a whole and to comparisons among countries, and (3) industrial relations in the course of economic development.

In brief outline the theoretical framework is concerned with analyzing the workings of industrial-relations *systems* which may vary in scope from an enterprise to a sector or to a country as a whole. Regardless of its scope, an industrial-relations system is regarded as having certain common properties and structure and as responding to specified influences. It is the concept of an industrial-relations system upon which generality is based in this volume. Every industrial-relations system involves three groups of actors: (1) workers and their organizations, (2) managers and their organizations, and (3) governmental agencies concerned with the work place and the work community. Every industrial-relations system creates a complex of rules to govern the work place and work community. These rules may take a variety of forms in different systems—agreements, statutes, orders, decrees, regulations, awards, policies, and practices and customs. The form of the rule does not alter its essential character: to define the status of the actors and to govern conduct of all the actors at the work place and work community. The actors in an industrial-relations system are regarded as confronting an environmental context at any one time. The environment is comprised of three interrelated contexts: the technology, the market or budgetary constraints, and the power relations and statuses of the actors. The system is bound together by an ideology or understandings shared by all the actors. The central task of a theory of industrial relations is to explain why particular rules are established in particular industrial-relations systems and how and why they change in response to changes affecting the system.

But the test of a theoretical structure, aside from internal consistency and congruence with other bodies of ideas, must be its usefulness. The present volume is as much concerned with the application of the body of ideas as with formal constructs. They must stand or fall on the test of the additional insights and understanding they provide of industrial-relations practices, the propositions they indicate for further testing, and the new facts organized in new categories they require to be gathered.

Chapter 1 presents the central concept of an industrial-relations system at a given point in time; the main characteristics and structure of a system are outlined, but there is no systematic concern with change in the system over time.[5] The next three chapters (Chapters 2 through 4) indicate the consequence of each of the three major features of the environmental context of a system upon its body of rules. The three chapters consider in turn the technological environment, the market or budgetary constraints, and the power status or relations among workers, managers, and governmental agencies. Extensive illustrations are used to illuminate specific problems and to develop the richness and the usefulness of the central concept.

Chapters 5 through 7 are designed both to illustrate the general theory developed in the first four chapters and to present results of research which need to be carried forward on a broad front to compare within countries and among countries the rules developed by different industrial-relations systems. Chapter 5 compares certain of the rules developed by industrial-relations systems in bituminous-coal mining in eight countries: United States, Great Britain, France, Germany (Federal Republic), Italy,

[5] For an early formulation of these ideas, see "Systems of Management-Employee Relations and Economic Development," *12th Annual Conference on Industrial Relations Research*, University of Minnesota, May 25–26, 1956 (mimeographed).

Australia, New Zealand, and Poland. Chapter 6 makes the same types of comparisons for rules developed by the building sectors in nine countries: United States, Great Britain, Switzerland, France, Germany, Spain, Yugoslavia, Australia, and the Netherlands. These studies probably constitute the first attempt to make such comprehensive comparisons among rules developed by industrial-relations systems. These results are significant because they permit careful study of the relative influence of technological and market or budgetary constraints on rules of the work place and work community compared to the influence of the national characteristics of an industrial-relations system. The chapters are designed to answer the question of the extent to which the rules regulating the work place and work community in bituminous-coal mining and building are similar among different countries and the extent to which they are unique to particular countries. Chapter 7 is an account of the Yugoslav national industrial-relations system and is presented both because of its intrinsic interest and as a further application of the central ideas of the volume. It also introduces the problems of an industrial-relations system in the course of economic development.

Chapters 8 and 9 are directed to a systematic treatment of industrial-relations systems in the process of change over time and in the course of economic growth. Chapter 8 is concerned with the emergence of national industrial-relations systems, and Chapter 9 treats changes in the rules of the work place and the work community in the course of economic development. These chapters are particularly related to the Inter-University Study of Labor Problems in Economic Development in that these chapters use the ideas of industrializing elites developed with my colleagues in that project. Chapter 10 is a summation of the theoretical core of the volume.

This study is at once both a product of five years of association with President Clark Kerr of the University of California, Professor Frederick H. Harbison of Princeton University, and Professor Charles A. Myers of the Massachusetts Institute of Technology in the inter-university research project and a longer period of research and practice in what has come to be called the field of industrial relations. It has been a most stimulating and fruitful experience to be associated systematically for such a period with these colleagues, and it is a pleasure to acknowledge my indebtedness to their courtesy and discipline. Professor Myers generously provided comments on the manuscript at the cost of considerable inconvenience to his schedule. This inter-university project is unique among university groups for it has been largely concerned with ideas and substance in contrast to the too-frequent academic gatherings which tend to be diverted too easily to administrative matters, and it has extended over a period of years to permit frequent and systematic interchange of ideas. We are indebted in large part to the Ford Foundation for financial support of the Inter-University Study of Labor Problems in Economic Development.

This volume was written during the academic year 1957–1958 while I was on leave in Geneva, Switzerland, under the financial auspices of the project. I am particularly indebted to Mr. David A. Morse, the director general of the International Labor Office, to Dr. E. J. Riches, Dr. Robert Myers, Mr. John Price, Mr. Robert Gavin, and Mr. Jean de Givry, respectively the chiefs of the ILO divisions of Economics, Statistics, Industrial Committees, Non-metropolitan Territories, and Labor-Management Relations, and to numerous other members of the staff of the ILO whose courtesy and gracious assistance made the period in Geneva so useful to this study. Other acknowledgments are made at the outset of particular chapters.

The typing of several drafts of the manuscript, under the handicap of correspondence, has been performed most conscientiously by Mrs. Nancy M. Richardson, who has also generously attended to a variety of details during this year of freedom from students, committees, and the telephone.

The extensive translations quoted in Chapters 5 and 6 have, in almost every case, been made particularly for this study by professional translators in Geneva experienced in this field. Their assistance is gratefully appreciated.

Two final words of caution are appropriate. First, it is often difficult to find concepts in one industrial-relations system that fully correspond to those in another. The problem is more than a matter of language. It arises from basic differences among industrial-relations systems and among the larger communities. An illustration is afforded by the apparently simple terms "worker" and "employee" which, in the United States, have no rigorous differentiation. The terms *arbeiter* and *angestellter* in Germany (F.R.) or *radnici* and *službenici* in Yugoslavia convey differences in groupings of people in jobs and even social differentiations that are only defined in the full setting of these national systems. Second, while every reasonable precaution has been taken, it is not unlikely that in handling the very large body of empirical material in Chapters 5 through 9 some minor factual misstatements or failure to present a situation with full understanding may have arisen. But such lapses could not affect the central purpose to present a general theory of industrial relations, to use the tools to illuminate specific industrial-relations experience, and to propose the collection of new facts and new studies.

J.T.D.

Geneva, Switzerland
June 30, 1958.

Contents

1 · An Industrial Relations System

THERE are marked differences in industrial relations among enterprises, industries, and countries. While each work place is to a degree unique, there are groups of situations with common industrial-relations features. A participant—be he manager, worker, representative of workers, neutral, or government agent —moving from one place to another will recognize familiar arrangements; other moves will reveal strange surroundings. Practical experience in the United States would identify a distinctive pattern of industrial relations within the railroad industry, the maritime field, basic steel, a construction site, the plants of General Motors, the newspaper offices in metropolitan New York City, the Bank of America in California, or the offices of federal government departments. Each of these cases constitutes a system of industrial relations. For some purposes these illustrations may be broken down into smaller and more distinctive systems, and for other purposes they may be integrated into still larger systems. Men with industrial-relations experience identify and distinguish among systems on the basis of rules of thumb developed out of experience.

Practitioners recognize that within a single industrial-relations system there are common problems, distinctive from those posed

1

in other systems; there tend to be distinctive solutions. A system has a certain unity; changes in one part of a system affect other parts of that system more directly than they affect other systems. The participants are more attuned to developments within the system than without; they share distinctive common beliefs and prejudices. The perceptions of the sensitive practitioner are no substitute for systematic analysis, but they are a suggestive starting point.

The literature on industrial relations has recently begun to make explicit use of the term "system," particularly to describe features characteristic of one country and distinguished from others.[1] Two studies are illustrative: *The System of Industrial Relations in Great Britain*[2] and "The American System of Industrial Relations."[3] "System" in these writings does not mean a planned order. ". . . We have chosen to deal with so vital a matter as the relations between employers and employed in an extremely involved and haphazard fashion. This is, after all, an age of planning. Yet in no part of our economic life is planning so strongly opposed by all classes in the community."[4] "The ardent advocates of economic planning may be shocked by the haphazard consequences of our voluntary system; they see power overriding equity, tradition barring the way to rational change, and muddled compromise being preferred to ordered consistency."[5] "Perhaps it is wrong to designate as a 'system' a group of arrangements that has grown up without being planned as a whole. . . . Our arrangements in the field of industrial relations may be regarded as a system in the sense that each of them more

---

[1] The term is used in the titles: Walter Galenson, *The Danish System of Labor Relations: A Study in Industrial Peace*, Cambridge, Mass., Harvard University Press, 1952; Paul H. Norgren, *The Swedish Collective Bargaining System*, Cambridge, Mass., Harvard University Press, 1941.

[2] Edited by Allan Flanders and H. A. Clegg, Oxford, Basil Blackwell and Mott, 1954. See pp. v, 260, 285.

[3] Sumner H. Slichter, in *Arbitration Today, Proceedings of the Eighth Annual Meeting, National Academy of Arbitrators*, Boston, Massachusetts, January 27 and 28, 1955 (BNA Inc., Washington, D. C., 1955), pp. 167–186.

[4] Flanders and Clegg, *loc. cit.*, p. 260.

[5] *Ibid.*, p. 315.

or less intimately affects each of the others so that they constitute a group of arrangements for dealing with certain matters and are collectively responsible for certain results." [6])

The present interest in industrial-relations systems is to be sharply distinguished from classifications of union-management relationships in the spectrum of labor peace and warfare.[7] These typologies use such terms as open conflict, armed truce, arms-length bargaining, and full cooperation; in one sense each may be regarded as a different system of relationships between parties. The concern with labor peace or warfare probably has stimulated interest in the larger subject of industrial-relations systems, but such classifications have almost no relevance to the present inquiry.

What meaning, then, is to be given to an "industrial-relations system"? In what sense is a "system" involved? Can the term be given rigorous and analytical definition, or shall it remain a perceptive phrase corresponding to the insights of practical experience? Are there characteristics common to all industrial-relations systems? What factors distinguish one industrial-relations situation from another? Can the same concept be used to facilitate analysis among sectors within a country and also among countries? These questions are suggestive of the major problem of this chapter: to provide *analytical* meaning to the idea of an industrial-relations system.

INDUSTRIAL RELATIONS AND INDUSTRIAL SOCIETY

In primitive and agrarian societies the analogue of industrial-relations problems arise—such as, who shall perform what work, what standards of discipline shall be applied at the work place, or

---

[6] Slichter, *loc. cit.*, p. 168.

[7] Benjamin M. Selekman, "Varieties of Labor Relations," *Harvard Business Review*, March 1949, pp. 175–199; F. H. Harbison and J. R. Coleman, *Goals and Strategy in Collective Bargaining*, New York, Harpers and Brothers, 1951; National Planning Association, *Causes of Industrial Peace*, New York, Harpers and Brothers, 1955.

how shall the fruits of labor be divided. These issues are typically handled within the extended family which is closely integrated into the society. In the plantation-slave society the corresponding problems are met by the political institutions that maintain slavery.[8] Thus, industrial-relations problems of a general type are not unique to modern industrial society. But industrial society, whatever its political form, creates a distinctive group of workers and managers. The relations among these workers and managers, and their organizations, are formally arranged in the industrial society outside the family and distinct from political institutions, although the family and political institutions may in fact be used to shape or control relations between managers and workers at the industrial work place.[9]

The full range of the complex interactions among groups and persons in a modern industrial society does not admit of ready description or explanation. The social system as a whole is ordinarily regarded as the province of sociology. Economics has carved out from the fullness of social action certain limited facets of behavior. Within the confines of these abstractions, it has developed rigorous theoretical models and analytical propositions relevant to these limited aspects of total social behavior. There is no purely economic behavior, but economists have developed significant and useful propositions about the economic aspects of behavior. They have also organized specialized collections of facts, often built around special-purpose concepts and definitions such as the national-income accounts or input-output tables. Thus has economics become highly developed as a discipline.

The economic system can be regarded as a subsystem of the more general total social system. Few scholars have explored the interrelations and boundary lines between a general system of social action and economics more comprehensively nor persist-

[8] W. Arthur Lewis, *The Theory of Economic Growth*, London, George Allen and Unwin, 1955, pp. 107–113.
[9] Clark Kerr, Frederick H. Harbison, John T. Dunlop and Charles A. Myers, "The Labour Problem in Economic Development," *International Labour Review*, March 1955, pp. 223–235.

ently than has Professor Talcott Parsons.[10] While it would be interesting to apply directly the general analytical scheme developed by Professor Parsons and various associates to the industrial-relations features of industrial society,[11] such an exercise is not the central interest here. Nonetheless, the analogy of economics, an economic system, and the relations between the economic aspects of behavior and the totality of social action is suggestive for organizing insights and observations about the industrial-relations aspects of behavior in industrial society.

1. An industrial-relations system is to be viewed as an analytical subsystem of an industrial society on the same logical plane as an economic system, regarded as another analytical subsystem. The industrial-relations system is not coterminus with the economic system; in some respects the two overlap and in other respects both have different scopes. The procurement of a work force and the setting of compensation for labor services are common centers of interest. A systematic explanation of production, however, is within economics but outside the scope of industrial relations. The full range of rule-making governing the work place is outside the scope of an economic system but central to an industrial-relations system.

2. An industrial-relations system is not a subsidiary part of an economic system but is rather a separate and distinctive subsystem of the society, on the same plane as an economic system. Thus, the theoretical tools designed to explain the economic system are not likely to be entirely suitable to another different analytical subsystem of society.

3. Just as there are relationships and boundary lines between a society and an economy, so also are there between a society

---

[10] Talcott Parsons and Neil J. Smelser, *Economy and Society, A Study in the Integration of Economy and Social Theory*, London, Routledge and Kegan Paul, 1956. A social system is defined as ". . . the system generated by any process of *interaction*, on the socio-cultural level, between two or more actors.' The actor is either a concrete human individual [a person] or a collectivity of which a plurality of persons are members" (p. 8).

[11] For a suggestion in this direction see the brief note at the end of this chapter.

and an industrial-relations system. All analysis of the economy makes some assumptions, explicitly or implicitly, about the remainder of the social system; so also must an analysis of an industrial-relations system make some assumptions about the rest of the social system.

4. An industrial-relations system is logically an abstraction just as an economic system is an abstraction. Neither is concerned with behavior as a whole. There are no actors whose whole activity is confined *solely* to the industrial-relations or economic spheres, although some may approach this limit. Neither an economic system nor an industrial-relations system is designed simply to describe in factual terms the real world of time and space. Both are abstractions designed to highlight relationships and to focus attention upon critical variables and to formulate propositions for historical inquiry and statistical testing.

5. This view of an industrial-relations system permits a distinctive analytical and theoretical subject matter. To date the study of industrial relations has had little theoretical content. At its origins and frequently at its best, it has been largely historical and descriptive. A number of studies have used the analysis of economics particularly in treating wages and related questions, and other studies, particularly of factory departments, have borrowed the apparatus of anthropology and sociology.[12] Although industrial relations aspires to be a discipline, and even though there exist separate professional societies, industrial relations has lacked any central analytical content. It has been a crossroads where a number of disciplines have met—history, economics, government, sociology, psychology, and law. Industrial relations requires a theoretical core in order to relate isolated facts, to point to new types of inquiries, and to make research more additive. The study of industrial-relations systems provides a genuine discipline.

[12] W. H. Scott, J. A. Banks, A. H. Halsey, and T. Lupton, *Technical Change and Industrial Relations, A Study of the Relations between Technical Change and the Social Structure of a Large Steelworks*, Liverpool, Liverpool University Press, 1956, pp. 263–281.

6. Three separate analytical problems are to be distinguished in this framework: (a) the relation of the industrial-relations system to the society as a whole, (b) the relation of the industrial-relations system to the subsystem known as the economic system, and (c) the inner structure and characteristics of the industrial-relations subsystem itself. These questions have not ordinarily been separated in industrial-relations discussion, and what is given and what is variable accordingly has not been clearly stated. These issues are quite distinct. The next section considers the structure and characteristics of the industrial-relations sub-system of industrial society.

STRUCTURE OF AN INDUSTRIAL-RELATIONS SYSTEM

An industrial-relations system at any one time in its development is regarded as comprised of certain actors, certain contexts, an ideology which binds the industrial-relations system together, and a body of rules created to govern the actors at the work place and work community.

The Actors in a System

The actors are: (1) a hierarchy of managers and their representatives in supervision, (2) a hierarchy of workers (nonmanagerial) and any spokesmen, and (3) specialized governmental agencies (and specialized private agencies created by the first two actors) concerned with workers, enterprises, and their relationships. These first two hierarchies are directly related to each other in that the managers have responsibilities at varying levels to issue instructions (manage), and the workers at each corresponding level have the duty to follow such instructions (work).

The hierarchy of workers does not necessarily imply formal organizations; they may be said to be "unorganized" in popular usage, but the fact is, that wherever they work together for any considerable period, at least an informal organization comes to be formulated among the workers with norms of conduct and attitudes toward the hierarchy of managers. In this sense workers in a continuing enterprise are never unorganized. The formal hierarchy of workers may be organized into several competing or complementary organizations, such as works councils, unions, and parties.

(The hierarchy of managers need have no relationship to the ownership of the capital assets of the work place; the managers may be public or private or a mixture in varying proportions. In the United States, for instance, consider the diverse character of management organizations in the executive departments of the federal government, local fire departments, the navy yards, the Tennessee Valley Authority, municipal transit operations and local utilities, government-owned and privately operated atomic-energy plants, railroads and public utilities, and other private enterprises. The range of combinations is greater where governments own varying amounts of shares of an enterprise and where special developmental programs have been adopted. The management hierarchy in some cases may be contained within an extended or a narrow family, and its activities largely explained in terms of the family system of the society.

(The specialized government agencies as actors may have functions in some industrial-relations systems so broad and decisive as to override the hierarchies of managers and workers on almost all matters. In other industrial-relations systems the role of the specialized governmental agencies, at least for many purposes, may be so minor or constricted as to permit consideration of the direct relationships between the two hierarchies without reference to governmental agencies, while in still other systems the worker hierarchy or even the managerial hierarchy may be assigned a relatively narrow role. But in every industrial-relations system these are the three actors.[13]

[13] The term "actor" may have the limitation that it conveys the unreality or pretense of the stage. But "participant" is too passive, and other terms are no more satisfactory. Actor is used in the sense of doer or reagent.

The Contexts of a System

The actors in an industrial-relations system interact in a setting which involves three sets of givens. These features of the environment of an industrial-relations system are determined by the larger society and its other subsystems and are not explained within an industrial-relations system. These contexts, however, are decisive in shaping the rules established by the actors in an industrial-relations system. The significant aspects of the environment [14] in which the actors interact are: (1) the technological characteristics of the work place and work community, (2) the market or budgetary constraints which impinge on the actors, and (3) the locus and distribution of power in the larger society.

The technological features of the work place have very far reaching consequences for an industrial-relations system, influencing the form of management and employee organization, the problems posed for supervision, many of the features of the required labor force, and the potentialities of public regulation. The mere listing of a few different work places reveals something of the range of industrial-relations systems within an industrial society and the influence of the technological characteristics: airlines, coal mines, steel mills, press and wire services, beauty parlors, merchant shipping, textile plants, banks, and food chain stores, to mention only a few. The technological characteristics of the work place, including the type of product or service created, go far to determine the size of the work force, its concentration in a narrow area or its diffusion, the duration of employment at one locale, the stability of the same working group, the isolation of the work place from urban areas, the proximity of work and living quarters, the contact with cus-

[14] ". . . There does always exist some organization of living matter whose function is to maintain itself in direct interaction with its environment. In the terminology of modern genetics, we may speak of this as the phenotypic system." Julian Huxley, "Evolution, Cultural and Biological," in *New Bottles For New Wine*, London, Chatto and Windus, 1957, p. 63.

tomers, the essentiality of the product to the health and safety or to the economic development of the community, the handling of money, the accident potential, the skill levels and education required, the proportions of various skills in the work force, and the possibilities of the employment of women and children. These and many other features of the technology of the work place are significant to the type of managerial and worker hierarchies and government agencies that arise. They also pose very different types of problems for the actors and constrain the types of solutions to these problems that may be invented and applied. Significant differences among industrial-relations systems are to be attributed to this facet of the environment, and, in turn, identical technological environments in quite different national societies may be regarded as exerting a strong tendency upon the actors (modified by other factors) to create quite similar sets of rules.

The market or budgetary constraints are a second feature of the environmental context which is fundamental to an industrial-relations system. These constraints often operate in the first instance directly upon the managerial hierarchy, but they necessarily condition all the actors in a particular system. The context may be a market for the output of the enterprise or a budgetary limitation or some combination of the two. The product market may vary in the degree and character of competition through the full spectrum from pure competition, monopolistic competition and product differentiation, to oligopoly and monopoly. A charitable institution or a nationalized plant is no less confronted by a financial restraint than a private business enterprise, and the harshness of the budgetary strictures which confront managements vary among nonmarket units in the same way that degrees of competition vary among market-oriented enterprises. These constraints are no less operative in socialist than in capitalist countries. The relevant market or budgetary constraints may be local, national, or international depending on the industrial-relations system; the balance of payments constitutes the form of the market restraint for nationwide systems.

The product market or budget is a decisive factor in shaping the rules established by an industrial-relations system.[15] The history in the past generation of the textile and coal industries around the world is testimony to the formative influence of the market or budgetary influence on the operation of industrial-relations systems. The contrasts between industries sheltered or exposed to international competition is another illustration. The interdependence of wage and price fixing in public utilities gives a distinctive characteristic to these systems of industrial relations. The degrees of cost and price freedom in monopolistic industries permeate these industrial-relations systems. The market or budgetary context also indirectly influences the technology and other characteristics of the work place: the scale and size of operations and the seasonal and cyclical fluctuations in demand and employment. An industrial-relations system created and administered by its actors is adaptive to its market and budgetary constraints.

The locus and distribution of power [16] in the larger society, of which the particular industrial-relations complex is a subsystem, is a third analytical feature of the environmental context. The relative distribution of power among the actors in the larger society tends to a degree to be reflected within the industrial-relations system; their prestige, position, and access to the ultimates of authority within the larger society shapes and constrains an industrial-relations system. At this juncture the concern is not with the distribution of power *within* the industrial-relations system, the relative bargaining powers among the actors, or their controls over the processes of interaction or rule setting. Rather the reference is to the distribution of power

---

[15] John T. Dunlop, *Wage Determination under Trade Unions*, New York, The Macmillan Company, 1944, pp. 95–121.

[16] S. K. and B. M. Selekman, *Power and Morality in a Business Society*, New York, McGraw-Hill Book Company, 1956.

outside the industrial-relations system, which is given to that system. It is, of course, possible that the distribution of power within the industrial-relations system corresponds exactly to that within the contextual society. But that this need not be so is illustrated by numerous instances of conflict between economic power within an industrial-relations system and political power within a society, or by the tendency for an actor to seek to transfer a conflict to the political or economic arena in which his control over the situation is thought to be relatively greater. The general strike and French and Italian experience for a period after World War II particularly illustrate the point. The dominance of an army group, a traditional and dynastic family elite, a dictator, the church, a colonial administrator, a political party, or public opinion are types of power orientation in the larger society that tend to shape an industrial-relations system.

The distribution of power in the larger society does not directly determine the interaction of the actors in the industrial-relations system. Rather, it is a context which helps to structure the industrial-relations system itself. The function of one of the actors in the industrial-relations system, the specialized governmental agencies, is likely to be particularly influenced by the distribution of power in the larger society. Industrial-relations systems national in scope as different as those in contemporary Spain, Egypt, USSR, Yugoslavia, and Sweden call attention to the distribution of power within the larger society. Industrial-relations systems of a lesser scope, such as those at the plant level, are also shaped by the distribution of power within the industrial-relations system which is exterior to the plant level. Thus, the industrial-relations system at a plant level which is part of a highly centralized industrywide arrangement is quite different from one which is decentralized to the plant level. The distribution of power in the society exterior to the industrial-relations system is regarded as given to that system and helps to shape its operations.

The full context of an industrial-relations system which is

given for the three actors consists at a given time in the development of that system of (1) the technological and work-community environment, (2) the market or budgetary constraints, and (3) the distribution of power in the contextual society.)

The Establishment of Rules

(The actors in given contexts establish rules for the work place and the work community, including those governing the contacts among the actors in an industrial-relations system. This network or web of rules [17] consists of procedures for establishing rules, the substantive rules, and the procedures for deciding their application to particular situations. The establishment of these procedures and rules—the procedures are themselves rules —is the center of attention in an industrial-relations system. Just as the "satisfaction of wants" through the production and exchange of goods and services is the locus of analysis in the economic subsystem of society, so the establishment and administration of these rules is the major concern or output of the industrial-relations subsystem of industrial society. In the course of time the rules may be expected to be altered as a consequence of changes in the contexts and in the relative statuses of the actors. In a dynamic society the rules, including their administration, are under frequent review and change.)

(There is a wide range of procedures possible for the establishment and the administration of the rules. In general terms the following ideal types can be distinguished: the managerial hierarchy may have a relatively free hand uninhibited in any overt way by the other two actors; the specialized governmental agencies may have the dominant role without substantial participation of the managerial or worker hierarchies; the worker hierarchy may even carry the major role in rule fixing; the manage-

---

[17] Clark Kerr and Abraham Siegel, "The Structuring of the Labor Force in Industrial Society: New Dimensions and New Questions," *Industrial and Labor Relations Review*, January 1955, pp. 163–164.

ment and worker hierarchies in some relationships may set the rules together without substantial participation of any specialized governmental agency; finally, the three actors may all play a consequential role in rule setting and administration. The procedures and the authority for the making and the administration of the rules governing the work place and the work community is a critical and central feature of an industrial-relations system, distinguishing one system from another.

The actors who set the web of rules interact in the context of an industrial-relations system taken as a whole, but some of the rules will be more closely related to the technical and market or budgetary constraints, while other rules will be more directly related to the distribution of power in the larger society. Thus maritime safety rules are related primarily to the technology of ships, while rules defining the relative rights of officers and crew aboard ship are related primarily to the distribution of power in a larger society. But safety rules are also influenced to a degree by the distribution of power in the full community, and the obligations and rights of officers and crew aboard ship are clearly conditioned to a degree by the technical problems of running a ship. While the context is an interdependent whole, some rules are more dependent upon one feature of this context than others.

A vast universe of substantive rules is established by industrial-relations systems apart from procedures governing the establishment and the administration of these rules. In general, this expanse can be charted to include (1) rules governing compensation in all its forms, (2) the duties and performance expected from workers including rules of discipline for failure to achieve these standards, and (3) rules defining the rights and duties of workers, including new or laid-off workers, to particular positions or jobs. The actual content of these rules varies enormously among systems, particularly, as will be shown, as a consequence of the technological and market contexts of the systems.

One of the major problems of this inquiry is to determine the extent to which similar rules are developed in different industrial-relations systems with common technological contexts and similar market or budgetary constraints. The inquiry also seeks to isolate in systems otherwise similar the separate influence of the locus of power in the larger society, the form of organization of the actors, and their relationships upon the substantive rules. In general terms the rules, including the procedures for establishing and administering them, may be treated as the independent variable to be "explained" theoretically in terms of other characteristics of the industrial-relations system.

Whatever the specific content of rules and regardless of the distribution of authority among the actors in the setting of the rules, the detailed and technical nature of the rules required in the operation of an industrial society tends to create a special group of experts or professionals [18] within the hierarchies of the actors. This group within each hierarchy has the immediate responsibility for the establishment and the administration of the vast network of rules. The existence of job-evaluation plans, incentive or piece-rate systems, engineering time studies, pension plans, or many seniority arrangements is ample evidence of the role of experts or professionals in rule-making. Indeed, one of the major problems within the hierarchies of actors is the difficulty of communication and genuine understanding between such experts and the rest of the hierarchy. There may be on occasion a greater community of interests and understanding among such experts in different hierarchies than between them and the lay members of their own hierarchy.[19]

The experts tend to place the interaction among organizations of workers and managers and special governmental agencies on a more factual basis with careful technical studies

[18] The term "professional" does not mean a member of one of the generally recognized established professions with access by formal education.

[19] George W. Brooks, "Reflections on the Changing Character of American Labor Unions," *Proceedings of the Ninth Annual Meeting, Industrial Relations Research Association*, December 28 and 29, 1956, pp. 33–43.

made within each of the various hierarchies, or on a cooperative basis. These expert or professional ties on specialized issues tend to add to the stability of the system and to bind the actors closer together. The resort to a study by experts is an established method of reducing, at least for a period, tensions that arise among the actors.

The rules of the system may be expressed in a variety of forms: the regulations and policies of the management hierarchy; the laws of any worker hierarchy; the regulations, decrees, decisions, awards, or orders of governmental agencies; the rules and decisions of specialized agencies created by the management and worker hierarchies; collective-bargaining agreements, and the customs and traditions of the work place and work community. In any particular system the rules may be incorporated in a number of these forms; they may be written, an oral tradition, or customary practice. But whatever form the rules may take, the industrial-relations system prescribes the rules of the work place and work community, including the procedures for their establishment and administration.

The Ideology of an Industrial-relations System

An industrial-relations system has been described so far in terms of actors who interact in a specified context and who in the process formulate a complex of rules at the work place and work community. A further element is required to complete the analytical system: an ideology [20] or a set of ideas and beliefs commonly held by the actors that helps to bind or to integrate the system together as an entity. The ideology of the industrial-relations system is a body of common ideas that defines the role and place of each actor and that defines the ideas which each actor holds toward the place and function of the others in the

[20] The term "shared understandings" has been suggested by Clark Kerr to characterize the English and American social scene. See Reinhard Bendix, *Work and Authority in Industry, Ideologies of Management in the Course of Industrialization*, New York, John Wiley & Sons, 1956, p. xii.

system. The ideology or philosophy of a stable system involves a congruence or compatibility among these views and the rest of the system. Thus, in a community in which the managers hold a highly paternalistic view toward workers and the workers hold there is no function for managers, there would be no common ideology in which each actor provided a legitimate role for the other; the relationships within such a work community would be regarded as volatile, and no stability would likely be achieved in the industrial-relations system. It is fruitful to distinguish disputes over the organization of an industrial-relations system or disputes that arise from basic inconsistencies in the system from disputes within an agreed or accepted framework.

Each of the actors in an industrial-relations system—managerial hierarchy, worker hierarchy, and specialized public agencies—may be said to have its own ideology.[21] An industrial-relations system requires that these ideologies be sufficiently compatible and consistent so as to permit a common set of ideas which recognize an acceptable role for each actor. Thus, in the industrial-relations system of Great Britain [22] the philosophy of "voluntarism" may be said in a general way to be common to all three actors; this accepted body of ideas defines the role for manager and worker hierarchies and defines their ideas toward each other within the system; it also prescribes the limited role for specialized public agencies. The ideologies which characterize the industrial-relations arrangements, for instance, of India [23] and the Soviet Union [24] are each different from the British.

The ideology of an industrial-relations system must be distinguished from the ideology of the larger society; but they can be expected to be similar or at least compatible in the developed industrial society. In the process of industrialization,

---

[21] For a discussion of managerial ideologies see *ibid.*

[22] Flanders and Clegg, *loc. cit.*, p. 260.

[23] Charles A. Myers, *Labor Problems in the Industrialization of India*, Cambridge, Mass., Harvard University Press, 1958.

[24] Isaac Deutscher, *Soviet Trade Unions*, London, Royal Institute of International Affairs, 1950; Joseph S. Berliner, *Factory and Manager in the USSR*, Cambridge, Mass., Harvard University Press, 1957, pp. 25–44, 271–278.

however, there may be marked differences between the ideology (relevant to the role of managers, workers, and public agencies) of the actors within the industrial-relations system and other segments of the larger society which may even be dominant, such as the ideology of the traditional agricultural landholders. Nonetheless, the ideology of an industrial-relations system comes to bear a close relationship to the ideology of the particular industrial society of which it is a subsystem. Indeed, in the absence of a general consistency of the two ideologies, changes may be expected in the ideologies or in other facets of the industrial-relations system.

The term ideology may convey a more rationalized and formalized body of ideas than is intended. The actors in the system are often inclined to be pragmatic and may hold ideas that are to a degree inconsistent or lack precision. But hierarchies of managers and workers (when formally organized) and public agencies also tend to develop or adopt intellectuals, publicists, or other specialists concerned with articulating systematically and making some form of order out of the discrete ideas of the principal actors. These statements, preachments, and creeds tend to be reworked and reiterated, and in the process even a fairly explicit ideology may emerge. Each industrial-relations system contains its ideology or shared understandings.

AN ILLUSTRATION

The preceding section has been concerned with developing in general outline the analytical concept of an industrial-relations system. It was a formal and definitional exercise, and no one looks for precise correspondence between the world of construct and the world of experience. But the concept may be clarified, and the unity and interdependence of a system may be more simply portrayed, if an illustration is very briefly presented at this stage of the exposition. For anyone familiar with the particular industrial-relations system, the description may appear more like a caricature.[25]

The railroads in the United States have a distinctive system of industrial relations. It gradually evolved over the past eighty years to its present form and has been relatively stable for almost three decades; there have been some changes in rules, of course, but the main structure of the system is well established. The actors are the Class I carriers, the national railway labor organizations, and the specialized governmental agencies including the National Mediation Board, the divisions of the National Railroad Adjustment Board, emergency boards, and the Railway Retirement Board.

The carriers above the management hierarchies of individual railroad companies are organized into three conference committees (Western, Eastern, and Southern railroads) and then usually into a negotiating committee for national cases. Within a single railroad the management structure is organized into divisions according to operating requirements, length of track, and other technological factors. At each level in the hierarchy from a division to all carriers as a group there are specialized personnel concerned with the formulation or administration of rules.

The labor organizations are comprised of some twenty-three national craft organizations which are federated together in several ways: the six shop crafts operate together on many problems of common concern in the repair shops; the fifteen nonoperating unions, including the shop crafts, negotiate together on general wage changes and fringe compensation; the operating unions have negotiated singly or in various combinations, but in no fixed grouping; almost all the organizations are affiliated to the Railway Labor Executives' Association. The union and management hierarchies from the division to the top levels have corresponding and opposite numbers at each level, and rule formu-

---

[25] Some readers may prefer to turn to the more detailed illustrative material of Chapters 5, 6, and 7.

lation and administration takes place at each level appropriate to the generality of the issue.

The specialized governmental agencies were established by national legislation in which both parties were actively involved in discussions and proposals, and on occasion the legislation reflected the agreed-upon views of the management and employee hierarchies. These agencies determine the bargaining representative for the craft or class, decide disputes over the administration of rules which cannot be directly resolved, and mediate and make recommendations on issues of new rules which cannot be otherwise settled. The parties are both very much involved in the processes by which policy-making appointments to these agencies are made.

The technological context of railroads has many distinctive features affecting the relations of managers and workers: the train operating divisions use small crews working together and in movement far from close and immediate supervision; complex and expensive equipment is utilized with a high ratio of capital to worker; the technology has produced steadily increasing speeds and longer trains; a very high degree of responsibility (and considerable skill) is required of the major operating positions; the costs of accidents can be consequential; the hours of operations for equipment may be around the clock, and they do not conform to normal factory schedules, although repair shops and many clerical operations conform to conventional workweeks; the transportation services are regarded as vital to many other industries and to the community generally; there is a high degree of continuity of operations in many departments, and the public-utility status of the railroads requires the maintenance of published service; there is intimate contact with the public in the train service and in the selling of tickets and at corresponding points with freight customers.

The market context may be characterized by the governmental determination of commodity and class freight rates and passenger fares (product prices), by the keen competition of other forms of transport, and by a high sensitivity to fluctuations in general levels of business activity.

The locus and distribution of power in the American community has had significant impacts on the structuring of the railroad industrial-relations system. The relatively larger role of governmental processes (legislative and administrative) in railroads for a very long period has led to the development of managerial and employee hierarchies particularly sensitive to and knowledgeable of the legislative and administrative bodies concerned with railroad matters as compared with most other management and labor organizations. The wide distribution of railroad workers across the country, even in agricultural states, combined with the significance of governmental agencies for railroads, has resulted in a legislative and administrative influence and expertise unrivaled among American labor organizations.

The ideological aspect of an industrial-relations system is likely to be most distinctive in considering a system of a whole country, and it has been suggested that the ideological character of a particular industrial-relations system within a country shares both many of the ideological features of the full industrial-relations system of the country and the ideological character of the whole society. The American railroad industrial-relations system does share much of the ideology of the American collective-bargaining system and society. All three actors have consistent ideas of their roles and the functions of the other actors. There are some distinctive ideas and interests which further help to bind this system together: the common concern with the growing competition of other forms of transportation has led on occasion to mutual discussions of common interests and to proposals for common action on such matters as state laws regulating the length of trains. There is some development of a sense of a common stake in a livelihood threatened by competition. Then, large sections of railway management have come from the ranks, perhaps more than in most industries, and this provides some sense of a common experience and a mutuality in looking at problems.

The rules developed by the railroad industrial-relations system are related to the contexts already noted: the historic rules on rates of compensation for operating personnel involve the "dual method of pay" under which elapsed time and mileage traveled affect earnings. The weight of engines and the length of train also affect earnings of some operating crafts. Nonoperating personnel have more conventional methods of compensation. These various methods of pay are tailor-made to the technological and market contexts. The rules regarding the rights and duties of employees are significantly affected by the continuity of railroad operations, by the difficulties of comparing individual workers over a whole railroad property, and by the large element of responsibility in many jobs. As a consequence "seniority" in specified "districts" has a distinctive role to play, and it permeates the whole system of rules. The rules on promotion, layoffs, and transfer were evolved from the technological and market contexts and are consonant with them and the rules on compensation. The procedures used for the administration of the complex of rules ending in the divisions of the boards of adjustment are likewise congenial to the other rules and to the geographical diversity of operations; the procedures work very slowly for there is less imperative for speed than in most other industrial-relations systems, and "retroactivity" to the date a claim is filed is a significant feature to the operation of the system. The procedures established by statute providing for the unique role of the government in the making of agreements, in the event the parties fail to agree (emergency boards), is derived from a common recognition within the system of the essential nature of railroad transportation to the national community. The absence of a fixed duration to collective-bargaining agreements and rules, except as occasionally otherwise specifically bargained, is a distinctive feature of the system attributable to the lengthy procedures used in making contracts and to the system of setting railroad rates and fares.

The railroad industrial-relations system has its own social customs. As distinct from formal channels, there are important informal and personal lines of communications among persons in all three groups of actors. The professionals in each group particularly develop distinctive habits in their interactions in conferences and formal hearings, in their places of meeting, and even in their social gatherings. "There is a great deal of affinity between those who were engaged in the same occupation . . .", ". . . the employers and workers . . . were bound together by a common experience and a common love for their occupation. . . ."[26] The railway industrial-relations system is a very human institution; flesh and blood soften analtyical bones.

Such a brief description of the American railroad industrial-relations system cannot adequately convey its distinctive features and internal unity since no systematic comparisons or contrasts have been drawn with other industrial-relations systems.[27] It is in the perspective of other systems that the reality and the distinctive characteristics of a system can be more fully appreciated and understood.

SOME IMPLICATIONS OF AN INDUSTRIAL-RELATIONS SYSTEM

In the preceding discussion, an industrial-relations system has been used on occasion to refer to a subsystem of a national society, at times to a system of industrywide scope, and in other settings to a system in a single enterprise. The term is designed

[26] International Labor Office, *Minutes of the Ninety-first Session of the Governing Body, London, 16–20 December, 1943*, p. 54; *Minutes of the 94th Session of the Governing Body, London, 25–31 January, 1945*, p. 61. (Sir Frederick Leggett, discussing the proposal of Mr. Ernest Bevin for industry committees.)

[27] For a more detailed treatment, see Jacob J. Kaufman, *Collective Bargaining in the Railroad Industry*, New York, King's Crown Press, 1954.

to be applied to each depending on the scope of the discussion. The smaller the unit to which the term is applied, the larger the context, and in general the larger the influence of givens outside the system. This multiple usage of the term only requires that the reference to scope be made clear in each instance. The formulation has the merit of facilitating comparisons (and contrasts) within a country, between comparable sectors of different countries, and between industrial-relations systems of countries taken as a whole.

The usage which has been developed recognizes that a group of allied systems may be integrated into a larger sector or into a national system. In turn many systems may be subdivided into specialized smaller systems depending upon the purpose at hand. The American railroad industrial-relations system is an integral part of the larger national system; it is also meaningful to explore the industrial-relations system on the Baltimore and Ohio Railroad or some other separable road and even in particular shops or a division. It must be recognized, however, that not all industrial-relations systems are equally compatible or divisible, and combinations and separations cannot be made arbitrarily which destroy the sense of unity in the resultant grouping.

The preceding formulation calls attention to the fact that a national industrial-relations system has a variety of more limited systems within it; they are not all the same, and the features that are ordinarily regarded as distinctive to a national system do not all enter equally into each industrial-relations system within its borders. It becomes evident that the industrial-relations system characteristic of a country or a region may arise because of the dominance of a particular industry. For instance, the relative influence of the automobile industry in Detroit and basic steel in Pittsburgh give industrial relations in these metropolitan areas a distinctive coloration. A company town is another illustration. In general terms, the industrial-relations system of any aggregate will be shaped by the relative prevalence of different types of the component systems.

The import of the discussion is that international comparisons of industrial-relations systems may be less fruitful, or even misleading, if confined solely to countrywide systems. It is essential to examine for comparable sectors and industries the component industrial-relations systems in the various countries. In such comparisons, with the technology and the market contexts relatively constant, it should be possible to highlight more sharply the separate effects and characteristics of the national industrial-relations systems. A comparison of industrial-relations systems across countries in such industries as maritime, coal mining, aviation, automobiles, textiles, basic steel, and construction, to mention a few which appear to have rather distinctive and decisive technological and market contexts, should permit some testing of the impact of national systems in these cases. Are the rules developed in these industries similar among countries or do they vary substantially? Which rules show considerable similarity and which reflect the diverse influences of the national industrial-relations systems? It may be suggested for exploration that in some industries, such as those just noted, the similar technological and market contexts result in a number of comparable rules, overriding the influence of national peculiarities, while in other sectors the influence of the national system is more paramount overriding any similarities in the technological and market context or reflecting significant differences in these elements of the context. A comparison of national industrial-relations systems and systems for particular sectors across national lines should accordingly prove of considerable theoretical interest. These issues are explored in considerable detail in Chapters 5 and 6.

It is suggested for further exploration that for industrial-relations systems of a lesser scope than a country, thus for an industry, the technological and market (or budgetary) contexts are likely to be most significant in influencing the comparative rules which emerge, and that in the comparison of national systems the locus and distribution of power in the larger communities, as given to the industrial-relations systems, is likely to be most significant in influencing the characteristics of the distinctive national rules. It may also be inferred, to be tested and explored later, that there is a higher degree of uniformity in the substantive content of rules among countries in comparable industries that concern the duties of employees, discipline, safety, and many aspects of compensation at the work place than the degree of similarity among rules concerning the establishment and administration of substantive rules. A diversity of procedures may still result in similar substantive rules.

The attention to industrial-relations systems places comparisons among systems on a basis to analyze differences (and similarities) of substance rather than form. The simple description of industrial relations in several countries (or in several industries in one country) tends to be concerned with institutional shapes and forms rather than with substantive operations of the systems. A description of practices in great Britain, for instance, would point out that rule-making is determined in some industries by voluntary private collective bargaining, in other industries by publicly established wages councils, and in still others by joint industrial councils (JIC). The description would go on to elaborate the differences in form, origins, and legislative background and the procedures that are used by these bodies. While these institutional variants are of interest for some administrative and historical purposes, they tend to obscure the unity of the British industrial-relations system. Allan Flanders has well said, "It is difficult to know where statutory regulation ends and voluntary regulation begins, it is still more difficult to discover any practical significance in the distinction between industries with JIC's and those with some other arrangements for collective bargaining." [28] The attention to rule-making in industrial-relations

[28] Flanders and Clegg, loc. cit., pp. 288–289.

systems provides a common denominator for the comparative analysis of systems of different forms.

The idea of an industrial-relations system implies a unity, an interdependence, and an internal balance which is likely to be restored if the system is displaced, provided there is no fundamental change in the actors, contexts, or ideology. Industrial-relations systems show considerable tenacity and persistence. The essential unity of an industrial-relations system raises doubts about the transfer of rules, practices, or arrangements from one system to another. There is, for example, a prima-facia case against the export of the terms of American collective-bargaining agreements or American-style trade unions to industrial-relations systems with essentially different actors, contexts, and ideologies. The same may be said, of course, for the export of features of any other industrial-relations system, except that in the spectrum of world experience the American arrangements are likely to be relatively more specialized.

In the preceding discussion, an industrial relations system was developed at one moment in time. But an industrial-relations system may also be thought of as moving through time, or, more rigorously, as responding to changes which affect the constitution of the system. The web of rules can be expected to change with variations in the three features of the context of the system. Changes may be expected in the complex of procedural and substantive rules with alterations in the technological context, in the market or budgetary constraints, and in the locus and distribution of power in the larger society. In this way Chapters 8 and 9 focus attention upon the consequences of economic development for industrial-relations systems. Changes may originate within the organizations of the actors, and the task of analysis is to indicate the consequences for the complex of rules. The formal analysis also suggests that changes in ideology, as a response to the larger society, may also come to have an impact upon the rules established by an industrial-relations system. An industrial-relations system provides a means of organizing inquiry into changes over time in the rules and other features of industrial relations.)

The chapter has set forth a formal theoretical framework with which to approach industrial-relations aspects of experience. The test of this concept of an industrial-relations system is to be found not primarily in its elegance (or lack of it) or even in its internal consistency but rather in the process of making detailed studies of industrial-relations systems among countries, on a countrywide and industry basis, and within a single country among different sectors. Only its application to particular situations will effectively show whether it usefully calls attention to significant relationships and enlightens new and neglected features of experience. The test of a model ultimately is in its use.)

NOTE

Professor Parsons regards every social system as differentiated into four primary functions or as confronted by four basic system problems: [29] (1) the adaptive function or the control of the environment for the attainment of the goals of the system—Adaptation (A); (2) the functional imperative of goal attainment or the mobilization of the necessary prerequisites for the attainment of given goals—Goal Gratification (G); (3) the function of maintaining solidarity among the actors in the system to permit effective operation—Integration (I), and (4) the function of maintaining the integrity of the system's value system and its institutionalization from pressures from cultural sources outside the value system and from motivational sources which may prevent persons from conforming to expected roles—Latent-pattern Maintenance and Tension Management (L).

As applied to a total (industrial) society these four functional imperatives correspond to four specialized structures or processes regarded as differentiated subsystems of society which themselves also possess the characteristics of social systems: (1)

[29] Parsons and Smelser, *loc. cit.*, pp. 18, 46–51.

the economy is the primary subsystem specialized to the adaptive function; its specialized output is the production of *income or wealth* as a contribution to the adaptive needs of society. (2) The polity or political functions of society is the subsystem specialized in achieving the capacity to attain the goals of the society; its specialized output is *power* as a contribution to the goal gratification needs of society. (3) The integrative subsystem relates the cultural value patterns to the motivational structures of individual actors to eliminate undue conflict and other failures of coordinations; its specialized output is *solidarity* as a contribution to the integration needs of society. (4) The pattern-maintenance and tension-management subsystem concerns the motivation of the actors and the integrity of the values of the system; its specialized output is *prestige* as a contribution to the needs of the society for tension management and pattern conformity.

Professor Parsons regards the economy as a social system and analyzes it in terms of the same four basic system problems. He then considers the relations between the economy as an analytical subsystem of society and the whole society in terms of each of the functions of a social system. That is, he develops the "boundary interchange" between the economy and the society. In this process the discipline of economics is placed analytically in reference to other social sciences concerned with society.

It should be possible in the general framework for social systems developed by Professor Parsons to treat the industrial-relations system (analogous to the economy) as an analytical subsystem of (industrial) society, to analyze an industrial-relations system in terms of the four functional imperatives of any social system, and to identify the corresponding specialized structures or processes. Finally it should be possible to explore the interchange at the boundary between the industrial-relations system and other subsystems of society. The exercise may provide an interesting application of the analysis of Professor Parsons and an indication of its usefulness in a different area, and at the same time it may illuminate the structure of the industrial-relations system and its relations to (industrial) society.[30]

The functional differentiation of an industrial-relations system and the corresponding specialized structures or processes may be defined as follows: (1) Adaptive—The regulatory processes or rule-making in which the specialized output is a complex of rules relating the actors to the technological and market environment and the frequent changes which pose problems of adaptation to the actors. (2) Goal Gratification—The polity or political functions in the subsystem are specialized toward the contribution of survival or stability of the industrial-relations system and to survival and stability of the hierarchies of the separate actors which is requisite for the attainment of goals by the actors. (3) Integration—The function of maintaining solidarity among the actors in the system is contributed by the shared understandings and common ideology of the system relating individual roles to the hierarchies and hierarchies to each other in turn. (4) Latent-pattern Maintenance and Tension Management—The function of preserving the values of the system against cultural and motivational pressures is provided by the role of the expert or professional in all three groups of actors in the system.

It can be seen how each of these functional differentiations contribute to each other and to the unity of an industrial-relations system. (A-G) The rule-making contributes to the attainment of stability and survival, and stability in turn requires a grid of rules. (A-L) The technical problems involved in rule-making contribute to enhance the role of the professional or expert, and his role in turn produces a reduction of tension (a literal drawing of the "heat") among the actors and is the repository and defender of the values of the system. (G-I) The attainment of stability and survival requires shared understandings relating the actors to each other, and an effective integra-

---

[30] The present application may not be acceptable to Professor Parsons, and it may reflect a lack of understanding of his theoretical system.

tion contributes to the achievement of stability and survival. (L-I) The reduction in tensions and the preservation of values contributed by the professionals is a force for integration, and the shared understandings contribute toward enhancing and maintaining the role of the professional or expert. The functional differentiations of the system reinforce each other and unify the industrial-relations system.

The industrial-relations system and the larger society can be related by the four basic problems of any social system and their boundaries and interrelations briefly stated. (1) The adaptive function of society, specialized in the economy, contributes wealth and income to the system while the adaptive function of an industrial-relations system contributes a grid of rules, including wage rates and other forms of compensation. In some respects these functions overlap; the rules on compensation or price of labor are common ground, but each is broader in scope. The economy contributes a context to the parties in the industrial-relations system, and the rules established by the industrial-relations system (other than compensation), such as manning rules and crew size, provide given technical coefficients for the economy. The subject of compensation is their common ground, and it is accordingly clear that the two subsystems have looked at wage determination in quite different terms. (2) The goal-gratification function of society and of the industrial-relations system are concerned with the contribution of power to the needs of the two social systems. The polity of society defines the power distribution and contributes an essential element to an industrial-relations system. The achievement of stability and survival in the industrial-relations system in turn contributes to the capacity of the society to achieve its goals. (3) The integration function of society and of an industrial-relations system may be closely related in an industrial society. A high degree of solidarity in the society may contribute to the industrial-relations system, and a large area of shared understandings integrating the industrial-relations system may contribute to the solidarity of the society. In the early stages of an industrial society, however, there may be marked conflicts between the ideology of the industrial-relations system and the society, and there is a low degree of integration in the society. (4) The pattern-maintenance and tension-management subsystems of the society and an industrial-relations system may also reinforce each other or be in conflict. The values and motivations within the industrial-relations system may be in congruence with those in the society or they may be for a period incompatible. Such conflicts contribute to instability in both systems and to change in one or the other or both.

2 · The Technical Context
of the Work Place

Mmanagers, workers, and specialized governmental agencies
—the actors in every industrial-relations system—were
represented in the preceding chapter as interacting in a specified
context. This environment is comprised of (1) technical conditions of the work place and work community, (2) the market or
budgetary constraints, and (3) the locus and distribution of
power in the larger society. The present chapter is concerned
with the first: the technical context of the work place. Chapters
3 and 4 respectively treat the other two features of the context.

The discussion in separate chapters of these three aspects of
the full context should not obscure their mutuality and interdependence. The reference to a single context emphasizes this
unity, and a system stresses the full range of interaction in a specific context. A three-part context (and a three-chapter discussion) is necessarily arbitrary to some degree. Thus, the size of the
work force at one work place is treated as a technical feature,
but it is clearly influenced by market constraints where economies
of scale are in part determined by relative factor prices; similarly,
the importance of labor costs to total costs is treated largely as a
market constraint although technological coefficients impose limitations on substitution among factors. The context is taken apart

33

in these three chapters and examined analytically in order to develop the ideas more clearly; later chapters that examine illustrative industrial-relations systems stress the unity of the context and a system.

To start with the technical context does not imply a rigid determinism or a form of social predestination in which the "modes of production," to use the Marxian phrase, precisely establish the superstructure of every social system. The technical context is only a part of the whole context and interacts with the other two aspects in varying patterns. Nonetheless, the present emphasis does upgrade the significance of the technical context, and indeed all aspects of the context, in the understanding of industrial-relations systems, in contrast to the current attention to "human relations" which too often appears to treat the interaction of the actors in a vacuum, as if the context made no difference to the results of their interaction.

The technical context of each industrial-relations system is to a degree unique, defined by a wide variety of particular facets. These technical conditions are decisive to the creation of the complex of rules by the actors. They are also significant to the form and operations of the hierarchies of the actors. At any one time the technical context is given, but over time it may be expected to change. Such changes tend to alter the rules, the organization of the hierarchies, and the operation of an industrial-relations system. These abstract propositions are developed and illustrated in the course of the present chapter.

CHARACTERISTICS OF THE WORK PLACE AND THE RULES

The technical context orients or places workers and managers in a specific place of work in which they perform certain particular operations and functions. Industrial society contains a vast variety of types of work places, infinitely more than any preceding society, and requires widely diverse operations and functions.

The range of rules of the work place is correspondingly multiplied. Seven characteristics of the technical context are to be distinguished; the first group of four characterize workers and managers relative to the type of their work place, and the second group of three are differentiated by the operations or functions the actors perform.

Types of Work Place

1. *A fixed or variable work place.* Technical conditions largely determine whether the work place is geographically fixed or variable, and, if it is variable, whether the fluctuations are through long or short distances, whether the variations involve a periodic or variable pattern, and whether the work place itself is mobile as in transportation industries. There is a tendency to think of industrial-relations systems in terms of fixed places of work, and it is true that a high proportion of factory and office jobs involve a stable work place. An electric-power generating station, a textile spinning plant, or a basic steel mill are illustrative. An industrial-relations system of the plant-level type evolves around such a fixed work place. There are, however, a significant number of industrial-relations systems which involve work places that are variable in a number of respects or even mobile. A significant proportion of employment in the following sectors is so characterized: transportation (railway, maritime, trucking, transit, and aviation); construction; some types of mining; many repair, service, and sales operations; some medical practitioners; many professional positions, and migratory agriculture and forestry. Perhaps as many as one out of four or five workers may be employed in geographically variable work places. Moreover, there are a variety of operations within fixed work places which involve a range of movement; the meter reader for the utilities and many maintenance and repairmen in industrial plants provide an illustration. These types of operations often create special features to industrial relations within the larger work place. The

mobility of maintenance personnel among plant workers makes them of special interest to union organizations for their wide contacts. Special problems frequently arise in the United States regarding the determination of the bargaining units for employees with variable work places, even when the pattern of movement is within a plant.

International airplane flight operations probably constitute the maximum in variability of the work place, while other industries, such as strip mining, involve only small changes in the work place. The pattern of change may be regular and hopefully predictable, as in a transportation system, or irregular and uncertain, as in many types of construction. In instances of regular variation in work place, the duration of work at any one place may be short, as in door-to-door selling, or substantial, as in oil drilling or periodic turbine overhauling. A relationship between given workers and managers may thus take place in a variety of work places which are differentiated solely with regard to whether they are fixed or variable in locale.

It is central to the present analysis that such differences are vital to the substantive rules. The variable work place, depending on the type of movement, clearly requires a range of rules not involved normally at the fixed work place. Where the work place itself is in motion, as in the transportation industries, a complex of specialized rules relate to this movement, speed, route, schedule, manning, safety, and emergencies. Regardless how these operating rules are set, whether by any one of the actors or by some combination of all three, special rules regarding the relations of managers and workers arise concerning supervision, special methods of compensation, rights to free transportation, manning schedules, hours, meals, lodging, and other problems posed by a mobile work place. In other than transportation industries where the work place is variable, rather than itself mobile, rules are frequently required regarding such topics as the cost and method of transportation between work places, provision for board and lodging, time and place of reporting, and special forms of reports and monitoring in view of the frequent complexities of supervision. The automatic machine installed in New York City on beer distributor's trucks in order to record the route and length of stops at taverns is one indication of the specialized problems of supervision that arise with a variable work place.

The technical context of a fixed or variable work place not only affects the substantive rules of the industrial-relations system but also shapes the internal organization and the operation of the hierarchies. The management or worker hierarchy or governmental agency treating transportation, or, more generally, variable work places, may be expected to be different from those designed for a fixed work place. The mere scope of the hierarchies is wider in variable work places; delegation to supervisors may have to be more complete and instructions may have to be more detailed when access to top levels in hierarchies is more remote; reporting takes on even greater significance; operating problems may frequently be more variable than in a single locale. Under union conditions the variable work place poses special problems of policing the agreed upon set of rules and involves distinct relations between union officers and members that are not so likely to be present in a fixed work place. Special arrangements or deviations from rules made among workers or between minor supervision and individual workers under shifting locale and variable work places are more difficult to detect.

If the fixed or variable character of the work place shapes in part a distinctive industrial-relations system, then changes in the technical context (which change a work place from fixed to variable, or vice versa, or which alter the nature of such variation) can be expected to change features of the rules and the organizations of the actors. The industrial relations of door-to-door selling is different from over-the-counter selling even if the same managers and workers were involved; wholesale milk delivery to depots at stores is a distinctive system from door-to-door milk delivery to individual customers. Changes in the work-place context of the industrial-relations system has an impact on the complex of rules and on the organization of the actors.

2. *Relation of work place to residence.* The technical context establishes a number of different possible relations between the work place, fixed or variable, and the residence of the workers and managers. The work place and residence, at least for considerable periods, may both be mobile as in the maritime [1] and sea-fishing [2] sectors. The work place may be variable but within such a territory that residence is not affected, as in the case of local trucking, delivery, some repair services, and local transit. The work place may be variable over such a wide territory, and in particular patterns, that some workers and managers are periodically away from normal residence, as in the case of airplane flight crews [3] and those in traveling sales organizations. In still other instances residence and work place are both migratory as in types of construction and agricultural labor contracting.[4] Finally, the place of work and residence may be relatively isolated as in mining, plantations, and timbering operations, concentrated in company towns and government reservations, or diffused in urban areas.

The complex of rules established in industrial-relations systems with these sorts of technical contexts are likely to develop provisions reflecting the special relation of work place to residence. Maritime contracts have spelled out in detail the living accommodations aboard ship including such details as how often

[1] Joseph P. Goldberg, *The Maritime Story, A Study in Labor-management Relations,* Cambridge, Mass., Harvard University Press, 1958.
[2] Bert Zoeteweij, *Fishermen's Remuneration,* Round Table on Fisheries, Rome, United Nations Food and Agriculture Organization, 13–19 September, 1956 (mimeographed); Donald J. White, *The New England Fishing Industry: A Study in Price and Wage Setting,* Cambridge, Mass., Harvard University Press, 1954.
[3] International Labor Office, *Review of Conditions of Employment in Civil Aviation,* Ad Hoc Meeting on Civil Aviation, Geneva, 1956 (mimeographed).
[4] Lloyd H. Fisher, *The Harvest Labor Market in California,* Cambridge, Mass., Harvard University Press, 1953.

clean sheets are provided and a new bar of soap furnished. Logging-camp industrial relations have on occasion been concerned with the menu and quality of meals. In the fishing industry where compensation is frequently related to value of the catch, the rules spell out which expenses of the voyage, including food and living expenses, may be deducted from the proceeds before the division between the workers, captain, and managers (owners). Provisions in rules regarding allowances for board and lodging are widely adopted where transportation or construction crews are required to be away over night. Provision for family transportation or home leave are general in government or private employment when a work place is separated from an established residence for long periods as in the oil companies, foreign service, or the civil service of United Nations organizations.

The technical context may involve a work place and normal residence which are both relatively isolated such as in many mining communities, on plantations, or on government reservations. In these instances industrial-relations rule-making tends to become concerned with problems of the community: the provision for housing and rents, medical services, transportation, perquisites, and payments in kind. A review of the history of collective agreements or regulations applicable to coal mining [5] or to plantations [6] illustrate rules which are related to the distinctive relationship of residence and work place.

The different scope of rule-making created by bringing issues of residence and the work place together also tends to affect the form and internal organization of the actors. It is apparent, for instance, that concern with the housing problems of a work force will create some specialized forms of management organiza-

[5] International Labor Office, *Principles and Methods of Wage Determination in Coal Mining, An International Survey*, Series D, No. 20, 1931; George B. Baldwin, *Beyond Nationalization: The Labor Problems of British Coal*, Cambridge, Mass., Harvard University Press, 1955.

[6] International Labor Office, *Conditions of Employment of Plantation Workers*, Fifth Item on Agenda, International Labour Conference, 42d Session, Geneva, 1958.

tion. The points of contact and potential issues among the actors will be broadened by consideration of rules related to residence, subsistence, and perquisites. Thus, company housing involves such questions as whether managers shall be distributed through the community or live close together; whether employees and managers shall be kept apart or integrated into the rest of the community; what shall be done with retired workers or those on strike. The levels of rents and wages become more closely intertwined, and developments in the community are probably even more directly reflected in the plant, and vice versa, than would be the case if plant managers did not also have formal community responsibilities. The significance of these issues is illustrated by the policies of Middle East oil companies,[7] and they were much in evidence in the period in which the United States government maintained Oak Ridge and Richland as isolated communities in the atomic-energy program.[8]

A change in the technical context, in the relations of the work place to residence, may be expected to change both the complex of rules and the organization of the actors in an industrial-relations system. In many plantations and isolated mining communities, managements have tended to establish more of a cash nexus and to reduce the extent of perquisites and services. Home-purchase arrangements have been widely encouraged. Such changes in the relation of the work place to residence have necessarily changed the complex of rules, creating more rules and organization for a period to handle home purchase although eventually decreasing the necessary regulations when employees have homes or homes are secured without assistance of the company. Home purchase also changes the relationships among the actors; there is less paternalism where industrial relations do not also include questions of the household. The change in community

---

[7] John Murray, "The Economic Impact of Oil on the Arab Middle East," reprinted from *The Institute of Petroleum Review*, 1956, pp. 21–32.

[8] *Report of the Secretary of Labor's Advisory Committee on Labor Management Relations in Atomic Energy Installations*, Washington, United States Government Printing Office, 1957.

status of Hanford and Richland directly affected the rules and the relations among the managements, the unions, and the specialized government agency (Atomic Energy Labor Relations Panel) by reducing the scope of interaction and the range of activities. By contrast the need to expand coal output after World War II in new communities and regions in Europe and the USSR was associated with an extension of enterprise housing to attract manpower.

3. *Stable or variable work force and work operations.* The technical context substantially determines whether an industrial-relations system involves a relatively stable work group or one in which the persons and the size of the group is in frequent flux. Several types of situations are to be distinguished. The work operations may be of short duration and associated with rapid turnover or changes in individuals as found in situations involving migratory agricultural labor, movie extras, the talent field generally, and some construction workers. The work operations may be of short duration but associated with a work group that is fairly steady from one hire to the next as illustrated by longshoring where a number of gangs, although by no means all, may be relatively stable over time. The work operations may be relatively steady but associated with a relatively high degree of turnover in the work force; a sales force of young girls in some department stores or restaurants would be illustrative. Some work operations may be relatively steady but fluctuations in the volume of work may result in a steady core of workers with a high degree of variation in employment for others. The seasonal garment, millinery, and tourist trades may be cited as examples. Some seasonality may arise for technical reasons (such as weather) and other seasonality is dependent upon styling and other considerations of more economic character. Finally, the limiting case of stable work operations associated with a stable work force should be mentioned. Among the great many illustrations that might be cited are large sectors of public employment in the civil service and the operation of power stations.

A stable or variable work force is one of the most significant conditions affecting the complex of rules of an industrial-relations system. The rules concern hiring and temporary or permanent layoffs. Few questions are of greater interest to all participants in an industrial-relations system. From what source and by what procedures are new employees to be engaged? What rights have previous employees? Who shall decide which workers shall be hired and in what sequence? Under what circumstances may there be any reduction in force? What procedures are to be followed in reductions of forces? Who shall have control over decisions on layoffs? Which workers shall be separated first and in what sequence? Which workers have superior rights? How shall limited job opportunities be shared? These decisions vitally affect costs and the managerial role; at the same time they are central to the degree of employment security of workers. These issues are of greatest urgency in a technical context with a high degree of variable operations since hirings and layoffs are more frequent than under stable conditions.

The substantive rules governing hirings and layoffs may take a variety of forms such as last-in-first-out, or first-in-first-out, or first-in-last-out, share-the-work-equally, or simply first-come-first-serve. The rules may also specify certain employees as having top priority, such as representatives of unions or works councils, and others who have least priority, such as temporary or foreign workers. Ability or competence to perform the particular position, or marriage status and number of dependents, or residence may be significant. The rules may involve the operation of a hiring hall, controlled by any one of the actors or by any combination of actors. Such hiring halls tend to develop more complex rules. A maritime radio-operators plan, for instance, assigned priority to a vacancy on the basis of a combination of duration of unemployment (first-in-first-out) and length of previous employment. A long stretch of employment under this plan delayed access to work compared to those with shorter periods of previous employment. A hiring hall, however, may be simply designed to facilitate information on job opportunities and may be associated with a variety of possible rules on priorities and relative rights for selecting the individuals.

Not only are a significant set of rules necessarily shaped by the stability or variability of persons at the work place, but so also are the structure and internal organization of the actors and their relationships. The frequent change in the size and scope of operations places an added premium on management whose central function is the building and continual rebuilding of the workplace organization. The premium on organizing ability is high where each new movie production, construction project, or voyage involves a new and different combination of workers and supervision faced with some new assignment. The new workers and supervision must quickly be fitted into a working organization. The frequent hiring of new workers and managers may require specialized departments within management and employee hierarchies, or hiring halls may become a governmental activity. Specialized procedures and information on workers, managers, their qualifications, and job opportunities are usually required where there are highly variable work operations. A number of forms of compensation, such as vacations with pay, health and welfare, and pension plans, pose special problems of administration where the work force is highly variable. Special administrative arrangements in a locality—on a regional, national, or even international basis—may be required.

The relations among workers and the relations with supervisors can be expected to be different when the work force is highly variable than under stable conditions where the same workers and managers work together steadily for many years. The forming and reforming of work groups for each production job, voyage, site, or other appropriate term for a work place involves human relations different from the more permanent patterns of the stable industrial plant or department. Where seasonal patterns are involved, there may be marked cleavages between the temporary groups and those of the hard core or more permanent group.

A change in the technical context of an industrial-relations system in respect to the stability or variability of the work force and work operation can be expected to create a tendency toward a change in the complex of rules bearing on hiring and layoffs and in the structure of the actors and their interaction. The contrast between the rules regarding general cargo ships and certain tanker operations with steadier employment illustrates the role of this feature of the technical context. Another example is the introduction of seniority and on occasion the wage-scale change when workers are switched from outside construction to a more steady captive department of a department store or plant. The displacement of migratory agricultural labor and contractors by the farm household or locally hired labor in the wheat harvest, associated with a change in machinery, is an even more striking case. A change in the stability or variability at the work place, including changes in seasonality, tends to result in new rules, new organizational structure of the actors, and new patterns of human relations.

4. *Size of the work group.* Technical conditions, in combination with market and budgetary constraints, substantially determine the size of the work group which in turn has a major impact on the rules established by the actors and the form of their hierarchies and relationships. In modern industrial society the size of the work group varies from single workers and managers to aggregates of tens of thousands in a single place of work.

The larger the number of workers and managers at the work place, in general, the greater the formalization of rules into written codification and policies. Informality and personal contacts among small groups is replaced by organizational channels in larger work places. Internal communications become more complex with the growth in size. Formal rules are more essential and characteristic of the larger work place.

The rules of compensation are particularly formalized in larger-sized work groups; personalized wage rates give way to the wage scale for occupations, to the job-evaluation plan, and to highly elaborate codifications of other forms of compensation. Differences in compensation among similarly situated workers becomes a source of complaints, and the tendency to correct such differences by establishing uniformities may be very costly. The establishment of acceptable rules of compensation, with uniformities among some workers and differences among others, is one of the central points of interest of any hierarchy of workers. The larger work places, with greater specialization, tend to have work operations and positions not characteristic of smaller establishments, and in smaller work places many different operations are assigned to the same person. Differences in managerial duties and skills also vary with the size of work place. Accordingly, the rules of compensation in contexts otherwise similar can be expected to involve more types of operations and to be more complex the larger the scale.

The impact of size on compensation rules can be illustrated in the hotel industry where the larger operations have the more elaborate dining rooms and kitchens; wage scales must make provision for types and skills of chefs and waiters unknown in smaller hotels. In textile weaving mills the division of duties among weavers, loom fixers, and various auxiliary help varies characteristically by the size of the weave shed. In some mills the weavers may have some responsibility even for minor repairs and maintenance, for cleaning, and for handling materials and product which are specialized to particular job classifications in larger mills. Compensation may be expected to vary by virtue of such differences in job content that are directly related to size of operations.

In a small-sized operation the handling of time off for funerals, leave for personal and family reasons, allocation of overtime, time off before holidays and eligibility for vacation pay, and a variety of other day-to-day questions affecting total compensation and relative pay among workers tends to be handled informally. But in larger-scale work places a large complex of rules tends to arise on these subjects. In the absence of formal rules, precedents in one situation may be extended to other cases, and the number of situations that arise are significant enough to warrant policy and assure a measure of uniformity.

In addition to compensation, size tends to influence the complex of rules on promotions and transfers and the relative rights in jobs of workers. There are more potential openings and more possible jobs into which a worker may be transferred the larger the scale. Indeed, the possible combinations increase exponentially with size. There are more potential problems of transfer and promotion that could arise and hence there tends to be a larger body of rules. In establishments with relatively fixed work forces, the scope of the group or seniority district which is canvassed in any promotion is an important rule vital to both managements and workers. The scope of the group reviewed, or the priority in which different groups are examined, is likely to make considerable difference to both actors. The scope of the groupings is influenced by size and specialization, regardless of the precise rule used to determine the priority of promotions or transfers in a given district.

The size of operations affects not only substantive rules but also very much the organization of the actors. Size is decisive to the shape and layers of the hierarchies of the actors and their internal decision-making processes. It is vital to the specialization of management and to the role of staff in all hierarchies. In particular, the large-scale managerial hierarchy tends to develop an elaborate specialized staff of personnel and industrial-relations departments to treat the development and administration of the system of rules. Among workers, a formal organization is more likely to emerge the larger the scale, and specialized personnel also emerge to treat the many aspects of rule-making and administration. In a small work place the manager personally performs industrial-relations functions, but with increasing scale a specialized staff emerges to perform a growing variety of distinctive industrial-relations activities under the general policy direction and review of top management.

In analyzing industrial-relations systems over time, the change in size of the work place is one of the factors in the technical context most likely to be reflected in variations in the system of rules and the form of organizations of the actors. Wartimes have afforded many illustrations of rapid changes in size, as in shipyards and aircraft and munitions plants in which small-scale operations have been transformed suddenly to large scale; such a change in the technical context has wide consequences for the complex of rules and the organization of the actors. Economic development has brought more gradual but no less consequential changes in the size of work places.

Types of Work Operations

The second group of features of the technical context of an industrial-relations system refers to the nature of the services performed by workers and managers, as distinct from characteristics of the place of work.

5. *The job content.* The technical context substantially influences the occupations, jobs, or operational content of services performed at the work place and the relative distribution of each type of work. This facet of the technical context indicates whether the work performed may be characterized as manual, clerical, or professional services and in what proportion these types of operations are found; it is an index of the skill composition and distribution at the work place. These general terms cannot adequately convey the diversity of work operations in modern industrial society. The aspects of the technical context here considered are those which normally enter as the factors in a job-evaluation plan, however defined and however finely subdivided. The headings of skill, effort, responsibility, and job conditions used to

summarize a group of eleven factors in the National Electrical Manufacturers' Association plan are illustrative.[9] Another list of factors is that used in the "Standardized Method of Job Evaluation," adopted in the Netherlands providing for ten factors: knowledge, self-reliance, contact with others, authority, power of expression, dexterity, material and machine sense, disadvantages accompanying the work, special qualifications, and risk of damage.[10] A variety of other listings of factors might be cited,[11] but these illustrations show that differences in job content take a variety of forms reflecting the technical context.

While it is widely recognized that differences in job content among work operations of the sort described in job-evaluation plans are likely to be reflected in differences in wage or compensation rates, it is not generally seen that such differences among jobs are also likely to be associated with differences in the complex of rules other than compensation. Thus, the technical context defines the extent of "unavoidable hazards" or "risks of accidents" or "responsibility for the safety of others," and these factors in job-evaluation plans are used to describe and to weigh one aspect of job conditions. But the actors do not typically limit their concern to hazards by some added element of compensation. Safety rules are prescribed. Lead shoes, goggles of certain color and thickness, metal hats, and various types of protective clothing against weather, radiation, altitude, acid, fumes, dust, cold, or heat may be specified. Periodic medical examinations may be required. Elaborate rules may also refer to the use of equipment and operating procedures: provision for guard rails, nets, gauges, and indicators, speeds of operation, testing procedures, and the like. The rules normally make provision for

[9] *Job Rating Manual. Definitions of the Factors Used in Evaluating Hourly Rated Jobs*, New York, NEMA, 1946.
[10] Ad. Vermeulen, *Job Evaluation in the Netherlands*, European Productivity Agency, Union Studies No. 5, pp. 14–15; Hoofdcommissie voor de Normalisatie in Nederland, *Standardized Method of Job Evaluation*, July 1953, (mimeographed).
[11] International Labor Office, Metal Trades Committee, Sixth Session, *Job Evaluation Methods in the Metal Trades*, Geneva, 1956 (mimeographed).

safety committes, steps to be taken in the event of accidents or a danger alert, and for the setting aside of normal operating rules, such as those that refer to hours, in the event of a safety emergency or accident. The authority to declare a condition unsafe and to remove workers and supervision from danger may be specified. In some work places customs have developed which shut down operations for the balance of the day when a fatal accident occurs. Such safety rules are not found in work places devoid of high degrees of risk to accidents. An elaborate web of rules thus may be expected to arise in a technical context prone to accidents or hazards.

The impact of job content on the rules developed for the work place can be further illustrated by what might appear to be a relatively minor feature of the technical context, the contact of workers with customers, or "conduct toward others" or "human contacts outside the company," to cite the terms employed in a Belgian and a French job-evaluation plan. In most types of factory work this experience probably arises infrequently, but in many work places such as retail trade, transportation, insurance, banking, repair operations, and many offices, this feature of the technical context may be extremely important. The economic or budgetary position of the enterprise may be significantly affected by the way in which these relations between workers and actual or potential customers are handled. Rules may relate to uniforms or other conditions of dress and appearance. Disciplinary regulations may be much affected, as in at least some hotels where a complaint from a known customer may invoke a heavy penalty, if not discharge, since "the customer is always right," and no procedures for redress between management and worker can involve resort to the customer without fear of loss of patronage. Relations with customers may involve the handling of money which tends to call forth a wide variety of specialized rules. Provision is made for responsibility in accepting counterfeit money or credit instruments that cannot be reclaimed and for shortages that arise from errors in transactions. There arise procedures for detecting dishonesty and for prescribing penalties. Special standards for recruiting and disciplinary rules may involve aspects of the personal life of a worker outside the work place on account of the importance of reputation to an enterprise; the cases of the bank teller who habituates the race track and the shoe clerk who has attracted publicity for sexual conduct are the classic illustrations. In a variety of ways the characteristic of the technical context which requires direct contact with customers tends to develop a specialized set of rules.

In similar fashion it would be possible to review each facet of job content and to illustrate how a particular feature of the technical context comes to stimulate particular rules of the work place: A high skill content and a high proportion of such operations tends to create apprenticeship and other programs for training a skilled work force. Professional requirements of a job result in the specification of formal education and degrees for entrance requirements as in education, scientific, and technical fields. A high responsibility for tools and product as in many custodial, guard, and watchman positions often create specialized hours of work and standards of discipline.

Job content has significance in an industrial-relations system beyond its impact on the content of the rules. Job content substantially defines the strategic position [12] of a group of workers in the (production) process at the work place or the strategic position of one work place in the technical flow of goods and services in the society. The opportunity in a given job classification at one work place, plant or other unit to curtail a flow of products is necessarily related to the content of the work performed. Thus, the ability of garment cutters as one occupation to shut down a whole garment factory, by leaving machine operators and pressers without work, contributes to the strategic position of the cutters. Similarly, the capacity of workers in the only engine-block plant in

---

[12] John T. Dunlop, "The Development of Labor Organization: A Theoretical Framework," in *Insights into Labor Issues*, Richard A. Lester and Joseph Shister, Eds., The Macmillan Company, New York, 1948, pp. 163–193.

an automobile company to shut down all automobile production of the company (aside from inventories of engine blocks) may provide the workers in such a plant with a degree of strategic power. From this perspective the production and distribution process of modern industrial society has some points that are more vulnerable than others to shutdown or stoppage. These points may be attributed to special skill requirements (patternmakers in a foundry), to channels of the flow of work operations (teamsters), or to temporary shortages of supply or capacity (coal miners in the postwar period). Within an industrial-relations system, at the plant or national level, the location of such strategic positions may have significant effects upon the relationships developed among the actors and consequently upon the precise rules that are established and how they are administered.

As in the case of other facets of the technical context, a change in the job content can be expected to result in a tendency toward a change in the complex of rules. Under a formal job-evaluation plan, changes in the values of the factors that are of sufficient magnitude (and not off-setting) result in a change in the ranking of the job and in its wage classification. Where no formal job-evaluation plan is operative, there is nonetheless a rough tendency for comparable changes to be reflected in changes in wage rates, although not in so discrete or mechanical a way. Changes in job content of a substantial character can be expected to result in changes in the rules that are more or less directly associated with the particular facet of job content. Thus, a marked increase in the levels of skill required of the maintenance department(s) in a large plant or industry may lead the actors to institute for the first time a formal apprenticeship program. While a shortage of skills and other factors may have also contributed to the same result, the considerable growth of formal apprenticeship programs in many mass-production plants in the American experience of the past decade is to be attributed largely to the rising levels of technology and skill required for maintenance operations. Such a program may require a grading of existing non-apprentice mechanics, provision for access of some of the present employees to the program (many may be too old or otherwise unsuited), and a variety of other rules.

The introduction of new types of machinery and equipment constitute a change in the technical context which may have far reaching consequences on the complex of rules. The complete introduction of mechanical cutting and loading equipment in coal mines frequently seems to have changed the methods of wage payment from a tonnage to a time basis. New types of looms in the textile industry, new furnaces in the steel and glass industries, and new printing presses have frequently involved new manning schedules. Higher speeds and new equipment may require new safety regulations. The problem of assignment and allocation of the existing work force to new equipment, such as pilots to new aircraft or papermakers to new machines, may evoke a substantial group of new or changed rules. The new equipment may be designed for continuous operations and lead to a change in the scheduled workweek involving rules assigning workers to shifts and affecting compensation. Indeed, some types of machine changes may so alter the technical context of the work place as to require sooner or later a rather widespread revision of the rules. The impact of the diesel engine on the railroads is illustrative.

A change in job content may also affect the strategic position of groups of workers and managers in an enterprise or in the community. The emergence of glass-cutting machines affected the strategic position of hand glass cutters and the bunching machine, the strength of the hand cigar makers. A change in strategic position is often associated with a change in market or competitive position as illustrated by the extent to which the community appears to have become somewhat less dependent upon the bus driver and coal miner. More substitutes for his product are available.

6. *Locus of attention of the actors at the work place.* An examination of a range of work places shows that in some the opera-

tions are paced and directed by the workers; in others the operations are machine paced and workers adjust and adapt to the pace and rhythm of the machine; in still others there may be little or no equipment or machinery and the center of attention may be customers. The orientation of a work place in these respects is significant to the rules that are established. A more detailed classification of work places according to the moving force or focal point of the attention of the actors follows:

a. Workers direct tools—a sweeper with a broom, a sewing-machine operator, or a surveyor with a transit. The tool may be simple or complex, and its operation may involve little or great skill.

b. Workers direct machines—cutting-machine operator in a coal mine, a truck driver, or a lathe operator. The relationship of the worker to the machine is not essentially different from the worker to a tool except that the machine is likely to be more expensive and involve a greater degree of responsibility.

c. Machine-paced operations—a routine punch-press operator, an assembler placing one part on a moving conveyor as in automobile assembly lines, or spinners in a textile mill. A narrow operation is performed, and its timing and position is determined by the machine.

d. Service operations to machines—these include maintenance and repair, custodial, and intermittent transportation. These operations could be assigned to (a) or (b) above on the basis of whether tools or machines were involved.

e. Customer services—a waiter in a restaurant, an entertainer, a bank teller, a sales person, or a professional man. In each of these instances the customer rather than a tool or machine is the focus of attention; he is being "acted upon" or "reacted to" by both the workers and managers.

It is recognized, of course, that a single actual work place typically contains a number, if not all, of these types of operations. Frequently, however, one type will be so prevalent as to represent the whole work place and provide a distinctive characteristic to the industrial-relations system. Assembly plants are likely to be characterized by machine-paced operations despite maintenance departments and basic steel mills by the type in which workers direct machines despite some tinplate and wire-mill operations that may be largely machine paced. Department stores have customer-service and maintenance operations. A newspaper has operations in which workers direct machines in the mechanical departments and customer service orients operations in the news-gathering and editorial departments. On occasions where the same enterprise contains more than one distinctive type of these operations, separate industrial-relations systems may arise. It is also recognized that some operations may be borderline and are not readily placed in this, or any other, classification scheme designed to call attention to the same relationships at the work place.

As a facet of the technical context, the locus of attention of the actors at the work place may well be regarded as simply another feature of job content. The relation of managers and workers to machines or customers deserves separate attention, however, since this characteristic of the technical context tends to give an industrial-relations system, its human relations and its complex of rules, some distinctive characteristics. Machine-paced jobs tend to be narrow in scope and highly repetitive with a cycle and pace imposed by the machine.[13] The rules of such a work place tend to have distinctive concern with rest periods and the speed of machines or assembly lines. Worker-paced tools or machines tend to involve a wider range of activities and more discretion by the single worker. Where the tools or machines and their manipulation are complex, formal training and apprenticeship rules tend to develop in view of the significance of the elements of judgment and discretion on the part of the worker. Consider, for instance, the impact on costs of the garment cutter with an

[13] Benjamin W. Niebel, *Motion and Time Study, An Introduction to Methods, Time Study and Wage Payment*, Homewood, Ill., Richard D. Irwin, 1955, pp. 110–150.

electric knife, a boner with a quarter of beef, or an operating engineer with a steam shovel. The managerial and supervisory arrangements place greater emphasis on hiring or training standards, and directions to skilled workers tend to be more general and less precise or detailed. Among members of a work crew there tends to develop a clear hierarchy of job operations for setting wage rates and for promotion within the machine crew (printing presses, paper machines, blast furnaces, or brass rolling mills). On the other hand, among machine-paced operations there is a tendency for much less of a hierarchy in wage rates or promotion; the semiskilled operators even on different machines tend to be more or less in the same category.

Service-type and maintenance operations tend to be less oriented to a particular department and the rules spread throughout the work place, partly because similar operations are found widely throughout an enterprise and partly because service operations are mobile (maintenance man and hand truckers) and comparisons are more readily made. The customer-services type of operation, as has been noted above, tends to produce a distinctive set of rules on discipline and may require unique regulations on the handling of money.

7. *Hours of operation of the work place.* The technical context of the work place has a major influence on the hours of the day and week that a work place is in operation. The hours a place of work operates need have no necessary fixed relationship to the schedule of hours worked by any individual or any group of actors. Some processes are to a large measure technologically continuous and are manned in shifts around the clock: certain processes in oil refineries, basic steel mills, aluminum-reduction pots, chemical plants, atomic-energy installations, power-generating stations, and long-distance transportation. Other operations have hours that reflect a structure of demand which is outside the typical work hours of the community: public scheduled local transportation, fire, police, doctor, and hospital services, restaurant and meal services, entertainment, and a variety of special

services such as offered by many drug stores, taxi cabs, and gasoline stations. There are other situations in which the hours of operation of the work place are particularly influenced by cost considerations or short-term fluctuations in demand so that shift work is scheduled outside the regular workday or workweek such as over the week end or for additional shifts through the week or at odd hours.

The hours of operation of the work place pose a wide variety of problems to the actors and a considerable web of rules arises to deal with this range of questions. Rules govern such problems as the authority to establish and to change scheduled hours, to institute new shifts and to set their hours, the criteria used to assign particular workers and managers to these scheduled work times, the premium compensation rates, if any, for scheduled hours and shifts which are outside the hours regarded as normal in the community (week end, shift premiums, and short periods before or after normal hours), the computation of such premiums in the light of other premiums or the question of whether premiums are to be compounded and the criteria and the authority to allocate overtime among the actors.

The local transit industry most strikingly illustrates the significance of the hours of operation and of scheduling problems in a complex of rules; a large proportion of the rules in this work place are directly concerned with the scheduling of runs and compensation for hours worked outside a specified spread of hours or outside the schedule of the runs. In the local-transit industry in metropolitan areas the demand for transportation tends to peak very markedly at a morning and evening rush hour; these peaks are further apart (ten hours or more in many cases) than the scheduled work day. Managements would probably prefer to provide for these peaks by runs which involved a period of compensated work and then an unpaid lapse of three or four hours with a second period of compensated work. In countries where the working population returns home during a prolonged lunch period, particularly in southern Europe, the peak periods may be expected to be different in magnitude and number. The desires of the workers for a regular day conflict with the needs to schedule shorter runs to man the peak periods without substantial periods of stand-by compensation. The scheduling rules in local-transit operations may specify a minimum proportion of the total number of runs which are to be straight runs of continuous compensation and a minimum proportion which can be broken into two or more pieces, in which event the rules are likely to specify the outside elapsed time between the start of the first piece of work and the end of the last piece. In view of the wide differences in the desirability of these working periods and differences in preferences among workers, the rules typically provide criteria for the allocation of runs among workers and for the periodic review of these assignments or choices. In an industry where traffic or weather may slow the completion of runs on schedule, the rules arc likely to be elaborate regarding overtime compensation and rates for work performed outside of the daily schedule, the allowed elapsed spread, or weekly scheduled hours.

In continuous-process industries the rules specify the criteria of allocation of workers among operations that may be on fixed shifts and the rotation principles used for workers and managers on rotating shifts, turns, watches, or other terms used to designate a regular daily work period. On late shifts special problems may arise regarding the provision of meals. Night work may also confront rules and regulations, some developed by the governmental actor, regarding the employment of women or employees below certain ages.

In some work places the question becomes urgent as to the place workers shall be expected to be at the start of the scheduled workday. In coal mines the portal-to-portal or bank-to-bank rules relate to whether the working day begins when miners have reached the working mine face, an entrance to the shaft, the cage, or some other check-in point on the mine property. In other types of operations in which locale of the work place shifts, such as lumbering and some construction, the issue arises whether the workday shall be construed to start at some central check-in point or closer to the place of actual work operations. In many industries the rules specify whether the workday shall include time for changing to work clothing, where specialized apparel is required, and whether time shall be allowed for cleaning and washing, where operations are dirty or hazardous.

The hours of operation of the work place mould the structure of the hierarchies in important respects. A continuous operation, for example, requires parallel levels in the hierarchies for each shift; it divides both management and workers into shift groups. It makes difficult simultaneous meetings of all workers and management personnel on account of operations always in process. It imposes additional problems of coordination among parts in each hierarchy; it becomes necessary to secure information, to establish uniformities, to make provision for emergencies in each time zone of operations and to make arrangements for transferring workers and supervision among shifts.

The change in the hours of operation of the work place, like all other features of the technical context, is to be seen as a dynamic element which leads to changes in the complex of rules when varied. In the case of a change of hours, a distinction is to be made between those changes within a given set of rules (such as the weekly variation in the amount of overtime) and a change in the rules governing the standard working day of the work place or a change involving new shifts or new methods of allocating workers among shifts. A change in the standard working day may have significant repercussions on the rules fixing the levels of compensation. The introduction of a new shift raises the issues, unless previously settled, of the criteria for the allocation of workers among shifts, rates of premium compensation, as well as the hours of the new shift. A new group of rules arises, and old rules may be altered by a change in the standard hours of operation of the work place.

IMPACT ON ORGANIZATION OF ACTORS

While the major interest of the preceding discussion has been to show the impact of the technical context of the work place on the substance of the rules developed by an industrial-relations system, there has been more limited reference to the impact of the technical context on the structure and organization of the hierarchies of the actors and their interaction. These latter points may be fruitfully pulled together at this juncture.

The characteristics of the work place itself—fixed or variable in locale, its relation to residence, the stability of the work place and work force, and the size of the work group—tend to establish, or at least to set limits to, many features of the hierarchies of workers and managers. The geographical spread of the organizations, the variability or permanence in their operations, the number and location of the tiers in the hierarchies, their scale of operations at a single work place, and many features of the internal-communications systems must be adapted to these facets of the work place. The operations performed at the work place—the job content, the orientation toward machines or customers, and the hours of scheduled operation—also tend to influence the hierarchies of workers and managers.

A variety of specialized organizations, committees, and staff are required to cope with problems presented by the different operations. A high degree of danger creates safety committees and may introduce professional engineers in this area; a high degree of skill tends to develop apprenticeship programs and other instrumentalities for training; the introduction of shift work develops some parallel organizations to cope with the spread of operations through time, and the handling of money tends to require specialized reporting procedures and investigating methods to check upon honesty.

There is no contention here that a few technical conditions rigidly or precisely determine every organization form; there are some differences in organization among actors confronted by similar technical contexts, and other facets than the technical features of the context also play a role. But many features of an organizational configuration are narrowly constrained by the particular technical context.

The technical context also has a good deal to do with the nature of the interaction between the actors; the concern here is much broader than the sole question of industrial peace or warfare. The technical conditions influence the points of contacts between the hierarchies, whether their interactions are geographically widely spread and diffused or more concentrated and whether large or small groups are involved. The nature of supervision varies in its detail with skilled labor who direct tools and equipment and with a mobile work place as in transportation as compared to semiskilled groups in one fixed work place who are machine paced. The importance of organizing ability in management is greater where the place of work changes frequently and new organizations and relationships must be created afresh. The internal solidarity of workers is affected by the isolation of the work place, its relationship to residence, and the homogeneity of skill.

The technical context also shapes the relations among the actors by indicating the extent of the power of strategic groups of workers to shut down an operation or enterprise. The capacity of a management organization to resist shutdown by being able to replace workers or by operating with supervisory and managerial personnel for short periods is often directly related to technical processes and their vulnerability to shutdown at strategic points. A highly technical work operation with considerable managerial personnel and highly automatic processes may have a high resistance to shutdown. The technical conditions also indicate whether sudden shutdowns without adequate precautions may involve substantial damage to plant and equipment as in the freezing of aluminum pots or glass furnaces. The capacity to shut down operations, or to resist shutdowns, by the withdrawal of strategic services is highly dependent upon the technical context. These relative capacities are a factor which shape the relations between workers and managers, or at least decisively influence their strategies in any conflict over the rules of the industrial-relations system.

The technical characteristics of the work place frequently are a major determinant of the extent of public interest and governmental role in an industrial-relations system. The operation of public transportation is of wide concern and particularly vital to the life of an interdependent industrial society. The technical vulnerability of the continuous operations in a gaseous diffusion plant in the atomic energy field provides an occasion for a special role for governmental agencies. The power to destroy major assets of a community by flooding a coal mine may call for drastic type of action by government. Some technical characteristics of a work place are significant to defining public interest and help to ascribe the role of governmental agencies.

The technical context is one of three environmental features of an industrial-relations system. The technical context defines the type of work place and the operations and functions of workers and managers and to some degree influences the role of specialized governmental agencies. The following facets of technical contexts were particularly distinguished: (1) fixed or variable work place, (2) relation of work place to residence, (3) stable or variable work force and operations, (4) size of the work group, (5) job content, (6) relation to machines or customers, and (7) the scheduled hours and shifts of the work place. Some of these facets are interrelated with the economic context and not determined by purely technical factors alone. The technical context is decisive both to the substantive rules established for the work place in the industrial-relations system and to the organizational configuration and the interaction of the actors.

3 · The Market Context
or Budgetary Constraints

THE second of the three facets of the context of an industrial-relations system is the market or budgetary constraints. The relevant markets or budgets differ for a plant or an enterprise, an industry or a regional sector, or a national industrial-relations system. Some plant or enterprise systems are oriented entirely toward local and domestic product markets or budgetary conditions as in the case of metropolitan transit operations; they typically face competition from automobiles, bicycles, motor contraptions of various sorts, and the pedestrian, and their fares and services are typically regulated by local public authorities. Other enterprises, such as diamond cutting and gold mining, are oriented largely toward international product markets. Similarly, some industrial or regional systems primarily confront domestic or sheltered markets while others face internationally open product competition in varying degrees. In considering national industrial-relations systems, international markets constitute the relevant market context, although differences in the degrees of domestic competition may also be significant to the characteristics of a national industrial-relations system. All industrial-relations systems confront a greater or a lesser degree of product-market competition or budgetary pressure which shapes—like

62

the technical context—the rules developed and the organizations and relations of the actors.

The market context refers not only to the product-market or budgetary constraints but also to conditions in the markets for factors or inputs, particularly in this study for varying types and skills of labor services. The product market, or budget, places the actors under various constraints and disposes them in certain directions toward the rules that are established in an industrial-relations system, given physical productivities and the survival of the enterprise or agency. For instance, competition in the relevant textile markets or the budget of a charitable institution limit and constrain the rules that can be established affecting employees at the work place. But the competitive conditions in the factor markets, such as the availability of employees and the rules applicable to other similarly situated employees in other systems, also constitute constraints upon the rules established in an industrial-relations system. The characteristics of workers themselves directly influence the rules established at a work place. The language facility of workers and supervisors, the age, sex, nationality and religious affiliation of workers, and the educational qualifications of the work force tend to be reflected in the rules of a work place.

The purpose of this chapter is to develop systematically the way in which the market context or the budgetary constraints, in product and labor markets, shape the rules of the work place and the organization and relationships of the actors in an industrial-relations system. Certain types of market and budgetary positions tend to be associated with certain types of rules. In analyzing any particular industrial-relations system the market context or budgetary constraint is only one of three facets of the full context.

The following characteristics of the market context or budgetary constraints of an industrial-relations system have different impacts on the complex of rules and on the organizations and relations of the actors.

FEATURES OF PRODUCT MARKETS
OR BUDGETARY CONSTRAINTS

Competitive Position or Budgetary Control

The competitive position in the relevant product markets (considering first an industrial-relations system confronting product markets rather than budgets) depends upon such well-known factors as the number of competitors, freedom of entry, the standardization of product, the availability of substitute products and sources of supply, and the postponability of demand. Indeed, all factors that affect the elasticity of demand for the goods and services supplied by the industrial-relations system, by definition, affect the character of competition.[1] These same factors are relevant for plant-level, industrywide, or national industrial-relations systems. The character of competition is a measure of the degree of control over product price or other aspects of sale which in turn is decisive to the control or elbow room and discretion which the actors have in setting the rules of the work place, including compensation.

In an industrial-relations system with highly competitive product markets, as in most branches of the cotton-textile or garment industries, the discretion in setting most rules, particularly those affecting compensation, is very narrow. In petroleum refining or steel production, on the other hand, the range of discretion is ordinarily considerably greater. Competition within a system (comprised of more than one enterprise) and competition among enterprises from different systems may prescribe a wide or a narrow latitude for rule-making. National systems differ widely in the extent to which they are exposed to international competition. In the Netherlands, for instance, exports of

[1] Joe S. Bain, *Barriers to New Competition, Their Character and Consequences in Manufacturing Industries,* Cambridge, Mass., Harvard University Press, 1956; William Fellner, *Competition Among the Few,* New York, Alfred A. Knopf, 1949.

goods and services constituted 50.4 percent of gross national product in 1954, compared to 23.8 percent in the United Kingdom, 15.2 percent in France, and less than 5 percent for the United States.[2] Industrial-relations systems differ widely in the number of firms which comprise the system, the ease of entry to markets, standardization of product, availability of substitutes—in brief, the character of competition in the product market.

The budgetary constraints that surround an industrial-relations system, not directly confronted by markets, also range from conditions which constitute a very tight limitation to those which afford considerable discretion in the setting of rules. Among French nationalized industries, for example, some make money while others require a subsidy. The Renault automobile plant has been earning a surplus and in practice has not been required to submit to detailed budgetary scrutiny. It appears to have greater discretion in the setting of rules at the work place than, for instance, electricity works with controlled rates (prices) which draw a subsidy from the national budget. The chronic budgetary constraints in electricity works constitute a severe limitation on the rules that may be established by any actor or combination of actors, including even the minister who has responsibility for the electric works.[3] The decision of the British government not to provide further funds for wage increases in nationalized industries significantly affected the railways wage settlement of May 1958 as well as other rules of the work place. Numerous illustrations may also be drawn from Soviet experience. There, managers, Communist party functionaries, and trade-union officials, in tacit understanding of their common interests at a plant, may seek to affect the plan and report on its fulfillment and operating practices not only to achieve a safety factor against untoward contingencies, but also to affect compensation, plant

[2] United Nations, *Economic Survey of Europe in 1955*, Geneva, February 1956, pp. 59–63.
[3] No. 4703, Assemblée Nationale, Troisième Législature, Session Ordinaire de 1956–57, Annexe au procès-verbal de la séance du 28 Mars 1957.

housing and amenities, and other rules of the work place.[4] In the United States the comparative levels of compensation and rates of promotion in special wartime agencies compared to regular government departments, or the levels of compensation in "crash programs" or high-priority agencies, is indicative of the influence of the budget upon the rules of the governmental work place. Commonly, universities, foundations, and charitable institutions tend to vary the levels of compensation, retirement plans, promotions, services, and amenities directly with budgetary stringency. The fact that labor organizations among state and municipal employees, firemen and policemen, postal workers, and employees in navy yards and arsenals tend to be lobbying organizations when concerned with influencing the rules of the work place is testimony to the same simple fact. A budget predisposes all the actors in the rule-making process no less than a market context.

There is nothing new in finding that the suit must be cut to fit the cloth. The significant task is rather to establish the ways in which the market context and budgetary constraints are related to rule-making. What rules are predisposed by the market or budgetary context, and in what respects are they shaped?

1. *Compensation rules.* There is little need to pause long to show the fundamental effects of the market or budgetary context on the compensation rules of an industrial-relations system. Both formal analysis and the experience of actors support this well-established proposition.[5] Despite the great difficulty of isolating the effects of any one analytical factor when a variety are operative, the differences in wage rates for comparable occupations between book and job and newspaper printing, among branches of a local trucking industry, and among classes of hotels

---

[4] Joseph S. Berliner, *Factory and Manager in the USSR,* Cambridge, Mass., Harvard University Press, 1957, pp. 67–70, 318–329.

[5] Joan Robinson, *The Economics of Imperfect Competition,* London, Macmillan and Co., 1933; John T. Dunlop, *Wage Determination Under Trade Unions,* New York, The Macmillan Company, 1944, pp. 45–121, and *Theory of Wage Determination,* London, Macmillan and Co., 1957.

in some cities is illustrative of the influence of different product-market competitive conditions upon wage rates. Differences in compensation by size of enterprise frequently constitute, at least in part, a reflection of different degrees of control over price and product-market conditions.[6] The timing of wage changes over a period of years among different industrial-relations systems is frequently a response to varying market and budgetary conditions. It is not to be implied, however, that every difference in product-market competition or budgetary constraint is reflected in differences in wages. Small differences in degrees of competition may have no effect, and there are strong labor-market pressures to equalize wage rates for comparable job classifications within an industrial-relations system. But pronounced and growing differences in product-market competitive conditions tend to strain previous contours of wage equality or uniformity of wage change.

In a single industrial-relations system which encompasses different product markets or budgets with different degrees of competition or constraint, these different conditions tend to influence the structure of internal wage rates.[7] Thus, in the women's garment industry the greater competitive pressure on low-price lines as compared to high-price lines tends to result in tighter piece rates where price competition is greater and looser piece rates on operations with less severe price competition. Another application of the principle is seen in the rubber industry where the major companies produce a wide variety of products including tires and footwear; the competitive conditions among these markets are quite different. There are significant tendencies for relative tightness or constraint in wage settling on operations producing more competitive lines and relative loose-

[6] *The Smaller Industry in Japan*, Asia Kyokai, Tokyo, Japan, 1957, pp. 1–7, 100.
[7] E. R. Livernash, "The Internal Wage Structure," in *New Concepts in Wage Determination*, George W. Taylor and Frank C. Pierson, Eds., New York, McGraw-Hill Book Co., 1957, pp. 140–173; G. P. Shultz and C. A. Myers, "Union Wage Decisions and Unemployment," *American Economic Review*, June 1950, pp. 362–380.

ness on less competitive lines. In national industrial-relations systems the contrast between wage setting in sheltered as compared to export industries has frequently been noted.[8]

2. *Product-market arrangements.* A wide variety of rules of the work place are explicitly designed as a response to market constrictions or to a tight budget. The rules of the fishing industry, for instance, often regulate the type of auction market in which the catch can be sold, specify the standards of quality for grades of fish, and define the conditions under which a catch may be downgraded to a lower quality and price. The limitation on the number of subcontractors that a manufacturer may use in the women's garment industry or restrictions on operations that may be subcontracted in the home-building field is a response by the actors to the consequences of highly competitive product markets characterized by great ease of entry. Indeed, more common rules which specify limitations on the subcontracting of work operations (such as maintenance and minor construction) are in part a response to the comparative costs of these operations when performed within an enterprise and when let out on contract. The prescription of grades of men's clothing and the limitation of output to specific standardized grades constitutes a complex set of rules developed in response to a highly competitive product market with wide variations in quality that are not readily distinguished by customers. Rules designed to limit owner-operators in trucking or to specify a minimum size for establishments are to some degree a response to highly competitive conditions; they are designed to control product-market competition by action at the work place.

The actors in an industrial-relations system may seek to establish public policies, aside from rules of the work place, designed to change the competitive conditions of the product market, and thereby gain discretion in rule-making at the work place. In the maritime industry the quest for governmental

---

[8] Henry Clay, *The Problem of Industrial Relations and Other Lectures,* London, Macmillan and Co., 1929, pp. 74, 142.

subsidies to make up the difference between foreign and domestic labor costs affects the rules established at the work place to a major degree. The support for tariffs, building codes, and appeals to rate-making or price-setting bodies by managers and workers constitute conduct outside the work place designed directly to influence the rules established at the work place by influencing the competitive conditions of the product market.

3. *The timing of revision of the rules.* The competitive characteristics of the product market significantly influence the time at which revisions in the rules are periodically considered. A good many product markets are seasonal, and output may involve important style and quality factors. Women's clothing, millinery, agricultural products, tourist and some travel services, and a variety of other activities are dependent upon the seasons or calendar. In seasonal activities the problem arises as to the date or period that rules shall be established or reviewed. If the rules are determined at the end of the season when output and employment are low, to apply to the next full season, then the managers would appear able to push an advantage since there is little need for workers. If the rules are set during the seasonal peak, to apply to the next full season, then the workers would appear able to secure an advantage since withdrawal of labor services would inflict the greatest loss to enterprises. In these types of markets, managers are frequently interested in having labor costs determined before substantial production is undertaken in order to be able to quote prices, secure orders, and schedule production.[9] In view of these conflicting preferences, the rules for the season are frequently determined just before or during the early stages of the season, to some extent offsetting the conflicting maximum timing advantages of the managers and workers. In many product markets the type of problem posed by such seasonal factors does not arise, and other strategic factors

---

[9] For an analysis of the problem, see Lloyd Ulman, *The Rise of the National Trade Union,* Cambridge, Mass., Harvard University Press, 1957, pp. 620–623.

including the timing of related settlements are significant to the actors. But where markets are seasonal, and particularly where they also involve perishable output by virtue of physical qualities or style, the timing of rule-making constitutes a significant impact of the product market upon the rules of the work place.

4. *The duration of rules.* The competitive characteristics of the product market also influence the duration between periods of rule reconsideration. In industrial-relations systems which are prone to experience substantial variations in economic conditions in short periods, relative to the resources of the system, the actors may be expected to make firm commitments for only relatively short periods. The rules may specify no fixed term and may be subject to review at will in the light of changed conditions, or a set of rules with a substantial fixed term may provide for periodic review at short-term intervals. Only a system of substantial strength, where the actors together or management alone have substantial control over product-market competition, can make rules providing for long intervals between reviews of the rules. It should also be noted that rules may have no fixed duration, and may be subject to review at will, in situations where it characteristically takes a considerable period of time to establish a new rule.

The English industrial-relations system is unique in that it has characteristically not provided for a fixed duration for rules.[10] The importance of international trade, with rapidly changing markets, the characteristics of industries in which collective bargaining developed early and the early resort to product-price sliding scales may have contributed to this peculiarity of British collective-bargaining arrangements. The procedures for setting rules by continuing bipartite or tripartite bodies placed less emphasis upon fixed-duration agreements, particularly when the process of settlement was of such variable and uncertain duration. In the United States the railroad industry has ordinarily

---

[10] Allan Flanders and H. A. Clegg, *The System of Industrial Relations in Great Britain*, Oxford, Basil Blackwell and Mott, 1954, pp. 291–292.

had no fixed duration of its rules [11] on account of the lengthy and uncertain duration of the process of setting new rules and as a consequence of the infrequent and slow procedures by which railroad freight and passenger rates have been reviewed by public authorities.

In a variety of ways decisions respecting the rules of the work place have come to be considered in many industrial-relations systems at the same time that decisions are made respecting prices in product markets or decisions on budgets. In public employment or in charitable institutions and other sectors confronted by budgets, the decisions affecting compensation tend to be made at the same time as decisions on the budget. Indeed, in many instances procedures are established to assure that they are made at the same time, so that expenditures are balanced by available income. The timing of compensation changes for municipal firemen, policemen, and teachers, for instance, is frequently tied to the date of budgetary changes. The Congress has provided for both increases in salaries for postal employees and increases in postal rates in the same legislation.[12] In the public-utility field, managements have sought to reduce the lag between increases in compensation and changes in regulated prices and explicitly to relate increases in compensation to increases in the regulated prices, rates, or fares. In industrial-relations systems confronting product markets where price leadership is developed and wages are a significant component of costs, there is a clear tendency to tie increases in prices to particular increases in compensation, as in the case of the basic steel industry. The competitive characteristics of the product market in this way influence the timing of rules changes at the work place.

5. *Job order versus market production.* The competitive characteristics of the product market, in conjunction with technical characteristics, indicate whether output is produced for a gen-

---

[11] In the period 1956–1959, however, most railroad agreements were subject to a fixed duration on money matters as a consequence of negotiations in which managements sought agreements with a three-year term.

[12] *The New York Times,* May 23, 1958.

eralized market or created on a custom or specialized job basis. The contrast, of course, constitutes more of a spectrum than a rigid demarcation, and job-lot production with minor variations in the assembly of parts may resemble production for a general market. The distinction, however, is useful for an understanding of certain rules of the work place. In custom or job-order production, the lesser degree of standardization of work operations, the greater degree of contact with the customer, and the tendency for greater instability in employment are of major consequence to rule-making. The work of a tailor, a hotel bellboy, a barber, a chartered-bus driver, many professional men, and a wide variety of repair operators is illustrative of these conditions. In many of these cases price and wage setting are closely tied together by formal practices or rules of thumb; the worker receives a fraction of the price. In work places with such instability in employment and with operations of quite variable duration, the rules tend to be concerned with the allocation of employees to discrete work opportunities (by rotation, customer preference, length of service, or some other explicit standard) and with the criteria by which particular layoffs and additions to the work force are made. The competitive character of a market, including its influence on the size of a market, in these ways affect the rules of the work place.

The Scope of an Industrial-relations System

The market context or budgetary constraint is a significant determinant of the scope of an industrial-relations system. Enterprises which confront identical or closely related product markets frequently tend to comprise the same industrial-relations system or their systems are closely related and interdependent. The market context or budgetary constraint, however, does not alone set the limits to a system since labor-market considerations are also relevant. But distinctive product-market conditions often create specialized rules at the work place.

The formal point can be understood more clearly with an illustration. In the maritime industry tankers confront a specialized market. While it is true that some technical conditions of work are relatively unique on tankers, such as hazards of fire and explosion, specialized job classifications, and regularity of employment, and they result in some specialized rules of the work place, the market for tanker services is significantly different from that for general dry-cargo and passenger ships and other branches of the maritime industry. The specialized market conditions for tanker services do not necessarily carve out an entirely separate industrial-relations system since labor-market factors and the magnitude of the differentiation in the product market are relevant. But the distinctive market conditions for tankers do create a tendency in this direction, resulting in a distinguishable industrial-relations system within the larger maritime arrangements or in some specialized rules for the tanker work place (quite apart from specialized rules occasioned by technological considerations).

While affinity or affiliation of an enterprise to a particular industrial-relations system is not solely determined by product market or budgetary attachment, this factor is frequently very significant since managers, public or private, are likely to fix their attention on their competition. The acceptance by workers and managers in an enterprise of the rules generally prevailing in the rest of the relevant industrial-relations system provides a standard which reduces arbitrary action, narrows the range of discretion, and orients the rules of one work place to a limited group of other enterprises.

In strict logic the product market or budget of every enterprise is to some degree unique, and as a consequence some specialized rules may be developed at each work place. But this observation does not alter the fact that some enterprises are more closely competitive with each other than with those outside the group. There are some groupings of enterprises (or plants), although they may participate in a number of different product markets, which are particularly significant for the determination of compensation and other rules of the work place.

When the formal organizations for rule setting are narrower in scope than the group of enterprises which comprises the principal product-market competition, as is frequently the case in the United States with collective bargaining at the plant and firm level, the industrial-relations systems tend to be broader than the enterprise on account of the high degree of market interdependence, and wage or industrial-relations leadership tends to develop. The steel, auto, rubber, and meat-packing industries are illustrative. When the formal organizations for rule setting, on the other hand, are wider in scope than an area of product-market competition, as is frequently the case in continental European countries, the industrial-relations systems that develop confront pressures for specialization of some rules along the contours of market competition. These specialized rules are often limited to particular plants and are created by managements alone or with workers councils or other plant-level organizations. In the extreme case of the metal trades in many countries where general rules have been developed across a large number of product markets, many specialized and more detailed rules come to be applied at the work places in significant product-market sectors such as automobile manufacturing, shipbuilding, aircraft production, machine-tool manufacturing, and others.[13] Regardless of the formal organization, the product-market context or budgetary constraint is likely to be significant in influencing the scope of a set of rules, that is, the sector of work places over which a common web of rules are in fact applicable.[14]

[13] International Labor Organization, Metal Trades Committee, *Factors Affecting Productivity in the Metal Trades*, Third Item on the Agenda, Geneva, 1952.

[14] H. A. Clegg and Rex Adams, *The Employers' Challenge, A Study of the National Shipbuilding and Engineering Dispute of 1957*, Oxford, Basil Blackwell and Mott, 1957; Knowles and Hill, "The Structure of Engineering Earnings," *Bulletin of the Oxford University Institute of Statistics*, September and October 1954; Milton Derber, *Labor-Management Relations at the Plant Level Under Industry-wide Bargaining, A Study of the Engineering Industry in Birmingham, England*, University of Illinois, Institute of Labor and Industrial Relations, 1955.

Basic changes in the product-market context or budgetary constraints may be expected to alter the scope of an industrial-relations system, and in extreme cases changes in competition associated with technical change may even disintegrate the particular system. As an illustration, the changing character of competition in the United States woolen and worsted industry, in part the consequence of new fibers, has substantially disintegrated the previous arrangements among managers and workers in this field. From the new technology and patterns of competition a new system may be expected eventually to arise.

An enlargement in the scope of many industrial-relations systems, on the other hand, may be expected from the development of the Common Market in Western Europe with a change in competitive product-market conditions brought about by the reduction or eventual elimination of tariffs.[15] Already there appears to be some discussion of joint negotiations of a single collective-bargaining agreement for coal and another for steel among the parties to the present agreements within the European Coal and Steel Community. New industrial-relations systems, supernational in scope, would be required to replace those which have been confined to individual countries or sectors of the industries in a country. A more uniform set of rules should be expected to arise in such a new system. As new competitive conditions are generally created in the Common Market, changes in the scope of the industrial-relations systems are to be expected. It should not be presumed that the direction of change is likely to be entirely toward an expansion in scope of industrial-relations systems. As sectors of present systems are exposed to increased product-market competition, despite labor-market considerations, a number of the larger sectors within some countries may be expected to show considerable strain at product-market contours, and some may split into separate industrial-relations systems which then develop some rules more specialized and appropriate to the narrower sector. Whichever of these two types of changes

[15] International Labor Office, *Social Aspects of European Economic Cooperation, Report of a Group of Experts*, Geneva, 1956 (Ohlin report).

may predominate as a direct consequence of the introduction of the Common Market, there can be little doubt that the associated changes in competitive conditions in product markets are likely to have significant effects both upon the substantive rules of the work place and upon the scope of industrial-relations systems.

The Market or Budgetary Homogeneity

The market context or budgetary constraint of an industrial-relations system includes the degree of similarity or homogeneity in the market or budgetary position of the constituent enterprises. This facet does not apply, of course, when the system only includes one enterprise, except that the different budgetary positions of departments create analogous problems. In some industrial-relations systems the enterprises have relatively similar market and cost positions while in others there are marked differences in these respects among the component enterprises. This characteristic of the market or budgetary context is significant to the degree of uniformity in these rules and to the degree of centralization or the location within the system at which the rules of the work place are determined.

In general, the more diversified the market and cost positions of the component enterprises, the less the degree of uniformity in the rules actually applied among the work places and the greater the actual decentralization in rule setting. In these circumstances, when uniform rules are formally established, they are likely to be of a most general nature with provision for more detailed and higher standards to be determined in more decentralized locations in the system. The uniform rules may be confined to a few limited items among the great many which constitute the full complex, and the balance may be formulated at more decentralized points. It should be recognized, however, that in some systems with marked diversity in market and cost positions, a highly centralized, detailed, and uniform set of rules is promulgated in order to attempt to regulate the disparate market conditions and to seek to develop more uniform market and cost positions among the constituent enterprises. A system of uniform piece rates in a highly competitive product market, such as did exist in the full-fashion hosiery field or does operate in the men's clothing field, or the establishment of the nationwide internal wage structure (CWS) in the basic steel industry are illustrative.

Some systems of rules may be so centralized that a single manual, centrally established, seeks to prescribe complete regulations for a wide variety of work places. A set of civil-service regulations for executive-department employees would perhaps approximate this case. In other systems some rules are established centrally while other rules are added at more decentralized positions. The complex of rules at a particular work place consists of layers created at different levels in the hierarchy. Thus, a master contract may provide that promotion is to be based on seniority provided that ability is sufficient, and local rules may specify the particular seniority districts and the relevant seniority lists. This type of successive rule-making, providing detailed rules within a framework of more general rules, is a very general arrangement, although the content of general rules and details vary greatly. Finally, in still other systems, few if any rules are made centrally and most rules are established close to the work places. The present interest is that the homogeneity of the market or budgetary context influences the type of rule setting in that highly divergent market or budgetary contexts tend to be associated with relatively more decentralized rule-making, or centralized rule-making becomes very general, at times so general that it may have little direct consequence for the actual rules applied at particular work places.

These principles are particularly evident in a comparison of national wage structures.[16] In some countries wage setting is

[16] John T. Dunlop and Melvin Rothbaum, "International Comparisons of Wage Structures," *International Labour Review*, April 1955, pp. 3–19; B. C. Roberts, *National Wages Policy in War and Peace*, London, George Allen &

highly centralized with national bargaining between a central confederation of employers and a central body representing workers; in other cases centralization is achieved through a special tribunal or by government edict, or various combinations of these methods may be utilized. The postwar experience of Sweden, the Netherlands, Australia, and Italy are illustrative. But the determination of wage rates for four or eight broad classifications on a nationwide basis for one industry or for all industry, or by a few major job titles in an industry, as is more generally the case in centrally determined wage structures, may be quite different from the wage rates actually established, paid, and received at a work place. In varying degrees these countries illustrate successive rule-making on wage rates from very broad classifications and groups of rates established on a national basis to more specific rates for particular jobs set at the work place. In many instances the nationally established rates and classifications are treated as minimum rates, and the competitive position of particular enterprises in product markets and the stringency in their labor markets result in higher earnings in practice at the work place. Indeed, in "high-wage" enterprises, the nationally determined rates have almost no significance. The discussion of the wage "drift" or "slide" reflects such deviations in earnings actually paid at the work place from those provided in centrally determined wage schedules.[17] In other cases, where en-

---

Unwin, 1958, pp. 83–144; H. A. Turner, *Wage Policy Abroad: And Conclusions for Britain*, London, Fabian Research Series No. 189, August 1957.

[17] *Report of the Basic Steel Panel*, October 15, 1944, 19 *War Labor Reports*, pp. 611–619; *The Termination Report of the National War Labor Board*, Vol. 1, pp. 536–559; Swedish Trade Union Federation, *Trade Unions and Full Employment* (English edition, 1953); B. Hansen and G. Rehn, "On Wage Drift, A Problem of Money-Wage Dynamics" in *Twenty-five Economic Essays in Honor of Eric Lindahl*, R. Bentzel, et al., Stockholm, Ekonomisk tidskrift, 1956, pp. 87–138; H. A. Turner, "Wages, Industry Rates, Workplace Rates and the Wage Drift," *The Manchester School*, May 1956, pp. 95–123; G. Rehn, "Swedish Wages and Wage Policies," *The Annals of the American Academy of Political and Social Sciences*, March 1957, pp. 87–98; Ely Devons and R. C. Ogley, "An Index of Wage-Rates by Industries," *The Manchester School*, May 1958, pp. 77–115. The term is not very useful for many purposes since it lumps together a wide variety of factors creating a difference between

terprises are confronted with constrictive product markets, considerable unemployment, and little effective organization in the labor market, the actual rates paid at the work place may be below those established in the national scale and classifications. The significant observation for the present purpose is that diverse market or budgetary conditions tend to exert a dispersive effect upon centrally determined wage structures. The extent of market or budgetary diversity affects the generality of the wage rates that can be established centrally and the extent of successive wage setting closer to the work place.

The influence of market or budgetary diversity is also seen in setting other rules of the work place than wage rates. While the diversity of the technical context is also significant, the general and nonoperational nature of many nationally determined rules on such items as production standards, manning requirements, transfers, and promotions suggest that there is difficulty in designing detailed and uniform rules to govern work places (in an industry) with widely different conditions, including diverse competitive constraints. It is relatively simpler to develop uniform procedural rules to be applied at diverse work places, concerning such items as steps to be followed in settling grievances, selecting representatives, or resorting to neutrals, than it is to provide detailed substantive rules.

In most Western European countries the role of the trade union in rule-making, including legislation, tends to be concentrated at the national or regional level rather than at the work place where works councils, or comparable bodies which have only an indirect hierarchical relation to the unions, are the instrumentality of worker concern or participation in the rulemaking process.[18] The larger the scope of the industrial-relations

gross weekly or hourly earnings and scheduled wage rates. It is often important to know the influence of each separate component affecting this divergence.

[18] Adolph Sturmthal, Ed., *Contemporary Collective Bargaining in Seven Countries*, Ithaca, N.Y., Cornell University Press, 1957; B. C. Roberts, *Trade Union Government and Administration in Great Britain*, Cambridge, Mass., Harvard University Press, 1956, pp. 57–79.

system—regional, industrywide, or national—with a given degree of diversity among enterprises, the more general the rules developed at the level in which trade unions participate. These national industrial-relations systems are thus internally consistent in that only generalized rules are established at the national or industrywide level and the details of rules of the actual work place involve separate organizations at the work place. Indeed, it may be suggested that the preoccupation of the unions with national or industrywide rules necessarily implies a lesser impact on the immediate rules of the actual work place, in the absence of subordinate bodies or local unions directly preoccupied with the rules of the work place. The traditional European dichotomy between the union and the works council is shaped by many factors including the political orientation of the unions, the dominance of localism over solidarity by industry, and the industrywide organization of employers, but it is strengthened by the fact that divergent competitive conditions among enterprises tend to create different rules at the work place. The problem is how to have national or industrial uniformity and still allow for the divergencies in rules required by lack of technical and market or budgetary homogeneity. Apparent uniformity on some issues, established with the unions, coexists with additional rules that are dissimilar and with quite different applications of the same general rules, established with the works councils.

The Size of Enterprises

In the preceding chapter on the technical context, the size of the work group at a single work place was treated as a significant factor shaping the complex of rules. It was there recognized that the market or budgetary context, in addition to technical factors, also influences the size of the single work place. The present concern is rather with the size of the enterprise, and while the technical context in turn plays a significant role, the consequence of the size of enterprise for the complex of rules will be discussed as a feature of the market or budgetary context. The size of the total market or budget, the character of competition or budgetary constraints, the prospects for long-term growth or retardation, and factor-market developments and prospects are well-recognized media through which the market context influences the size of an enterprise.

The larger the enterprise, the more necessary formal rules and the more complex the formal grid of communications within the hierarchies of the managers and workers and between them. The larger the enterprise, the greater the likelihood of specialized personnel among managers and workers to participate in the formulation and administration of the complex of rules. Rule-making and administartion may almost become the exclusive province of a group of specialists or professionals in the hierarchies associated with the largest enterprises. The larger the enterprise, the more likely that public-relations considerations play a role in the relationships between workers and managers, and the greater is the likelihood of direct governmental participation in rule-making.

In larger enterprises with more than one work place additional problems are created for rule-making and administration. Work places in a number of localities require balancing local conditions against enterprisewide uniformity in rule setting. Shall wage rates be set in each establishment in accordance with that locality or shall a uniform enterprisewide scale be established? A uniform scale may be higher than comparable work in some localities and lower than in others, but the policy of different scales within the same enterprise may well create considerable pressure for uniformity by raising the wage levels of the lower-rated work places to the highest. The same type of problem may arise with respect to holidays, health and welfare, and pension plans, manning schedules, seniority rules, and, indeed, almost any major rule of a work place. Moreover, enterprises with many work places must decide what rules shall be settled on an enterprisewide basis and which may be determined more or less independently at each particular work place.

The rules of an enterprise with a number of work places frequently must deal with the problems of transferring work operations and workers from one work place to another, problems that are absent, at least in this form, in the single work place. The rules may concern costs of transportation, moving expenses, family provisions, or the relative rights to jobs in one work place by workers normally attached to different work places.

Secular Expansion or Contraction

The market or budgetary context may be said to encompass the characteristic of a long-term expanding or contracting product demand or budget. Industrial-relations systems that are secularly expanding or contracting in employment often confront specialized problems which may result in distinctive rules at these work places. Thus, a shrinking system may be expected particularly to be concerned with rules on severance pay and on procedures and compensation to be applied in shutting down operations and work places. The relative rights among employees in the remaining jobs become of primary interest. The severance pay rules applicable to the editorial departments of newspapers are a response to the merger of newspapers and the decline in their numbers. In some contracting systems a variety of rules may be attempted to arrest the decline and to reduce costs or to shift output into new markets. A number of union-management cooperation plans were originated in this fashion.[19] The elaborate regulations regarding the transfer of workers, including the costs of moving, housing, and family expenses and compensation, in the rationalization of the British coal industry and the activities of the European Coal and Steel Community are significant illustrations of the impact of the market context on the rules of

---

[19] Sumner H. Slichter, *Union Policies and Industrial Management*, Washington, D. C., The Brookings Institution, 1941, pp. 393–571.

the work place. A contracting market may raise special problems for pension plans and other deferred-type compensation specialized to the industrial-relations system. The liquidation of the hosiery-industry pension plan is a startling instance of the need for special rules, although in this case the decline was concentrated in the unionized sector of the industry.

But all the problems do not lie with the industrial-relations system that is contracting; even expansion has its measure of specialized rules created by this feature of the market context. The experience of new industries affords many illustrations. A labor force which is specialized in some new skills or operations is often required, and rules regarding recruitment, hiring, and training (including unlearning of some practices) are likely to receive special emphasis. Special inducements for skills in particularly short supply have frequently been supplied. The development of work standards and norms for discipline may receive special attention. Safety rules in a new technology, as in atomic-energy installations, may require great concern at the outset. The whole structure of organization of the hierarchies of managers and workers are likely to require frequent appraisal and rearrangement in a rapidly expanding sector. The selection and training of leadership in these hierarchies under these market or budgetary conditions is often in a state of flux. One of the major problems of rule-making under conditions of rapid expansion arises from balancing the immediate needs for expansion against rules which are likely to persist when expansion ceases to be so urgent. Rapid recruitment may be achieved at the cost of compensation levels and work practices which later prove embarrassing, or new employees may receive advantages which create friction and resentment among longer-service employees. The war period provided many illustrations of these problems. The characteristic of long-term expansion or contraction of product markets or budgets may require specialized rules at the work place and may significantly influence the substance of more ordinary rules.

FEATURES OF LABOR AND OTHER FACTOR MARKETS

Characteristics of the Labor Force

The rules of a work place are formulated in the light of special characteristics of the actual and potential labor force. The interest at this point is not in those features of a labor force determined by the technical context, such as qualities of skill or location of the working place relative to residence and other points noted in Chapter 2, but rather in those characteristics of the labor force which are shaped largely by the labor market and its influence on the rules of the work place.

A simple illustration is afforded by the problem of the languages in which the rules of the work place are to be promulgated and the languages to be used in issuing orders within the hierarchies. When the work force is comprised of several different linguistic groups and when the native language of managers is different from that of the workers, a variety of problems of communication, rule setting, and administration inevitably arise: there are new dimensions to discipline; special training is required of both managers and workers; if language groups are stratified in the hierarchies, standards for promotion are affected, and the prospects of discrimination and tension are certain to arise. The communication problems of managers are greater, and the solidarity of the work force is affected by linguistic division. Linguistic characteristics of the work force thus affect the rules of the work place.

In analogous ways racial and nationalistic characteristics of the work force complicate the substance of rule-making. Many of the conflicts, prejudices and tensions of the local or regional community may be carried over into the work place. The question of whether there shall continue to be separate toilets for Negroes and whites in many industrial plants in Southern communities has frequently been an issue in collective bargaining; the active program of the United Packinghouse Workers in the meat-packing industry to seek to eliminate discrimination with respect to promotions, hiring, and other conditions of employment has received widespread attention. Middle East oil companies are frequently required by governmental regulation to confine foreigners to particular staff occupations and to expand the use of their nationals into these jobs, in some cases at a prescribed rate. The diverse cultural and racial backgrounds within many of these countries has created policies and practices in these companies allocating the scarce and highly regarded industrial job opportunities among these diverse groups within the labor market. Nationality may be an explicit factor in rules assigning priority to employment, as it is in the coal mines in many Western European countries or in construction in Switzerland. Racial, nationalist, and linguistic factors may also be significant to the organization of workers; separate organizations may be created for each group as existed for years among the German typographical workers and has existed for many years in the New York garment industry for Italian and Jewish groups.

The cultural and religious affiliations of a work force may have significant effects upon the rules of the work place. The scheduled days of work in the week are Saturday through Thursday in the Moslem world, and during the sacred month of Ramadhan the work days and hours may be curtailed. A break in scheduled hours of work may be required for specified calls to prayer. Both the number and the selection of holidays with pay will be significantly influenced by these characteristics of the work force and community. Only in Boston is Patriots Day celebrated.

The characteristics of the labor-market area from which a labor force is recruited may have significant effects upon the rules of the industrial work place regarding training and discipline. Agricultural workers without industrial experience may necessitate a relatively long probationary or learning period and special rules may be required regarding absenteeism, at least during certain seasons of the year.

> The South African coal-mining industry has special characteristics, which are due neither to geological conditions nor to technical factors. Its major problem arises from the manpower structure . . . when a Native came to the mine for the first time; he merely underwent a period of adjustment which could last up to two months. This period aimed at initiating him to the special conditions of underground work rather than giving him vocational training.[20]

Some communities are noted for a high degree of tension and conflict and for a high propensity to feuds, violence, and radicalism. Whatever the social relations and experiences which have created such communities, these features are likely to be reflected within the work place. Special rules respecting discipline, slowdowns, and work stoppages may arise to constrain this state of affairs at the work place. The highlighting of such "trouble spots" in surveys of industrial location is one indication of the significance of community and labor-force characteristics to the rules of a work place.

Labor-market Stringency

Just as product-market competition or the extent of budgetary stringency influences the freedom that the actors have in setting the rules of the work place, so the stringency of the labor market for the relevant skills or occupations has an impact on the rules determined. It is well established that the extent of competition in the labor market has some impact on particular wage rates. In regard to rules other than for compensation, the more stringent the labor market the more likely that uniform rules will

[20] International Labor Organization, Coal Mines Committee, Fifth Session, Düsseldorf, 1953, *Productivity in Coal Mines,* Second Item on the Agenda, Geneva, p. 31.

develop at different work places in the same locality, particularly among those which are a part of the same industrial-relations system.

The stringency of a labor market changes from day to day, but it should not be presumed that the rules likewise tend to change daily. Rather, a longer-period level of demand for labor, relative to supply, affects rule setting. The prolonged period of high-employment levels during the war and the postwar period no doubt did change rules in a number of work places, in addition to wage rates, that had been developed in a prolonged period of underemployment in the thirties. Thus, the spread of vacation and holiday practices into the maritime and construction fields, rather than corresponding increases in wage rates, is largely to be explained as labor-market imitations of more general practices in a period of comparative tightness in the labor market.[21] Indeed, the dramatic transformation in the labor force and rules of the work place of the maritime industry, including its lesser isolation from the rest of the community, is to be attributed to high levels of employment in the economy which deprived the industry of the type of work force it previously employed, to the cessation of immigration, and to the activities of the union.[22]

A number of industries which were adapted to low wages and a loose labor market in the Great Depression have since had to make drastic changes to accommodate a period of high wages and a tighter labor market. In the process the rules of the work place are transformed. Perhaps the most dramatic changes have come in the work place of family agriculture where many farms are no longer beset with surplus and unpaid family labor and a supply of cheap hired labor. The increased size of farms and mechanization of operations, with consequent changes in the practices and rules of the work place, have been associated

[21] International Labor Conference, Forty-first Session, 1958, First Item on the Agenda, *Report of the Director General*, Geneva, 1957, pp. 18–24.

[22] Joseph P. Goldberg, *The Maritime Story, A Study in Labor-Management Relations*, Cambridge, Mass., Harvard University Press, 1958.

with the postwar conditions of the labor market. Major changes have also occurred in other industries such as larkspur mining, many timbering operations, agricultural processing, and enterprises which depended upon low wage rates and a ready supply of labor.

Ratio of Labor Costs to Total Costs

Labor costs as a percentage of total costs vary widely among enterprises. In petroleum refining and meat packing, for instance, it tends to be a small figure, around 10 percent; in coal mining labor costs approximate two thirds of total costs, while in some service industries where almost all costs are labor costs the figure may even be higher. These ratios are significant for rule-making in that they show, in conjunction with other features of competitive position or budgetary control, how severe the impact of any change in labor costs may be on total costs and prices or budgets. This feature of the context of an industrial-relations system is influenced by a variety of technical and market factors, but its consequence for rule-making cannot be overlooked.

This ratio is a rough index of the concern of management at the work place with labor costs and the rules of the work place. This factor supplements the competitive or budgetary position as an indication of the degree of freedom available to the actors in making rules. A high ratio, unless offset by a considerable degree of control over product markets or budgets, tends to constrict greatly the capacity to determine rules of the work place and tends to focus management's attention upon compensation and all rules influencing labor productivity and labor costs. A low ratio, particularly when combined with a high degree of control over product markets or budgets, creates a wide range of discretion in the setting of rules and often appears to result in a variety of more favorable benefits than generally prevail in other industrial-relations systems. Where labor costs are a low percentage of total costs, the major energies and the principal attention of the management organization is more likely to be directed toward the purchase of raw materials or the capital structure than toward labor costs and the rules of the work place. On the other hand, where labor costs are a high percentage, management cannot escape the dominant impact of compensation, labor productivity, and rules of the work place upon its economic destiny. Such differences in the orientation of managements, created by the technical and market contexts, are significant to rule-making at the work place.

THE ATTACHMENT TO AN INDUSTRIAL-RELATIONS SYSTEM

In a sense, the most fundamental decision confronting rule-makers at a single work place or enterprise is the choice of the industrial-relations system to which they are to be a part.[23] In highly centralized national industrial-relations systems, the problem may take the form of prescribing the boundary to each industry or the enterprises to which each regulation applies. This choice should be construed to include the alternative of constituting a separate industrial-relations system for an enterprise or work place with some major deviations from the rules established in other systems. This decision may not always be made self-consciously, but a well-established practice of following or adopting the rules established in other work places may in fact constitute a commitment to the future, the recognition of common interests, and a sense of belonging to a particular industrial-relations system. The common rules frequently develop out of common contexts without detailed knowledge of the rules adopted elsewhere. The allegiance to a particular industrial-relations system

[23] In respect to the rules on compensation, the decision may be described as a choice of "wage contours," to use the concepts developed elsewhere. The scope of a wage contour tends to be equivalent to that of the relevant industrial-relations system within a country. John T. Dunlop, Ed., *The Theory of Wage Determination*, London, Macmillan and Co., 1957, pp. 16–22.

need not be irrevocable, as the technical and market contexts change, but in an industrial society these attachments are fairly stable for the vast proportion of work places and enterprises for considerable periods.

The normal preference of managers is to select an identification with an industrial-relations system defined in terms of enterprises or work places subject to the same or similar product-market competition or budgetary constraints. The normal orientation of workers and their representatives is to choose attachment to other work places in terms of similarity of differentiated labor-market characteristics with more favorable rules. It is, of course, to be recognized that managers are concerned with labor-market developments and workers with product market or budgetary constraints as previously noted. In many situations there is little conflict between these standards of selection of comparable work places, and the actors readily identify the work places and enterprises with which one is to be associated (formally or informally) for purposes of rule-making. Railroad managers and workers readily regard all sectors of the railroad network of a country, for instance, as part of one major industrial-relations system. In other cases, there may be conflict over whether an enterprise or work place is to be identified with others in terms of product-market or labor-market characteristics. The managers are concerned with the limitations imposed by their product market or budget and ordinarily prefer the rules established in the work places of their product-market competitors or by their fellow managers subject to the same budgetary constraints; the workers ordinarily prefer to adopt the rules established in the work places of other enterprises in the same differentiated labor market or under agreement with their same union. For instance, the issue whether the steel fabricators should follow the basic-steel wage pattern in 1946 involved just such a conflict over the scope of the basic-steel industrial-relations pattern, or in other terms, whether the fabricators were to establish in small groups or individually their own industrial-relations systems or be affiliated against their wishes to the basic-steel system.

There is no simple way, in theoretical terms or in practice,[24] to resolve such conflicts over the placement of a work place or enterprise in an industrial-relations system. Sometimes the differences in the rules established in the "competing" systems are minor and confined to a few issues which may be compromised, resulting in some unique rules. At times the compromise may take the form of aligning with the product-market grouping and accepting such rules subject to minor variations reflecting the imprint of labor-market characteristics; or the converse compromise may prevail accepting the rules established in the differentiated labor market or union grouping subject to minor variations in the direction of the rules adopted by the product-market competitors. In other instances, the complex of rules may be drawn partially from each of the systems toward which the actors were pushing. In still other cases, one group of actors may prevail fully, and the whole complex of rules of a system, or significant groups of rules, are imposed on a work place despite significant differences in its product or labor-market position from other work places governed by the same complex of rules. The promulgation of rules for a work place or enterprise, and thereby the attachment to an industrial-relations system, may be made by the third actor—specialized government agencies—rather than by decision of managers or workers.

Where managers or workers are highly dissatisfied with the industrial-relations system and the associated rules which may have been "imposed" on them, or which may have become onerous on account of changes in the technical and market or budgetary contexts, they may attempt a variety of action, aside from direct changes in the rules. Managers may liquidate the enterprise or work place or change the character of output to be more consonant with the product market or budget, and workers may

[24] Refer to Regulation No. 16 of the National Wage Stabilization Board.

"strike in detail" by leaving or may seek to change affiliation to an organization capable of imposing the desired system of rules.

The attachment or identification of a particular work place to an industrial-relations system tends to be well established at any given time for the vast majority of work places or enterprises. In a dynamic world, changes in technical and market or budgetary conditions are to be seen as gradually loosening the identification of some work places or enterprises to one industrial-relations system and creating new identifications with another system; the actual shift or recognition of the change is likely to be a discrete event. Work places and enterprises which themselves constitute isolated systems may attach themselves to larger systems, or those with marginal identification to a system may break away and develop their own rules, distinctive in some respects. The present paragraph is intended to avoid the twin errors of regarding, on the one hand, all work places in an industrial society as neatly divided or assigned into a small group of permanent industrial-relations systems, and on the other, envisaging each work place as somehow autonomously establishing rules which have little or no relation to others determined in an industrial society. It is sufficient for the present purposes to hold that the world of actual industrial-relations experience has sufficient stability and order to warrant the use of the concept of an industrial-relations system as a fruitful instrument in organizing and understanding the establishment of the rules of the work place.

The actors in an industrial-relations system in approaching the task of establishing rules for the work place have given to them at one time not only the technical context, discussed in the previous chapter, but they also confront given product-market or budgetary constraints and labor-market characteristics. A number of features of the market or budgetary context are to be distinguished: (1) competitive position or budgetary control, (2) the scope of the market or budget, (3) market or budget homogeneity among enterprises, (4) the size of enterprises, (5) secular expansion or contraction, (6) the characteristics of the labor force, (7) labor-market stringency, and (8) the ratio of labor costs to total costs. These features of the market or budgetary context decisively shape and influence the complex of rules developed to govern the work place. A complex of rules cannot be exclusively related to the market or budget context since the technical context and the locus and distribution of power in the larger community are also operative. But the market or budgetary context is an analytically significant determinant of the complex of rules.

The product-market or budgetary constraints and labor-market characteristics of a work place are significant to the definition of the scope of its industrial-relations system and to the long-term identification or attachment of the particular work place or enterprise to a system. The product-market or budgetary constraints and the labor-market characteristics may point to the same attachment. Common or similar conditions may prevail in the product and factor markets for a group of enterprises, and all actors in each may come to recognize, formally or informally, the tacit identification for purposes of rule-making. There may exist, however, conflict over the identification or attachment of a work place to one rather than to another industrial-relations system with different sets of rules. However these conflicts may be resolved, with stability in the market and technical context, the attachment or identification of a work place to an industrial-relations system tends to be relatively stable.

4 · The Power Context and
the Status of the Actors

IN addition to the technical context and the market or budgetary constraints, the third analytical dimension to the environment of an industrial-relations system is the locus and distribution of power in the larger society. This facet of the context
is decisive for defining the status of the actors: workers and their
organizations, managerial hierarchies, and governmental agencies. The complex of rules established for the work place, particularly those defining formal interrelations among the actors and
those providing arrangements for setting new rules and procedures for administering old ones, are often substantially shaped
by this feature of the total context.

A review of the full complex of rules applicable to a work
place shows that certain rules are only most remotely related to
the technical and market or budgetary context. For instance, in
most industrial-relations systems with labor unions in the United
States the rules provide for the "exclusive representation" by a
union in a defined "bargaining unit"; in most Western European
countries detailed rules applicable to the same technology and
markets specify the method of selection and the functions of
works councils. In Denmark the rules establish a Permanent

Court of Arbitration, selected by the confederations of employers and unions, to decide cases involving "breeches of agreement."[1] In a number of countries rules set forth a procedure extending agreements from the parties who make the agreements to all managers and workers in an industry with the binding force of law.[2] There is a wide variety of limitations on strikes and lock-outs.[3] The rules in national programs of factory legislation, social security, and family allowances involve basic differences among countries. These differences in rules among national industrial-relations systems can be seen more clearly when sets of rules from similar technological and market or budgetary contexts are compared.

A collection of rules for coal mining, for instance, shows a high degree of similarity among many coal-producing countries on such topics as house coal, mine-safety committees, provision of tools, housing or rents, measurement of hours from portal to portal or bank to bank, prohibition of payment in script, physical examinations, the structure of wage rates by occupations, and a variety of other matters. In this comparison of national coal rules, however, a number of other rules that relate more to the status of the actors and the procedures for establishing and administering rules at the work place reflect considerably greater differences and many unique features among countries. Examples of such

[1] *Industrial Relations in Denmark, Basic Collective Agreements and Laws on Labor Disputes,* edited and published by Social Tidsskrift, Copenhagen, 1947, pp. 14–22; Walter Galenson, *The Danish System of Labor Relations, A Study in Industrial Peace,* Cambridge, Mass., Harvard University Press, 1952, pp. 209–226.

[2] Adolph Sturmthal, *Contemporary Collective Bargaining in Seven Countries,* Ithaca, N.Y., Cornell University, 1957, pp. 327–334; Second International Congress of Labor Law, *National Reports, Content, Legal Effects, Application and Execution of Collective Agreements,* (Japan, p. 5), Geneva, 1957.

[3] International Labor Office, *Report of the Committee on Freedom of Employers' and Workers' Organizations,* 131st Session, Governing Body, Seventh Item on the Agenda, 6–10 March, 1956 (Cited hereafter as the *McNair Report*), pp. 178–196 (mimeographed); C. W. Jenks, *The International Protection of Trade Union Freedom,* London, Stevens and Sons, 1957.

rules are those which pertain to machinery for the settlement of disputes, status of workers' organizations, and social-security items (see Chapter 5).

In industrial-relations systems confined to a single enterprise, some rules are likely to reflect the position of the actors in the industry outside the work place as well as rules which have a distinctive countrywide flavor. As an illustration, a local plant outside the automobile-assembly or parts field, organized by the United Automobile Workers (UAW), is likely to have some rules distinctive to UAW affiliation, quite apart from the distinctive technical or market context of the enterprise. In the same way a single plant of a multiplant company in a specialized market and in a different technical context from its other plants may be expected to show rules which reflect its affiliation with the company.

It is in the analysis of countrywide systems of industrial relations, however, that the power context and the prescribed status of the actors attracts most attention. Indeed, it is almost these factors alone which have received attention in discussions of industrial-relations practices among countries. In countrywide comparisons, such as those examining the industrial-relations practices of the United States, France, Italy, or Germany (F.R.),[4] the rules of the work place that are peculiarly influenced by the technical context receive almost no attention. There are too many different technical contexts within a country to make comparisons very readily on a countrywide basis, and they may be fairly similar among countries.[5] The market context of a country as a whole has received only occasional attention in treating the consequences on wage rates and industrial peace of a

[4] National Planning Association, *Trade Unions and Democracy—A Comparative Study of United States, French, Italian, and West German Unions,* Planning Pamphlet 100, Washington, D. C., October 1957.

[5] A few studies of industrial relations of particular industries in one or more countries have noted the significance of technical and market factors, both in creating similarities and differences. A notable example is George B. Baldwin, *Beyond Nationalization: The Labor Problems of British Coal,* Cambridge, Mass., Harvard University Press, 1955.

high proportion of national product derived from export industries.[6] Detailed comparisons of industrial relations among countries based upon a market by market review have not been made.

The comparisons of industrial-relations practices among countries that have been made have tended to leave an exaggerated impression of the differences; the comparisons of industrial-relations systems as a whole do not reflect the impact of similar technical and market or budgetary contexts on the web of rules.[7] It is understandable that comparisons of countrywide industrial-relations systems should have concentrated largely on the power context and the prescribed status of the actors; these features of a countrywide industrial-relations system are considerably more uniform within a country than the technical and market or budgetary contexts. It is in the rules most directly derived from the power context that there exist the greatest differences among countries. The rules most dependent upon the technical and market contexts require much grubbing, and they have not concerned most experts in comparative industrial relations.

The primary objective of the present chapter is to develop the variety of features of the power context and to indicate the consequences of this feature for the work-place rules. In the previous two chapters, changes in the technical conditions and in the market or budgetary context were related to changes in the complex of rules. In the present chapter, changes in the power context and the status of the actors also tends to have significant consequences for the rules established at the work place. It is well understood that economic development changes the technical and market context, but it brings just as pronounced changes in the status of the actors. Economic development changes the rules of the industrial work place through recasting all three

[6] Mark Leiserson, *Post-war Wage Policy in Norway*, Cambridge, Mass., Harvard University Press, 1959.

[7] On the problems of making comparisons among national industrial-relations systems, refer to the delightful comments of Val R. Lorwin, *The French Labor Movement*, Cambridge, Mass., Harvard University Press, 1954, p. xvii.

features of the context of an industrial-relations system (see Chapters 8 and 9).

This third feature of the context of an industrial-relations system, at least in a system that is countrywide, is peculiarly the product of public policy, including the history and traditions of a country. Public policy may have minor direct effects on the technical contexts and somewhat greater effects upon the market or budgetary context through measures to control product and labor-market competition. But the status of the actors in a national industrial-relations system is largely within the explicit decision of the larger society by political processes, although all alternative forms are not to be regarded as equally congenial in the light of the traditions of a country.

When considering the power context of national industrial-relations systems, it is most important to distinguish between differences of form or style and those which have significant consequences for the complex of rules and the operation of a system. One illustration is afforded by the Danish Permanent Court of Arbitration; it is perhaps less significant to note that the court has the form of a governmental tribunal in contrast, say, to private arbitration in the United States than to observe that the court was established by agreement between the confederations of unions and employers, and that they effectively choose the members, including the neutral chairman who is appointed (or reappointed) each year.[8] The contrast in the degree of centralization and continuity in the two machineries is also to be noted. Differences in form, private or public, may be of concern to students of law, but they cannot be the primary interest of attempts to treat industrial relations more analytically.

A "rule" of the work place has been defined to include a wide variety of forms; a rule may be expressed in the form of an

---

[8] Only once since 1910 has it been necessary to invoke the alternate procedure by which the chairman is elected by the presiding justice of the Supreme Court and the other Copenhagen courts. Second International Congress of Labor Law, *Labor Law in Denmark*, Geneva, September 12–14, 1957, pp. 8–9.

agreement, a regulation, an award, a decree, a law, or an established custom or practice. At times an established or recognized practice is at variance with the stated regulations.

The status of any one of the actors in an industrial-relations system is defined to mean the prescribed functions of that actor and the relations with the other actors in the same system. These prescribed functions and relations may be largely imposed upon an industrial-relations system from outside by the community, as in the case of legislation affecting a countrywide system, or they may develop within the industrial-relations system and then be confirmed by community sanction or recognition. These prescribed functions and relations are treated as given at one period in time and constitute a context logically analogous to the technical and market or budgetary features of the whole context. The three sections of this chapter consider the status of each of the actors in an industrial-relations system.

THE STATUS OF WORKERS AND THEIR ORGANIZATIONS

The status of the workers and their organizations in a national industrial-relations system is depicted logically by the network of proscribed interrelations with: (1) the management hierarchy, (2) rival or potentially rival organizations of workers, (3) workers and their organizations, and (4) agencies of government. These are not autonomous or independently paired relations, and in a social system with a limited number of actors, often one prescribed relation defines others. Thus, in the United States the "exclusive bargaining representative" certified by a specialized governmental agency and granted to a union as the representative of the workers defines its status in relation to the management hierarchy; it also prescribes substantial limitations on the status of rival or potentially rival organizations of workers, and it further defines in some respects relations between workers and their organization.

1. *Relation to management.* The status of workers' organizations in respect to management in different national industrial-relations systems reveals a vast spectrum of experience.[9] In some few systems any form of worker organization is prohibited; the ancient master-servant relationship is unqualified. At times the master-servant relationship is harsh and dictatorial, and in other cases it is softened with paternalistic responsibility. In some instances worker organizations are tolerated solely in so far as they are strong enough, influential enough, or servile enough to secure attention by management. The spectrum encompasses cases in which formal recognition by management is permissive depending upon governmental registration, certification, approval, or designation. Formal recognition may be mandatory in accordance with countrywide agreements or with a governmental award, certification, or regulation.

The wide range of experience in the status of worker organizations, usually described by governmental regulation, is illustrated by a few brief citations from the *McNair Report.* No attempt is made in these quotations, or those which follow, to present a complete picture of the status of the actors in the national system. The status of workers' organizations with respect to management is at times implied rather than explicitly stated:

> Application for authorisation of a trade union must be submitted to the Ministry of Economic Affairs (Department of Social Affairs). The Ministry, after consultation with the Ministry of the Interior, issues an order granting or refusing the authorisation. . . . No appeal against the decision of the Minister is provided by the Labour Code. It would appear, therefore, that the administrative authorisation is discretionary in character. (Lebanon, Appendix II, Supplement, p. 281.)
>
> . . . the exclusive right to represent the interests of the em-

[9] *McNair Report,* pp. 101–105 and the cited country reports in the extensive Appendix II (1698 pp.) and Supplement (372 pp.), *Monographs Relating to State Members of the Organization.* The comparisons are made among countries at different stages of economic development. Logically it would be preferable for the present purposes to confine the comparisons to countries at approximately the same level of economic development.

ployers and workers in their particular categories, both in dealing with the public authorities and in making collective agreements, is accorded to registered organisations that have been "approved" by the Minister of Labour. (Brazil, p. 102.)

Trade union organisations are not, then, compelled to be registered. . . . In fact the relations between organisations of employers and workers, particularly with a view to the conclusion of collective labour contracts, are based on the appraisal made by these organisations of each other's *de facto* representative character. (Italy, Appendix II, pp. 905–906.)

In order that a trade union may conclude certain types of agreements with the employer, it must represent the majority of the workers in the establishment. . . . In order that a trade union shall be one by which the employer is required to consult on the formulation or amendment of the rules of employment, it must also represent the majority of the employees in the establishment. (Japan, Appendix II, p. 937.)

In 1936 legislative provision was made for compulsory unionism. This provision establishes the rule that workers who are subject to any award or industrial agreement registered under the Act must become members of a union, and it is not lawful for an employer to employ or continue in employment in any position subject to an award or industrial agreement any adult person who is not a member of a workers' union to which the award or agreement applies. . . . The main benefit from registration is that it enables a union of workers to compel employers to take part with it in negotiations in a Council of Conciliation or, if no agreement is reached, before the Court of Arbitration, which may make an award prescribing rates of wages and working conditions applicable to all employees in the industry. (New Zealand, Appendix II, pp. 1067–1068, 1070.)

The above rules refer to trade unions, and in a number of countries the status of works councils, by whatever term they are called, is separately prescribed. In Germany, France, and the Netherlands, for instance, statutes require works councils in plants with more than a specified minimum number of employees, and managements are required to treat with them on specified topics. In Sweden, on the other hand, the status of enterprise councils in relation to management was established through a

1946 agreement between the confederation of employers and unions.[10] In England "shop stewards and works councils are not known to the law"; [11] their status is not established by a single agreement but rather by separate agreements and by custom and practice.[12]

The status of workers' organizations in relation to management in particular sectors or specialized groups of employees reflects another spectrum of rules.[13] By regulation or by agreement, workers' organizations may be precluded from representing certain groups of employees in dealings with managements or limited in their representation: such is the case with employees performing certain supervisory duties,[14] agricultural employees, various categories of public employees, foreigners, and certain racial groups.[15]

The status of worker organizations in respect to management in different national industrial-relations systems is also reflected in the functions prescribed for the union, works council, or other worker organizations. In some countries these functions are very narrow while in others they constitute a very wide range of duties and responsibilities. Among those countries with the widest functions for workers' organizations is Israel where they ". . . have developed activities [16] which affect nearly every phase

[10] Lennart Vallstrand, *Works Councils in Sweden,* European Productivity Agency, Union Studies, No. 1 (n.d.).

[11] O. Kahn-Freund, "Legal Framework" in *The System of Industrial Relations in Great Britain,* Allan Flanders and H. A. Clegg, Eds., Oxford, Basil Blackwell and Mott, 1954, p. 50.

[12] B. C. Roberts, *Trade Union Government and Administration in Great Britain,* Cambridge, Mass., Harvard University Press, 1956, pp. 57–79.

[13] *McNair Report,* pp. 92–100 and the cited country reports in Appendix II.

[14] The September Agreement made in 1899 in Denmark provides in Section 5: "Salaried foremen, as such, shall have full liberty not to become members of a trade union. By salaried foremen is understood persons who are the employers' chosen representatives in relation to the workers, who do not undertake piecework, and who are not interested in piecework earnings."

[15] ". . . in the Union of South Africa, natives are debarred from forming or joining organizations under the Industrial Conciliation Act, 1937." *McNair Report,* p. 93.

[16] "In 1954 Histadrut was providing medical attention through its sickness

of the social and working life of the people, largely as a result of the fact that the Histadrut especially was, from the beginning and through sheer force of circumstances, a veritable partner of the Government in the building up of the life of the new State." [17] In Yugoslavia since the Basic Law of July 2, 1950, the workers' councils constitute a "system of worker self-management." [18] Each enterprise above a very nominal size is run by management bodies proceeding from and directly responsible to all the working force through elected workers councils. Each workers council makes decisions on the organization of the enterprise, the quantity and type of output, the purchase of raw materials and equipment, the sale of products, and sales prices, and it has a voice in the selection of the manager. In a number of countries the functions of the workers' organizations in some enterprises include a consultative, but not a decisional, role with regard to production, costs, safety, and other matters vital to the enterprise through joint consultative committees [19] or joint productivity committees.

The function of worker organizations in respect to management in many industrial-relations systems is formulated in terms of the "rights" of management. The September Agreement in Denmark (1899) provided, for instance, "The employer's right to direct and distribute the work and to use what labor may in

---

fund for 56 percent of the population. Seventy percent of Israel's cooperatives are affiliated with the Workers' Society, the economic organ of the Histadrut. All the enterprises associated with the Workers' Society taken together provide 18 percent of all employment for wage-earners in commerce and industry, including agriculture. Undertakings affiliated with the Workers' Society of Histadrut include five transport cooperatives, an airline, the biggest building enterprise, brick factories, an iron foundry, cement works, a glass factory, flour mills, an oil factory, fruit-processing plants, shipping interests, a bank, and an insurance company."

[17] McNair Report, Appendix II, pp. 877–878.

[18] McNair Report, Appendix II, pp. 1645–1698; R. Uvalic, "The Management of Undertakings by the Workers in Yugoslavia," International Labour Review, March 1954, pp. 235–254. For a fuller discussion of the Yugoslav industrial-relations system, see Chapter 7.

[19] H. A. Clegg and T. E. Chester, "Joint Consultation," in Flanders and Clegg, loc. cit. pp. 323–364.

his judgment be suitable at any time is acknowledged by, and if necessary must be supported by, the workers' central organization. . . . ." [20]

While every industrial-relations system requires managers and workers, these illustrations reveal the diversity among national systems in the status of workers' organizations with respect to management and the differences in functions performed by workers' organizations in the management direction.

2. *Relation to rival workers' organizations.* The status of worker organizations in an industrial relations system is partly prescribed by the relation to rival or potential rival organizations of workers, by the extent and form of competition for the loyalty and affiliation of workers, and by recognition by managements and governmental agencies. In some systems there is little rivalry while in others there is a great deal, and the prescribed rules of a countrywide system frequently constrict and channel the scope of such competition. As has already been noted the status of workers' organizations in relation to any one group is frequently intertwined and defined in terms of its relations with other groups in the system.

There may be rivalry among union organizations for authority to represent workers in making agreements with management, in appearing before arbitration bodies and labor courts on behalf of workers, and in occupying positions of consultation and membership on governmental boards. Some illustrations of the range of these experiences is afforded by the following brief quotations from the *McNair Report:*

> The registration of a union does not make any fundamental difference to its powers. An unregistered union has equal rights with a registered union to represent workers or employers respectively in collective bargaining and in relations with the public authorities. . . . No distinction is made in law between the various trade unions organisations on the ground of their representative character and no particular organisation of work-

---

[20] Galenson, *loc. cit.,* Appendix B, p. 291.

ers or employers enjoys a legal monopoly of representation of workers or employers, respectively. (United Kingdom, Appendix II, pp. 1537, 1539.)

The granting of legal status to an employers' or workers' organisation does not constitute an obstacle to the subsequent granting of legal personality to another employers' or workers' organisation the members of which are engaged in the same activity or district.

The following Acts thus provide for the admission of occupational organisations to organised consultations for the study of certain questions only if these organisations are considered sufficiently representative; these are the Economic Organisation Act of 1950, the Works Councils Act and the Act on the Organisation of Social Insurance of 1952. . . . The Government maintains that an industrial organisation must be representative in order to take part in the procedure for consultation and cooperation in the field of decisions taken by the Board of Conciliation, following the finding of the Labour Foundation. (Netherlands, Appendix II, pp. 1027, 1028.)

The constitution of representative organisations (*sindicatos*) on the other hand is subject to the preliminary condition of recognition on the part of the State and of the limitation that not more than one such organisation per occupation is allowed in any given area. Only recognised organisations may exercise the function of collective representation for the occupational category concerned and other functions typical of industrial organisations. . . . Brazilian law permits of any number of parallel associations but, for purposes of the representation of an "occupational or economic category," it calls for the single union. (Brazil, Appendix, Supplement, pp. 83–84.)

If, however, two or more unions fulfilling the conditions necessary for registration apply for registration in respect of the same industry in any local area, the union having the largest membership of workers employed in the industry is registered. . . . Representative unions are the sole bargaining agents in all proceedings in which they are entitled to appear. (India, Bombay Act, Appendix II, p. 764.)

. . . there may be, in respect of any undertaking, only one trade union of wage earners and one trade union of salaried employees (but these may combine) and, in respect of the same occupation, craft or trade, only one trade union in a particular locality. The formation of one union or federation precludes the establishment of another for the same undertaking or for the same occupation and locality. . . . The law provides that only one central confederation may be formed. (Egypt, Appendix II, pp. 485–486.)

. . . restrictions are imposed on the formation of new unions of workers or of employers in a district where a union in the same industry exists. No such union may be registered unless the Minister of Labour concurs. This safeguard against the formation of rival unions was strengthened in 1951 by requiring the Minister's approval before any registered industrial union may alter its rules so as to include in its membership any employers or workers who could already properly belong to another existing registered industrial union or trade union. (New Zealand, Appendix II, pp. 1070–1071.)

In view of the fact that the percentage of organisation is very high both for employers and workers in Denmark, in particular within the fields covered by the Danish Employers' Confederation and the Confederation of Danish Trade Unions, the law generally provides for these central organisations to enjoy the right to appoint a certain number of members to commissions, committees, etc., dealing with questions of labour law. (Denmark, Appendix II, p. 430.)

The status of labor unions is not alone defined in terms of competition with other unions but also by the relations between the unions and works councils or other organizations of workers at the immediate work place. There may also be competition between union organizations or workers' councils and an "unorganized" work place in which individual workers press problems on their own behalf, sometimes through machinery established by the government. In the United States and Canada the workers' organization at the work place is the local union, and there is a direct line of communication and authority from the national union to the individual member at the work place. In other national systems, at least for some periods, the immediate work place organizations have resisted control by the unions and have asserted varying degrees of independence from the unions, as was the case with the "shop stewards movement" in Great Britain during the first World War.[21] In France "there is no lack of grievance channels; in fact there is a proliferation of channels created by government regulation": *conseil de prud'hommes*, ministry of labor inspectors, bipartite discipline committees, *délégué du personnel*, *comité d'entreprise*, and the approach of individual workers.[22] The Hungarian government apparently found the elected workers' councils too independent and replaced them with shop-stewards councils, two thirds of whose members are appointed from the trade unions, the party, and the youth movement.[23] In defining the status of the workers' hierarchy in an industrial-relations system it is imperative to specify the relations, including the extent of competition, between the immediate work-place organization and the unions.

In most national industrial-relations systems the relations between the work-place organizations and the unions is complex: [24] in some the unions select a slate of candidates for the works councils; they may maintain schools for training candidates; they may hold meetings with members of such councils and provide more or less effective leadership and programs, and in other cases the members of the work-place committees may be designated by the unions. In general, the greater the degree of independence of the works councils and comparable work-place committees from control by the unions, the greater is the degree of potential competition and the narrower the scope of the function of the unions. In a single country the practice typically varies widely among plants as to the extent of control exercised by the unions and the extent of competition they face from the works councils.

[21] G. D. H. Cole, *Workshop Organisation*, London, Oxford University Press, 1923.

[22] Lorwin, *loc. cit.*, pp. 255–276. See, Henry W. Ehrmann, *Organized Business in France*, Princeton, N.J., Princeton University Press, 1957, pp. 420–471.

[23] "Worker Councils Ended in Hungary," *The New York Times*, International Edition, November 18, 1957.

[24] Marcel David, *La Participation des Travailleurs à la Gestion des Entreprises privées, dans les Principaux Pays D'Europe Occidentale*, Paris, Librairie Dalloz, 1954. The study considers the experience of France, Italy, Belgium, Western Germany, Norway, and Great Britain.

As would be expected, when the status of the works council is established in detail by agreement between employers' federations and national unions or confederations, there is probably less occasion for conflict and competition, as is the case in Sweden and in Italy. The *Commissioni Interne* in Italy historically tended to be responsive to trade unions, although after World War I, particularly in the Turin metallurgical plants, they were the instrument through which the revolutionary elements made their bid for challenging the leadership of the dominant reformist trade-union movement. Prior to the splits in the trade unions of 1948–1949,

> The distribution of power within the Commissions would appear to have been parallel to that of the trade-union movement itself. Under these circumstances and the general supporting role played by the trade union provincial offices in grievance matters, there was little manifestation of competition between the trade unions as an institution and the Commissions.[25]

In this view, the split up of the Italian trade-union movement in 1948–1949 changed the relations between the unions and commissions, but it brought no more competition between the unions and commissions. Rather, the commissions became a principal focal point of interunion rivalry; they were now a prize to be won by competition.

Where the status of the works councils is established pursuant to legislation and their existence is independent of the unions, there appears to be more occasion for rivalry. The circumstances under which the legislation establishing the works councils is adopted affect the status of the work-level bodies.[26] In Germany

[25] Daniel L. Horowitz, "Structural and Internal Organization," an unpublished chapter in a manuscript on Italian labor history. For a view which emphasizes a greater degree of competition between the Commissions and the trade unions in Italy, see Maurice Neufeld, *Italian Unions and National Politics in Italian Industrial Plants*, Ithaca, N.Y., Cornell University Press, 1954.

[26] On occasion, as in Denmark, the status of works councils may be formulated directly by unions and managers and then confirmed by governmental action. Galenson, *loc. cit.*, pp. 247–254. For an account of the intro-

the role of the unions has been narrowly constricted, in large part by the statutory functions exercised by the works councils but also by the operations of the political parties linked with the trade unions. "The German trade-union movement . . . found itself in an environmental context which limited greatly its sphere of action. . . . It could not get into close contact with the workers in the plants because the works councils were there already. It could not gain support of all workers since the German employee group is highly stratified. . . ."[27]

In the election to works councils in Belgium, the act of September 20, 1948 states that ". . . the employees' representatives and substitutes shall be elected by secret ballot from lists of candidates submitted by the most representative organizations of employed persons."[28] This affords the "most representative organisations" the opportunity for control over the designation of slates. The relations between the works councils and the unions will also depend upon whether independent candidates may also run and what is their record of success against union-designated and -backed candidates.

One of the most significant features of a national industrial-relations system is the relations between national labor organizations and groups at the immediate work place. In Western Europe works councils exist with varying degrees of independence from the unions. This arrangement of workers' organizations may be explained in the following terms. A working force which is deeply split by ideological, confessional, and class lines (including the distinction between white-collar and manual workers or employees and workers) requires some mechanism for a degree

---

duction of the French *comités d'entreprise,* see Henry W. Ehrmann, *loc. cit.,* pp. 446–460.

[27] Clark Kerr, "The Trade Union Movement and the Redistribution of Power in Postwar Germany," *Quarterly Journal of Economics,* November 1954, p. 562. See also Herbert J. Spiro, *The Politics of German Codetermination,* Cambridge, Mass., Harvard University Press, 1958; Werner M. Blumenthal, *Codetermination in the German Steel Industry,* Industrial Relations Section, Princeton, 1956.

[28] *McNair Report,* Appendix II, p. 123.

of unity of action in dealing with managers at the work place. The works council permits such unity while preserving the traditional trade-union cleavages. The trade-union attachment to political activities and the high degree of industrywide organization of employers with which the unions deal on a national basis have been contributing factors making for the independent role of the works councils. In the United States, on the other hand, exclusive representation is associated with a single line of union organization from the national level to the immediate work place. This is probably the most distinctive and fundamental characteristic of the industrial-relations system of the United States. In countries in the Soviet orbit, there is likewise a single line of authority from the national level to the immediate work place, but the authority of the Communist party is decisive.

The rules that define the status of workers' organizations, in terms of their relations to rival organizations, are a most significant characteristic of an industrial-relations system arising from the power context of the larger society. These arrangements are given to a national industrial-relations system at one point in time.

3. *Relation to workers.* The status of workers' organizations in an industrial-relations system is further prescribed by the relations between labor organizations and the workers. In some national systems the rules regarding the relations of members (workers) to officers and to the organization are determined purely by the internal processes of the organization. In other cases these relations are partially specified in collective agreements as in the United States in regard to union security and the check off, and in many countries there are varying forms of governmental regulations specifying aspects of the relations between workers and their organizations. Some illustrations of the range of these experiences is provided in the following brief quotations from the *McNair Report:*

> There is nothing in the legislation which restricts the right of members of workers' and employers' organisations to elect

their representatives freely and to organise their administration. There is no supervision or approval of their rules, and the law does not prescribe any subjects which must necessarily be dealt with therein. The organisations may freely draw up their programmes and policies and take decisions on any matters that concern them, including questions of a political nature. (Sweden, Appendix II, Supplement, pp. 154–155.)

Trade union organisations are not, then, compelled to be registered. They may freely draw up their rules, regulate their administration, and elect their executive organs, without having to conform to any rules decreed by the State; they are free from any control or interference by the State. (Italy, Appendix II, p. 905.)

If a works' union represents 60 percent of those employed there, the remainder are deemed to be members. . . . Law No. 319/1952 provides for minors, persons under disability, members of unions who retain their membership after leaving their employment and persons convicted of a felony . . . may not be members of a union executive committee. . . . The law requires that trade unions shall conduct their business in conformity with their rules, which must include rules on a number of stated subjects. They must also maintain their minutes of meetings and books of account, in accordance with rules prescribed by the Minister. (Egypt, Appendix II, pp. 485–486.)

With respect to registered trade unions, the Indian Trade Unions Act lays it down that not less than half of the total number of its officers shall be persons actually engaged or employed in the industry with which the union is connected. . . . The general funds of a registered trade union can be spent only in furtherance of certain objects specified under Section 15 of the Indian Trade Unions Act. It may constitute a separate fund for political purposes but no member may be compelled to contribute to such a fund. . . . The constitution of a registered trade union must contain provisions for certain prescribed matters. . . . Registered trade unions have to comply with the requirement concerning the submission of properly audited annual statements of receipts and expenditure to the Registrar. (India, Appendix II, pp. 766–767.)

Entrance fees, subscriptions and levies of unions are regulated by statute. . . . The rules of industrial unions must provide that the election of officers of industrial unions shall be by secret ballot of financial members, or by such other democratic method as the Registrar may approve. The Registrar may, on application by at least ten financial members of a union, refer to the Court of Arbitration for inquiry a disputed election of union officials. . . . Section 70 of the 1954 Act empowers the Registrar to refuse to record any rule of amendment on the grounds that it is unreasonable or oppressive, but his decision is subject to appeal to the Court of Arbitration. (New Zealand, Appendix II, pp. 1071–1072.)

The internal elections of "sindicatos" are subject to detailed regulations. . . . The ballot is counted by a committee presided over by a representative of the Labour Ministry. . . . The right of the Minister to intervene is provided for in Article 528 which states that "Should disputes arise or circumstances occur which may disturb the working of the organisation, the Minister of Labour, Industries and Commerce may intervene through a delegate empowered to take over the administration of the association and to execute or propose the measures necessary in order that it should function normally. . . ."

But the main source of income is the contribution which is payable to the organisations by all the members of the occupational and economic categories concerned, even if they are not members of the organisation. . . . The financial affairs of the organisations are subject to supervision by the Ministry of Labour. (Brazil, Appendix II, Supplement, pp. 89–92.)

These illustrations show that in defining the status of workers' organzations in a national system the status of leaders and their relations to members have often received attention. In a number of the countries which have only recently begun to industrialize, rules have frequently been prescribed providing that leadership be restricted in some ways to workers; the objective is apparently to preclude intellectuals, professional groups, and politicians with the advantages of formal education from gaining elective office. In other countries the same results have been achieved by hard experience and tradition, while in still others intellectuals have played a significant role in the leadership of the labor organizations directly or through their political associations. The limitations on the political affiliations of the leadership, either that it cannot be or that it is required to be affiliated with a particular political party, is another feature defining the status of workers' organizations in an industrial-relations system. The large number of rules—constitutions and bylaws—which are essential to the internal operation of any organization, as has been illustrated, may be left entirely to workers or may be prescribed in varying degrees by governments. These diverse arrangements for workers' organizations are likely to affect their relation with the other actors and are presumed to influence the web of rules which are particularly related to the power context.

4. *Relation to agencies of government.* The status of workers' organizations finally is defined with reference to governmental agencies. In some considerable degree the role of government is made evident by defining, as has already been done, the relations of workers' organizations to management, to rival organizations of workers, and to their members since governmental regulations and agencies have been one of the principal means of defining these relations and hence the status of workers' organizations. The concern now is with the definition of the status of workers' organizations in their direct relations to governmental agencies rather than in the definition of their relations to management, rivals, or members through governmental regulation. Some illustrations of the variety of these relations among countries is suggested by the following brief quotations from the *McNair Report.*

> The legislation contains no provision for the control by public authorities of the financial management of the workers' and employers' organisations and the Government does not grant any subsidies to these organisations . . . there is no legislative provision which empowers administrative authority to resort to dissolution or suspension of employers' or workers' organisations. (Norway, Appendix II, p. 1115.)
> There is no general arrangement for the granting of subsidies to employers' or workers' organisations, but assistance is given in certain cases. For instance, it is reported that the Government

of Orissa distributed a sum of Rs. 6 lakhs amongst certain unions in February 1955 for expansion of library facilities and for providing recreational facilities for their members. . . .

. . . grants are being made to workers' unions or associations for purposes of recreation, education, etc. (India, Appendix II, p. 767.)

The Minister may return the budget to the union with such observations as he considers necessary. The Committee of the organisation must amend the budget in accordance with these observations and submit it to the General Meeting of the Union. . . . Subsidies may be granted for various purposes in the following order of priority: (a) workmen's compensation in case of accident; (b) the organisation of vocational and technical studies for workers; (c) campaigns against illiteracy; (d) publicity and the production of workers' bulletins; (e) the construction of buildings for workers' dwellings and for the offices of trade union organisations; (f) promotion of the welfare of the workers and the establishment of workers' clubs. The Ministry of National Economy may, under the penalty of depriving the organisation of subsidies, determine by Ministerial Order the principles for collecting, paying, and allocating expenditure. (Syria, Appendix II, p. 1352.)

The organisations may be dissolved against the will of the members either by the authority which legalised their existence, or by law "if they are considered contrary to public policy, law or good behaviour; or if they do not fulfil the objects for which they were formed or fail to comply with instructions given to them by the General Directorate of Labour in virtue of its powers." (Chile, Appendix II, p. 298.)

The preamble to the Statutes of the Trade Unions of the U.S.S.R. . . . provides . . . "they conduct all their activities under the guidance of the Communist party of the Soviet Union, the organising and directing force of Soviet society." . . .

In a group of countries of which the U.S.S.R. is the leading example, one of the distinctive features is that the workers' organisations perform certain functions elsewhere more commonly exercised by the Government, in the field of social security, occupational safety and health, and labour inspection, or some of these matters. . . .

The Soviet trade unions also manage a considerable part of the national property set aside for education and the leisure of the workers. (USSR, Appendix II, p. 1472; p. 125; Appendix II, p. 1498.)

The power of governments to direct the affairs of labor organizations, to control their finances, to prevent their formation or to dissolve the organizations, or to enhance their standing and functions in the community varies widely and in minute detail among the seventy countries covered by the *McNair Report*. This comprehensive comparative survey undoubtedly provides the most extensive data thus far compiled on the status of workers and their organizations in national industrial-relations systems. Although the data were marshalled and organized around the problem of freedom of association, the individual-country reports are a major source of data and convenient reference for the comparative study of the power context and the status of labor organizations, managements, and governments in national industrial-relations systems. These data leave the impression of a wide diversity of arrangements; the status of the workers and their organizations at any one time are set forth in the laws, practices, and traditions of each country.

THE STATUS OF MANAGEMENT HIERARCHIES

The status of management in an industrial-relations system may be logically described in terms of the network of prescribed interrelations with (1) the workers and their organizations when such organizations exist, (2) rival or other management hierarchies, and (3) agencies of government. These are not entirely separate or autonomous relations, and one relationship is frequently expressed in terms of the others or associated with them. The discussion in the preceding section of the spectrum of relationships between workers and their organizations and managements, which go to define the status of workers and their organizations in an industrial-relations system, is the converse of the relationship of managers to workers which goes to define the status of managers in an industrial-relations system.

1. *Relation to workers' organizations.* The status of management with reference to workers and their organizations is reflected in the nature of the authority exercised by managers over workers at the work place.[29] National industrial-relations systems range in a spectrum from countries where managerial authority at the work place has few, if any, restraints to those in which it is very narrowly constrained by workers' organizations, governments, and managerial associations. A countrywide system is likely to show considerable internal variations; all managers at comparable points in hierarchies do not have the same authority in a country, even if allowance is made for differences in the technical and market contexts.

A classification of managers according to the status of their authority toward workers has been developed elsewhere,[30] as a part of the larger project on Labor Problems in Economic Development which can be fruitfully adapted to make more tractable the full spectrum of actual experience. The status of the managerial hierarchy with reference to workers or their organizations may be designated:

1. *Dictatorial.* Managerial authority is exercised without any formal constraint or redress from the workers. A distinction is to be drawn between systems in which authority is arbitrarily or capriciously exercised and systems in which authority is asserted only strictly in accordance with a web of rules which has been solely imposed by management.

2. *Paternal.* Managerial authority is exercised with little or no constraint or redress from the workers through a web of rules which are designed to reflect an acknowledgment of obligations by the managerial hierarchy to workers, that naked managerial authority often creates unproductive re-

---

[29] Reinhardt Bendix, *Work and Authority in Industry, Ideologies of Management in the Course of Industrialization,* New York, John Wiley and Sons, 1956.

[30] Frederick H. Harbison and Charles A. Myers, *Management in Industrial Societies,* New York, McGraw-Hill Book Company, 1959, Chs. 3–4.

actions on the part of workers, and that the objective is to secure the loyal service of workers.

3. *Constitutional.* Managerial authority is exercised only in accordance with a web of rules which the management hierarchy did not formulate alone. A distinction is to be drawn between the pure case in which governments exercise some role in the formulation of parts of the web of rules and the pure case in which workers' organizations exercise some role in the formulation of the web of rules. In actual systems both governments and workers are involved in varying degrees in the rule-setting and rule-administering process.

4. *Worker-participative management.* Managerial authority is exercised to draw from individual workers and their organizations the largest possible participation in consultations and suggestions prior to decision-making on a wide range of matters affecting the enterprise and prior to the application of the established web of rules to particular situations.

The classification defines the status of managerial authority in the industrial-relations system with respect to workers. The present chapter is interested in the character of managerial determination of the rules of the work place rather than in managerial philosophies or ideologies that may be associated with each type. The references cited include numerous illustrations of each status of management, and so no cases need be described at this point.

2. *Relation to other managements.* The status of managerial hierarchies in an industrial-relations system is also prescribed in part by their relations to managerial rivals and competitors and to the extent of competition among managements in the determination of the rules of the work place applicable to their workers. In some circumstances there may be rivalry or competition among managements or their associations for authority to make agreements with workers, to represent managements before tribunals, or to hold positions of consultation on governmental boards or commissions. Some indication of the range of experi-

ence on the status of managements in this respect is apparent from the illustrations quoted above from the *McNair Report*. The status of worker and managerial organizations are frequently defined simultaneously and by comparable standards. The regulations of government typically determine whether an association of managers shall have exclusive rights to enter into agreements with workers' organizations in an industry, sector, or locality, or whether they face open competition from others. Moreover, in many national systems certain conditions and regulations are prescribed for managerial associations in registration or in order to participate before tribunals just as conditions are prescribed for workers' organizations.

In many national systems managerial hierarchies, even in the same industry, have been split by differences along confessional and ideological lines which preclude unity of organization in treating organizations of workers. In the Netherlands, for instance, the Foundation of Labor and the Social and Economic Council are instrumentalities where national organizations of employers organized into three groups along denominational and ideological lines may treat with workers' organizations similarly divided in a single forum.[31] Differences in competitive position, dependence on foreign trade, and size of operations may also be divisive influences among managements. Racial and nationalistic differences may be important, particularly in affecting the affiliation of foreign enterprises.

The division between public or private managements may also affect the solidarity of management organizations in their dealings with workers' organizations. "In general, it does not seem to be customary for government-controlled corporations or undertakings to join employers' associations."[32] There are significant

[31] The Central Social Employers' associations, the General Catholic Association of Employers' trade unions, and an association of Protestant Christian Employers. P. S. Pels, "The Development of Collective Employment Agreements in the Netherlands," in *Contemporary Collective Bargaining in Seven Countries*, Adolph Sturmthal, Ed., Ithaca, N.Y., Cornell University Press, 1957, p. 105.

[32] *McNair Report*, p. 71.

exceptions to this generalization, however, such as the Canadian National Railways, the Renault factories in France and some sixteen Finnish companies, of which the state is the principal stockholder, with 10 percent of the employees of members of the Finnish Employers' Confederation. But affiliation with an employers' association does not establish a full identity of interests nor does it guarantee in all instances conformity to policies in regard to workers' organizations.

3. *Relation to government agencies.* The status of managerial hierarchies in an industrial-relations system is finally defined in terms of the relation to government. The concern here is not with the governmental prescription of the relations of managements to workers or their organizations or to managerial rivals but rather with the direct status of managerial hierarchies in their relationship to government. Here again there is a wide spectrum of experience [33] ranging from national systems largely characterized by private enterprises to countries in which the public sector covers virtually the entire field of economic enterprise. Within many countries there is a mixture in varying proportions of public and private management; the relative size of the public sector has grown in most countries in the past two decades.

The variabilities in the status of managements with respect to government in industrial-relations systems is illustrated by the following types of experience ranging away from purely private management. In the same product markets public enterprises may compete with private enterprises. Enterprises may be organized as public utilities subject to public regulation of all major decisions including those affecting workers. The enterprise may be owned partially, to a greater or lesser degree, by government as a mixed company and subject to varying degrees of direction by governmental agencies. The French National Railways and the Italian Industrial Reconstruction Institution are well-known instances. The enterprise may be organized as a government corporation with control exercised through government-appointed

[33] *McNair Report*, pp. 27–70.

directors and managers as are many Indian government enterprises. The enterprise may be a regular unit of the government, as a nationalized industry or the mint, reporting directly to a minister or cabinet officer. There are a variety of special development plans, such as those under the Iraq Development Board, the Peruvian Corporation for the Santa Region, or the Pakistan Industrial Development Corporation, which establish a distinctive status to the management hierarchy. In this array, mention must also be made of the status of management in the USSR and countries with similar economic organization.[34] There is also the unusual position of managers in respect to workers' councils in Yugoslavia which is particularly difficult to classify.

The status of the managerial hierarchy, as defined by its position in such an array, is significant to its relations with the workers or their organizations. When managers are more or less directly responsible or susceptible to pressure from governmental authorities, additional avenues of influencing managers are opened to workers' organizations. The status of managers and their enterprises in the industrial-relations systems may depend upon their standing with bureaucrats, ministers, legislators, or party leaders and their relative influence compared to leaders of worker organizations. The concern here is apart from the degree of budgetary constraint already regarded as a different facet of the context. The public character of an enterprise may be a measure of the extent to which public opinion, wide attention, and publicity attend the actors in the particular industrial-relations system. In such cases the public posture of the actors becomes a feature of the context that is significant to the status of the actors and the operation of the system. The time horizons or perspective of the managers may be influenced by the position of an enterprise in the above array of types of public managements; public enterprises may have longer horizons and consider a wider range of social costs while in other cases, particularly those which have a high degree of turnover, they may be im-

---

[34] Berliner, *loc. cit.*; *McNair Report*, Appendix II, pp. 1456–1527.

pelled to achieve the immediate plan without regard to social costs or longer-run interests of the enterprise and those more permanently associated with it.[35] Thus, the motivations for public managers built into the system and the methods of social accounting [36] may have significant consequences for an industrial-relations system. The differences between public managers and private managers, experience appears to show, is not in any one single direction, and the differences depend largely upon the system of rewards and penalties built into the national industrial-relations system.

THE STATUS OF GOVERNMENTAL AGENCIES

The status of the government as an actor in an industrial-relations system finally must be defined before the status of all the actors is complete. The preceding discussion of the network of relations which defines the status of workers' organizations and managerial hierarchies included, however, their separate relationships to government. In proceeding now to the government as an actor, the two earlier sections have already separately treated the interrelations between each of the two actors and government. The task that remains is to define the role of the government itself in determining substantive rules directly or through determining the rules of the interaction between workers and managers. This section encompasses accordingly the status of the right to strike and lock out, and the agreement, award, or substantive regulation of the work place by government, its extension, and the procedures for its administration or application to particular cases.

A distinction must be drawn between systems in which the

---

[35] "It is with the short run that the manager is concerned and only the premiums vary in the short run," Berliner, loc. cit., p. 49.

[36] In decisions on expansion of plant, for instance, whether or not the costs of additional housing for workers and community facilities are included may well affect the methods of production selected and the basic decision to expand.

status of government is defined and prescribed in statutes or constitutions and is reasonably predictable by tradition and practice from systems in which the actions of government are largely unrestrained and unpredictable and are frequently arbitrary or capricious. This distinction is analogous to the reference above to dictatorial and constitutional management. The present concern is necessarily with systems in which the role of government no matter how absolute or constrained has some stability and predictability. A further distinction must be made between the status of government in industrial-relations systems during periods of war or similar crises and during periods without armed conflict. The present concern is with nonwar periods; experience demonstrates that during war periods the role of government in an industrial-relations system tends to be enhanced.

National industrial-relations systems reveal a wide variety of experience in the role of government directly in rule setting, as distinct from prescribing the relations of managers and workers. It is possible, however, to classify the rules prescribed by government into three types: (1) One or more rules, or the full complex of rules, takes the form of a legislative enactment, an award of a tribunal, or a decision of an administrative agency. These determinations usually apply to all managers and workers or to those in specified sectors, industries or other groupings. Occasionally such a determination may apply solely to a particular dispute. The provisions for social security in most countries, the legislative enactment of vacations with pay in France and Sweden, many of the rules for maritime employment in many countries, and the awards of arbitration courts in Australia and New Zealand are of this type. In some instances governmental action may be used to settle a particular dispute in an *ad hoc* fashion.[37] (2) A form of a rule may be specified as permissive by government and then included in appropriate collective agreements or actual rules of employment when adopted by workers and managers. The

---

[37] See, for instance, legislative enactments in Denmark, Galenson, *loc. cit.*, pp. 130–138. The Canadian parliament has directed arbitration within specified limits in a particular railway dispute.

rules in the United States as to the check off and union security are of this nature. The provisions of collective contracts in the USSR appear to be somewhat of this character.[38] (3) The rules may be formulated by managers and workers, and then may require the approval of governmental agencies before they are put into effect. This has been the situation, for instance, in the Netherlands since 1945. These three types of governmental rule fixing constitute a descending order in the directness of governmental prescription.

But behind these differences in the form of governmental rule-making lie the substance of the extent to which governmentally prescribed rules are in fact determined by managers and workers' organizations and then adopted by the governmental agency. Even when no agreement is reached between managers and workers, governmental rules may arise from extended consultation and approach a consensus. Or the government may not have accepted the precise agreement. There may well be a variety of very subtle relations among the actors in a national industrial-relations system, and it is most significant for students of industrial-relations systems to see through such veils of governmental rule-making.[39] The actors in the system seldom confuse form with the reality. Thus, in Australia it appears that awards of the arbitration court, in at least some industries, constitute agreement between the managers and unions.[40] In the Netherlands the Government Board of Mediators before acting upon collective agreements is required to secure the advice of the Labor Foundation comprised of representatives of management and union organizations.[41]

[38] *McNair Report*, pp. 166–169; Appendix II, pp. 1507–1516.

[39] It is recognized that rules which take the form of agreements between managers and workers' organizations, on the other hand, may reflect a considerable extent of *de facto* governmental decision-making.

[40] Kenneth F. Walker, *Industrial Relations in Australia*, Cambridge, Mass., Harvard University Press, 1956, pp. 39–76.

[41] Pels, *loc. cit.*, pp. 119–120. There are normally joint meetings between the chairman of the Board of Mediators and the representatives of labor and management organizations on the wage committee of the Social and Economic Council.

The preceding discussion on substantive rules can be repeated with regard to those rules which concern the procedures for settling disputes. They may be formally incorporated in government enactments or awards of tribunals, decreed for incorporation in agreements, or submitted for governmental approval. Again the distinction between the formal status of such rules of procedures and the subtleties of their possible relations to managers and workers must be recognized. Referring to the arrangements for the adjudication of disputes over the interpretation of collective agreements in Denmark, Professor Galenson concluded: "It is entirely the work of the Federation of Labor and the Employers' Association and their affiliates, the state serving the function of formalizing what had already been agreed upon." [42] In regard to England it has been said: "If it is difficult to know where statutory regulation ends and voluntary regulation begins, it is still more difficult to discover any practical significance in the distinction between industries with JIC's [Joint Industrial Councils] and those with some other arrangements for collective bargaining." [43] In the United States the enactment of the Railway Labor Act (1926) comes readily to mind as an illustration. It is not contended, it should be observed, that there is no significance in the difference between a private agreement and the same rules of the working place incorporated into government prescription. There may be differences in responsibility, for credit or for blame, and there are likely to be differences in enforcement and in the scope of application. Nonetheless, the substantive or procedural rules of the work place are no different.

It is particularly in the field of social security, including disability and family allowance, [44] factory inspection, compensation for accidents at the work place, and minimum wage rates that rule setting by governments has developed in most countrywide

[42] Ibid., p. 232.
[43] Flanders and Clegg, loc. cit., pp. 288–289.
[44] International Social Security Association, XIth General Meeting, Paris, 7–11 September 1953, Family Allowances, Geneva, 1954, pp. 87–311.

systems. Even in this sector of the rules of a work place, there are vast differences in the role of government in the prescription of such rules, and the formal and the *de facto* processes of rule-making in this sector may likewise involve subtle differences.

While the extent and the substance of governmental rule-making varies widely among systems, some rules are more readily made centrally, or with a lesser degree of centralization, than other rules. Such rules may more readily be prescribed by governments. For instance, some rules regarding pensions and retirement tend to be centrally made by governments in most systems; there is need for central actuarial studies and record keeping. These centrally established rules are the effective rules at the work place. In contrast the rules on discipline or transfers or rules required by a distinctive technical and market context tend to be made at more decentralized points in the system, and their actual operation frequently depends upon the characteristics of the particular work place. Even with specialized tribunals and agencies that may formulate general rules by sectors, the more immediate managers and workers or their organizations are likely to have a greater role in the actual determination of the operative rules. The essential point is that some rules lend themselves more readily than others to central determination and thus to governmental prescription. Where some of the more specialized problems are made the subject of rules more centrally determined, such rules are formulated only in general terms and their specific content is often provided at successively more decentralized positions in the system where government may be expected to exercise a lesser role. The Spanish experience provides many instances of regulations for an industry issued by the Ministry of Labor which are so general as to have relatively little effect at the work place.

The rules that lend themselves most readily to central determination would appear to include those which define the formal relations of the managers and workers' organizations, the procedures for settlement of disputes, social-security matters of all types, factory inspection, and the prescription of other minimum or maximum standards. It should be expected that among rules treating these subjects there is greatest variability in the formal role of government among national industrial-relations systems, since there is considerable discretion for substitution between prescription by government and a greater role for managers and workers or their organizations, and there are subtle variations in the actual role of managers and workers in rule-making. In contrast, the formal role of managers and workers or their organizations may be expected to be greater, and any role of governmental agencies relatively general in treating the rules concerned with specialized problems of particular technical and market contexts.

The conclusion at this stage of the discussion must be that the status of all three groups of actors in a national industrial-relations system is not readily summarized or classified. At any one time in each national system there is a network of relations among managerial hierarchies, workers and their organizations, and governmental agencies that is highly complex. To understand the operation of a national industrial-relations system and its rule-making requires a sensitivity to the complex status of the actors and their interrelations. At one time these statuses and relations are given by the power context of the larger society.

It is to be observed that those rules of a single national industrial-relations system which are particularly dependent upon the power context and define the status of the actors tend to have considerable stability over time. The continuity in the status of the arbitration court in Australia for over fifty years and the position of the labor court in Denmark in relation to managers and workers' organizations for almost fifty years are illustrations of the stability in major features of a national industrial-relations system. The rule of exclusive representation in the United States, formulated in the 1920's and 1930's, is related to exclusive jurisdiction originated in the 1880's. There have been changes in minor respects in these institutions, and long-term tendencies may be found, but it would apparently require a major change in the power context of these countries to alter drastically these features of the web of rules. Chapters 8 and 9 seek an explanation for the establishment of particular relations among the actors in the course of economic development and for the general stability of arrangements once established. An initial and formative period of the relations among the actors in an emerging industrial society will be found to be particularly significant as are periods of major crises, such as war and immediate postwar years when the power context of many national industrial-relations systems have been significantly altered.

The environment of the actors in an industrial-relations system consists not only of the technical context and the market or budgetary constraints but also of the power context of the larger society and the derived status of the managerial hierarchy, workers and their organizations, and governmental agencies reflected in specific rules of the system. The status of these actors in any industrial-relations system is defined in terms of their prescribed functions and the full network of interrelations among them and with rival organizations of workers and managers. While the full complex of rules of a work place is to be regarded as influenced by the total context, some rules are more particularly related to the technical and market context and others to the power context and define the status of the actors. The power context is particularly significant to national systems and to those rules which ordinarily define on a countrywide basis the formal relations among managers and workers (and their organizations) and specialized governmental agencies, the right to strike and lock out, the procedures for settling disputes, the status of rival organizations of workers and managers, and the relations between the organizations of the parties and their members. Among the rules of the work place these matters are most frequently treated by governmental prescription, although in some systems they may largely reflect custom and practice, and in all countries the relations between formal laws and consensus is complex. The forms of governmental regulation may conceal the reality of complex interrelations among the actors, and a high degree of generality in governmental prescription may be associated with substantial detail left to managers and workers or their organizations. In order to understand the rules and the operation of an industrial-relations system, the full environment of that system consisting of the technical conditions, the market or budgetary context, and the power context, and the derived status of the actors is always to be appreciated.

5 · Bituminous-coal Industrial Relations Systems

THE first four chapters developed the idea of an industrial-relations system as a way of looking at the facts of everyday industrial-relations experience and of thinking systematically about the interrelations among managers, workers, and governments. The rules of the work place in any industrial-relations system are explained in terms of the composite of the technological context, the market or budgetary constraints, and the status of the principal actors of that system. It was suggested that a comparison of the rules developed in a number of different countries for one industry or sector that constituted a coherent industrial-relations system would highlight the relative influence of the national power contexts as compared to the technological contexts and market or budgetary constraints in setting the rules. By considering a relatively constant technical and market context, both the common elements and the differences in the complex of rules are more sharply presented. While a variety of brief illustrations was provided in sketching the general framework, a more intensive comparative analysis of the rules of industrial-relations systems for one industry in a number of countries should provide both a better understanding

129

of the central ideas and some more searching test of their usefulness. The present chapter examines some of the major substantive rules applicable to work places in the bituminous-coal industry in a number of countries and seeks to understand these rules comparatively with the assistance of the theoretical framework.

The facts and experience to be explained are the very large bulk of rules developed for the work place in bituminous-coal mining in different coal-producing countries. A comparison of the rules suggests three broad types of situations: (1) Some very similar rules have been developed in the different countries reflecting similar technological and market contexts even though major features of the national industrial-relations systems differ radically. (2) Some rules in the different countries treat the same type of problem, but differences in technology and market or budgetary constraints lead to some differences in the rules established. (3) Some rules in various countries may be very different, largely reflecting the influence of the distinctive national industrial-relations systems. As was emphasized earlier, the technological, market, and power features of the context of a system are not to be understood separately nor merely at one moment in time; they are to be interpreted as one context and as a development over time.

Not all industries or sectors compared among countries would show the same relative importance of the technological and market contexts in the determination of substantial rules. In some sectors the technological and market contexts prescribe a high proportion of all rules, reflecting common technological and market features or those which vary in a recognized fashion. In other sectors the technological and market factors will be subordinated to a more dominant influence of the respective national industrial-relations systems. In these terms, bituminous coal is probably toward the end of the spectrum at which the distinctive technological and market contexts produce a large number of similar rules. The rules on which the national industrial-relations systems tends to have a distinctive influence may the more readily be isolated.

The rules of the work place or work community in the bituminous-coal sector in various countries take a wide variety of forms: legislative statutes and governmental regulations, decrees, awards, orders and decisions of tribunals, agreements, arbitration awards, recommendations and interpretations, rulings of inspectors, policies of managements, and customs and practices. These forms of rules may be applicable on a national, district, or local basis. The rules concern the interaction of workers, managers, and specialized governmental agencies; the rules that are of interest here arise in an industrial-relations system. They do not ordinarily include the more technical or administrative rules relating to the operation of equipment or the internal operation of any organization. The comparison of a complex of rules developed by different national industrial-relations systems for coal mining tends to assume that all such rules are uniform within a country. This is, of course, not the case although there probably tends to be relatively more standardization in many of the formal rules applicable to bituminous coal than in many other industries on account of the extent of nationalization or the prevalence of industrywide bargaining. Agreements, awards, and regulations tend to be national in scope. In any event, the differences in rules within a country are neglected for present purposes.

A note appended to this chapter provides a listing by country of the sources of the texts of rules that have been quoted.[1] These data constitute only a fraction of the full complex of detailed rules applicable to managers, workers, and officials of specialized governmental agencies in their interactions in coal

---

[1] Grateful acknowledgment is made for discussions particularly with Dr. W. E. Stoermann, Mr. Hervey G. de Bivort and Miss A. Fidler of the Industrial Committees Division of the International Labor Office, with officials of the National Coal Board and Charbonnages de France. Officials of the New South Wales Department of Mines, the Coal Industry Tribunal, and the Joint Coal Board have provided information in correspondence.

production. But they do provide some opportunity for comparisons among a number of major rules. The present chapter cannot be more than a preliminary treatment of coal-mining rules, an appropriate subject for a separate volume. A full treatment would also trace the course of the historical development of each rule in the industrial-relations system.

The section which immediately follows briefly sketches the technological and market or budgetary contexts for coal mining. There next follow comparisons among countries for a group of eight rules which may be more or less directly related to the technological and market context of coal mining. Excerpts from the text of the rules are quoted in so far as is practicable. It is essential to compare the actual language of these rules. The detailed study of the text of rules is central to the major objectives of this volume, although no seasoned observer will fail to remember the distinction between the language of a rule and actual practice. A final section is concerned with rules which are more directly related to the power context and status of the coal actors in each of their national systems. Such detailed raw material provides a challenge to the comparative analysis of industrial-relations systems.

TECHNOLOGICAL AND MARKET CONTEXTS

Despite the growth of substitutes in recent decades, iron and steel—using coking coal—have provided the material foundation of industrial society. "From the beginning of the modern process of industrial change, coal and iron have moved ever closer together, like two leading and opposite characters in a play, until they have come to dominate the complex history of the European economy."[2] "This affinity of steelworks for coal-mining areas has been a continuing element in the pattern of

---

[2] Norman J. G. Pounds and William N. Parker, *Coal and Steel in Western Europe, The Influence of Resources and Techniques on Production*, Bloomington, Indiana University Press, 1957, p. 13.

industrial development for over two hundred years."[3] Moreover, coal is still the largest single source of industrial energy, and per-capita energy consumption is directly related to per-capita output and income.[4]

The major producing countries of bituminous coal are shown in the following listing. The world production has aggregated approximately 1.5 billion tons a year.[5]

| Country | Production in thousand metric tons | |
	1955	1956
United States	421,839	454,000
USSR	276,100	303,700
Great Britain	225,350	225,583
Western Germany	130,727	134,407
Poland	94,500	95,636
China	1954(67,000)	—
France	55,336	55,129
Japan	42,420	
India	38,832	—
Union of South Africa	32,256	—
Belgium	29,975	29,555
Hungary	22,300	—
Czechoslovakia	22,135	23,411
Australia	19,596	—
Saar	17,330	17,090

Source: *Colliery Year Book and Coal Trades Directory 1957*, London, Iliffe and Sons Ltd., 1957, pp. 592–593 and United Nations, *Quarterly Bulletin of Coal Statistics for Europe.*

Smaller amounts of coal (from 12,000 down to 2,000 metric tons per year) are produced in Spain, the Netherlands, Canada, Turkey, Southern Rhodesia, New Zealand and Brazil.[6] These data do

[3] C. L. Christenson, *Economic Redevelopment in Bituminous Coal*, unpublished manuscript, 1957, Ch. I, p. 17.

[4] E. S. Mason, *Energy Requirements and Economic Growth*, National Planning Association, Washington, D. C., 1955.

[5] OEEC, *The Coal Industry in Europe*, Paris, April 1956, p. 65.

[6] The listings have been ranked on the basis of bituminous-coal production; in some cases, however, the data do not permit a separation between coal and lignite production, and in these few cases the combined production has been treated as coal production. Other countries would be included in the

not directly reflect corresponding variations in employment on account of differences in output per man shift.

In geological terms coal is the product of submersion under water of forest growth and vegetable matter during the *carboniferous* period, two- to three-hundred million years ago. In general terms, anthracite was laid down at the earlier stages of this period and contains a higher proportion of fixed carbon and a smaller proportion of moisture and volatile content. Lignites were generally sedimented very much later, in the tertiary period fifteen- to sixty-million years ago, and they contain very much less fixed carbon and more oxygen and natural moisture. Coal deposits vary widely in their qualities within the bituminous classification: in the amount of heat they develop (measured in BTU) and the proportion of fixed carbon, volatile matter, moisture, ash, sulphur, or other impurities. These qualities particularly influence the relative selling price (average revenue) per ton of coal.

Coal deposits also vary among countries and within fields in the thickness of the seams in which coal was sedimented, the depth below the surface, the degree of inclination of the seams, the extent of faults, the rock formations which surround the coal seams, the presence of water, inflammable gas, or high temperatures.[7] Mines vary in their access to the transportation system, particularly by water, and in their distances to major markets for particular types and grades of coal. The continued exploitation of a coal field ordinarily requires resort to deeper mines, narrower seams, and less desirable coal. These factors are decisive for relative labor productivities,[8] the possibilities of mechanization, and the direct costs of mining and transporting a ton of coal.

second listing if the combined production was always to be counted, and the ranking of the first fifteen countries would be altered in minor respects.

[7] For an international comparison in tabular form, see *Colliery Year Book and Coal Trades Directory 1957, loc. cit.,* pp. 628–629.

[8] International Labor Organization, Coal Mines Committee, Fifth Session, Düsseldorf, 1953, *Productivity in Coal Mines,* Second Item on the Agenda, Geneva, 1953, pp. 4–95 and Appendixes I–IV.

The markets for bituminous coal are highly competitive in that coal is standardized by grade and heating properties, and oil, gas, water power, and atomic energy (potentially) are increasingly competitive substitutes for a range of purposes. There has been substantial international trade in bituminous coal during periods of high demand.[9] The extent of competitive conditions in coal markets vary widely within different countries. In some countries (the United States) the large number of producing units are organized into a number of competing enterprises; some may be "captive" of integrated companies facing quite different market competition than commercial mines. In other countries (England and France) there is for practical purposes a single nationalized seller of coal; in still other countries cartels or marketing arrangements may pool differential earnings among mines in quite different cost and market positions. The proportion of labor costs to total costs of production is high; the figure for Great Britain on the average in 1955 was 61 percent.[10]

These technological and market contexts for winning bituminous coal present workers, managers, and governments with distinctive problems at the work place and shape the web of rules that has emerged in the various coal-producing countries. There is a large measure of validity in the proposition ". . . that geological differentials will determine the ownership, financial pattern, and employment relations in the bituminous-coal industry."[11] Some of the principal problems posed by the technological and market environment may be briefly listed as follows.

1. The working conditions are hazardous and accident rates, including fatalities, are high compared to other work places. Thus, fatal accident rates (relative to exposure) in coal mines

[9] In 1956 European countries imported approximately 104 million metric tons of bituminous coal and coke from each other and the United States and exported 62 million metric tons. United Nations, *Quarterly Bulletin of Coal Statistics for Europe.*

[10] *Colliery Year Book and Coal Trades Directory 1957, loc. cit.,* p. 517.

[11] C. L. Christenson, *Economic Redevelopment in Bituminous Coal,* unpublished manuscript, 1957, Ch. II, p. 44.

in the United States are twenty times higher than in manufacturing on the average and six times higher than on railways. In India the figures have been at rates ten times higher than in manufacturing and at rates four times those in railways.[12] The psychological consequences of these hazards have permeated the relations of managers and workers in the work place and mine community. Dramatic instances of mine disasters have forced mine-safety problems upon the community. Under these circumstances specialized rules arise in all coal-producing countries to deal with underground accidents and safety problems.

2. Miners need coal for their domestic use in the relatively isolated mining communities. The custom no doubt originated in the earliest days of the industry of allowing workers to take, to purchase at a reduced price, or to mine after hours, coal for domestic purposes known as house or concessionary coal. A variety of problems arise concerning eligibility to this right, such as the status of retired miners and widows, the relative benefits among underground, surface, and white-collar workers, and the terms of distribution. These have become the subject of a group of rules.

3. Mining communities have frequently been isloated from more urban areas and create special problems in human relations. Historically this has raised a range of questions concerning housing, stores, community services, and welfare activities which are frequently beyond the rules of the work place in many other sectors. In coal mining, however, the special relations between the work place and the work community [13] are the subject of a variety of rules.

4. Working conditions in underground mines may involve operations in wet places with either stagnant or dripping water,

[12] International Labor Organization, Coal Mines Committee, Sixth Session, Istanbul, 1956, *Safety in Coal Mines*, Second Item on the Agenda, Geneva, 1956, p. 17.
[13] W. H. Sales, "Human Relations and Welfare," in *National Coal Board, The First Ten Years*, London, The Colliery Guardian Company Limited, 1957, p. 105.

or in high temperatures. Aside from safety problems, such conditions involve added discomfiture and may create the need for special clothing or hours of work. The occurrence of this common condition of work is also the subject of rules.

5. The problem of measuring the work day from portal to portal (bank to bank) or by time spent at the mine face arises from the fact that it may take considerable time to reach the place of actual work operations as shafts are deepened and as drifts are lengthened. At what point in the journey from his home to the mine face shall an underground miner begin to receive compensation, or at what point shall the working day begin? This general problem requires a clear set of rules.

6. Mining operations require certain tools and certain protective clothing. Shall the management be expected to furnish these items, or shall they be provided by the man? If the management is to provide some items, which ones shall they be, and what shall be done to assure that the practice is not abused?

7. The competitive character of the industry particularly creates variations in production, and workers are laid off or rehired not infrequently. This fact creates the problem of which men are to be laid off or rehired first, or how the unemployment or slack time is to be distributed. While many industries confront similar problems, this comparison concerns only the rules developed in the coal-mining industry in various countries.

8. The distribution of the work force among operations throughout the mine tends to divide the work force into groups of jobs and specifies the operations for which wage rates, by the day or piece, are to be established. The distribution of the work force among occupations will vary among mines but particularly according to whether the mine is open pit (or open cast) or underground. For British mines as a whole 21 percent of the work force were engaged in surface operations and 79 percent were underground. About half the underground staff were face workers (at the mine face) and the other half were supervisory personnel, maintenance workers, or those engaged in transport-

ing coal and other operations throughout the mine. A very elaborate set of rules develops to govern the compensation of the work force engaged in these various operations. Where piece rate or tonnage rates are in effect, additional rules are required. The rules establish a variety of elements of compensation, such as holiday or vacation pay. One of the most challenging problems of comparative analysis is to ascertain the extent to which technological and market conditions among countries establish similar compensation rules (or those which vary explicitly with technological and market differences among countries) and the extent to which unique features of national industrial-relations systems influence quite different compensation rules.

This list does not begin to exhaust the subject matter of rules. There are certain operations in many mines, in particular the operation of the pumps to control water flows and levels, which are indispensable to the mine and should they be stopped, as during a labor dispute, irreparable damage would follow. This situation poses a problem to be met by practice or by formal rules.[14] Mention might also be made of the rules for wash houses and lockers for clothing arising from the dirty nature of many work operations and the rules for firing explosives in view of the hazards of gas, fire, and explosions.

ACCIDENT AND SAFETY RULES

A relatively unique type of institution has arisen in the rules of coal-producing countries to deal with the accident-prone character of the industry. Apart from inspections by management safety departments and governmental inspectors, there is widespread provision for some variant of regular inspection by work-

[14] It should be emphasized that the interest here is with the substance of rules treating the problems raised by the technological and market contexts; the quality of labor peace or warfare is not of primary interest. For a comparative study which is oriented to the problem of labor peace, see G. V. Rimlinger, "Environmental and Historical Factors in Industrial Relations: Some International Comparisons in Coal Mining," 1957, unpublished manuscript.

men devoting part of their time to safety inspection. Although there are minor differences in their qualifications, in the methods of their appointment, in the responsibility for their compensation, and in their powers, rules for safety inspection by workmen are general. They periodically inspect to verify compliance with safety regulations, normally investigate accidents, file a variety of reports, and may be called to check a safety complaint of a worker.

In Belgium these workmen's delegates to mine inspectorates are elected by the workers, and for this service they are treated as state employees under the direction and supervision of mine inspectors; they may not be trade-union officials.[15] In France safety delegates are elected; they also serve as *délégués du personnel*. The number of days a year workmen's inspectors are to spend in regular inspections and their compensation is fixed by the prefect.[16] Representatives of the elected works council and particularly safety delegates perform these functions in the Saar. In Germany elected workmen's representatives perform the functions as a part of the duties of the works council, and other workers' representatives are appointed to the mine-inspection service (*Bergämter*) upon the proposal of the trade unions. The Netherlands arrangement provides for workmen inspectors appointed by the Coal Industry Council on the proposal of the mine-workers unions.

In Great Britain safety inspection is performed by teams of two inspectors selected by the workmen; one of each team must be employed by the mine while the other may be a full-time workmen's inspector. The form in the United States is a mine-safety committee selected by the local union; committee members are paid by the union when performing inspection duties.

[15] For a tabular summary of "Workmen's Contribution to Supervision of Safety Measures," see European Coal and Steel Community, *Report on the Conference on Safety in Coalmines*, March 1957, Doc. No. S 360/57e, p. 95ff. The tables compare the experience of Belgium, France, the Saar, Germany, Italy, the Netherlands, and the United Kingdom.

[16] International Labor Office, *Safety in Coal Mines*, Vol. 1, *Studies and Reports*, New Series, No. 33, Geneva, 1953, pp. 70–74.

It appears that some provision for workers' supervision of safety also exists in Canada, Mexico, Poland, and Japan.[17]

The following excerpts illustrate the rules of various countries —terms of agreements and provisions of laws or regulations— showing both the common policy and variations in details in regard to workers' inspections for safety.

United States

At each mine there shall be a Mine Safety Committee selected by the Local Union. The Committee Members while engaged in the performance of their duties shall be paid by the Union, but shall be deemed to be acting within the scope of their employment in the mine within the meaning of the Workmen's Compensation Law of the state where such duties are performed.

The Mine Safety Committee may inspect any mine development or equipment used in producing coal. If the Committee believes conditions found endanger the life and bodies of the mine workers, it shall report its findings and recommendations to the management. In those special instances where the Committee believes an immediate danger exists and the Committee recommends that the management remove all mine workers from the unsafe area, the Operator is required to follow the recommendation of the Committee.

If the Safety Committee in closing down an unsafe area acts arbitrarily and capriciously, members of such Committee may be removed from the Committee. Grievances that may arise as a result of a request for removal of a member of the Safety Committee under this section shall be handled in accordance with the provisions providing for settlement of disputes.[18]

Great Britain

Legislation on workmen's inspections apparently originated in the nineteenth century; the present legislation [19] requires the mine owner to permit such inspections if there is an association

---

[17] International Labor Organization, *Safety in Coal Mines, loc. cit.*, p. 71.

[18] *National Bituminous Coal Wage Agreement of 1950*, Mine Safety Committee, pp. 2–3.

[19] Mines and Quarries Act, 1954, Part III, Section 123, 2 and 3 Eliz. 2, Ch. 70.

or body representative of the majority of employees which wishes to select a panel of workmen inspectors. The statute envisages agreements between managements and unions on the subject. The regulations issued under the statute apparently leave the operation of workmen's inspectors to collective bargaining despite very detailed regulations on such subjects as the status of government mine inspectors and pages on the care and killing of horses underground. The National Coal Board and the National Union of Mineworkers have continued with minor revisions earlier agreements on this subject. From time to time the national collective bargaining agreement has changed the level of compensation of these workmen's inspectors. Excerpts from the legislation and the agreements provide as follows:

(1) For the purpose of enabling inspections to be carried out at a mine or quarry on behalf of the persons employed thereat, a panel of persons each of whom has had not less than five years practical experience of mining, or as the case may be of quarrying operations may be appointed for that mine or quarry—

> (a) in a case where there is an association or body representative of a majority of the total number of persons employed at the mine or quarry, by that association or body; [20]

1. For the purpose of considering questions in relation to safety in coal mines and in order to facilitate the operation of the compulsory partial inspections by workmen in pursuance of the recommendations of the Royal Commission on Safety in Coal Mines there shall be established a National Safety Board and District Safety Boards. . . .

9. (a) The appointment of inspectors shall be in the hands of the workmen.

> (b) The workmen may, where they so desire, appoint full-time inspectors; any person so appointed shall have at least ten years practical experience as a working miner in a coal mine.

> (c) When a full-time inspector examines a mine, he shall be accompanied by a person whose occupation is at the

[20] Mines and Quarries Act, 1954, Part III, Section 123.

mine, who is or who has been a practical working miner and has had not less than ten years' experience of underground work and who has been appointed by the workmen for the purpose.[21]

France

The French Labor Code differs from the British statute or regulations in prescribing in detail the arrangements for the operation of *délégués mineurs*.[22] A few quotations indicate some of the main features:

> Art. 121 The workmen's inspector and deputy inspector shall exercise their functions in an underground area the boundaries of which shall be fixed by an order of the prefect issued under the authority of the minister of labor on the basis of a report from the inspectors of mines, after the mine owner has been heard and the workers concerned who fulfill the conditions required by Art. 135, and the trade unions (if any) to which they belong have been called upon by means of a public notice to submit their observations; the notice shall be posted in the usual places for announcements to the workers. . . .

> Art. 126 The workmen's inspector shall inspect the shafts, workings, and work places of his area twice a month. . . .

> Art. 135 The workers employed underground in an area shall be the electors for that area, provided. . . .

> Art. 136 The following persons shall be eligible in an area. . . .
> 1. electors as specified above who have attained the age of twenty-five years, have been employed underground for at least five years and for the last two years at least in the area or in one of the adjacent areas belonging to the same mine owner;

[21] National Coal Board, *Memorandum of Agreements, Arbitration Awards and Decisions, Recommendations, and Interpretations Relating to National Questions Concerning Wages and Conditions of Employment in the Coalmining Industry of Great Britain*, Part I, Period 20th March 1940 to 31st July 1946. Agreement Between Mining Association of Great Britain and Mine-Workers' Federation of Great Britain, *Safety in Coal Mines*. Workmen's Inspections, 3d March, 1941, May 1947, pp. 26(i)–(ii).

[22] Code du Travail (*Textes codifiés et textes annexes*), Paris, Jurisprudence Générale Dalloz, 1956, Bk. II, Title III, Ch. IV, Art. 120–157.

2. former workers, provided that they have attained the age of twenty-five years, are in possession of their political rights and have been employed underground for not less than five years, . . . and finally, that not more than ten years have elapsed since they were last employed either as underground workers or as workmen's inspectors or deputy inspectors. . . .

Art. 153 bis. A workmen's inspector or deputy inspector working in his own or in a neighbouring area operated by the same mine owner shall not be dismissed owing to shortage of work in the undertaking until after all the workers of the occupational group to which he belongs.

Art. 153 ter. After their election, workmen's inspectors and deputy inspectors shall be required to attend the courses of vocational instruction organised by the mine services, under conditions laid down in orders issued by the minister for mines.[23]

In the French coal industry which is largely nationalized, agreements reached between unions and the *Charbonnages de France* require the approval of appropriate governmental ministries. The decrees may adopt or follow such formal agreements,[24] or they may constitute a general set of regulations arrived at without formal agreement within which operating rules may be established at a national or mine level.[25] These decrees extended to surface workers in mining the same type of workmen's inspectors which were originally developed in the labor code for underground workers. "These delegates replace the *délégués du personnel* provided by the general legislation." [26] Rules common to a national system are modified to fit the coal industry.

[23] For an earlier version, see *France 4* in International Labor Office, *Legislative Series*, Montreal, 1941.
[24] Thus, the decree of April 9, 1956 on housing bonuses in mining contains the same provisions as the agreement of February 20, 1956 made with the *Fédération Nationale des Mineurs* (F. O.) and the *Fédération des Mineurs* (CFTC).
[25] *Statut du Mineur, Statut du Personnel des Exploitations Minières et Assimilées,* Décret No. 46. 1433 du 14 juin 1946. Mis à jour au 1er octobre 1957.
[26] *Ibid.,* Art. 27 (a), p. 24.

Germany

A distinction must be made between the arrangement for appointing full-time mining inspectors to the *Bergämter* upon the nomination of the trade union and the safety and accident responsibilities of members of the works council (*Betriebsrat*) who continue to work in the mine. The works council duties are of particular comparative interest. The law assigns to works councils an interest in accidents and safety in most general language:

> 57. The following matters, *inter alia*, may be governed by works agreements:
>   (a) action to prevent industrial accidents and injury to health; . . . .
> 58. (1) The works council shall devote attention to the combating of accident risks and dangers to health, shall give assistance in such matters to the industrial inspection officials and other competent bodies by means of suggestions, advice and information, and shall promote implementation of the provisions respecting the protection of labour.
>   (2) The works council shall be invited to participate whenever safety appliances are installed or tested, and also whenever an inquiry into an accident is undertaken by the employer, the industrial inspection officials or other competent bodies.[27]

In this legislative framework, industrywide collective bargaining agreements between the *Industriegewerkschaft Bergbau* and the *Gewerkschaft der Bergbauangestellten* on the one side and associations of coal operators on the other have prescribed in detail an expanded role for the works council in regard to safety and accidents.[28] The following excerpts may be noted:

[27] Works Constitution Act, October 11, 1952. Quoted from *Germany 6* (Federal Republic), in International Labor Office, *Legislative Series 1952*, Geneva, 1955.
[28] *Tarifvertrag über die Betriebsverfassung des rheinisch-westfälischen Steinkohlenbergbaus*, Gültig ab 1. April 1955, pars. 8–20.

8. Every underground section and every surface department of the undertaking shall be inspected once a week by a member of the works council. Further visits of inspection shall be permitted in so far as they are necessary to investigate complaints or to discharge particular duties. . . .

15. (1) The works council shall assist in ensuring that all provisions and instructions issued to prevent or counter accidents and health risks are enforced. It shall further be associated in the introduction and testing of equipment for the protection of labor and safety in the mines. It shall transmit all suggestions, proposals and objections to the management. . . .

16. (1) A member of the works council shall be appointed from time to time to participate in accident inquiries, special tests of winding, and the approval of technical facilities which are of essential importance for the protection of the workers. The management shall give due notice to the chairman of the works committee for the purpose. . . .

17. (1) The temperatures in the mine shall be measured in the presence of an authorized representative of the works council if the works council so requests. . . .

Australia

Rule 39. (1) The majority of the persons employed in or about a mine may from time to time appoint two of their number or any two persons who are practical miners and one of whom is the holder of at least a third-class certificate of competency or of service under this Act to inspect the mine at their own cost, and the persons so appointed shall be allowed from time to time on giving reasonable notice to the manager, accompanied, if the owner, agent, or manager of the mine thinks fit, by himself or one or more officers of the mine, to go at any time to every part of the mine, and to inspect the shafts, levels, planes, working-places, return air-ways, ventilating apparatus, old workings, and machinery, ...

Provided that such inspection shall not be conducted so as to impede or obstruct the working of the mine. . . .

If any report made under this general rule states the existence or apprehended existence of any danger, the owner, agent or manager shall forthwith cause a true copy of the report to be sent to the inspector of the district.[29]

Poland

2. The Social Inspectorate of Labor shall be responsible for supervising observance, by the management of the establishment, of the statutory provisions and terms of collective agreements and rules of employment relating to industrial safety and hygiene, the protection of workers' health, the employment of women and young persons, hours of work, and the supervision of plant, equipment, and sanitary installations from the point of view of labor protection. . . .

5. (1) Any worker of the establishment who is a member of the trade union, and who does not hold a managerial position in the establishment or perform duties on behalf of the management which are subject to supervision by the Social Inspectorate of Labor, may be appointed to the post of social inspector of labor. . . .

6. (1) The social inspectors of labor shall be appointed by means of annual elections.

(2) The establishment social inspectors of labor shall be elected (a) by the general assembly of the staff, in the case of establishments employing up to 500 workers; (b) by a meeting of the authorized representatives (i.e., the representatives acting as a link between the employees in each department and the works council), in the case of establishments employing over 500 workers. . . .

15. (1) The establishment social inspectors of labor shall have power to give written notice to the head of the establishment requiring him to remedy certain irregularities within a specified time. Such notice shall require the approval of the works council. . . .[30]

---

[29] *Coal Mines Regulation Act, 1912–1953*, Certified September 2, 1957, New South Wales, Section 54, Rule 39, pp. 110–111.

[30] From *Poland 1*, Worker Inspectors, in International Labor Office, *Legislative Series 1950*, Geneva, 1953.

The Polish rules providing for worker inspectors apply to industry generally, but they tend to be more significant in coal mining.

Regardless of whether these rules take the form of statutes, regulations or agreements, the provisions for workmen's inspectors differ from safety rules in other industries. They are a response to the special accident-prone experience of coal mining; the rules cited on occasion run in the face of dominant national patterns establishing the relations of workers, managers, and governmental agencies in industry generally. Thus, in the United States where management prerogatives are ordinarily thought to be highly regarded, the agreement gives a safety committee appointed by the local union the authority to shut down a mine if the committee believes "an immediate danger exists" even against the judgment of management. This type of provision no doubt is the special consequence of dramatic accidents; the fatal-accident rate is higher in the United States than in any other reported country. In Belgium the elected workers' delegates to mine inspectorates have a more limited right to shut down work in imminent danger in their judgment, subject to review in twenty-four hours by regular mine inspectors. It is to be recognized that Belgium mines, which are the deepest in Europe with many natural unfavorable working conditions, had many spectacular and costly accidents: ". . . nowhere on the Continent were explosions more numerous or more disastrous." [31] In other countries the authority of workmen inspectors in this regard is limited to urgent reports to the regular governmental mine inspectorate.

Aside from workmen's inspectors, another set of rules may be compared in the accident field. What is to happen when a fatal or serious accident occurs? Work inevitably tends to stop in the near locality of the accident. There are adverse psycho-

[31] Pounds and Parker, *loc. cit.*, p. 131. The reference is to the experience in the latter half of the nineteenth century.

logical reactions. Friends and the family are to be notified in a closely knit mining community. Other workers may be required to carry out a seriously injured workman. No doubt this whole area of conduct became the subject of customs and practices established in the mores of the work community. It is to be remembered that the United States Congress adjourns for the day on news of the death of one of its members.

In many coal-producing countries, these problems posed by the place of work are now the subject of explicit rules as the following excerpts attest, although in other countries the rules no doubt remain in the area of unwritten custom.

United States

> On the day that death by accident occurs in a mine, for that shift only the Mine Workers may cease work, but under no circumstances shall a mine be laid idle for a funeral. This is, however, not to prevent individuals from attending a funeral.[32]

Great Britain

> Whereas:
> (A) The parties hereto are desirous of establishing a special fatal accident fund for the purpose of providing benefits to the widows and other dependents or nominees of men fatally injured in the pits.
> (B) The proposal is intended to substitute a more practical mark of sympathy for the custom now existing at some pits by reason of which work ceases on one or more shifts after a fatal accident and is intended to replace all such customs.

This agreement establishes a contributory fund to be jointly administered. The agreement further provides:

> 4 (a) No man shall be entitled to refuse to descend the pit by reason only of the fact that a fatal accident has taken place on a preceding shift provided that the body of the person fatally

[32] *Williamson District Agreement*, July 5, 1941.

injured has been removed from the pit by the commencement of the shift on which such workman is required to descend.

(b) If the body of any person fatally injured has not been removed from the pit by the commencement of any subsequent shift, the extent to which work shall be resumed during that shift shall be determined by the manager. Men who remove the body of the deceased during a shift shall not be called up to resume work during that shift.[33]

2. In the case of an accident underground only the pit or drift in which the accident occurred shall be affected, unless it can be shown that at 1st January, 1906, it was the custom at any particular colliery for all the pits or drifts drawing on to the same heapstead to be laid idle for an accident underground, then such custom shall continue at the colliery. . . .[34]

New Zealand

4. *Injured Workers.* In the case of any accident occurring in the mine and the man or men injured thereby having to be carried out, the deputies shall select the men required as stretcher bearers, and these men shall be paid for time lost at agreement day-wage rates in the case of day-wage men, or at their average daily contract earnings in the case of contract workers. In the case of serious accidents the stretcher bearers shall not be required to go back into the mine.[35]

8. *Fatal Accidents.* In the event of any fatal accident occurring in or about the mine, it shall be lawful for the workers to cease work for the remainder of the day on which the accident occurs. It shall also be lawful for the workers, excepting pumpmen, fan

[33] National Coal Board, *Memorandum of Agreements, Arbitration Awards and Decisions, Recommendations, and Interpretations Relating to National Questions concerning Wages and Conditions of Employment in the Coalmining Industry of Great Britain,* Fatal Accident Agreements, February 1, 1950. Part V, 1st January to 31st December, 1950, January 1951, pp. 480–493. Also see, National Coal Board, *Mineworkers' Special Fatal Accident Scheme* (as amended with effect from November 18, 1954), April 1957.

[34] National Coal Board, Northern Division, *National and District Agreements (Durham Area) To January 1948,* Conciliation Board Arrangement, 8th November 1907, p. 62.

[35] *National Coal Mines Agreement,* May 11–14, 1954.

attendants, or men required to maintain the safety of the mine, to cease work for one whole day to attend the funeral of the deceased worker, but not further or otherwise.[36]

The theme to be stressed is that a relatively common and unique context in coal mining in different countries over the years has created a distinctive set of similar rules, although the role of the separate national conditions is by no means eliminated. The source of payments for workmen's inspectors, for instance, is likely to reflect larger national arrangements. In the combination of unity and diversity, safety and accident rules of the coal-mining industry tend to show a relatively strong influence of the technological and market context making for an underlying similarity among countries, although the forms and details are shaped by the diverse national industrial-relations systems and by the intensity of the objective safety problems.

CONCESSIONARY OR HOUSE COAL

In coal-producing countries, rules develop to govern the distribution of coal without charge or at less than full market price to employees of mining enterprises, to retired or disabled miners, to their widows, or to other members of their family. This practice, formalized into a complex of detailed rules, grows out of the relatively isolated location of many mining communities, the example of the use of coal at the mines for a variety of heating and power purposes, the difficulties of preventing miners taking some coal, and the need to establish administrable arrangements. In Great Britain miners' coal constitutes over 5 million tons or almost 2.5 percent of total annual consumption.[37] The practice

---

[36] Department of Labor, New Zealand, *Awards, Agreements, Orders, and Decisions Made under the Industrial Conciliation and Arbitration Act, the Apprentices Act, the Labour Disputes Investigation Act, and Other Industrial Legislation, For the Year 1956,* Canterbury Coal-mine Employees-Award, August 30, 1956, Vol. 56, p. 1324. Also see Runanga District Coal-mine Employees, Industrial Agreement, November 26, 1956, *Ibid.,* pp. 1953–1958.

[37] *Colliery Year Book and Coal Trades Directory, 1957, Loc. cit.,* p. 541.

of concessionary coal once instituted poses a variety of problems respecting the relative claims and equities of different groups of present or past employees. The issues arise whether such coal may be sold or given away and whether concessionary coal shall be made available to workers who may not directly use coal in a household. These problems are solved in slightly different ways in various countries, but the main outlines of the arrangements reflect a common situation.[38] The common elements and the differences reflecting separate national labor-management characteristics are evident in the following excerpts from agreements and regulations:

United States

House coal shall be sold to all employees (including retired employees) of the mine, who live within a reasonable distance of the mine, for their own household use, at the cost of production, exclusive of sales and administrative costs. Should any differences arise between the mine workers and the operator of any mine as to the price so to be charged for said coal, such differences shall be settled under the terms of the Settlement of Disputes section of this Agreement.[39]

Great Britain

3. For the purposes of this agreement: (a) Concessionary coal means coal which is supplied by the Board to their employees for their personal domestic consumption free or at a nominal or reduced price and which is exempt from the provisions of the Coal Distribution Order, ...

6. In any office in which at the date of this Agreement there is a practice or arrangement to supply concessionary coal to staff to whom this Agreement applies such practice or arrangement shall continue to be applied in order to determine which

[38] For an earlier brief survey, see International Labor Office, *Principles and Methods of Wage Determination in the Coal-mining Industry, An International Survey*, Series D, No. 20, Geneva, 1931, pp. 72–73.

[39] *National Bituminous Coal Wage Agreement of 1950 as Amended September 29, 1952.*

members of such staff employed in that office shall be eligible for concessionary coal under this Agreement.

Provided that no person under the age of 21 to whom this Agreement applies shall be eligible for concessionary coal under this Clause unless

either (i) he or she is entitled to concessionary coal at the date of this agreement,

or (ii) he or she is regarded under such practice or arrangement as having householder responsibilities and therefore entitled to concessionary coal.

7. Staff to whom this Agreement applies who are or may become eligible for concessionary coal under Clause 6 above shall have their annual entitlements under the practice or arrangement referred to in that Clause modified as follows: . . .

    (a) Staff who occupy separate self-contained domestic establishments.

      (i) 13 tons and above, or an unspecified entitlement, the modified annual entitlement shall be 9 tons; . . .

    (b) Staff who do not occupy separate self-contained domestic establishments. . . .

      (i) not less than 5 tons, or an unspecified entitlement, the modified annual entitlement shall be 5 tons, . . .

8. Staff who receive concessionary coal under Clauses 6 and 7 above shall pay for the purchase and delivery of such coal at the following rates: . . .[40]

[40] National Coal Board, Agreement between the National Coal Board, the National Union of Mineworkers, the Clerical and Administrative Workers' Union, and the National Association of Clerical and Supervisory Staff, May 28, 1953. *Loc. cit.*, Part VIII, 1st January to 31st December 1953, pp. 550–556. This agreement governs clerical and junior administrative staff. For other references on concessionary coal, see Part VII, pp. 306–311 (nonindustrial staff); Part VI, pp. 44–45 (nonindustrial staff); Part V, pp. 502–506 (managers, agents, surveyors, and engineers); Part III, p. 398 (men transferred from one district to another); Part IV, p. 436 (interpretation on whether a claim is a national question). Also see National Coal Board (South-Western Division) and National Union of Mineworkers (South Wales Area), *Workmen's Housecoal Agreement,* December 17, 1953; Industrial Relations Department, National Coal Board, *Free and Concessionary Coal,* October 1957, a tabular summary of divisional and area agreements. The regional agreements specify the quantity of coal furnished to varying classifications and occupations, the charges, if any, made for the concessionary coal and the quality of the coal. Householders are allotted more coal than subtenants; only in Durham do allotments vary with the number in a household.

France

Art. 22. In those enterprises where the allocation of coal is the custom and is granted to persons in the active labor force or those retired, the amount and the conditions under which coal is allocated will be fixed jointly by decision of the minister of mines and of the minister of economics. In case this allocation is not possible, a compensating indemnity will be fixed under the same conditions.

In those enterprises where the allocation of coal is not the custom, a heating premium will be allocated by the joint decision of the minister of mines and of the minister of economics.[41]

Germany

61. The following shall be entitled to an allocation:
  (a) married workers, provided they are living with their families or can prove that they are supporting them,
  (b) widowed or divorced workers, if they are living with their children or can prove that they are supporting their divorced wife or their children,
  (c) widowed or divorced workers with no children, if they can prove that they are keeping on their home,
  (d) unmarried workers who are the main support of their families.

62. The workers indicated in 61 shall receive annually on request, for their own requirements, up to 100 cwt, for a household of more than four persons up to 110 cwt, for one of more than seven persons up to 120 cwt of domestic coal at a rate of .40 DM. *ex* mine. The management may not limit the personal requirements of a worker entitled to an allocation. The only condition shall be that the worker must actually use it in his own household. . . .

70. Domestic coal allocations shall be granted exclusively for the worker's own needs and only *ex* mine. Without prejudice to other legal consequences, the penalty for disposing of them to unauthorized persons, either for payment or free of charge, shall

---

[41] *Statut du Mineur, loc. cit.,* p. 23

be the suspension of the domestic fuel allocation for a period of six months.[42]

Australia

19. One load of coal of approximately one ton shall be allowed free of charge, except for transport, each calendar month to each deputy or shotfirer who is a householder.[43]

The Coal Industry Tribunal advises that this provision ". . . by custom and practice of many years standing has general application."

New Zealand

5. Where a maximum tonnage is not specified in agreements, the maximum quantity of house coal a workman who is a householder shall be entitled to receive at reduced rates to be 10 tons per annum, provided that any particular cases in which there are exceptional circumstances may be considered on their merits for an additional tonnage. . . .[44]

20. Workers shall be given the right to purchase for their own use only not more than one ton of coal every three weeks from the first day of May to the 31st day of October, and one ton per month from the 1st day of November to the 30th day of April, from the mine at which they are employed, at 13 s. per ton at the tip. This privilege shall not apply to men living in boarding-houses.

Retired mine workers who have had not less than twenty years' service may be supplied from the mine last worked at with a maximum of four tons of coal per annum at miners' rates for their own personal use and consumption, provided delivery is taken by or on behalf of the person concerned at the colliery bins or screens.

A maximum of four tons of coal per annum at miners' rates

[42] *Manteltarifvertrag für die Arbeiter des rheinisch-westfälischen Steinkohlenbergbaus,* Gültig ab 1. Mai 1953, Section D, Domestic Fuel, Sections 61–80, pp. 19–25.

[43] *The Coal Mining Industry (Deputies and Shotfires)* Award, 1954, New South Wales, (Dispute No. 75 of 1952), p. 7.

[44] *National Coal Mines Agreement,* May 8–10, 1956.

will be supplied to widows whose husbands were at the time of death in receipt of the retired mine workers' house-coal allowance, provided that the widows reside in the mining township adjacent to the colliery from which their husbands retired. This concession shall cease in the event of remarriage.[45]

Poland

Art. 21. Coal Allowance. . . .

Manual Workers: Workers in pay category 1, six tons, two of which shall be provided in the form of their cash equivalent.

Workers in pay category 2, seven tons, two of which shall be provided in the form of their cash equivalent.

Workers in pay category 3, eight tons, two of which shall be provided in the form of their cash equivalent. . . .

The following shall receive the equivalent of two tons:
  (a) all workers living alone [unmarried, widowed, or separated] who are not entitled under any of the foregoing paragraphs;
  (b) married women whose husbands are entitled to an allocation of coal in kind.[46]

Art. 49. Former workers of the coal industry and the widows of such workers shall be entitled to free coal for heating purposes of the quantity and subject to the rules given below. . . .

It is always difficult to compare such rules in detail since there are significant variations in the tendency at the national level to make general and procedural rules as compared to detailed substantive rules. The degree of centralization in the organizations, the size of countries and the internal diversity among coal fields also influence the choice of approaches. Ideally, the actual rules in effect at representative mines should be compared. The rules cited above indicate a common concern with a limitation of concessionary coal to household use, the eligibility of retired as well as active miners and the purchase of coal at a price

---

[45] Department of Labor, New Zealand, Canterbury Coal-mine Employees Award, August 30, 1956, *loc. cit.*, p. 1327.

[46] *Zbiorowy Uklad Pracy dla pracowników fizycznych i umyslowych zatrudnionych w zakladach pracy Ministerstwa Górnictwa i Energetyki obowiązujący od dnia 1 kwietnia 1957 r.*, pp. 13–14, 28.

less than the market price. Variations in the rules concerning the eligibility of widows and disabled miners, the limitations on quantity, the special problems of young miners, and the inequities between those who receive concessionary coal and those who do not are instructive of the characteristics of the various national industrial-relations systems, particularly when a number of different rules are compared. The variation in coal allowances in accordance with the size of the household in France and Germany in contrast to the arrangements in the United States and Great Britain, for instance, constitutes an effect of the national industrial-relations system upon the form of the rule on concessionary coal.

HOUSING OR RENTS

The relatively isolated character of coal mining has led to rules on housing or rents. In order to attract labor to mining operations enterprises have had to be concerned with housing, and frequently housing has been built by the enterprise, even in countries where the practice of company housing is not general. In any event some rules on housing emerge, but the differences among the rules are instructive of other features of the national systems. Thus in the United States the concern is solely with the level of rents, while in France there is provision for housing accommodation or a housing allowance for miners, which increases with the size of family. Many of the same types of problems concerning standards of eligibility for retired miners and members of families and the priority among groups of mine workers that were observed in the case of house coal also arise with housing. The following rules may be compared:

United States

> Equitable adjustment of housing rents shall be made in District Conferences.[47]

[47] *Southern Wage Agreement, July 5, 1941.*

Great Britain

(1) Where the appropriate Authorities recognise tenancies by "Squatters" of vacant hutments, etc., and the occupants of these premises produce evidence that they are paying rent to the Authorities, then, if the occupants were previously in receipt of house-rent and a certain quantity of firecoal, they shall continue to receive these allowances. . . .

2. Allocation of Colliery Houses (a) Early steps will be taken to draw up a provisional schedule of colliery houses attaching to each colliery. . . .

(c) Preference shall be given to those workmen who are employed at a particular colliery for the occupation of a colliery house scheduled to that colliery.

(d) Where a workman of 65 years of age or over or such earlier age as may be agreed between the National Coal Board and the National Union of Mineworkers retires by reason of old age or infirmity and does not take up other gainful occupation, he shall be allowed to continue the occupancy of a colliery house for a period of not more than six months. . . .

(f) Where widows or families of deceased workmen are living in a colliery house, they should be allowed to continue the occupancy of such a house for a period not exceeding six months. . . .[48]

France

Article 23—(1)   Personnel in Employment Status
Employees who are married or are the breadwinners of a

---

[48] National Coal Board, Northern Division, *National and District Agreements* (*Durham Area*) *to January 1948*, Agreement, September 17, 1946 and Agreement, August 1, 1947, pp. 136–138. Also see National Wage Structure for the Coal-mining Industry, Agreement dated April 20, 1955, National Coal Board, *loc. cit.*, Part X, p. 1033, par. 37.
"By the end of 1957, 588 houses had been built in the East and West Midlands Divisions, additional to the original building programme of the Coal Industry Housing Association. The Board's view has always been that houses in mining areas should properly be provided by Local Authorities. Some Authorities have agreed to build houses for mineworkers, but it became clear in 1957 that all the Board's requirements could not be met in this way." National Coal Board, *A Summary of the Report and Accounts for 1957*, May 1958, p. 13.

family shall be provided free of charge with accommodation by the undertaking or, failing this, shall receive a monthly accommodation allowance in an amount to be fixed by order of the minister responsible for mines and the minister responsible for economic affairs.

This allowance shall not be payable to persons who for no valid reason decline a dwelling offered by the mine operator.

If the spouse is in the wage-earning employ of the mine operator only one such allowance shall be payable.

If the spouse, being a wage earner in the employ of another employer, is in receipt of an accommodation allowance from the latter, the amount of the said allowance shall be deducted from the accommodation allowance provided for herein; if the spouse is accommodated free of charge, the allowance provided for in this article shall not be payable.

Priority for vacant dwellings, making due allowance for operational requirements and the grade of each employee, will be given to entitled employees having the largest number of dependent children and in consideration of seniority.

(2) *Pensioners and Widows*

In the event of the husband's death before reaching the retiring age the widow who does not marry again shall continue to be accommodated free of charge or to draw the allowance in lieu thereof. Retired employees shall retain the same privileges.

Retired employees may not keep the dwelling they occupied during their working life without the assent of the undertaking; the same provision applies to the widows who have not married again to whom reference is made above.

The undertaking may offer retired employees the choice between free accommodation and entitlement to the allowance in lieu thereof.

An order by the minister responsible for mines and the minister responsible for economic affairs will lay down the conditions on which former members of the staff in receipt of pensions from the Autonomous Mining Social Security Fund or a supplemental retirement benefit scheme as provided for in Article 26 below will be entitled to such accommodation or the allowance in lieu thereof.[49]

[49] *Statut du Mineur, loc. cit.*, pp. 23-24.

A very detailed agreement [50] (thirteen single-spaced pages) specified the eligibility to free housing and the allocation of available housing. A subsequent decree [51] authorized the agreement and provided that the director of mines was given responsibility for the administration of the decree.

Germany

2. (1) The miners' lodging allowance shall amount to
16.50 DM. for underground workers
12.50 DM. for surface workers
per calendar month.
In addition, the following supplements shall be payable:
    i. to workers entitled under the agreement to an allowance for children or brothers and sisters, a supplement for each child (sec. 40, 42 of the Master Agreement for mine workers) 2 DM.
    ii. to owners of their own homes and small holdings, a supplement of 2.50 DM.
(2) Workers who have worked underground for 15 years shall continue to be entitled to the higher lodging allowance for underground workers, even if they are employed on the surface. . . .

4. Having regard to general legal requirements, workers absent through illness shall remain entitled to the miners' lodging allowance for a period up to six weeks. In addition, the lodging allowance shall continue to be paid to such workers for a period up to thirteen weeks, if they have been in the German coal industry for over three years, and for a period up to twenty-six weeks, if they have been in the German coal industry for over fifteen years. . . .[52]

[50] *Protocole d'Accord Relatif aux Conditions D'Attribution des Prestations de Logement aux Membres ou anciens Membres du Personnel des Houilleres de Bassin et Aux Veuves,* 22 janvier 1957.

[51] *Autorisant a Titre Provisoire L'Application du Protocole D'Accord du 22 janvier 1957, Relatif aux Conditions d'Attribution des Prestations de Logement aux Membres et Anciens Membres du Personnel des Houilleres de Bassin et aux Veuves,* 10 juillet 1957.

[52] *Tarifvertrag über das "Bergmannswohnungsgeld für den rheinischwestfälischen Steinkohlenbergbau,"* Essen, 10 Juli 1957.

Australia

The existence of mine-workers' housing is indicated by the following excerpts from the report of the Joint Coal Board:

7. With the object of encouraging mineworkers to acquire new homes, the Board pays a subsidy towards the management costs of the Miners' Cooperative Building Societies. . . .

9. The Miners' Cooperative Building Societies scheme (which was organized by the Board) has resulted in the completion of 994 houses of good standard. Additional houses totalling 561 were under construction at the 30th June, 1956.[53]

New Zealand

21. *Accommodation.* Suitable accommodation shall be provided for single men.[54]

Italy

Article 27 (d) Accommodation. In the case of workmen accommodated in company-owned houses, the lease shall terminate *ipso jure* upon the cessation of employment relations; the workman shall, however, be granted two months in which to vacate the premises.[55]

Poland

Art. 43. The management of the establishment shall be bound to utilize in the most suitable manner the funds set aside for the construction and repair of dwelling houses. The statutory

[53] *Ninth Annual Report of the Joint Coal Board for the Financial Year 1955–1956*, pp. 52–53; *First Report of the Joint Coal Board*, 1st March 1947 to 30th June 1947 and 1947–1948, p. 19.

[54] *Nightcaps District Opencast Agreement*, 1954–1956, March 8, 1954. The agreement is signed by the United Mine Workers of New Zealand, the minister of mines, and the Ohai Coal Company, Ltd.

[55] *Contratto nazionale di lavoro 28 marzo 1953 per gli operai addetti all'industria mineraria.*

provisions shall apply with regard to the renting of dwelling houses belonging to the establishment.[56]

In the distribution of flats, primary consideration is given to the needs of newly recruited workers (80 percent of the total number of flats built for mines).[57]

WET CONDITIONS OR HIGH TEMPERATURES

The special physical conditions of the work place in coal mining create problems which are frequently the subject of rules. Two of the most common groups of rules concern working in wet conditions or under high temperatures. These conditions require precise definition. When are conditions wet or temperatures high? The rules concern what shall be done under such unfavorable working conditions; hours of work may be affected, special clothing and rest periods may be required, and increased compensation may be provided. The importance of these conditions varies among fields and countries. In some, high temperatures may be relatively unknown or wet conditions seldom encountered. These variations in physical conditions of work, in the technological context, may be expected to be reflected in the rules of the work place.

Great Britain

(1) Underground pieceworkmen and datallers working wet in their working place or places shall be paid as follows:

Persons 18 years and over, 6d. per shift (basis).

Persons under 18 years, 3d. per shift (basis).

These rates to be paid in addition to the piecework earnings, minimum wage rates as fixed under the Coal Mines (Minimum

---

[56] *Zbiorowy Uklad Pracy dla pracowników fizycznych i umysłowych zatrudnionych w zakladach pracy Ministerstwa Górnictwa i Energetyki obowiązujący od dnia 1 kwietnia 1957 r.*, p. 26.

[57] Economic Commission for Europe, Coal Committee, *Fundamental Policy Questions Facing Governments in Regard to the Future Development of the Coal Industry and Trade in Europe*, Geneva, Switzerland, 1958.

Wage) Act, 1912, county standard rates or datal rates applicable to the classes concerned.

(2) Any question arising as to whether or not an underground workman is working wet shall be referred first to the colliery manager for decision and, failing agreement, to the usual machinery for the settlement of local disputes. . . .[58]

9. The aforementioned rates will be all-inclusive rates and will not be subject to any additions by way of bonuses, flat rates, or allowances, whether national or local, temporary or permanent, except for temporary allowances *in respect of men working wet*, the Five Day Week bonus, and rent allowances made as an addition to wages.[59] [Emphasis added]

Italy

Article 15. In the case of underground work performed under particularly arduous conditions, such as the presence of toxic gases, great heat, infiltration of water, etc., there shall be granted a progressive scale of percentage increases on basic pay or on the task-work rates, to be determined in the supplementary agreements.[60]

France

Art. 146. With exceptions for which there must be sound reasons, the rate of draught at the place of work must be such that the temperatures by dry thermometer and wet thermometer shall be appropriate to the work to be done. . . .[61]

Work sites where the resulting temperature reaches 28° must be regarded as particularly hot; at this temperature the effective physical work of the average worker cannot exceed 4,500 kilogram-meters per hour on a continuing basis. . . .[62]

---

[58] National Coal Board, Northern Division, *National and District Agreements (Durham Area) to January 1948*, agreement, August 19, 1942, p. 252.

[59] National Coal Board, National Wage Structure for the Coal-mining Industry, agreement, April 21, 1955, *loc. cit.*, Part X, p. 999.

[60] *Contratto nazionale di lavoro 28 marzo 1953 per gli operai addetti all'industria mineraria.*

[61] *Règlement Général sur L'Exploitation des Mines de Combustibles Minéraux Solides*, Décret du 4 mai 1951, p. 67.

[62] *Annexe, Les Conditions Physiologiques du Travail Au Chantier en Relation avec L'Aérage*, Instruction du 30–7–1951, p. 55.

Germany

4. (1) At work points underground with a temperature of over 28°C, daily working time in the drift shall not exceed six hours, and the daily shift shall not in principle exceed seven hours.

(2) In mines where as many as 50 percent of the underground workers are working at temperatures over 28°C, miners employed at these work points must be allowed rest shifts in accordance with the attached "Guiding Principles for the Curtailing of Shifts in Special Cases," which form a part of this master agreement.

5. (1) In the case of mines in which more than 50 percent of the underground workers have been working at temperatures above 28°C only subsequent to 1 April 1953, the Collective Agreement Committee may fix the daily shift for miners employed at such work points at 7½ hours, on the proposal of the management or of the works council.[63]

As the coal mines grew deeper in the Ruhr around 1900, the problems of greater walking distance and hotter working conditions led to the strike of January 1905. The law of July 14, 1905, was enacted to mitigate these working conditions which had been deteriorating. The 28-degree rule was developed in these circumstances [64] and spread to other countries.

Australia

(s) (i) Where in the course of his duties an employee's clothing becomes wet through no fault of his own, he shall be paid water money at 2 s. 6 d. per shift.

(ii) The employee shall as soon as possible notify the manager or his representative of his intention of making a claim for water money and of his reasons for making it.[65]

---

[63] *Manteltarifvertrag für die Arbeiter des rheinisch-westfälischen Steinkohlenbergbaus,* Gültig ab 1. Mai 1953, p. 4.

[64] Herman Isay and Rudolf Isay, *Allgemeines Berggesetz für die Preuszischen Staaten,* Mannheim, J. Bensheimer, 1919, Vol. I, p. 406.

[65] *The Coal Mining Industry (Miners) Award, 1954, New South Wales,* p. 7.

New Zealand

12. Wet Time: If any dispute shall arise at any time concerning wet time or dust time it shall be referred to an independent umpire to be mutually approved between the management and the Union and the decision of such umpire shall be final and binding. . . .

When water is laid on in a place to lay dust it shall not of itself be deemed to make the place a wet place.[66]

4.(a) Men in wet places shall work six hours bank to bank and shall be paid a full shift. A "wet place" shall mean a place in which a workman cannot avoid his clothing becoming saturated with water within three hours of starting time. Men in such places shall report to an official before leaving the mine.

(b) In extra-wet places a five-hour shift shall be worked. . . .

(d) In cases in which outside workers cannot avoid becoming wet in the performance of their duties, they shall be granted an allowance of 1 s. 6 d. per shift for each shift worked. This provision shall supersede and replace any previous arrangement in respect of wet time allowances for outside workers and/or oilskins or oilskin allowance.[67]

Poland

Art. 4. . . .

(6). The hours of work of workers employed underground in particularly heavy or unhealthy operations, inter alia—

. . . . (b) in the deepening of shafts and in the building, repair and maintenance of shafts, or of apparatus in and at the shafts, if the conditions make it necessary for the work to be done in waterproof clothing;

. . . shall be seven hours, paid as a full working day.

(7) The hours of work of workers employed underground—

(a) in workings where the temperature is above 28° Centigrade,

[66] National Coal Mines Agreement, May 11–14, 1954.

[67] Department of Labor, New Zealand, Canterbury Coal-mine Employees Award, August 30, 1956, loc. cit., p. 1322.

(b) in frozen shafts shall be six per 24 hours, paid as a full working day. . . .[68]

THE MEASUREMENT OF THE WORKING DAY

Since underground miners may have a long distance to travel from the entrance of the mine to their actual place of work operations, a problem arises as to the precise measurement of the work day. As mines deepen this distance may increase. Where is the employee required to be at the start of the shift? At the entrance to the mine on the surface, at the mine face, or at some intermediate point? On whose time shall he travel at the close of the shift from the mine face to the exit of the mine on the surface? Wartime history in the United States records the dispute over "portal-to-portal" pay. The rules developed to meet this common problem are cited in the following excerpts.

United States

For all inside employes, work shall begin at the portal and end at the portal; but in shaft mines, for the purpose of making the operations of lowering and hoisting men orderly and safe, the mantrips shall leave the bottom ten minutes after the start of each nine-hour shift [69] and shall arrive at the shaft bottom five minutes before the end of each nine-hour shift. Employes shall be at the shaft collar in time for all of them to be lowered so as to be in the mantrip at the scheduled departure time. The operator shall have the right to designate the portal or portals and may move or establish new portals if adequate facilities, conveniences, and safety are furnished the mine workers at such new portals, subject to the right of review on the part of the mine workers under existing grievance machinery.[70]

An illustration of the older arrangement is provided by the following agreement provision:

[68] *Zbiorowy Uklad Pracy dla pracowników fizycznych i umyslowych zatrudnionych w zakladach pracy Ministerstwa Górnictwa i Energetyki obowiązujący od dnia 1 kwietnia 1957 r.*, pp. 6–7.

[69] These hours were subsequently reduced.

[70] *National Bituminous Coal Wage Agreement*, Effective April 1, 1945.

Drivers shall take their mules to and from stables, and the time required in so doing shall not include any part of the day's labor, their work beginning when they reach the change at which they receive empty cars, but in no case shall the driver's time be docked while he is waiting for such cars at the point named.[71]

Great Britain

2. That the hours per shift of coal hewers shall be 7 hours 10 minutes, calculated from the time of the first man going down to the time of the first man commencing to ride.[72]

1. The normal working week for underground workers shall be one of 5 consecutive shifts of 7½ hours plus one winding time. . . .

15. The management may, in co-operation with the appropriate representatives of the workmen and with the approval of H. M. Inspectors determine (on a rota basis or otherwise) separate winding times for different sections or districts of a pit so that the workmen will descend by sections in a specified order and ascend in the same order and their obligation to present themselves within the separate winding times so determined for them respectively, shall be as it now is as regards existing winding times.[73]

Germany

3. The hours of work of a shift for underground workers shall be 7½ hours for each individual to be counted from the time the cage starts down until the time it starts upwards including rest periods.[74]

In coalmining, working time means shift time; it is calculated from the beginning of the winding (Seilfahrt) at the start until

[71] *Southern Wage Agreement,* July 5, 1941.
[72] National Coal Board, Northern Division, *National and District Agreements (Durham Area) to January 1948,* Eight Hours Agreement, December 13, 1909, p. 112.
[73] National Coal Board, *Five Day Week Agreement,* April 18, 1947, *loc. cit.,* Part II, pp. 183, 185.
[74] *Manteltarifvertrag für die Arbeiter des rheinisch-westfälischen Steinkohlenbergbaus,* Gültig ab 1. Mai 1953, p. 4.

the beginning of winding on the return, or from the entry of the individual worker into the mouth of the drift until his exit.[75]

Australia

13(a) The ordinary hours of work without payment of overtime for underground employees shall be 40 per week to be worked in shifts of eight hours each bank to bank, including crib time of 30 minutes counted as time worked, Monday to Friday inclusive. . . .

(c) Bank to bank shall be reckoned from the time the first person working on a shift leaves the surface to the time the last person working on the same shift returns to the surface. . . .

12(r) (i) Contract workers who walk in excess of one mile to their working place from the inbye end of the underground transport shall be paid for the time so occupied at the appropriate day rate for their class of work.

(ii) For walking from their working place in excess of one mile to the inbye end of the transport contract workers shall be paid for the time so occupied at the rate prescribed in sub-clause (i) hereof provided they fill the approved darg or work a full shift.

(iii) Walking time shall be assessed on the basis of 20 minutes to the mile.[76]

New Zealand

(4). The hours of work in mechanised mines shall be seven hours *bank to bank* for *all* underground workers, and there shall be no shorter shifts permitted.[77] [Emphasis added on bank to bank]

Italy

Article 7 . . .

In mines and quarries time worked shall be reckoned from

[75] *Arbeitzeitordnung*, 30 April 1938, par. 2.
[76] *The Coal Mining Industry (Miners) Award, 1954, New South Wales*, pp. 7–8.
[77] *National Coal Mines Agreement*, May 11–14, 1954.

the time of entering to that of leaving the shaft or access gallery.[78]

Poland

Art. 4.

. . . . (4) The hours of work of underground workers shall be calculated from the time at which they enter the cage at the surface until the time at which they leave the cage at the surface.

(5) Signalmen, machinemen, firemen, and all manual workers employed underground to operate machines that are constantly running shall be required to await the arrival of the relieving shift at the work place.

Such workers shall receive the following supplementary remuneration in respect of a prolonged stay underground:

If the distance from the shaft bottom to their work place is between 500 metres and 1500 metres, half the basic hourly rate of pay for each day of work, not including the bonus for overtime on such account. The special remuneration shall be increased by a further one half of the basic hourly remuneration in respect of each additional kilometer or part of a kilometer.[79]

Analogous rules defining the measurement of the working day exist in France.[80]

TOOLS AND PROTECTIVE CLOTHING

The special conditions of the work place in coal mining have raised a range of issues concerning clothing, hand tools, lamps, and other specialized equipment required for the person of mine workers. A variety of questions in this area are the subject of rules:

[78] *Contratto nazionale di lavoro 28 marzo 1953 per gli operai addetti all'industria mineraria.*

[79] *Zbiorowy Uklad Pracy dla pracowników fizycznych i umyslowych zatrudnionych w zakladach pracy Ministerstwa Górnictwa i Energetyki obowiązujący od dnia 1 kwietnia 1957 r.,* p. 6.

[80] Communauté Européenne du Charbon et de L'Acier, Haute Autorité, *Quelques aspects des conditions de travail dans les industries de la Communauté, Monographie du conditions applicables en France,* février 1956, p. 12.

United States

The management shall furnish all necessary mine workers' tools. Safety equipment and devices, including electric cap lamps, and also carbide lamps, shall be furnished by the management without charge. This shall not include, however, personal wearing apparel such as hats, clothing, shoes, and goggles. In lieu of furnishing carbide lamps and carbide, the operator may, at his option, pay to the mine workers who use carbide lamps at their work place six cents per day, and the mine workers shall continue to furnish their own carbide lamps and carbide.[81]

Great Britain

1. A pair of safety boots and a safety helmet shall be issued free of charge to each new entrant to the Coalmining Industry at the beginning of his training.

2. Replacements will be charged to mineworkers at cost price in the case of safety boots and at one-quarter of cost price in the case of safety helmets.

3. In cases in which the management orders any of the articles of protective clothing set out in the Schedule hereto to be worn by a workman on grounds of safety or to protect his health in wet, dusty, or other abnormal conditions the following principles shall apply:

    i. the articles shall be provided on loan to the workman free of charge;

    ii. replacements required due to fair wear and tear shall also be provided on loan to the workmen free of charge;

    Provided that the workman will be held responsible for any damage due to his own negligence or for any loss.[82]

[The schedule contains 18 items including duffle coats, goggles, oilskins, and rubber gloves.]

[81] *National Bituminous Coal Agreement,* Effective April 1, 1945.

[82] National Coal Board, Agreement, December 31, 1955, *loc. cit.*, Part X, p. 1176.

France

Art. 195 The lamps shall be provided by the mine operator who is responsible for their maintenance.[83]

New Zealand

10. The Company shall provide free all tools for day-wage men; and each man shall be held responsible for tools supplied to him. Carbide shall be provided free to all workers.[84]

Italy

Art. 16. All tools, including safety lamps—but excluding ordinary lamps, where it is customary to use them—together with the maintenance thereof, and all equipment and any other articles required by the workman in the performance of his work shall be supplied by the undertaking at its own expense.

The workman shall be responsible for the tools issued to him in the proper way; it must, however, be made possible for him to look after the articles on charge to him.

The workman shall be required to exercise every care in the use of tools and equipment, and shall be answerable for any damage for which he is to blame, within the meaning of Articles 36 and 37 [Discipline and discharge articles].

Art. 17. Carbide, explosives, caps, and fuses shall be supplied by the undertakings at their expense.

Art. 18. Both underground and outdoor workers engaged in jobs where there is water seepage or in the handling of poisonous or highly corrosive substances shall be supplied with suitable protective equipment free of charge by the undertaking.

The workman shall take care of the protective clothing issued to him and shall return it at the end of the day's work.[85]

[83] *Règlement Général sur L'Exploitation des Mines de Combustibles Mineraux Solides*, Décret du 4 mai 1951, p. 80.

[84] Department of Labor, New Zealand, Canterbury Coal-Mine Employees Award, August 30, 1956, *loc. cit.*, Vol. 56, p. 1324.

[85] National Agreement of March 28, 1953. It is to be remembered that the Italian agreement governs mining in general.

Poland

Art. 24. If a recruited worker provides his own tools he shall be paid compensation, of an amount fixed by the establishment, for the wear and tear of such tools. . . .

Art. 26. . . . (b) Carbide in the following quantities: miners at the face, young miners, colliers, loaders, and other skilled workers underground, with the exception of machinemen, assistant surveyors, the drivers of electric locomotives and other locomotives, persons responsible for the issue of explosives and signalmen, 300 grams in respect of each full day worked; all other workers employed in the places specified in paragraph 2, 200 grams in respect of each full day worked; skilled surface workers, 40 grams in respect of each hour worked in the places specified in paragraph 2.[86]

Similar arrangements exist for other countries.[87]

HIRING, LAYOFFS, AND RIGHTS TO JOBS

There are a wide variety of rules concerning these subjects. In the postwar period the labor market has been tight, and a number of countries have imported miners, notably Belgium, France, and England. The status, or lack of status, of these foreign miners compared to nationals is the subject of rules. In periods with greater unemployment, the principles on which a reduction of work opportunities, temporarily or permanently, were to be handled elicited a more extensive body of local and national rules. In some countries explicit standards or principles have been adopted (seniority and the superior rights of certain workers such as officials of labor organizations or injured miners), while in other cases only procedures exist to contest a

[86] *Zbiorowy Uklad Pracy dla pracowników fizycznych i umysłowych zatrudnionych w zakladach pracy Ministerstwa Górnictwa i Energetyki obowiązujący od dnia 1 kwietnia 1957 r.*, pp. 17–18.

[87] In the USSR, "Working clothes consisting of a light canvas jacket and trousers and rubber knee boots, are issued free." National Coal Board, *The Coal Industry of the USSR*, A Report by the Technical Mission of the National Coal Board, Part 1, 1957, p. 92.

decision by management. There may not in fact be as great a difference between these sets of rules as might appear; they may work out to about the same decisions.

United States

1. Seniority in principle and practice shall be recognized in the industry.

2. In all cases where the working force is to be reduced, employees in each job classification at a mine with the least service shall be laid off first.

3. Employees who are idle because of a reduction in the working force shall be placed in a panel from which they shall be returned to employment on the basis of seniority. . . .

9. Any person in the panel list who secures casual or intermittent employment during the period when no work is available for him at the operation shall in no way jeopardize his seniority rights while engaged in such temporary employment. However, any person on the panel list who secures regular employment at another operation, or outside the industry, and does not return to work when there is available employment at the mine for those in said panel, shall sacrifice his seniority rights at the operation and shall have his name removed from the panel list.[88]

Great Britain

. . . it is agreed that the Union will raise no objection to Polish workers being employed as civilians in British coal mines on terms and conditions identical with those applicable to British workers provided that:

    i. No Polish worker shall be placed in employment at any colliery without the agreement of the local Branch of the Union;

    ii. Polish workers who enter the industry shall join the Union and any who fail to do so shall be dismissed.

    iii. In the event of redundancy Polish workers shall be the

---

[88] *National Bituminous Coal Wage Agreement of 1950 as Amended September 29, 1952.*

first to go. They shall be transferred or dismissed whenever their continued employment at a particular pit would prevent the continued employment or re-employment of a British mine worker who is capable of and willing to do the work on which the Polish worker is employed and who might otherwise be displaced by redundancy at that pit or at another pit.[89]

Australia

5. (c) . . . . employment shall be terminated by a week's notice on either side given at any time during the week or by the payment or forfeiture of a week's wages as the case may be.

21. When in the Northern or Southern District of New South Wales a reduction of hands is decided upon by the management it shall be regulated by the principle "the last to come the first to go" in the respective classes according to length of service at the mine.

22. (a) When in the Northern District of New South Wales an increase of hands is decided upon by the management, former employees who apply shall be re-engaged in order of their seniority in the respective classes according to length of service at the mine.

(b) In the event of the closure and subsequent reopening of a mine in the Southern District of New South Wales the management shall give notice of such re-opening in the local press and the employees previously employed shall have preference of re-employment provided they make application within two weeks after the said notice.[90]

---

[89] National Coal Board. Agreement, 31 January 1947, Part II, p. 180.
As to the more general application of seniority, in layoffs of considerable duration, the National Coal Board advised as follows: "Supposing a shaft collapsed and it was evident that no work would be available for six months, in such circumstances endeavours would be made to give these men immediate employment at other collieries and where that was not possible notice of termination of contract would be given, and in certain circumstances, men might be entitled to redundancy pay. There is a general understanding that senior miners would have priority according to custom and practice which varies locally." (Letter of June 25, 1958).
[90] *The Coal Mining Industry* (*Miners*) *Award, 1954, New South Wales,* pp. 3, 13.

New Zealand

14. When the services of any worker are to be dispensed with for any reason other than some fault of his own, he shall be entitled to a fortnight's notice before dismissal, and any worker desiring to leave his employment shall be required to give a fortnight's notice of his intention to do so. In the event of shortening of hands it is provided:

  i. That the management of every mine shall have the right to shorten hands when necessary to meet trade conditions.

 ii. That when it is necessary to shorten hands the management shall have the right to select the men to be retained in consideration of their suitability for the work to be done.

iii. When at any time there are ex-workers of the mine waiting for employment who in the opinion of the management are competent to fill any vacancy that may require to be filled, they shall have preference of employment according to seniority of service. If there are no ex-workers waiting for employment at any time where a vacancy requires to be filled, preference shall be given to unemployed members of the union. . . .[91]

13. When the services of any worker are to be dispensed with for any reason other than some fault of his own, he shall be entitled to a weeks notice before dismissal, and any worker desiring to leave his employment shall be required to give a weeks notice of his intention to do so.

When it is necessary to shorten hands the general rule shall be the last on, first off.[92]

Italy

Article 11. In the event of a slack period, the management shall endeavour, whenever it considers it to be compatible with the exigencies of the industry, to introduce short-time working or work sharing between the work people in turns before issuing dismissal notices. . . .

[91] Department of Labor, New Zealand, Canterbury Coal-Mine Employees Award, August 30, 1956, loc. cit., Vol. 56, p. 1325.

[92] Runanga District Coal-Mine Employees—Industrial Agreement, filed in the Office of the Clerk of Awards, November 26, 1956, ibid., p. 1955.

Article 43. The dismissal of a workman (not being a worker on trial), otherwise than under the provisions of Article 37 [discharge for misconduct], or the resignation of a worker (not being a worker on trial) may be given at any time with six working days' notice.

It is, however, optional for the management to dispense with a worker's services for the period notice by paying him the wages for the six working days (48 hours) or for so many hours as remain to run to complete the period of notice. . . .

Article 45. A worker terminated for other than disciplinary reasons shall be paid an indemnity on dismissal, calculated as follows: . . . .[93]

Poland

Art. 3. (1) Workers shall be recruited and dismissed by the management of the establishment with the prior consent of the works council. This does not apply in establishments to persons appointed by the higher authority, namely the director (or manager) of the establishment, his deputies, as provided for in the regulations, or to the chief (or senior) accountant. In the event of disagreement the question shall be decided by the higher organ for the establishment and the works (or local) council. . . .

(3) A contract of employment concluded with a member of the works council or the works arbitration committee or with the social inspector of labor may not be terminated without the consent of the said trade-union bodies; such consent must be confirmed by the Central Executive of the Miners' Union. . . .

(5) The employer shall not have the right to terminate the contract of employment during the first 26 weeks of a worker's incapacity for work where such incapacity is the result of an industrial accident or an illness.[94]

[93] *Contratto nazionale di lavoro 28 marzo 1953 per gli operai addetti all'industria mineraria.*

[94] *Zbiorowy Układ Pracy dla pracowników fizycznych i umysłowych zatrudnionych w zakladach pracy Ministerstwa Górnictwa i Energetyki obowiązujący od dnia 1 kwietnia 1957 r.,* p. 3.

RULES ON WAGES AND OTHER ELEMENTS OF COMPENSATION

The largest group of rules in the industrial-relations systems of coal mining probably concerns wages and other elements of compensation. The setting of these rules and their administration are decisive to the income and living standards of workers and to the costs and financial position of private or nationalized mining enterprises. The complex web of compensation rules significantly illustrates both a number of common characteristics among countries derived from similar technological and market contexts and also a variety of features distinctive to the respective national industrial-relations systems.[95] Compensation rules particularly well illustrate the combination of common technological and market influences as compared and contrasted to the role of distinctive features of a national system.

COMMON INDUSTRY FEATURES

Job Classifications

The occupational and job-classification list of scheduled wage rates is largely reflective of technology in its broadest sense. Dislodging coal by explosives creates the sensitive position of shotfirer; the use of coal plows or continuous miners requires skilled machine operators. Open-cast (open-pit) mining requires operators for the giant shovels to strip the overburden. The use of horses or mules to transport coal underground means different operating and servicing jobs than when electric cars or conveyors are used. In general underground mining creates clusters of related jobs: surface workers, underground workers at the mine

---

[95] For a general discussion of wage structure, see Communauté Européenne du Carbon et de L'Acier, Haute Autorité, *Salaires des Ouvriers Dans les Industries de la Communauté, Principales tendances de la politique salariale dans chacun des pays*, Luxembourg, septembre 1956.

face, underground maintenance and service operators, and underground transport workers. In a more complete view of the coal-mining wage structure reference should also be made to supervisory and managerial jobs, professional groups, and clerical operations. Such groupings are frequently used in setting wage schedules, and there is a considerable degree of interdependence of wage rates within these clusters.[96]

Not only does common technology create common groupings of jobs, but there is a relatively high degree of similarity in the ranking or ordering of wage rates by occupations or job classifications. Underground jobs have higher rates than those on the surface performing similar work operations, such as maintenance. In Italian mining there is an explicit "underground allowance," [97] while in other countries the wage schedules reflect the differences.[98] The factors of skill, responsibility, and hazards are commonly operative, and while implicit valuations and relative labor supplies vary, these considerations operate as a rough rule of thumb yielding fairly uniform wage schedules, at least for key jobs. The development of a single or relatively uniform wage schedule for coal mining within a country [99] reinforces this tendency toward a common ordering of wage schedules. There are differences in the extent of differentials between unskilled and skilled jobs, between the scheduled rates for face workers and for maintenance jobs, and the yields of pieceworkers over their minimum rates. But the relative ranking of major job classifications is essentially similar.[100] There are, of course, in any single country a variety of deviations and specialized job classifications,

---

[96] John T. Dunlop, "The Task of Contemporary Wage Theory," in *The Theory of Wage Determination*, London, Macmillan and Co., 1957, pp. 16–20.

[97] Article 19 (3) of the 1953 Agreement.

[98] National Coal Board, *loc. cit.*, Part X, pp. 998–999.

[99] W. H. Sales and J. L. Davis, "Introducing a New Wage Structure into Coal Mining," *Bulletin of the Oxford University Institute of Statistics*, August 1957, pp. 202–224.

[100] For the USSR, National Coal Board, *The Coal Industry of the USSR*, A Report by the Technical Mission of the National Coal Board, Part 1, 1957, p. 84, Table VI.

reflecting unique technology, advanced or retrogressive, and distinctive geology or traditions of a labor-market area.

Wage Levels

The level of wage rates in coal mining has been particularly sensitive to longer-run changes in the competitive position of the industry in both product and labor markets. In the thirties the relative position of coal wages declined in national wage structures under the impact of falling coal prices and profits and as a response to unemployment in mining communities with few alternatives for work. In the war and postwar periods the relative position of coal wages has risen to the very top of the wage structure among major industries in almost all countries in the face of a period of shortages of coal and of full employment with attractive alternatives to mining employment. The relatively much higher ranking of coal wages (and other compensation and amenities) has thus far been necessary to hold the existing work force and to attract new recruits simply for replacements.[101]

Supplements to Wages

The compensation system in coal mining involves a higher proportion of various supplements and a lower proportion in basic-wage rates. This is true despite the relatively high basic-wage rates noted immediately above. Special payments in kind in the form of concessionary coal and housing allowances, arising from the nature of the industry and further from the shortages of manpower in the past decade, have operated to create this observed feature of compensation in mining. An excellent study of labor-cost components in nine European countries with almost complete coverage for coal production concludes:

[101] Economic Commission for Europe, Coal Committee, *Fundamental Policy Questions Facing Governments in Regard to the Future Development of the Coal Industry and Trade in Europe* (Manpower problems), Geneva, Switzerland, 1958.

Wage supplements in percentage terms were consistently higher than in the manufacturing industries studied, with Greece the only exception.[102] There were a number of striking differences in the pattern of labor costs as compared with that in manufacturing industries. Wages in kind were generally very important, amounting in France to 12 percent of the total cost measured and in Germany to 10 percent. Social-security contributions were also substantially larger in coal mines. . . .[103]

In coal mining the nonwage elements of labor costs,[104] expressed as a percentage of total labor costs, ranged between 16.4 percent in Great Britain, 27.4 percent in Belgium, 39.8 percent in Germany, 41.4 percent in France, and 49 percent in Italy. While this spectrum is characteristic of the respective national systems, as shown in the consistency among the eight industries studied, the coal-mining industry in the various countries reflected a relatively greater proportion of supplements or fringes in addition to basic wages.

Piecework

A substantial proportion of employees, particularly those engaged in direct production at the coal face have historically been paid on piece rates, task work, or tonnage rates.[105] This fact is common to different countries but the incentive systems (including the extent of guarantees, incentive pull, and allowances for "unproductive" or "dead" work such as timbering) are highly variable even within countries and coal fields.

[102] Lignite production in 1955 was only 900 thousand metric tons.

[103] "Wages and Related Elements of Labor Cost in European Industry, 1955: A Preliminary Report," *International Labour Review*, December 1957, pp. 558–587. See Tables I and IX.

[104] Other than premium pay for overtime, late-shift, and holiday work. The nonwage elements consisted of bonuses and gratuities, payments in kind, time paid for but not worked, obligatory and nonobligatory social-security contributions, direct benefits, and subsidies.

[105] International Labor Office, *Principles and Methods of Wage Determination in the Coal-mining Industry, An International Survey*, Series D, No. 20, Geneva, 1931, pp. 51–57.

The institution of piecework in coal mining has created another distinctive coal-mining institution, the checkweighman, an employee to check the weight of coal produced since the scales are at the surface at a distance from the miners paid by the coal produced. The following rules governing the checkweighman may be cited:

United States

The Mine Workers shall have the right to a checkweighman, of their own choosing, to inspect the weighing of coal, provided that in any case where on account of physical conditions and mutual agreement, wages are based on measure or other method than on actual weights, the Mine Workers shall have the right to check the accuracy and fairness of such method, by a representative of their own choosing. . . .

The wages of checkweighmen will be collected through the pay office semimonthly, upon a statement of time made by the checkweighmen, and approved by the Mine Committee. The amount so collected shall be deducted on a percentage basis, agreed upon by the checkweighman and clerk, from the earnings of the Mine Workers engaged in mining coal and shall be sufficient only to pay the wages and legitimate expenses incident to the office. . . .

The checkweighman, or checkmeasurer, as the case may require, shall be permitted at all times to be present at the weighing or measuring of coal, also have power to checkweigh or checkmeasure the same, and during the regular working hours to have the privilege to balance and examine the scales or measure the cars. . . . It shall be the further duty of the checkweighman or checkmeasurer to credit each Mine Worker with all merchantable coal mined by him on a proper sheet or book kept by him for that purpose. . . .[106]

Great Britain

The existence of checkweighmen is confirmed by a rule regarding compensation for redundancy.

[106] Southern Wage Agreement, July 5, 1941.

Checkweighers, provided that they have been formerly in the employ of the Board or their predecessors, shall receive redundancy compensation on the same terms and subject to the same conditions as redundant mineworkers . . . but on an *ex-gratia* basis, it being understood that this concession shall not form a precedent and that the National Union of Mineworkers will not later apply for the admission of checkweighers to the Supplementary Injuries Scheme or the Fatal Accident Scheme or any other similar scheme.[107]

Germany

37. The workers are enabled to request according to par. 80 c of the General Mining Law the inspection of the measuring of the wagons by a man of their own choice and at their expense.[108]

Australia

47(1) The persons who are employed in a mine, and are paid according to the weight of the mineral gotten by them, may, at their own cost, station a person, in this Act referred to as "a check-weigher," at each place appointed for the weighing of the mineral, and at each place appointed for determining the deductions, in order that he may, on behalf of the persons by whom he is so stationed, take a correct account of the weight of the mineral, or determine correctly the deductions, as the case may be.[109]

The extension of mechanization in continuous mining operations, and an increase in the size or capacity of these machines, has a tendency to reduce the extent of piecework by individuals or small groups. ". . . The growth of mechanization . . . as a result of these the piecework system has in a number of instances

[107] National Coal Board, N.C.B. Circular L.R. (General) No. 32, 26 February, 1951, *loc. cit.*, Part VI, p. 38.

[108] *Arbeitsordnung für die im Aachener, Niedersächsischen und Rheinisch-Westfälischen Steinkohlenbergbau tätigen Arbeiter und Tarifangestellten,* Gültig ab. 1 November 1950, p. 27.

[109] *Coal Mines Regulation Act, 1912–1953.* New South Wales, Certified September 2, 1957, p. 55. See Part I, ss. 47–49, pp. 55–59.

been dropped or substantially cut." [110] "With the advent of mechanization, tonnage payments have declined [in the United States] to the point of covering only about 10 to 15 percent of the work force." [111] There is a less direct relation between individual effort and coal mined at the face. The fact that tonnage rates have been a major source of disputes with frequent variations in mining conditions is another factor working in the same direction. There has been some tendency for experiment with production bonuses which constitute a modest addition to the basic wage variable with output for underground miners as a group. A French agreement provides for a bonus formula in which payments are made when underground output averages 1075 kilograms per man per shift or more during a half-year.[112] But the bonus based upon production of underground workers of a mine averaged over a period as a supplement to basic wages is quite different from piece or tonnage rates.

There are other elements of compensation in coal mining which show common features: shift premiums for the second (back) shift or for night work after a designated hour. These various dimensions to compensation are particularly influenced by the common technological characteristics and similar product-market conditions. Other features of compensation are more influenced by the separate national industrial-relations systems.

SPECIALIZED NATIONAL FEATURES

Wage Differentials for Young Miners

The wage schedules of most countries include explicit differentiation by age below twenty-one years. Sometimes the differentiation is by half years and in other cases only by full years.

---

[110] European Coal and Steel Community, *Report on the Conference on Safety in Coalmines*, March 1957, Doc. No. S 360/57e, p. 124.
[111] Gerald G. Somers, *Grievance Settlement in Coal Mining*, Bureau of Business Research, Morgantown, West Virginia University, June 1956, p. 34.
[112] *Protocole D'Accord*, 27 décembre 1955, Article 6.

In England the wage schedule steps are by half years from fifteen to seventeen-and-one-half and by full years from eighteen to twenty-one.[113] In some countries, the full adult rate is achieved earlier (in New Zealand it is reached at nineteen [114]) and lower rates apply to the age bracket sixteen to nineteen. In some cases the wage progression by age is moderate while in other cases the wage steps are proportionately larger; they differ as to the age brackets in which rates are increased most rapidly. A differentiation by age may also be applied to the vacation, holiday, and housing-allowance components of compensation. Differentiation in the wage schedule by age brackets is common in these countries among many industries.

It appears that the United States is unique in providing no wage variation by age brackets in industry generally including coal mining. This difference is to be attributed to the later age of school attendance and the later age of recruitment to the industry. As with many other features of national industrial-relations systems, this distinctive feature of the rules of the United States industrial-relations system is not to be regarded as capricious nor as arising from the accidents of legislation; it has its roots deep in the characteristics and history of the nation. The absence of wage differentiation by age in the compensation system of coal mining in the United States is a consequence and reflection of the national industrial-relations system.

Family Allowances

Family allowances are characteristic of the compensation arrangements in some countries but not in others. The family allowance provisions apply to industry generally although the amounts may be increased in some industries, and variations in compensation by family status may be extended to housing allowances and

---

[113] National Coal Board, *loc. cit.*, Part X, Agreement of April 21, 1955, p. 1025; also see Part I, p. 29 for yearly intervals.

[114] 1956 *National Coal Mines Agrement.*

other elements of compensation. The French and German housing allowances in coal mining include provision for the size of the dependent family. Among countries there are, of course, wide variations in the relative size of family allowances to total compensation, in the incremental payments for additional children in families of different sizes, in the ages of dependency, and in other features of family allowances.[115] The presence or absence of family-allowance systems is rooted in a variety of features of a country, including the levels of real income, inflation experience, population policy, and religious persuasions. The presence of family allowances in the compensation rules of coal miners reflects characteristics of the national industrial-relations system rather than common features of the technological and market environment.

Wage Categories

In a number of countries the occupational or job-classification wage schedules in an industry or enterprise are grouped into a limited number of grades or categories which are standard across industries for manual workers; a similar group of categories ordinarily applies to white-collar classifications or jobs filled by "employees" as distinct from "workers." In Italy and Yugoslavia there are four categories by skill [116] and in France there are five. In the Netherlands the initial postwar reconstruction of the wage structure by resort to three categories of skill gave way to a national system of job evaluation with a larger number of labor grades more or less standardized across industries. These nationwide categories do not in themselves affect the relative ordering of wage schedules for job classifications, but they do affect the

---

[115] International Social Security Association, XIth General Meeting, Paris, 7–11 September 1953, *Family Allowances*, Geneva, 1954, pp. 87–311.

[116] In Italy the categories for manual workers are: *operai specializzati* (skilled tradesmen), *operai qualificati* (tradesmen), *manovali specializzati* (semiskilled workers), and *manovali communi* (laborers). In Yugoslavia there are four categories of workers and four for employees.

final grouping of jobs and the presentation of the occupational wage structure. Thus, coal wage-rate schedules in countries with such nationwide categories are presented in terms of these headings although the relative ranking of occupations in coal industries among countries, including those without such uniform groupings, is not necessarily affected.

Social Security

The main features of social-security programs—pensions, unemployment insurance, health programs, and the like—tend on the whole to be standardized across industry in most countries. The comparison of compensation in the coal industry in different countries thus reveals differences in the national social-security programs.

Other Features

There are a variety of elements or forms of compensation in coal mining in the various countries which reflect relatively specialized adjustments to coal problems rather than common characteristics of the national compensation system. The attendance bonus in French coal mining,[117] the underground allowance in Italian mining, and the health and welfare program for coal miners, including the building of hospitals, in the United States are illustrative. There are also further instances of elements or forms of compensation in coal mining which are common to other industries in the same country but distinctive to that country that have not been noted: the Christmas bonus,[118] or thirteenth month pay, in Italy; the disposition of funds by the workers' management in Yugoslavia; the selection of some particular holidays with pay,[119] and many overtime provisions.

[117] *Protocole D'Accord,* 27 décembre 1955, Article 6.
[118] *Contratto nazionale di lavoro 28 marzo 1953 per gli operai addetti all'industria mineraria.*
[119] Anzac Day in New Zealand or Day of National Unity in Italy.

While a variety of forces no doubt impinge on the arrangements for compensation of coal miners, it is significant to seek to separate, with the assistance of comparative analysis, those elements of compensation which are relatively common in coal mining in different coal-producing countries, those which are distinctive to the compensation practices of a particular country and generally common among its industries, and those elements of compensation which are distinctive to coal mining in a particular country. These comparisons are instructive, for they help to show which forces in wage determination are common among countries and have their roots in the technology and labor and product markets for coal and which forces in wage determination tend to be particularly influenced by the distinctive features of national industrial-relations systems.

THE POWER CONTEXTS AND THE STATUS OF THE ACTORS

A review of the web of rules of the work places in these coal-producing countries reveals a group of rules (different from those considered thus far) that are particularly reflective of the status of workers, managers, and governmental agencies in the respective national industrial-relations systems. These rules have few uniform features across countries except that they define the relative statuses and relationships of the three groups of actors. It is these rules which have attracted most attention in international comparisons of industrial relations. Some of the more important of these rules may be reviewed comparatively and the extent of impact of the coal environment, if any, may be observed.

Status of Actors

The formal relationships among workers' organizations, managers and governmental agencies, indicative of national practices, are reflected in the various collective agreements, regulations, awards, or other rules of coal mining. In New Zealand the awards and agreements in coal mining conform to the national policies of compulsory union membership:

> 11(a) It shall not be lawful for any employer bound by this award to employ or to continue to employ in any position or employment subject to this award any person who is not for the time being a member of an industrial union of workers bound by this award: Provided, however, that any non-unionist may be continued in any position or employment by an employer bound by this award during any time while there is no member of a union bound by this award who is available to perform the particular work required to be done and is ready and willing to undertake it.
>
> (b) This clause shall not apply to managers and underviewers, nor shall it apply to lorry-drivers where such workers are members of a union other than the Canterbury Coal Mine Workers Industrial Union of Workers and are provided for in another award.[120]

This clause not only defines the relations between workers (members and nonmembers) and a labor organization but also specifies responsibilities of the management, the status accorded to the labor organization by a specialized governmental agency, the relations between rival or potentially rival labor organizations, and the status of certain occupational groups in managerial positions.

The status of the actors is different in the United States where the agreement provides for "exclusive representation" of the union, not by explicit reference to certification by the National Labor Relations Board (or corresponding state agency) as would generally be the case, but rather solely by agreement of the parties.[121] The agreement also includes a "union-security" clause

[120] Department of Labor, New Zealand, Canterbury Coal-Mine Employees Award, August 30, 1956, *loc. cit.*, Vol. 56, p. 1324. Also see, *Nightcaps District Opencast Agreement*, 1954–1956, March 8, 1954, Clause No. 18; *Westland Engine-drivers' Firemen, Pumpmen, Etc. (State Coal Mines) Agreement*, 1954–1956, October 21, 1954, Clause No. 18.

[121] The provision for exclusive representation follows the language of the statute, first adopted in 1935, which in turn reflected the earlier industrial-relations traditions, the principle of majority rule, and the institutions of the labor movement (exclusive jurisdiction).

requiring membership in the union after thirty days of employment in conformity with the maximum union-security conditions permitted by statute; indeed, an earlier provision requiring the "closed shop" was similar in this respect to the above-cited New Zealand clause but was changed following the passage of the Taft-Hartley law. The agreement and statutes define the relations between workers (members and nonmembers) and the union, the responsibility of management in continuing this status, the status of rival or potential rival unions, and the status of certain occupational groups in managerial positions.

In sharp contrast the coal-mining rules in France, Germany, and Italy do not provide for "exclusive representation" or "compulsory membership"; indeed, they provide for no preferred positions among unions; they do not seek to regulate competition for members; nor do they regulate the relations between unions and their members. The French coal-mining national agreements are signed by two unions, *Fédération Nationale des Mineurs* (F.O.) and *Fédération des Mineurs* (CFTC), and subsequently the same rules have been incorporated in a decree, as required in nationalized industries, and thereby their provisions are made applicable to all employees in the industry. The Italian mining agreement is signed by three unions: *Confederazione Italiana Sindacati Lavoratori* (CISL), *Confederazione Italiana del Lavoro* (CIL), and *Unione Italiana del Lavoro* (UIL). The German agreements are often signed jointly by the union of manual workers and that for white-collar workers: *Industriegewerkschaft Bergbau* and *Gewerkschaft der Bergbauangestellten*. The signatory unions to these French, German, and Italian agreements may or may not necessarily have a majority of workers in any or all mines.

In Great Britain coal mining has neither "exclusive representation," "compulsory membership," nor multi-unions in the same occupations; there are separate unions among manual workers, clerical and administrative employees, those in supervisory positions, and other groupings of mine employees. The agreements do not regulate the relations between the workers (members or non-members) and the union except for trade-union contributions:

> 6. (a) Where an employee's contribution is payable to the Union or to a constituent association the rules of which do not provide for the level of a separate contribution for the political fund the Board will if authorised by him deduct that contribution from his salary or wages.
>
> (b) Where an employee's contribution is payable to a constituent association the rules of which do provide for the levy of a separate contribution for the political fund the Board will if authorised by him deduct from his salary or wages his contributions to the general fund of that trade union and will if separately authorised by him deduct his contributions to the political fund of that trade union. . . .
>
> 12. The Union will contribute towards the cost of operating the provisions of this Agreement at the rate of Eightpence-halfpenny (8½d.) per annum for each member whose contributions are deducted under this Agreement.[122]

The status of the various actors in the Polish coal-mining industry differs from that in other countries, and the relations among workers, trade unions, workers' councils, managing boards, and directors are prescribed by statute and supplemented within this framework by the rules adopted for the enterprise.

Thus the status of the rule-makers and administrators in coal mining, as reflected in the complex of rules, is highly variable among coal-producing countries and in this respect tends to be reflective of the respective national industrial-relations systems.

Scope of the Rules

In an industry with a large number of producing units or pits in a country, the web of rules typically treats the scope of the rule-making. In an industry with a high proportion of labor costs

---

[122] National Coal Board, Agreement, April 29, 1953, *loc. cit.*, Part VIII, pp. 541–542. Also see Part IV, pp. 420–425.

to total costs each enterprise is concerned whether other enterprises have more or less favorable terms in the labor market. These common concerns with the scope and with the uniformity of labor conditions are approached quite differently according to major features of the respective national industrial-relations systems.

In Australia and New Zealand these problems are handled by the Coal Industry Tribunal and arbitration court respectively which may make an advanced extension of an award to other enterprises in the same industry:

> 1. This award shall be binding upon employers respondent to coal-mining industry awards for New South Wales, Queensland, Tasmania, or for the privately owned mines in Victoria in respect to each and every member of the Australian Coal and Shale Employees' Federation employed by them in the coalmining industry, and upon the Australian Coal and Shale Employees' Federation and the members thereof.[123]

> 24. This award shall apply to the original parties named, herein, and shall extend to and bind as subsequent party hereto every industrial union, industrial association, or employer who, not being an original party hereto, is, when this award comes into force or at any time whilst this award is in force, connected with or engaged in the industry to which this award applies within the industrial district to which this award relates.[124]

In the industrial-relations systems of Australia and New Zealand the arbitration awards, not infrequently based upon an agreement, may be extended throughout an industry, particularly a highly competitive one.[125] In the United States the agreement applies solely to the enterprises which are signatory or which have explicitly granted authority to an association to bind the

---

[123] The Australian Coal and Shale Employees' Federation and J. & A. Brown and Abermain Seaham Collieries Limited and Others, No. 66 of 1952 and No. 41 of 1954, *Coal Industry Tribunal*, effective March 14, 1955.

[124] Department of Labor, New Zealand, *loc. cit.*, Vol. 56, p. 1328. This award "embodies the terms of settlement arrived at by the assessors in Conciliation Council."

[125] Kenneth F. Walker, *Industrial Relations in Australia*, Cambridge, Mass., Harvard University Press, 1956, pp. 39–76; 200–254.

enterprise. There is no procedure for extension of the rules.[126] The national agreement, however, contains a one-way most-favored-nation clause under which the union assures each enterprise that the same conditions will be available to it if more favorable terms (less favorable to the workers) are granted to competitors.

The Italian arrangements also contain no mechanism for automatic extension, but the national agreement contains a two-way most-favored-nation clause:

> Should the national organizations of workers who are parties to this agreement covenant for less onerous conditions than those laid down in this agreement with other associations of employers or artisans, the said conditions (after their scope has been determined in a minute drawn up by the organizations concerned) shall be deemed to extend to workers belonging to the organizations entering into the said less onerous agreements who are employed by those undertakings which are of the same description and which are members of organizations belonging to the Italian General Confederation of Industry.
>
> Similarly should the employers' associations signatory to this agreement enter into compact with other workers' associations that are more favorable to the workers than the provisions of this agreement, the said more favorable compacts shall be deemed to extend to the workers who belong to the national organizations that are parties to this agreement and who are employed by undertakings of the same description as those covered by the more favorable compacts, again after the said conditions have been determined in a written minute.[127]

The rules of the French coal-mining industry, largely nationalized, provide that conditions established by agreement are to be incorporated in decrees. The problems of scope and uniformity of conditions are not significant questions under nationalization in France and in England.

---

[126] The Walsh-Healy act may be regarded as establishing procedures under which the Secretary of Labor may in effect extend the basic-wage provisions of an agreement on contracts for purchases by the federal government.

[127] *Contratto nazionale di lavoro 28 marzo 1953 per gli operai addetti all'industria mineraria.*

Dispute Settlement

The rules which provide procedures for settling disputes over both the application of existing rules and the formulation of new rules are particularly characteristic of the various national industrial-relations systems rather than standardized by technological and market similarities in coal mining. In Great Britain the procedures for national and pit-level conciliation have been established by agreements which terminate at the pit level in an impartial umpire (assisted by one nonvoting assessor selected by each side) and at the national level in an impartial permanent three-man National Tribunal.[128] In the United States disputes over the application of the agreements are settled by local and district grievance-procedure steps including arbitration.[129] There are no procedures, aside from direct negotiations, for the settlement of disputes over the terms of a new or reopened national agreement.[130] In Australia and New Zealand the awards and agreements provide for a disputes procedure ending in the arbitration court or Coal Industry Tribunal or joint committees with a neutral chairman. In France a wide variety of procedures established by law are available depending on the nature of the dispute and the recourse selected by the party raising an issue.[131] In Germany disputes during the term of an agreement may be taken to the labor courts. There are procedures for arbitration committees in Poland.[132] All these sundry arrangements tend to be characteristic of the national industrial-relations systems.

[128] National Coal Board, Part II, pp. 140–159, 166–171.

[129] Gerald G. Somers, *loc. cit.*, pp. 7–10.

[130] Title II of the Labor-Management Relations Act, 1947, was in large part designed with coal disputes in mind. These procedures cannot be said to have contributed to the settlement of such disputes on the occasions they have been invoked.

[131] Val R. Lorwin, *The French Labor Movement*, Cambridge, Mass., Harvard University Press, 1954, pp. 255–276.

[132] "Decree respecting works arbitration committees, Dated 24 February 1954," *Poland 1*, International Labor Office, *Legislative Series 1954*, Geneva, 1957.

RULES AS COMMON RESPONSE OR IMITATION

A comparison of the web of rules of the work place developed in different countries in an industry raises the question of the process by which the similar rules were developed. Were the similar rules developed as a common response to similar environmental conditions? Or, were the similar rules simply spread from one country to another by imitation? Coal-mining technology has been widely transferred and adapted or selected, in accordance with local conditions. In recent years there have been many formally organized international missions, productivity teams, and committees. Among some countries there has been historically significant migration of miners, and some coal managers, mining companies and mining-machinery companies have had wide international experience. It is to be recalled that one of the early uses for the Watt steam engine was for pumping water in the Belgium coal mines. All of these different media can be regarded as carriers of rules.

The question whether the similar rules are a common response or an instance of borrowing basically involves very fundamental questions. Both mechanisms may be involved in the experience of coal mining reviewed in this chapter. Even where careful historical studies could establish the importance of direct borrowing of rules, however, the point is to be made that some rules were borrowed and not others, and the environmental conditions in a country were more receptive in the case of some rules and unfavorable to others.

The role of international borrowing of working rules is not inconsistent with the central interpretation. Some rules are largely the response to the common technological and market environments of the industry, modified or adapted to meet special national conditions. Other rules are largely the consequence of the particular national industrial-relations system. International borrowing may have played a role in some instances of common rules, but the national contexts would have to be congenial or permissive to the rule.

This chapter has intensely compared a limited number of rules applicable to the coal mining industrial-relations systems of eight countries. Industrial relations needs to pay relatively more attention to such data and relatively less to interviews with participants.

These rich details have shown the dominant influence of a common technology and similar market or budgetary constraints across countries in the shaping of certain rules. Attention was directed particularly to those providing for safety inspectors drawn from miners, concessionary or house coal, provision for housing or rents, treating problems created by wet conditions or high temperatures, the need for measuring the starting place of the work day for underground miners, provision for tools and protective clothing, procedures and standards for layoffs and some aspects of the wage structure and compensation. In their development over time, these rules also indicate the consequences of changing technology and markets upon the substance of rules, as in the case of higher temperatures created by deeper mines in some geological formations and the relative rise of coal-mining wages in the period of war and postwar shortage of fuel.

No rule is shaped exclusively by one feature of the context of an industrial-relations system, and even those which are related mainly to the technical and market context also reflect the influence of the status of the actors in the national system. The rules on concessionary coal, for instance, in France and Poland have the imprint of a family-allowance feature which is absent in these rules developed in England and the United States. In such fashion does the web of rules reflect the intertwining of the context as a whole.

Still other rules, particularly those defining the status of workers and managers (and their organizations) and specialized governmental agencies, tend to be largely influenced by the special features of the several national industrial-relations systems. The rules defining the rights of rival organizations, procedures for disputes settlement, the scope of rule setting, and some features of compensation are illustrative.

SOURCES

United States

Southern Wage Agreement, July 5, 1941.
Appalachian Joint Wage Agreement, June 19, 1941.
National Bituminous Coal Wage Agreement, Effective April 1, 1945.
National Bituminous Coal Wage Agreement of 1950.
National Bituminous Coal Wage Agreement of 1950 as Amended September 29, 1952.
Williamson District Agreement (Districts No. 17 and 28 and Operators' Association of Williamson Field, July 5, 1941).

Great Britain

National Coal Board, *Memorandum of Agreements, Arbitration Awards and Decisions, Recommendations and Interpretations Relating to National Questions Concerning Wages and Conditions of Employment in the Coalmining Industry of Great Britain.* Parts I–XII.
National Coal Board, Northern Division, *National and District Agreements* (*Durham Area*) *To January 1948.*
Concessionary Coal Agreement Between National Coal Board (*Scottish Division*) *and National Union of Mineworkers* (*Scottish Area*), *7th January 1955.*
The National Coal Board (South-Western Division) and National Union of Mineworkers (South Wales Area), *Workmen's Housecoal Agreement, 17 December, 1953.*
National Coal Board, *Handbook on the Wage Structure of the Coalmining Industry, Amended December 1955.*
Mines and Quarries Act, 1954.

France

Code du Travail (Textes codifiés et textes annexes), Paris, Jurisprudence Générale Dalloz, 1956.
Statut du Mineur, Statut du Personnel Des Expoloitations Minières et Assimilées, Décret No. 46.1433 du 14 juin 1946, Mis à jour au 1ᵉʳ octobre 1957.

Règlement Général sur L'Exploitation des Mines de Combustibles Minéraux Solides, Décret du 4 mai 1951, Charbonnages de France, octobre 1951.
Protocole D'Accord, 27 décembre 1955; Arrêté, 23 janvier 1956.
Protocole D'Accord Relatif aux Conditions D'Attribution des Prestations de Logement aux Membres ou anciens Membres du Personnel des Houilleres de Bassin et Aux Veuves, 22 janvier 1957.
Arrêté, Autorisant à Titre Provisoire L'Application du Protocole D'Accord du 22 janvier 1957, Relatif Aux Conditions D'Attribution Des Prestations de Logement Aux Membres et Anciens Membres du Personnel des Houilleres de Bassin et Aux Veuves, 10 juillet 1957.
Protocole D'Accord, 20 février 1956; Arrêté, *Indemnités de logement des personnels ouvriers et employés des exploitations minières,* 9 avril 1956.

Germany

Zusammenstellung des Tarifrechts im rheinisch-westfälischen Steinkohlenbergbau nach dem Stande vom Februar 1955.
Works Constitution Act, 11 October 1952, International Labour Office, *Legislative Series 1952,* Geneva, 1955, Germany (Federal Republic) 6.

Italy

Contratto nazionale di lavoro 28 marzo 1953 per gli operai addetti all'industria mineraria.

Australia

New South Wales, *Coal Mines Regulation Act, 1912–1953,* Certified 2nd September, 1957.
New South Wales, *Mines Rescue Act, 1925–1955*
The Australian Coal and Shale Employees' Federation and Northern Colliery Proprietors' Association and Others, *The Coal Mining Industry (Miners) Award, 1954, New South Wales* (Disposal No. 66 of 1952) and other awards.
Ninth Annual Report of the Joint Coal Board for the Financial Year, 1955–1956.

New Zealand

1954 National Coal Mines Agreement.
1956 National Coal Mines Agreement.
Westland Engine-drivers' Firemen, Pumpmen, Etc. (State Coal Mines) *Agreement,* 1954–56.
Nightcaps District Opencast Agreement, 1954–56.
Department of Labour, New Zealand, *Awards, Agreements, Orders and Decisions Made under the Industrial Conciliation and Arbitration Act, the Apprentices Act, the Labour Disputes Investigation Act, and Other Industrial Legislation. For the year 1956,* Vol. 56 (Canterbury Coal-Mine

Employees Award, August 30, 1956, pp. 1321–28; Runanga District Coal-Mine Employees—Industrial Agreement, Filed in the Office of the Clerk of Awards, November 26, 1956, pp. 1953–58).

Poland

Zbiorowy Uklad Pracy dla pracowników fizycznych i umyslowych zatrudnionych w zakladach pracy Ministrstwa Górnictwa i Energetyki obowiązujący od dnia 1 kwietnia 1957 r.

6 · Building Industrial
Relations Systems

THE present chapter is analogous to the last one; it examines
the rules of building and construction instead of bituminous
coal mining. It provides another application of the central concept of industrial-relations systems and the theoretical framework
developed in Chapters 1 through 4. The rules of the work place
and work community for the building industry are compared for
a number of countries.

Some of these rules largely reflect common problems posed
by similar technological and market contexts or they vary systematically with differences in these features of the environment.
Other rules show in the main the imprint of the status of workers
(and their organizations), managers (and their organizations),
and governmental agencies characteristic of the particular country. While the relative strength of the technological and market
contexts, as compared to the national industrial-relations characteristics, varies widely among industries, the complex of building
rules provides another instance, like the bituminous-coal industry,
in which many rules are shaped by distinctive features of the
technological and market environment.

The compilation of rules for the building industry is more
difficult than for bituminous-coal mining since there is likely to

be a lesser degree of uniformity within a country for most rules in building. In both industries there may be considerable delegation from national to regional or local levels of rule-making, but in building there tends to be a greater number of formal sets of rules than in coal mining, at least in recent years for most countries. The building rules, where they are not uniform or codified for a country, have been gathered for one or two major metropolitan centers or regions; these rules are treated as representative of the industry in the country as a whole. The present comparative study of building rules cannot be exhaustive; it is designed to be suggestive for further research in this and other industries. A note appended to this chapter provides a detailed listing of the sources of the rules that are cited.[1]

The term "building" is used to mean the same thing as the longer expressions "building and construction" in the United States or "building and civil engineering" in Great Britain.[2] In the Netherlands the terms *Burgerlijke- en Utiliteitsbouw* and *Water-, Spoor- en Wegenbouw* cover very roughly the same divisions of the industry. These terms include not only housing and commercial construction but also industrial plants, highways, dams, and heavy construction. They do not, however, dispose of

[1] Discussions with Dr. H. Umrath of the *Algemene Nederlandse Bouwbedrijfsbond* and Mr. Michael O'Callaghan of the Industrial Committees Division of the International Labor Office have been helpful in the preparation of this chapter. Grateful acknowledgment is made for many documents and informative discussion on rules in the building industry with members of the staff and officers of the following organizations. In England, National Federation of Building Trades Operatives, Amalgamated Union of Building Trade Workers, the Federation of Civil Engineering Contractors, and The National Federation of Building Trades Employers. In the Netherlands, *Stichting Vakopleiding Bouwbedrijf* and *Algemene Nederlandse Bouwbedrijfsbond*. In France, the *Fédération Nationale du Bâtiment et des Activités Annexes*. In Yugoslavia, the Building Enterprise "Rad" in Belgrade. In Geneva, Switzerland, *Fédération Suisse des Ouvriers du Bâtiment et du Bois*, and in Spain, the Construction Syndicate.

[2] The Joint Demarcation Agreement of July 4, 1934 specifies whether civil engineering or building rules are to apply to a particular type of project. Although the agreement between The National Federations of Building Operatives and The National Federation of Building Trades Employees and The Federation of Civil Engineering Contractors has been abrogated, its provisions are still largely operative.

the very difficult problem in every country of defining the limits of the industry and the boundary of the activities to which uniform or specialized rules apply. There is, for instance, the question of where maintenance and change-over activity in industrial plants ends and building begins and the question of what, if any, maintenance work shall be performed under building rules. There is the analogous question of whether building rules apply to workers and enterprises which normally operate industrial plants but which make installations on construction sites of machinery or equipment they manufacture, such as turbines or kitchen equipment. Such differences in the scope of the industry may be expected to influence some of the substantive rules revealed in comparisons among countries. The complex of rules developed in one country for building, confined to housing, may be expected to differ in some important respects from rules in other countries designed for housing, commercial and industrial buildings, and heavy construction. The rules in still other countries may be partly specialized to govern significant maintenance work.

Rules may take a variety of forms in different countries: legislative statutes and administrative regulations, awards, orders or decisions of tribunals, agreements, memoranda, policies of managements or accepted internal laws of labor organizations, and recognized customs and practices. The substance of the rule is of greater interest than its form. These rules may be formulated at different levels in various countries: national, regional, or local. The rules examined in this chapter are only a small fraction —albeit significant ones—of the large universe of rules designed to specify conditions and relations among workers (their organizations), managers (their organizations), and governmental agencies in building. The source material for this chapter leaves the strong impression of the great detail in which industrial society, through the interaction of all three groups of actors, comes to prescribe conduct at the work place and work community.

The first part of the chapter considers the technological context and market or budgetary constraints in building and their influence on particular rules. The latter part of the chapter is concerned with the impact of the distinctive features of the power context and the status of the actors in the national industrial-relations system upon the building rules.

THE TECHNOLOGICAL CONTEXT AND MARKET CONSTRAINTS

The major technological characteristics of the building work place relevant to rule-making may be very briefly summarized.[3] Work operations on a particular site are characteristically of a short duration; at times they may last only a few hours or days; on other sites they may run some months or even a few years. Some projects have a large number of separate enterprises and workers; others may involve only one enterprise and a single worker. The size and craft composition of the work force is likely to change markedly in the course of construction. Sites tend to be geographically variable; some are isolated from urban areas. A number of operations take place out of doors, and the weather has a significant effect upon the regularity of these work operations. The technology of building, which is not independent of its market characteristics, requires a very wide range of different skills of a high order, many of which may be necessary on a single project, such as a steam-generating plant, or only one of which may be used, as on a repainting job. Construction operations as a whole are relatively hazardous, although not to the same degree as underground coal mining, as a consequence of heights, material handling, temporary installations, and the interdependence of workers of different contractors on a job site. There are very wide differences in physical working conditions and in the tech-

[3] John T. Dunlop and Arthur D. Hill, *The Wage Adjustment Board, War-Time Stabilization in the Building and Construction Industry,* Cambridge, Mass., Harvard University Press, 1950, pp. 1–15; International Labor Office, Building, Civil Engineering, and Public Works Committee, *Factors Affecting Productivity in the Construction Industry,* Third Item on the Agenda, Fourth Session, Geneva, 1953, pp. 7–15; Anglo-American Council on Productivity, *Productivity Team Report on Building,* May 1950.

nological characteristics of different construction sites and operations; the wide variety of sites poses special problems in rule-making designed to cover such diverse conditions.

The market or budgetary constraints of the building industry likewise show wide variation. Many enterprises are very small; indeed, the self-employed worker frequently becomes the subject of explicit rule-making. In Great Britain, in May 1953, 78 percent of the contracting enterprises hired no more than five employees, 42 percent of the firms were one-man businesses, and only 1 percent of the firms employed 100 or more men.[4]

The pricing arrangements between a contracting enterprise and an owner, architect, or another contractor may be of various types. Bidding procedures vary widely among countries and in branches of the industry affecting conspicuously the extent of competition. A lump-sum bid may be secured in open competition with many other bidders. In most European countries the architect plays a much larger role, relative to the contractor, in subcontracting and price setting than in the United States. The British institution of the quantity surveyor affects the breakdown of the project into separate contracts and work operations and standardizes the quantity estimates for bidding. There have been a variety of bid-pooling arrangements such as the "London Conference." In the Netherlands, for instance, it is said that the bidding contractors meet after preparing their estimates. An average cost of bid preparation is added to all bids. The bids are then averaged, and the bids more than 10 percent above or below the average are excluded. The lowest remaining bid is declared low bidder for the project. A variety of arrangements exist by which general contractors secure estimates or bids from specialty contractors, and there are a variety of practices concerning the subsequent transactions between the successful general contractor and subcontractors or specialty contractors which affect the competitive character of building contracts. There are also cost-plus-

[4] The British Productivity Council, *A Review of Productivity in the Building Industry*, n.d., pp. 6–8.

fee contracts of many kinds secured by bidding or by a steady preferred arrangement for performing work for a particular owner. Private or public owners may themselves engage in construction work without resort to a contractor.

In Sweden the long-established role of cooperatives, trade unions, and municipal corporations in housing construction significantly affects the market conditions in this branch of construction. "In 1955 all nonprofit enterprises together built or supervised the building of . . . about 80 percent of all urban housing projects." [5] In Great Britain the direct labor departments of local authorities are a significant factor (one sixth) in new housing construction, in addition to their role in maintenance and repair operations.[6] The competitive conditions in the product market for housing will further be markedly affected according as the national traditions and tastes favor individual homes or flats.

The market for construction contracts not only differs in these forms, but each specialized type of construction has its specialized market conditions. Thus, the number of sellers, the degree of standardization, and the requirements for entry into the markets for painting, pier building, and turbine installation are likely to be quite different; construction is comprised of a variety of submarkets. While enterprises tend to be relatively specialized by type of construction, there is a degree of shifting, and there is considerable freedom of entry into most branches of the industry.

The labor market in construction likewise tends to be subdivided, and different market conditions may prevail for various crafts and forms of specialization. In many localities and types of operations there is significant seasonal fluctuation in employment,[7] although the seasonal pattern has been affected in a num-

[5] Algemene Nederlandse Bouwbedrijfsbond, *Report of EPA Mission of Trade Unionists from the Netherlands*, August 1957, p. 16. Also see Heinz Umrath, *European Labor Movement and Housing*, European Regional Organization of ICFTU, Brussels, Belgium, 1953, pp. 9–17.

[6] *Ibid.*, p. 7.

[7] Byggfackens Industriutredning, *The Building Labour Market in Sweden*, Stockholm, 1956; William Haber, *Industrial Relations in the Building Industry*, Cambridge, Mass., Harvard University Press, 1930, pp. 95–126.

ber of countries in recent years by technological changes designed to facilitate winter construction. While many of the skilled workers have served formal apprenticeship programs, there is wide variation in the quality of the work force which tends to complicate the pricing of labor services. The isolated location of many sites, the changing working conditions, and the small size of many operations make difficult the supervision of the work force and the securing of uniform quality and amounts of services from a work force. A variety of methods of supervision and piecework compensation (in most countries) has been designed to cope with these variations in the work force under variable working conditions. The short duration of many construction sites tends to create considerable interest in some countries in the arrangements used for hiring of the skilled work force for a particular site.

The principal characteristics of the technological environment and the product and labor markets in construction may be regarded as posing a number of problems to the actors which come to be the subject of a number of rules in the building industry. The major problems may be identified as follows.

1. *Variability of site location.* The variability in location of building sites requires that workers and managers be highly mobile, and some projects may even require that the work force maintain temporary living quarters apart from residence. This fundamental characteristic of building sites calls forth a large group of rules dealing with payment for time spent in traveling, transportation expenses, and living expenses and compensation for temporary residence away from home. The first of these types of rules called forth by the building environment is analogous to the measurement of the work day in coal mining. In the building context the question is the precise location to which a worker shall report at the start of the normal working day. Shall he be at the construction site ready to work at starting time? Or shall he report to a central shop of the contractor or some other designated location and travel to the site on the enterprise's time? On

a large construction site there are similar questions concerning the location of a worker at the start of the working day or shift. The body of rules specifies not only the amount of compensation or reimbursement involved but the eligibility conditions under which such payments are made. Are distinctions to be made between workers who live in the same community as the project and those whose residence is at a greater distance? A comparison of rules among regions or metropolitan centers in a number of countries shows common responses to these problems as well as certain other features characteristic of the separate national industrial-relations systems.

2. *Weather*. The weather poses a variety of problems to workers and managers at the building site, at least for exposed operations, which becomes the subject of a body of rules. Changes in weather may take place suddenly, and it is difficult to forecast the working conditions on a building site. What happens if men are required to report for work and after a short period the weather makes working conditions impossible? What compensation, if any, are the workers to receive—the actual period worked, some minimum period, or a full day? Shall they be paid for such time not worked at the regular rate, at past incentive earnings, or at some lesser rate? In the event that building operations are not started, or if workers are told not to report for work on account of the weather, are they to receive any compensation for being available to work other than normal unemployment compensation, in accordance with the eligibility requirements and waiting periods of the national social-insurance arrangements? The environment of building sites leads to a distinctive group of rules dealing with the consequences of unfavorable weather.

3. *Apprenticeship*. Apprenticeship arrangements permeate the building industry in all countries although many workmen are recruited, particularly for some operations, outside the apprenticeship rules. The wide variety of skills required in the industry, the shifting character of work opportunities that place a premium upon a broad training both to managers and to workers as a form

of job protection, and the traditions of an industry which go back in many countries to preindustrial conditions are all factors making for a significant role of apprenticeship. The group of rules surrounding apprenticeship concern the training period and types of instruction, the progression in wages by years prior to the journeyman status, the examination for journeyman, and in many cases the determination of the number or ratio of apprentices. The concern with apprenticeship often involves a good deal of feeling and ritual; the future of the trade or craft and the character of the supply of skilled labor in the generation ahead are at stake.

4. *Small-scale operations.* The characteristics of the industry encourage many small-scale operations which create special problems that become the subject matter of a number of rules. It is often difficult to police and to enforce rules in the smallest enterprises, and the administrability of rules in view of a large number of small enterprises and isolated work places must be taken into account in the formulation of all rules in building. Members of the same family may constitute both the managers and the work force, complicating the strict enforcement of the rules. In some cases there may be no separation between workers and managers, as self-employed craftsmen perform both groups of functions on a job site. The organizations of workers and managers tend to develop rules to limit such arrangements and to seek compliance with the whole complex of rules which might otherwise be circumvented. These rules may seek to limit one-man operations, to provide that subcontracts can only be let to those who conform to the rules of the prime contractor or to provide for nonworking supervision on a site or group of sites.

5. *Hiring.* The short duration of construction jobs and the necessary migratory character of employment opportunities and workers create problems of rationalizing the repeated hiring of a work force for different projects. The frequent matching of job opportunities and workers tends to create a group of rules to structure the labor market and hiring decisions particularly. The

task of matching demand and supply is further complicated by the fine degrees of specialization by craft and within craft by operation or type of machine. Moreover, there are differences in skill, performance, and output among workers of a given craft. The construction labor market seldom operates as a pure bourse in which a separate price is set each day for each skill to clear the market. Rules arise which report the available job opportunities to workers and register the demands of enterprises. There also emerges a variety of rules which govern the selection of particular individuals or workers with particular characteristics, such as designated skills, length of experience, or membership in labor organizations, for specific vacancies. The substance of these rules may vary, but some distinctive set of rules or practices are often formulated to order the hiring process in building activity in a locality, at least for skilled operations.

6. *Provision of tools.* The craft specialization of the work force and the variability of locations and types of projects create problems regarding the provision of tools which tend to become the subject of rules of the work place. Unlike many other industries workers are typically expected to provide themselves with a range of hand tools used by their craft. Other tools and equipment may be specified as furnished by the enterprise. The problem of tools becomes a center around which a variety of rules may be expected to grow.

7. *Area wage rates.* The short duration of most building projects means that wage rates are typically established for a designated geographical area. However, where piece rates exist, they are often fixed for each site,[8] but the piece rates tend to be built upon an explicit time rate for an area. In countries with centralized wage-setting machinery, such as Great Britain and the Netherlands, the rules for building fully rank or classify cities and areas into a limited number of wage brackets. Provisions

---

[8] In some countries, such as Sweden, the piece rates are also established on a nationwide or regional basis with elaborate manuals containing prices for various work operations.

in these rules recognize that there may be occasions for temporarily upgrading a city or area or branch of the industry in view of a temporarily large demand for construction workers.[9] The area basis of wage setting also provides the opportunity for vacations with pay, holiday pay, pensions, and other such supplementary compensation by assessing contributions over and above basic-wage rates in proportion to hours worked among a number of enterprises which may have engaged a particular worker.[10] These contributions are typically paid into a central fund for later disbursement in accordance with a schedule of eligibility. These wage practices are built upon the premise that the normal attachment of a large number of workers is to the industry in a locality or region, or even to the industry nationally, rather than to a single enterprise.

A number of other types of rules might be mentioned that can be ascribed directly to the technological and market characteristics of building operations. The provision of sanitary facilities, drinking water, and facilities in which to change clothes are illustrative. Other types of rules may be related more directly to specialized types of building operations such as safety in connection with scaffolding,[11] the use of specialized tools such as spray guns, plaster guns, or pipe-threading machines, and provisions for safety in connection with electrical circuits and heavy lifts.

[9] For Great Britain, see National Joint Council for the Building Industry, *National Working Rules for the Building Industry* (*as at October, 1956*), Exceptional Rates, Rule 11 (b) (iii) and (iv), p. 8.

[10] "A compensation fund to be known as the 'Compensation Fund for Building, Public Works and Allied Occupations in the Canton of Geneva,' and referred to in this agreement as 'The Geneva Fund of the Building Trade,' has been set up for the purpose of ensuring a fair distribution of the benefits to be provided by employers in accordance with articles . . . [holidays, public holidays, military inspection, family allowances, health insurance, and justified absence]." *Maçonnerie Travaux Publics et Branches Annexes, Contrat Collectif, réglant les conditions de travail pour l'ensemble de la profession dans le Canton de Genève, 1954–1955*, Article 18, p. 14. Similar arrangements on a national or regional basis are found in the other countries cited in this chapter.

[11] Convention 62, 1937, Part II, "General Rules as to Scaffolds," International Labour Conference, *Conventions and Recommendations 1919–1949*, Geneva, International Labor Office, 1949, pp. 428–430.

In the following sections a comparison is made of some of the rules in the building industry for a number of countries (or metropolitan centers or regions) dealing with each of the above group of distinctive problems (except the last) posed by the technological and market context of building operations. In the selection of excerpts, consideration has been given to the rules applicable to general contractors and to specialty contractors and to building construction as well as to heavy construction or civil engineering. In a number of instances several quotations or citations are used for a country.

TRAVEL TIME AND TRAVEL EXPENSES

The rules which arise from the variable and distant location of many construction sites reflect two types of situations. (1) In the first, the project site is within the community in which the workers reside or at a distance which permits daily commuting. The rules typically prescribe that when the site is beyond some minimum distance or commuting time the workers shall be compensated for some part of their transportation costs and may be compensated for some of the time spent in traveling. This type of rule may be expected to show variants among countries depending on whether lunch hours are long and workers normally return to their homes for a midday meal and on whether workers typically own their own transportation (automobiles, motorcycles, or bicycles) or use public transportation or that furnished by the enterprise. In some regions and countries normal commuting distances may be much greater than in others; fifty miles in Massachusetts is longer than in Texas, and the equivalent 82 kilometers is even longer in Switzerland. The distances included in the following rules in various countries are a significant indicator of geographical mobility. Apart from the physical conditions of roads and the speed and availability of transportation, there are no doubt differences in the resistances to movement among workers arising out of traditions and experience. A greater inducement to movement may be required in some cases than in others. These different circumstances will be reflected in the group of rules.

(2) In the second case workers are required to be away from their normal or temporary residence over night or for extended periods on distant or isolated projects. The rules typically prescribe allowances or reimbursement for transportation and living expenses and compensation for some time spent in traveling. The rules also ordinarily provide for periodic return home with expenses in the event work operations at the distant site continue for an extended period. In some countries the rules provide for transportation expenses of the workers' families. The common purpose of these types of rules as well as their variations among countries are illustrated in the following excerpts.

United States

> The Employer shall pay for traveling time and furnish transportation from shop to shop, job to job, and job to shop, within the jurisdiction of the Union. On work outside the jurisdiction of the Union, the Employer shall furnish transportation, board, and all other necessary expense.
>
> No traveling time or transportation shall be paid before or after working hours to workmen for traveling to or from any job in the jurisdiction of the Union when workmen are ordered to report to the job. . . .[12]

> G. Employees shall travel to and from their work on their own time and by means of their own transportation.

> H.1. . . . in the subsistence area as hereafter defined. . . , living facilities for the workmen on or immediately adjacent to the project, which living facilities shall comply with the standards established by California State Law governing camps, and board (seven days per week) will be furnished by the Contractor; or at the option of the Contractor and in lieu thereof,

---

[12] *Agreement between Southeast Texas Chapter, National Electrical Contractors Association and Local Union 716, International Brotherhood of Electrical Workers*, August 1, 1957, Article III, Sections 19 and 20. The jurisdiction referred to is the territorial boundaries allotted to the local union.

per diem payment of $5.00 per scheduled workday . . . will be made. (Subsistence shall apply to workmen ordered to report and for whom no work is provided.)[13]

Great Britain

National Working Rule 6A—Daily Journeys. . . .

Time spent in daily travelling is not to be reckoned as part of the working day and nothing in this Rule shall modify the condition upon which guarantee payments are granted under National Working Rule 2A—namely, that, unless otherwise instructed by the Employer, each man has to present himself at the usual starting time and be available for work throughout the normal daily working hours. . . .

Operatives Sent Out Daily.

When an operative is sent out daily by his Employer to a job beyond the appropriate "walking-time boundary" (or daily travelling time limit) as determined by the Local Joint Committee, the provisions of Alternative (a) hereunder may be operated at the option of the Employer; if that option is not exercised the provisions of Alternative (b) hereunder shall apply.

Alternative (a) Conveyance at Employer's Option.

At the option of the Employer such an Operative may be conveyed to and from the job daily by road, rail, tram or other conveyance, in which event the expenses of such conveyance shall be borne by the Employer, the Operative being paid for the actual time spent (one way) in travelling therein to the job from the said "walking-time boundary."

Alternative (b) Walking-time Allowance.

If the Employer's option to adopt Alternative (a) is not exercised such an Operative shall, in respect of each such day upon which he so travels, be paid a "walking-time" allowance of one third of the hourly rate for each mile of the distance (one way) between that (walking-time) boundary and the job, the distance between these points being measured along the shortest practicable route.

---

[13] *Labor Agreement between Southern California General Contractors and United Brotherhood of Carpenters and Joiners of America,* May 1, 1955, p. 23. The subsistence section contains 8 numbered paragraphs; only one is quoted above. The agreement also contains an article applicable to "Remote Projects."

Operatives Recruited Outside the District Boundary and Sent in Daily by Conveyance . . .

National Working Rule 6B—Operatives Sent Out Who Do Not Travel Daily.

B(1) Travelling Expenses (Fares or Conveyance)

Where an Operative, engaged by an Employer in the (Local Joint Committee) district where the Employer's shop or yard is situated, is sent out for a period (i.e., not under Rule 6A) to a job outside the district boundary his fares shall be paid— or he shall be conveyed—(a) to the job at commencement, (b) from the job on completion, (c) to and from the job, at "periodic leave" intervals of:

1 week —jobs up to 20 miles (in a straight line) from the district boundary.

2 weeks—jobs between 20 and 40 miles (in a straight line) from the district boundary.

3 weeks—jobs between 40 and 60 miles (in a straight line) from the district boundary.

Over 60 miles—an interval fixed by mutual arrangement between Employer and Operatives before going to the job.

B(2) Traveling Time.

In the circumstances specified in 6B(1) above, travelling time, at plain-time rates only, shall be paid for in respect of the following journeys:

(a) To the job from the boundary of the district from which the Operative was sent:
   (i) At commencement
   (ii) On return to the job after periodic leave.

(b) At completion—from the job to the boundary of the district from which the Operative was sent.

Time spent in such travelling shall not be reckoned as part of the working day.

B(3) Lodging Allowances.

Lodging Allowance shall be paid (while available for work) to any Operative sent to a job which necessitates his living away from his home in lodgings. The rate of allowance shall be 8s. for each night on which lodgings are necessitated. . . .[14]

[14] National Joint Council for the Building Industry, *National Working Rules for the Building Industry* (*as of 26th October, 1956*), pp. 47, 49.

In the case of the civil-engineering branch of the industry in Great Britain a different form of rule has been developed, particularly for daily travel, that is expressed in terms of mileage instead of boundary lines established by local committees. A man shall be paid 3 d. per mile or 6 d. per mile for travel in excess of four miles one way (not to exceed 7 s. per day) depending on whether transportation is furnished by the employer or the worker uses public transport.[15]

Switzerland (Geneva)

Neither maintenance allowance nor traveling allowance will be paid within Zone I on the plan adopted by the building trades. This zone falls within an approximate radius of three kilometres from the Ile Rousseau.

Transportation at the lowest rate will be paid four times a day in the second zone shown on the same plan.

If, within this zone, a worker is unable to eat at home without loss of time, the conditions of the following zone will be applied.

Beyond Zone II transport at the lowest rate will be paid twice a day together with a maintenance allowance of Fr. 3.50 per day. . . .

If the worker has to cover more than a kilometre on arrival from the nearest transport stop, the transport allowance will be increased by 30 centimes per day. . . .

In all cases the worker must arrive at his place of work on time and leave it on time so as to constitute an effective day's work.

When the worker must be lodged at his place of work he will receive a minimum daily allowance of Frs. 8. In the latter case he is entitled to a return ticket once a fortnight at his employer's expense. For distances of over 100 kilometres the worker can only return home once a month. As an exception, for work in these distant localities, normal working hours that are spent in traveling will be remunerated at the usual rate.[16]

[15] The Federation of Civil Engineering Contractors, *Handbook, Administrative Year, 1957–1958*, pp. 149–152.

[16] *Maçonnerie Travaux Publics et Branches Annexes, Contrat Collectif, réglant les conditions de travail pour l'ensemble de la profession dans le Canton de Genève, 1954–1955*, Art. 5, pp. 6–7.

Germany

1. Workers in travel status who are employed so far away from their place of residence that it cannot be regarded as practicable for them to return home daily from the building site shall receive an allowance per calendar day as compensation for the additional expense.

2. It shall be regarded as practicable for them to return home daily if the normal time required to travel one way from the center of the place of residence to the center of the building site, making use of the form of transport most suitable from the point of view of time (train, bus, tram, steamer, ferry) does not amount to more than 1½ hours. . . .

1. Workers in travel status who return to their place of residence daily, or for whom it is practicable to return, shall be entitled to journey money for each day of work away from home. . . .

5. Journey money shall be calculated on the basis of the distance between the building site and the center of the locality in which the firm has its seat. A distance of 8 kilometers or less shall not be taken into account.
Journey money shall amount to
    0.70 DM for a distance of over 8 and up to 15 km. . . .
    2.60 DM for a distance of over 50 km. . . .

1. Workers receiving compensation shall be entitled to free weekend travel home to their place of residence and back to the building site, as follows:
    Married workers or workers placed on the same footing, every five weeks.
    Unmarried workers, every 13 weeks. . . .

12. If canteens are set up, the employer must not realize any profit from running them. . . .[17]

France

Article 30.   The meal allowance shall be fixed at 120 percent of the hourly rate for category V, brought to the nearest franc. It shall be payable:

[17] *Bundesrahmentarifvertrag für das Baugewerbe im Gebiet der Bundesrepublik Deutschland vom 6. Juli 1956,* pp. 26–33. Only a few excerpts from the extensive section have been quoted.

(a) at Nantes, where a map has been prepared when the place of work is outside the specified area, the said place being more than 3 km from the workshop, site, or office where the workman was taken on. . . .

The allowance shall not be payable:
. . . 2. In cases . . . when the distance between the place of work and the workman's home is less than 1 km 500 meters as the crow flies, or when the workers have been engaged on the spot. . . .

Article 31. Minor traveling expenses shall be confined to cases where the workman can return home every night. . . .

When the worker is sent by the firm to work at a distance beyond the limits specified in Art. 30, par. a, and transport is not provided by the employer, a daily allowance equal to 4 percent of the hourly rate of pay for a workman in category V shall be payable, provided the distance between the place of work and the worker's home exceeds 1 km 500 meters as the crow flies. . . .

When the distance between the place of work and the outer boundaries of town with map or the administrative boundaries of the commune, as the case may be, is greater than 6 kilometers, the time spent on travel beyond the 6 kilometer limit, outside normal working hours, shall be subject to compensation on the basis of 50 percent of the worker's hourly wage. . . .[18]

Major Travel. The decree applies to workers who are required to travel either by their employers or by the competent labor exchanges, or with the latter's approval and who . . . are unable to return home daily. . . .

Workers in travel status receive a daily allowance for board and lodging, the amount of which is fixed, either for the whole "department" or for certain localities by decision of the minister of labor and social insurance. . . .

The traveling expenses incurred by the workers in order to reach their homes and return to their place of employment are refunded, 3d-class fare. According to the distance from home or from the usual place of residence, such journeys are authorized as follows:

up to a distance of 50 km inclusive, one return trip every week; . . . .

---

[18] *Convention Collective des Ouvriers du Bâtiment et des Travaux Publics de la Loire-Inférieure, 1ᵉʳ février 1956.*

beyond 400 km inclusive, one return trip every two months.[19]

Spain

Art. 67. Journey Money and Fares. When the building site on which the workman is employed is situated more than two kilometers away from the locality where he lives, a journey-money allowance of 0.30 pesetas for each additional kilometer shall be made to workmen who make the journey under their own arrangements; fares for travel in public transport vehicles shall also be refunded. These allowances shall be paid in accordance with the following rules: . . .

b. Where there exists a public transportation service from a point two kilometers outside the boundaries of the locality of residence to the place of work, no journey money shall be paid; instead the amount by which the fare by the said service exceeds one peseta for the round trip shall be refunded.

c. If rail travel is involved, the cost shall be calculated on the basis of the third-class fare in the case of workmen or maintenance personnel, second class for salaried employees with the grade of clerk, etc., and first class for senior grades. . . .

h. Journey money and transportation costs shall not be payable in the case of long-term building projects where the undertakings provide the workers with accommodation in suitable buildings close to the site, provided that such accommodation satisfies the minimum standards of capacity and hygiene for permanent accommodation, having regard to the matrimonial status and the number of dependents who normally live with the worker, and provided that such accommodation is provided free or at a rent not in excess of that for a cheap house befitting the occupational status of the person occupying it.[20]

[19] Fédération Nationale du Bâtiment et des Activités Annexes, *Mémento du Chef d'Entreprise, Le Chef d'Entreprise du Bâtiment et des Travaux Publics et Ses Salariés*, pp. 77–78. This quotation is from the decree of August 6, 1947.

[20] Carlos M. Fernandez Chaperon, *El Trabajo en la Construcción y Obras Públicas Al Día*, Editorial Goñi, Madrid, 1957, pp. 127–130.

Yugoslavia (Building Enterprise "Rad," Belgrade)

Art. 45. Workers and employees appointed to make a business trip can use the following means of transportation:
1. Workers and employees of the first and second categories: first class of fast or passenger train or first class on ship.
2. Other workers and employees: second class of fast or passenger train or ship.

Art. 48. Amount of the daily traveling allowance for business trips for workers and employees:

1. in managing positions. . . .	1,300 dinars
4. in jobs for highly skilled workers	1,200 dinars
5. in jobs with middle professional training of employees with more than five years of service . . .	1,200 dinars
7. apprentices, up to	700 dinars.

Art. 50. Workers and employees who are sent on business to work in other places, are paid all actual expenses for moving to new places of living.

A worker or an employee, whose expenditures for the transportation and the moving to another place are paid, cannot have the traveling allowance.

Art. 51. Individual transportation expenses for family members are paid, same as for worker or employee. . . .

Art. 53. Those workers and employees who support their families when moved to another place of living, without an apartment immediately supplied for them, are given allowance for the separated life from the families, the decision brought by the managing board:

		net	gross	
Workers: employees,	first category	5,000	5,600	dinars
	second category	3,500	3,900	dinars
	third	2,500	2,800	dinars
	fourth	1,500	1,700	dinars

The amount is paid every month from the day of entering the job in the new place of work, with a certificate from the municipality about the common households. This allowance ceases when a new flat is provided. This allowance is not granted during vacations. . . .

Art. 56. Workers and employees who live further than 15–30 kilometers from the place of work receive monthly 50 percent allowance from that which belongs to them according to the determined category. If they live further than 30 kilometers from the place of work, they receive the full amount of the allowance.

An exception to the preceding item is made for sites and trade shops in Belgrade. Here, those workers and employees who live over 15 kilometers out of Belgrade receive the full allowance. . . .

Semiskilled and unskilled workers also have no right to this allowance. An exception can be made, if this manpower is needed on a site, and the local authority asserts that such manpower cannot be found in the locality of the construction site. . . .

Art. 67. Workers and employees who every day have to use a transportation means for coming to and returning from the place of work, pay these transportation expenses themselves up to the amount of 600 dinars monthly. The amount over 600 dinars is paid by the enterprise.[21]

Australia

17(i) The following allowances shall be paid by employers to compensate for excess fares and travelling time to and from places of work. On places of work within the radii respectively stated herein below treating the G.P.O., Sydney, or the principal Post Office at Newcastle or Wollongong, as centres from which they are to be measured:

	s.	d.	
Up to and including 12 miles	3	0	per day
Over 12 and up to 20 miles	3	9	
Over 20 and up to 30 miles	4	6	

Provided that

(a) The above stated allowance shall not be payable if the employer provides or offers to provide transport free of charge to the employee, in which case an allowance of 2 s. per day shall be paid. . . .

(c) Subject to the foregoing provisions a fare shall be deemed

---

[21] "Recompense for Traveling Expenses and Moving from One Place of Living to Another," Articles 40–52; "Allowance for Separated Life," Article 53; "Allowance for Work Out of Place of Living," *Gradevinsko Preduzeće "Rad," Tarifni Pravilnik, za 1957 godinu.* The enterprise is one of the largest and does construction work throughout the country and abroad.

to have been incurred if the employee has used a bicycle or other means of locomotion or has walked instead of using a public conveyance.

(ii) Where an employee is sent during working hours from a shop to a job, or a job to a shop or from a shop to a shop, or from a job to a job the employer shall pay all travelling time and fares incurred in addition to the amounts he may be liable to pay under sub-clause (i) hereof.

18.(a) For the purposes of this clause a "distant job" is one in respect of which the distance of which or the travelling facilities available to and from which make it reasonably necessary that the employee should live and sleep at some place other than his usual place or residence.

(b) An employee who is directed by his employer to proceed to construction work on a distant job and who complies with such direction shall be paid the following allowances in order to enable him to provide himself with suitable board and accommodation:

If employed on the job for less than a full working week — £1 10s. per day; If employed on the job for a full working week or longer, at the rate of £4 17s. 6d. per week (of seven days).

If the employee satisfies his employer that he reasonably incurred a greater amount for board and lodging than the amount fixed, the employer shall pay the difference. . . .

(d) An employee who has been directed by his employer to proceed to construction work on a distant job, may, after three months continuous service thereon and thereafter at three monthly periods of continuous service thereon, return to his home at a week end. If he does so, he shall be paid the amount of a second-class railway fare. . . .[22]

Netherlands

Article 13. Work Away from the Worker's Place of Residence.

[22] *Memorandum of Agreement between The Master Builders Association of New South Wales and The Australian Builders Labourers Federation,* July 14, 1955, *Commonwealth Arbitration Reports,* 1955, Vol. 82, pp. 791–793. The text of the agreement is pp. 787–797.

(1) If a worker is, on the instructions of the employer (or his representative) by whom he is employed, assigned to work in another commune or another part of a commune than that for which he was engaged, he shall receive the wage payable for the former commune or part of a commune: Provided that the wage paid shall not be lower than that prescribed in this Agreement for the commune or part thereof for which the worker was engaged.

(2) (a) If a worker is engaged for work away from his place of residence he shall receive the wage payable for the commune or part of the commune where the work is situated: Provided that the wage paid shall not be lower than that prescribed in this Agreement for the commune or part of the commune where the work is resident.

(b) Departures may be made from the concluding provision of paragraph (a) if an agreement is entered into by an employer and a worker whereby the work is to be carried out at the wage payable in the locality and notice of such agreement is given within two weeks by means of a declaration signed by the employer and the worker to the Trade Council for the Painting Trade; in such event the provisions of paragraph (3) of this article shall likewise not apply.

(3) In the case of every worker covered by paragraph (1), if the commune or part thereof where he is assigned to work is farther from his place of residence than the commune or part of the commune for which the employment relationship has been entered into, and every worker covered by paragraph (2),

(a) If in the employer's opinion the worker must use public transport, the worker shall be paid the necessary traveling expenses (third class or equivalent) by the employer;

(b) the worker shall be paid for the duration of the journey mentioned in (a) and the journey made in a means of transport provided by the employer at the hourly rate applicable in his case. The expression "duration of the journey" means the time elapsing between the departure of the means of transport for the work and back from the work to the starting point, excluding the first 60 minutes, which shall not be remunerated by the employer;

(c) if in the employer's opinion the worker must use a bicycle to travel to and from work and the distance to be cycled each day as measured from the boundary of the built-up area exceeds 10 kilometers the worker shall be paid an allowance of 40 cents a day by the employer; . . .

(e) if the total duration of working time, rest breaks, and traveling time, calculated from the time of departure of the public-transport vehicle mentioned in paragraph (b) until the return of the said vehicle or (where the worker cycles or walks) from the time of crossing the boundary mentioned in paragraph (d) until the time of return to the said boundary is more than 12 hours a day on working days from Monday to Friday and 8 hours a day on Saturdays, the normal working time shall be reduced by the amount in excess.

(f) if the work is situated at such a distance from the place for which the worker was engaged or his place of residence that he is unable to go home each evening the worker shall be provided with adequate food and accommodation at the employer's expense.

Once a week workers covered by this paragraph shall be allowed to go home. . . . The resultant traveling expenses (third class or equivalent) shall be defrayed by the employer. The worker shall be paid in respect of necessary traveling time at the hourly rate payable in his case. It shall be lawful for the employer to deduct from the wages of an unmarried worker, who is not a breadwinner, one guilder in respect of each full period of 24 hours during which he receives food and accommodation. . . .[23]

These detailed rules reflect a very common approach to the problems of shifting a work force in the building industry with changing sites at varying locations. In the event a project is located in the community in which a worker lives, a certain distance or time or expense for commuting to work is expected of workers, and they are to report at the project at the start of the work day. In the event that a project is beyond a certain distance or time or

[23] *Landelijke Collectieve Arbeidsovereenkomst voor het Schildersbedrijf in Nederland,* 1 Febr. 1954–30 April 1955, pp. 15–18. Identical language appears in *Landelijke Collective Arbeidsovereenkomst voor het Bouwedrijf,* June 10, 1958, Article 18. This agreement is signed by general contractors.

expense, workers will be compensated or reimbursed for traveling expenses. When workers are assigned to more distant or isolated projects, the rules provide for traveling expenses, lodging and subsistence, periodic return transportation, and in some countries for transportation or accommodation for the family. These rules in all their variegated detail and complexity are created by the common problems posed to workers and managers by the technology and labor market of the industry.

UNFAVORABLE WEATHER CONDITIONS

The adjustment to unfavorable weather conditions in building activity appears to create two broad groupings of rules. The first are concerned with compensation for the inconvenience of reporting to work and being unable to work or to work for only a short period as a consequence of weather. The second group of rules are primarily designed to provide some degree of insurance against the full loss of wages attributed to periods of unfavorable weather conditions, over and above the compensation for loss of wages arising from unemployment generally. The rules of this type typically provide for some fraction of the regular rate in the event of inclement weather. This fraction varies between 90 percent and 25 percent in the countries examined which have this type of rule, although there are also variations in the duration of these payments. They may apply to all workers or only to selected groups. The following excerpts are drawn from the same body of rules used in the preceding section.

United States

When men are directed to report to the job and do not start work due to weather conditions, lack of material, or other causes beyond their control, they shall receive two hours at the prevailing rate of pay, unless notified before leaving home, or in the event men are put to work, they shall receive a minimum of four hours' work. When men are directed to report to a job and are instructed to go to work by the Employer or the Employer's representative, weather conditions permitting, and they refuse, they shall not receive the two hours' show-up time.[24]

Great Britain

National Working Rule 2A Time Lost Through Causes Beyond the Control of the Parties.

1. . . . .

(b) If, in the shop or on the job, work is temporarily not available for an operative in his own occupation, he shall hold himself ready and willing to perform work in any other building industry occupation of which he is capable or at any other site or shop where work is available. . . .

(d) In cases where abnormal weather conditions interrupt work over a period, suitable arrangements, appropriate to the circumstances of each case, may be made by the employer by which operatives shall register or establish that they are available for work on each day. . . .

2. Where in any pay-week an operative, being in the employer's employment, has kept himself available for work throughout the normal working hours of each working day of that week and has otherwise conformed with Section 1 of this Rule, but during any part of that week has been prevented from working by reason of inclement weather, plant breakdown, nonarrival of materials, or other similar causes beyond the control of the parties,

(a) he shall receive payment at his current hourly rate for half the time lost by him on that account during his normal working hours.

(b) his total payments in respect of (i) normal working hours worked in that week, and (ii) any payments under 2(a) above shall together be not less than 36 times the hourly wage rate applicable to him in that week (this amount being referred to hereinafter as the "guaranteed weekly minimum").[25]

If in any pay-week during any part of which a man has performed actual work on the job, time within normal working

---

[24] *Basic Agreement between the Southeast Texas Chapter of the National Electrical Contractors Association and Local Union 716 of the International Brotherhood of Electrical Workers*, August 1, 1957, Article III, Section 11.

[25] National Joint Council for the Building Industry, *National Working Rules for the Building Industry (as at 26th October, 1956)*, pp. 17, 19.

hours during which the man being in the employer's employment has kept himself available for work is not worked due to inclement weather, the man shall be paid for half the time so lost at the ordinary rate.[26]

Germany

An elaborate plan with detailed administrative rules has been established to provide for compensation for time lost on account of weather during the winter period.[27]

France

Work is stopped on a site only when bad weather (frost, rain, snow, etc.) makes it genuinely dangerous or impossible to carry out the work, in consideration either of the health or the safety of the workers, or of the nature or technique of the work to be done.

The stopping of work and the length of time for which it is interrupted are decided on by the employer or by his representative at the site after consulting the delegates of the employees (if any). . . .

The law grants compensation only if the interruption of work brought about by bad weather continues during the first working day following the day during which it was decided to stop work. . . .

The daily bad weather allowance is equal to the product of a certain number of working hours by three quarters of the amount of an hourly wage fixed in accordance with regulations. . . .

Under the terms of the decrees of 16 August 1949 and 25 July 1952, the wage is the real wage being drawn by the worker the day before work is interrupted, including, where appropriate, allowances accompanying the wage, and the output bonus, but excluding expense or danger allowances and extra pay for overtime, and providing that the total does not exceed 25 percent

---

[26] The Federation of Civil Engineering Contractors, *Handbook, Administrative Year, 1957–1958*, pp. 144–145.

[27] R. Blumensaat, C. Geerling, and G. Leber, *Lohnausgleich Winterlicher Arbeitsausfälle im Baugewerbe*, Schriftenreihe der Lohnausgleichskasse für die Bauwirtschaft Wiesbaden, 1956. For the text of the agreements, see pp. 5–26.

of the minimum wage of the professional category to which the person concerned belongs.[28]

Spain

1. Where work is suspended on account of inclement weather the undertakings shall pay the workers full wages in respect of the hours or days lost as a result thereof, the term "wages" being taken to mean the wages they are actually in receipt of; that is to say, the rate laid down in Article 42, plus any cost-of-living allowances, long-service increments, and initial seniority bonus, or such greater sums as may be paid voluntarily by the undertakings. . . .

This provision shall not be deemed to cover suspensions of work of indefinite duration due to the fact that climatic conditions in the area make normal working impossible during certain periods of the year.

2. . . . . In order to qualify for payment of wages, the workers shall be required to report at the work site at the usual time to begin work, unless expressly directed otherwise by the undertaking.

3. If so decided by the undertaking, workers shall be required to make up time lost on account of inclement weather, such time to be spread over the working days in subsequent weeks. . . . If the time is not made up through the fault of the worker, the latter shall refund to the undertaking the wages for time not made up, which may be deducted from the pay packet. . . .[29]

Switzerland

In accordance with the decree of the Federal Council dated 15 May 1954, which renders universally compulsory the terms of the agreement providing for the payment of an allowance for time lost in the building trade and public works on account of

[28] Fédération Nationale du Bâtiment et des Activités Annexes, *loc. cit.*, pp. 153–159. This section summarizes the relevant legal enactments: Article 47, Livre I, *Code du Travail;* the statute of October 21, 1946 and the decrees of December 11, 1946, August 16, 1949, July 25, 1952, and November 24, 1953.

[29] *Disposición Adicional Redactada Según la Orden de 25 de septiembre de 1951, Boletín Oficial de Estado de 2 octubre del Mismo Año.*

the weather, the loss of pay resulting from odd hours lost on account of bad weather (and not exceeding half a day) will entitle the worker to 80 percent compensation from the employer. Suspension of work will be ordered by the foreman. The worker will remain at the disposal of his employer to carry out any work that can reasonably be demanded.[30]

Yugoslavia

Stoppage is every interruption of work during the working hours and directly caused by:
1. Sudden and unexpected cut of electricity which is not a result of the enterprise's or its workers' fault, and
2. National disturbances.

During the occasional interruption of work, not caused by any worker's fault, if a worker can not be given another job, he receives 70 percent of the wage rate, which he has according to his qualification. . . .

If it is possible to give a worker another job, the responsible manager is obliged to do that, and the worker is obliged to work in that job. The work in this job is paid according to the wage rate of the worker. If the worker refuses to work in this job, he is not given the recompense.[31]

Australia

11. An employer shall be allowed to deduct from the wages of "weekly employees" all time lost through wet weather in excess of 8 hours in any one week subject to the following conditions:
(a) that weather shall not be regarded as inclement for the purposes of this clause unless the employer or his representative on the job and the employee or a representative of the employee agrees that it shall be so regarded. Failing such agreement weather shall not be regarded as inclement and work shall continue.

[30] *Maçonnerie Travaux Publics et Branches Annexes, Contrat Collectif, réglant les conditions de travail pour l'ensemble de la profession dans le Canton de Genève, 1954–1955*, Art. 16, p. 13. The 80-percent figure only applies to two days out of fifteen, and unemployment compensation applies thereafter. Immigrant construction workers are not eligible for unemployment compensation.
[31] *Gradevinsko Preduzeće "Rad," Tarifni Pravilnik za 1957 godinu*, Art. 27, 28.

(b) that any intermission of work owing to inclement weather, regarded as such aforesaid shall immediately cease and work shall be immediately resumed on the employer or his representative calling for a resumption of work.

(c) that an employee shall not be entitled to payment as provided for in this clause unless he remains on the job until a decision to cease work for the day has been made by agreement between the employer or his representative and the employee or his representative.

(d) that the intermission of work by employees who would be exposed to or working in inclement weather so regarded in accordance with this clause shall not be a ground for intermission of work in places where employees are not so exposed to, or are not called upon to work in such inclement weather.[32]

Netherlands

Article 15. Bad Weather

(1) The employer shall pay the worker 80 percent of the hourly rate fixed in this agreement when and for such time as (both subject to the judgment of the employer) work is prevented by adverse weather conditions (excluding frost and the consequences of frost).

(2) The worker shall, if the employer provides alternative work of which he is capable during the time mentioned in paragraph (1) of this article, perform such alternative work, on condition that the employer is prepared to pay the worker the hourly rate fixed for him in this agreement.

(3) A worker who leaves the work place without permission shall not be entitled to the remuneration prescribed in this article.

Article 15a. Wage Compensation Fund

(1) A fund exists for combatting loss of wages where workers are unable to work because of frost or failing light, namely the foundation called the "Wage Compensation Fund for the Painting Trade in the Netherlands" whose head office is in Amsterdam. . . .

[32] *Memorandum of Agreement between The Master Builders Association of New South Wales and The Australian Builders Labourers Federation,* 14 July 1955, *Commonwealth Arbitration Reports,* Vol. 82, p. 790.

(2) Employers shall have the following obligations towards their workers of 18 years or over: . . .

    (b) if and for such time as the workers (in the opinion of the employer but subject to the approval of the management of the Fund) work less hours than their normal hours of work because of frost or the consequences of frost, in so far as the performance of painting operations is directly affected thereby, to pay them a sum equal to 90 percent of the hourly rate fixed in their case, on condition that in respect of the 12 months preceding the date on which the said climatic conditions begin they are able to produce 26 vouchers . . . [one for each week worked] and further that they qualify under the constitution and rules of the Fund;

    (c) if the hours of work during the period from 1 November to 12 February inclusive must continually be reduced as a result of darkness, to pay them a sum equal to the full wage in respect of a maximum of 52½ hours which shall be distributed over the said period each year by the Industrial Council for the Painting Trades.[33]

While the United States appears to have limited rules dealing with weather conditions, the provisions for compensation in the event of inclement weather are much less extensive than in the other countries cited. In part this is to be attributed to the fact that an essential feature of the weather-compensation schemes would create considerable difficulty in the United States, in particular, the general requirement that men be shifted to other work and be willing to perform other work during periods of unfavorable weather. Such a rule would be inconsistent with the emphasis upon jurisdictional rules in the United States.

[33] *Landelijke Collectieve Arbeidsovereenkomst voor het Schildersbedrijf in Nederland, 1 February 1954–30 April 1955*, pp. 19–21. Identical language appears in *Landelijke Collectieve Arbeidsovereenkomst voor het Bouwbedrijf*, June 10, 1958, Art. 23, 24. This latter agreement is signed by general contractors.

Attention is directed to the separate arrangements for treating with general bad weather, under which the enterprise pays 80 percent of the hourly wage, and the special fund for frost, when the temperature falls to zero degree Centigrade.

See, "Methods of Compensating Construction Workers in Europe for Loss of Working Time Caused by Bad Weather," *International Labour Review*, August 1958, pp. 195–208.

APPRENTICESHIP

The rules on apprenticeship are particularly significant in an industry in which such a large fraction of the workers are skilled.[34] There are significant differences among countries in the proportion of building workers regarded as skilled; thus, in Yugoslavia the percentage is approximately a third while in the United States the figure would be two thirds. A group of rules is primarily directed toward the control over the standards of skill. In the written formulation of these rules, some are most general and others are detailed, although the actual operation of both sets of rules may be very similar. The rules may only differ with respect to the extent they are committed to writing. The wage scales typically provide for a step increase from the first year of apprenticeship until the journeyman's rate is achieved on the successful completion of the apprenticeship. These wage rules are not considered in this section. Governmental agencies invariably have a significant role in the apprenticeship arrangements, in the setting of standards and in registering apprentices. The following excerpts provide some indication of the regulation of apprenticeship.

United States

There shall be a Joint Apprenticeship Committee of three members representing the Employers and three members representing the Union. This Committee shall, in conformity with the National Apprenticeship Standards for the Electrical Construction Industry, make local rules and requirements governing the qualifications, education, and training of all apprentices.

There shall be allowed to each firm one apprentice when two journeymen are employed; two apprentices when five journeymen are employed; three apprentices when ten journeymen are employed; four apprentices when fifteen journeymen are employed; and five apprentices when twenty journeymen are employed. However, no Employer shall be permitted to have more than

[34] International Federation of Building and Woodworkers, *Apprenticeship Schemes in Various Countries*, Copenhagen, 1955.

five apprentices at any one time. There shall not at any time be more than three apprentices on any one job. . . .

Apprentices shall be registered with the Joint Apprenticeship Committee.[35]

Great Britain

The Bodies adherent to the National Joint Council for the Building Industry have given consideration to the need for the early establishment of a more comprehensive National Scheme of Building Crafts Apprenticeship administered upon a local and regional basis, for the better training of building craftsmen with particular regard to the encouragement and promotion of building crafts apprenticeship; recognition of specific terms and conditions of indentures; registration and certification of apprentices; transfer of apprentices in certain circumstances from one employer to another; surveillance of technical and general educational courses and facilities; and the making, from time to time, of regulations for the general betterment of building crafts apprenticeship in all its aspects. In the light of such consideration by the Adherent Bodies it has been decided that:

1. There shall be established by the National Joint Council for the Building Industry . . . a Standing Committee of the Council to be known as the National Joint Apprenticeship Board . . . for the purpose of administering a National Joint Apprenticeship Scheme. . . .[36]

Switzerland

Both parties to the agreement undertake to promote the training of apprentices, as well as the practical organization of post-apprenticeship examinations, according to the conditions stipulated in the agreement of 8 May 1950 and additional clause No. 2 to the present agreement.

No apprentice can be employed by any firm and no apprentice-

---

[35] *Basic Agreement between the Southeast Texas Chapter of the National Electrical Contractors Association and Local Union 716 of the International Brotherhood of Electrical Workers*, August 1, 1957, Article I, Section 11; Article III, Sections 7, 8.

[36] National Joint Council for the Building Industry, *National Joint Apprenticeship Scheme. National Form of Apprenticeship Agreement*, as amended October 2, 1950, p. 3.

ship contract can be signed unless the candidate has passed the preapprenticeship examination. . . .

The Examination Committee will eliminate candidates who fail to fulfill the following conditions: . . .

The Committee will organize a one-day examination without documents and under supervision. The examination will be on the following subjects: . . .

The Apprenticeship Committee will set an intermediate examination every year for all apprentices to attend and again, after two years of apprenticeship, in order to determine whether the apprenticeship is proceeding satisfactorily in accordance with the Federal Apprenticeship Regulations for the building trade.[37]

Germany

The provisions of the federal master collective agreement shall apply to apprentices and trainees learning semiskilled trades, in so far as expressly stipulated below.

An apprentice (*Lehrling*) is one who is being instructed in a recognized trade on the basis of articles of apprenticeship.

A trainee for a semiskilled trade (*Anlernling*) is one who is being instructed in a recognized semiskilled trade on the basis of a training contract.[38]

France

The French Labor Code provides for an apprenticeship program including a model contract for indenture.[39] It regulates their hours and conditions of work and sets their wages on the basis of a ratio of journeymen's wages, starting with 50 percent at the age of fourteen to fifteen.

[37] *Maçonnerie Travaux Publics et Branches Annexes, Contrat Collectif réglant les conditions de travail pour l'ensemble de la profession dans le Canton de Genève, 1954–1955*, Art. 23, Additional Clause No. 2, and Regulations for the Pre-Apprenticeship and Intermediary Examinations for the Trade of Builder, pp. 18, 25–30.

[38] *Bundesrahmentarifvertrag für das Baugewerbe im Gebiet der Bundesrepublik Deutschland vom 6. Juli 1956*, Annex I, pp. 46–51.

[39] Fédération National du Bâtiment et des Activités Annexes, *loc. cit.*, pp. 87–98; Livre II, *Code du Travail; Apprentissage, accord du 15 novembre 1957.*

Spain

Art. 27 In accordance with the policy of social legislation in the new state, undertakings in the construction and public-works industries shall devote the fullest attention to apprenticeship training, accepting apprentices for the trades belonging to these industries in the proportion of at least 5 percent of the corresponding tradesmen employed, as laid down in the Order of 23 September 1939, and affording them the requisite tuition to improve their knowledge of their trades. . . .

Art. 28 Certificates of training issued by official labor schools or similar institutions, or by the vocational-training schools set up by the guilds concerned, shall be regarded as a preferential qualification for appointment or promotion in undertakings covered by these regulations.

Apprenticeship in the trades belonging to the industries subject to these Regulations shall be for a period of four years.[40]

Yugoslavia

Apprentices who work in the enterprise in individual trades are paid during the apprenticeship—practical work and attendance at school—monthly, according to the year of school training: . . .

In addition to these earnings, the managing board of the enterprise can decide, on the suggestion of the director, to give grants to apprentices for some needs, such as: supply of clothes, shoes and textbooks, school utensils, study excursions, improvement of food, supply of work, and protective clothing, as well as other payments, but they can not exceed a monthly amount of: . . .

For professional advancement of workers, temporary vocational courses in the enterprise can be established by the decision of the managing board of the enterprise. During the attendance of these courses, workers are paid according to the wage rate for their job.[41]

[40] Chaperon, loc. cit., pp. 84–86.
[41] Gradevinsko Preduzeće "Rad," Tarifni Pravilnik za 1957 godinu, Article 38.

Australia

(a) All apprenticed junior employees shall be indentured for five years in accordance with the form of indenture set out in the appendix of this award: provided that a period of probation of three months shall be allowed to each such junior employee, which shall be reckoned as part of the period of his apprenticeship should he at the commencement thereof or during or at the termination thereof become indentured as aforesaid.

(b) All documents of indentures and transfers thereof shall be lodged with the Industrial Registrar. . . .

(c) (ii) The proportion of apprenticed junior employees to journeymen employed elsewhere than in shops or joinery mills shall be as prescribed in the legislation of the state in which the work is being carried out or by a relevant apprenticeship commission, board or authority vested with power to regulate such proportion by the legislation of such state.[42]

Netherlands

Article 8. Boys and Assistants

(1) The expression "boys" (*jongmaatjes*) means young men under 18 years and the expression "assistants" (*jonge gezellen*) means workers between the ages of 18 and 22 years.

(2) The number of boys and assistants to be admitted to the painting trade shall be determined by the number of adult persons engaged in the trade. . . .

(3) The number of boys and assistants who may be employed in any one undertaking shall be as follows: one boy or one assistant where the number of adult persons engaged in the trade is between one and three; one boy and one assistant for four or five adult persons engaged in the trade; two boys and one assistant for six to ten adult persons engaged in the trade; for every five additional adult persons engaged in the trade (or fraction of five) one additional boy and one additional assistant may be employed. . . .

[42] *The Amalgamated Society of Carpenters and Joiners of Australia and R. F. Anderson and Others,* Award, 30 January 1953, *Commonwealth Arbitration Reports,* Vol. 75, p. 561. "In this matter the parties have reached agreement on most points and in due course an award will be issued in the terms of the agreement . . ." (p. 536).

(5) It shall be the duty of the employer to enter into a contract of apprenticeship with an apprentice who is in his service in accordance with the statutory apprenticeship system. The provisions of this collective agreement shall also apply to such apprentices.[43]

THE PROTECTION OF STANDARD CONDITIONS

In the field of construction the highly competitive characteristics of the product market—many enterprises, small-size, easy entry, lack of standardized product, subcontracting—and of the unstructured labor market—short duration of jobs, self-employment, family employment, difficulties of enforcing rules when work places are variable—tend to create a variety of rules designed to regulate the forms of competition in both markets. Two of the most common rules of this type are (1) those designed to protect standard conditions in the event of subcontracting by requiring any subcontractor to comply with the established rules, and (2) prohibitions on individual workers from engaging in construction work on their own account, particularly after hours or on holidays and weekends. The following rules illustrate both the problem and the common measures designed to protect the standard conditions determined in other rules.

United States

Members of the Union, except those meeting the requirements of Employer as defined herein, shall not contract for any electrical work.

No individual connected with an employing concern as owner, manager, partner, or member of a board of directors, shall perform any manual electrical work.

The Union agrees that if during the life of this Agreement,

[43] *Landelijke Collectieve Arbeidsovereenkomst voor het Schildersbedrijf in Nederland,* 1 Febr. 1954–30 April 1955, pp. 10–11; see *Landelijke Collectieve Arbeidsovereenkomst voor het Bouwbedrijf,* June 10, 1958, Articles 30, 31. For a description of the apprenticeship system, Stichting Vakopleiding Bouwbedrijf, *Historical Background of the Apprenticeship-System in the Building Industry,* The Hague, (mimeographed), 1957.

it grants to any other Employer in the Electrical Contracting Industry any better terms or conditions than those set forth in this Agreement; such better terms or conditions shall be made available to the Employer under this Agreement and the Union shall immediately notify the Employer of any such concessions.

Certain qualifications, knowledge, experience, and financial responsibility are required of everyone desiring to be an employer in the Electrical Industry. Therefore, an employer who contracts for electrical work is a person, firm, or corporation having these qualifications, maintaining a permanent place of business with a business telephone, and not connected with or a part of a domestic establishment and with a suitable financial status to meet payroll requirements.

. . . the subletting, assigning, or the transfer of any work in connection with electrical work to any person, firm, or corporation not complying with the terms of this Agreement by the Employer, will be sufficient cause for cancellation of this Agreement, after the facts have been determined by the International Office of the Union.[44]

Great Britain

The problems of regulating competition in the product market for building have resulted in a variety of rules, policies, and informal practices. The *Joint Demarcation Agreement*,[45] now formally repudiated but still largely in effect, was an attempt to standardize competition by indicating what type of operations would be subject to building wages and rules and which would be subject to civil-engineering wages and rules. Various methods have been tried to discourage "labor-only subcontracting" by which owners make direct arrangements with workers to supply labor services without a contractor.[46] Local authorities have been

[44] *Basic Agreement between the Southeast Texas Chapter of the National Electrical Contractors Association and Local Union 716 of the International Brotherhood of Electrical Workers*, August 1, 1957, Article II, Sections 1, 2, 3, 5, and 11.

[45] Civil Engineering Works and Building Works, *Joint Demarcation Agreement*, July 4, 1934.

[46] National Federation of Building Trades Operatives, *Minutes of the Meeting of the General Council Held at The Royal Station Hotel, York, on 15th March, 1956*, "The Secretary said the London Regional Secretary had

a particularly knotty problem in this respect. The practice of workers performing work after hours or over week ends on their own account is termed "doing a foreigner," and a variety of informal pressures have been utilized to discourage such arrangements. These various devices to curb forms of competition have proven difficult to administer.

Switzerland

Duties of Employers and Workers.
Illicit Work.
1. Workers regularly employed under the aforementioned conditions are expressly forbidden to perform any remunerated or nonremunerated work outside working hours or during the holiday period for any other person, with the exception of agricultural labor or private or public functions.

Any violation of this rule will constitute grounds for the immediate termination of the labor contract in accordance with article 352 C.O., and the immediate withdrawal of the worker's card.

If the violation takes place in the holidays or on a paid holiday the Geneva Fund of the Building Trade can demand the reimbursement of any allowance paid and the round-table committee will decide whether the worker should be deprived, for a certain length of time, of the benefits of holidays with pay or allowances for public holidays. . . .

The workers, on the other hand, must undertake no professional activity under inferior conditions to those specified here and must not work for any employer who has not formally adhered to this agreement. . . .

Both parties to the agreement must do their utmost to safeguard their common professional interests, and will make special efforts:

(a) to obtain acceptable conditions concerning the promulgation and submission of work;

---

sent out a circular to the local authorities in London informing them that the Federation had terminated their arrangements with the NFBTE for the examination of the bona fides of labour only subcontractors, and therefore all reference to the matter contained in the 1954/55 Working Rule Agreement no longer applied. The Employers' Regional Secretary had sent out a circular contradicting that statement, some local authorities accepted that, and many did not" (p. 11).

STANDARD CONDITIONS · 237

(b) to obtain adequate time for completion of the work and as regular a flow of work as possible in the trade;
(c) to oppose any execution or completion of work involving harmful pressure for the trade;
(d) to combat illicit labour and unfair competition resulting especially from inadequate offers. . . .[47]

Germany

6. The contract of employment may be terminated without observing a period of notice if the worker performs "black work" [Schwarzarbeit] in spite of a written warning.[48]

France

The first point that should be made clear is that "black labor" [le travail noir] appears in France primarily in two forms: (1) "Black labor" for a building firm, and (2) "black labor" done directly on behalf of a private individual. . . .

(1) There is very often jobbing or subcontracting, however, without any suggestion of "black labor," for it is quite normal for a contractor to subcontract part of the work he has to do to a fellow contractor or a tradesman with his own business, duly registered on the Trade Register, even when the latter does not supply any material and uses the material of the principal contractor. . . .

On the other hand, there is indubitably "black labor" when a firm, although duly entered on the Commercial Register or the Trade Register, enters into an agreement with some of its workers with a view of employing them clandestinely, often in return for extra pay, and thus evading all the social charges resulting from the employment of manpower.

There is also "black labor" when the same firm, wishing to evade all or part of its social responsibilities, uses the services of a worker regularly employed by another firm, over and above

---

[47] Maçonnerie Travaux Publics et Branches Annexes, Contrat Collectif, réglant les conditions de travail pour l'ensemble de la profession dans le Canton de Genève, 1954–1955, Article 22, pp. 17–18.
[48] Bundesrahmentarifvertrag für das Baugewerbe im Gebiet der Bundesrepublik Deutschland vom 6. Juli 1956, p. 6. "Black work" is defined in "Gesetz zur Bekämpfung der Schwarzarbeit," March 3, 1957, BGB Bl. I Seite 315. The concept of "black work" is roughly equivalent to "labor-only subcontracting."

the maximum working hours permitted [60 hours per week] and without putting him on its lists of employees.

(2) It is becoming more and more common for a customer to give a worker in a building firm jobs to carry out outside his normal working hours, or for a worker not employed by any firm to undertake full-time work for a private person; this is how many industrialists or farmers have their buildings repaired, a wall or fences put up, or all kinds of other jobs done which unquestionably form part of the work of building firms. . . .

Odd jobs done by building trade workers in their leisure . . . free of charge, cannot be regarded as "black" labor.[49]

No one may carry on for himself an industrial or commercial profession or a trade if he is not entered either on the Commercial Register or on the Trade Register, and if he evades the social and fiscal responsibilities imposed on that profession or trade.

No wage-earner in industry, commerce, or trade may carry out paid work in his profession or trade over and above maximum working hours as stipulated in the laws and regulations governing his profession or trade.[50]

Australia

28 (a) No employer shall permit any of the classes of work covered by this agreement to be carried on by a contractor or other person except in accordance with the terms and conditions of this agreement as if the contractor or other person were himself an employer and bound by this agreement.

(b) No employer shall enter into any contract for the carrying on of any of the classes of work covered by this agreement by any contractor unless the contract contains a clause binding the contractor to pay the rates and observe the conditions set out in this agreement in respect of the work contracted for and unless a clause is inserted in any such contract to the effect that the employer can determine the contract if there is any breach of the conditions above referred.[51]

[49] Fédération Nationale du Bâtiment et des Activités Annexes, *loc. cit.*, pp. 243–244.

[50] Statute, October 11, 1940; Fédération Nationale du Bâtiment et des Activités Annexes, *loc. cit.*, p. 244.

[51] *Memorandum of Agreement between The Master Builders Association of New South Wales and The Australian Builders Labourers Federation,* 14th July, 1955, *Commonwealth Arbitration Reports,* Vol. 82, p. 794.

Netherlands

Article 3. Work Undertaken by Worker on His Own Account. (1) It shall be unlawful for a worker to work at his trade on his own account for third parties. A worker who violates the foregoing provision shall be liable to suspension without pay for between one and six days. . . .

(3) It shall also be unlawful for a worker after completing his day's work in the service of his employer to perform work in the service of an employer other than his own employer.[52]

Section 4. Employer's Responsibility.

(1) The employer having the status of principal employer shall be responsible for the proper application of the conditions of employment prescribed in this Agreement by his subcontractor or subcontractors. . . .

(2) The principal contractors hereby undertake to ensure that the provisions of this agreement are observed in the subcontracting contracts. In addition, it shall be expressly stipulated in the contract governing the relationship between the principal contractor and the subcontractor that where subcontractors are engaged in operations for a contractor who is a party to a dispute they undertake to comply with decisions given by the Arbitration Board and agree that whenever a dispute of the aforementioned nature occurs the final settlement of accounts in respect of the amount in dispute shall not take place before the obligations stipulated in the award of the Arbitration Board have been discharged. . . .[53]

THE EMPLOYMENT RELATIONS: LAYOFF AND HIRING

The short duration of construction projects and the variability in employment opportunities mean that hiring and layoff take place in building much more frequently than in industry generally. Layoffs have been rather strictly circumscribed by rules in

[52] *Landelijke Collectieve Arbeidsovereenkomst voor het Schildersbedrijf in Nederland, 1 Febr. 1954–30 April 1955*, p. 5.

[53] *Landelijke Collectieve Arbeidsovereenkomst voor het Bouwbedrijf*, June 10, 1958, Article 11.

employment in industrial plants: long periods of notice, outright prohibitions, severance or indemnity pay. The rules in building stand out in sharp contrast to factory rules, and in this respect there is a high degree of similarity among different countries. Workers can be laid off on relatively short notice, a matter of a few hours, a day, or a week; a little longer notice period may be required for long-service employees with the same enterprise. But building rules everywhere recognize the need for greater flexibility in layoffs than in industry generally.

Hiring arrangements are more variable, although a variety of devices are often used to assure preferential treatment to those workers regularly following the craft against foreigners, temporary or casual workers, or nonmembers of workers' organizations, in this respect reflecting different problems in the building labor market of the various countries. Where no rule is cited, hiring takes place in a wide variety of ways: through employment exchanges, at the job site by individual arrangements, occasionally through labor organizations, and through gang leaders of groups who work as an incentive team. The following excerpts of rules for each country provide some indication first of the layoff and then of the hiring rules.

United States

1. Layoff

> Subject to this understanding [exclusive bargaining rights] the Employer shall have entire freedom of selectivity in hiring and may discharge any employees for any cause which he may deem sufficient, provided that there shall be no discrimination on the part of the employer against any employee, nor shall any such employee be discharged, by reason of any union activity not interfering with the proper performance of his work.

2. Hiring

> (1) The local unions shall establish and maintain open and nondiscriminatory employment lists for employment of workmen in the work and area jurisdiction of each respective local union of each particular trade.

(2) The employer shall first call upon the respective local unions having work and area jurisdiction, or their agents, for such men as they may from time to time need, and the respective local unions or their agents, shall immediately furnish to the employers the required number of qualified and competent workmen and skilled mechanics of the classifications needed by the employers.

(3) The respective local unions, or their agents, will furnish each such required competent workman or skilled mechanic entered on their lists, to the employers by use of a written referral, and will furnish such workmen or skilled mechanics from the respective local unions' listings in the following manner:

(a) Workmen who have been recently laid off or terminated in that respective local union's work and area jurisdiction by employers now desiring to re-employ the same workmen in that same area provided they are available for employment.

(b) Workmen who have been employed by employers in the respective local union's work and area jurisdiction within the multi-employer unit during the previous ten (10) years and are available for employment.

(c) Workmen whose names are entered on the list of the respective local union having work and area jurisdiction and who are available for employment.

(d) Reasonable advance notice (but not less than 24 hours) will be given by the employers to the unions, or their agents, upon ordering such workmen or mechanics; and in the event that 48 hours after such notice, the unions, or their agents, shall not furnish such workmen, the employers may procure workmen from any other source or sources. . . .[54]

Great Britain
1. Layoff

National Working Rule 2B—Termination of Employment.
During the first six working days of employment, termination of service shall be upon the tendering of two hours' notice by either employer or workman, such notice to expire at the end of the normal working day.

[54] *Labor Agreement between Associated General Contractors of America, San Diego Chapter . . . and A.F. of L. Building and Construction Trades Unions*, May 1, 1955, Article II, pp. 9–10.

Thereafter, termination of service shall be upon the tendering of two hours' notice by either employer or workman, such notice to expire at the normal finishing time on Fridays. Provided always

(i) that at the discretion of the employer an operative may be transferred, at any time during the period of his employment, from one job to another;

(ii) that the contract of employment shall be deemed a contract from hour to hour and that payments other than as prescribed in Working Rule 2A shall be for time actually worked;

(iii) that in cases of misconduct an operative may be summarily discharged at any time;

(iv) that on termination of the particular operation for which the operative has been engaged, or when work is stopped on the instructions of a recognised competent authority, employment may be terminated at two hours' notice expiring at the end of any day.[55]

Switzerland

1. Layoff

In case of dismissal or departure, preliminary notice must be given in the evening for the following evening. When a worker has been employed by the same firm for over a year a fortnight's notice of termination must be given. . . .

The labor contract cannot be terminated: (a) during a period of total or partial incapacity for work resulting from accident or sickness of a kind accepted by the insurance organizations, providing that the incapacity cannot be ascribed to the worker's own fault and does not exceed four weeks; (b) while the worker is performing his military service and during the fortnight following his release. . . .

The worker must give his employer 24 hours' notice before return to work.

The employer may send the worker to work with another employer.

In case of unemployment in the profession, workers with seniority rights will receive employment priority in their occupational category.

[55] National Joint Council for the Building Industry, *National Working Rules for the Building Industry* (*as of 26th October, 1956*), p. 21.

2. Hiring

For the purpose of ensuring security of employment and regularity of production in the building trade and public works in the Canton of Geneva, a card, known as a "worker's card" will be instituted and given to workers regularly employed in building and public-works concerns in the Canton of Geneva. Conditions of issue of this card are set out in additional clause No. 1 appended to the present agreement.

The worker's card can be withdrawn by the round-table committee in case of violation of the collective agreement. . . .

The professional card will be delivered to workers regularly employed by building and public-works enterprises in the Canton of Geneva. This card will bear a single serial number which will be the same as that of the Workers Compensation Fund book, as well as the bearer's personal particulars, occupation, and domicile. Under no circumstances will the card give details of such matters as pay, religion, membership of professional organizations, family commitments, etc. . . .

The professional card gives the bearer priority in matters of employment.[56]

Germany

1. *Layoff.* Three-days notice is required for reductions in force arising from a lack of work; in the winter period from October 15th to March 31st no notice is required.

France

1. Layoff

Art. 8. (a) In the event of breach of the work contract after the trial period has expired, the length of the period of notice to be given by either party shall be fixed as follows:

One hour for employees who have been with the firm for less than three months, any day started being due in full within the limits of working hours for the day in question. . . .

[56] *Maçonnerie Travaux Publics et Branches Annexes, Contrat Collectif, réglant les conditions de travail pour l'ensemble de la profession dans le Canton de Genève, 1954–1955,* Articles 8, 19, and Articles I and VI of Additional Clause No. 1, pp. 8, 15, 22–23.

Three working days for employees who have been with the firm for a period ranging from one to five years.

One week for employees who have been with the firm for more than five years. . . .

(c) Where a serious offence has been committed, the employee may be paid off or sent away immediately. . . .[57]

Spain
1. Layoff

Art. 14 (a) During the probationary period [two weeks for skilled workers], the undertakings may dispense with the services of an employee of any class whenever they think fit, if such employee is unsuited for or does not possess the necessary ability for his job. . . .

(d) The employment contract of permanent-project workers shall be terminated without entitlement to compensation when the work in their trade is completed in the works project on which they have been employed. Such termination shall be communicated with one week's notice by the undertaking to the workers and to the Provincial Building Union, . . .

(e) In building projects of long duration, permanent-project workers having more than four years' service with the undertaking on the same project shall have the option, on the termination of the project, either of being transferred with the permanent status of "permanent established workers" to other projects of the undertaking in the same or a different locality, if a vacancy exists . . . or of terminating their contracts with compensation of one week's wages for each year of service.[58]

Australia
1. Layoff

10. A "casual employee" shall mean an employee employed for less than one week. Employment may be terminated by the employer on giving not less than one hour's notice or by forfeiture or payment of one hour's pay respectively.

[57] *Ouvriers du Bâtiment, Accord National du 21 octobre 1954*, p. 10; Fédération Nationale du Bâtiment et des Activités Annexes, *loc. cit.*, pp. 109–118.
[58] Chaperon, *loc. cit.*, pp. 74–76.

A "weekly employee" . . . unless . . . dismissed for dishonesty, drunkenness, or incompetency shall be entitled to one day's notice or to one day's pay in lieu of notice and any "weekly employee" on leaving his employer's service shall give one day's notice or forfeit one day's pay. Provided that no employee shall be deemed to be dismissed for incompetency after he has worked one week continuously for one employer.

2. Hiring

35. Subject to the provisions of Re-establishment and Employment Act 1945, as between members of The Australian Builders Labourers Federation and other persons offering or desiring service or employment at the same time, preference shall be given to such members, other things being equal.[59]

Netherlands
1. Layoff

Article 12.   Employment Relationship and Termination Thereof.
(1) The employment relationship shall be entered into for an unspecified period. . . .
(3) Except in the cases specified in articles 1639 p and 1639 q of the Civil Code employers and workers shall give notice of at least one working day before terminating the employment relationship.
Notice of the termination of the employment relationship shall be given in writing against a receipt.
(4) Where an employment relationship has lasted three years or more a period of notice of one week shall be observed by both parties. . . .[60]

2. Hiring

Employers who are members of employer's organizations signing this agreement shall in engaging workers who are not members of the workers' organization signing the agreement grant

---

[59] *Memorandum of Agreement between The Master Builders Association of New South Wales and The Australian Builders Labourers Federation,* 14 July, 1955, *Commonwealth Arbitration Reports,* Vol. 82, pp. 789–790, 796.
[60] *Landelijke Collectieve Arbeidsovereenkomst voor het Schildersbedrijf in Nederland,* 1 Febr. 1954–30 April 1955, pp. 14–15.

such workers conditions at least as favorable as those prescribed in this agreement.[61]

PROVISION OF TOOLS

The craft character of work in building means that skilled workers in many operations typically provide at least some of their own hand tools. With increased mechanization in many fields and with the emergence of more expensive tools, however, enterprises tend to furnish such items. The rules of the work place in building accordingly tend to define rather specifically the tools to be furnished by workers, sometimes with a specific allowance. Other tools and equipment are provided by the enterprise. The precise tool lists vary with the craft. In many countries rules arise regarding arrangements for keeping tools sharp and in order and for the safekeeping of tools on the site. In the following comparison, as far as possible the single craft of carpenters has been used although more elaborate rules often exist for bricklayers, electricians, and painters.

United States

1. The employers agree to furnish substantial and weatherproof tool shed or box equipped with lock for the protection of carpenters' tools.
2. All power-driven, pneumatic, or electrical tools or electrical cords, and all tools other than hand tools shall be furnished by the Employer. Carpenters shall not be permitted to provide such tools to their employers.[62]

Great Britain

The following allowances which shall not be deemed to be a payment of wages and which shall not therefore be enhanced when calculating overtime payments shall be paid in respect of

---

[61] *Landelijke Collectieve Arbeidsovereenkomst voor het Bouwbedrijf*, June 10, 1958, Article 9 (3).

[62] *Labor Agreement between Associated General Contractors of America, San Diego Chapter . . . and A.F. of L. Building and Construction Trades Unions*, May 1, 1955, pp. 31–32 (Special Craft Working Rules, Carpenters).

the provision, maintenance, and upkeep by the operative of such tools as may be required in the execution of his work:

Carpenters and Joiners   4d. per day.[63]

Switzerland

Art. 5.   All workers who utilize their tools in good conditions in conformance with the lists appended to the present collective contract shall receive allowance of 2 fr. for an entire fortnight (fr. 1—for an entire week). The tools of the worker shall be insured against fire by the employer for their real value.[64]

Germany

10. Compensation for wear and tear and maintenance of tools supplied by the workers shall be fixed, in places where payment of such compensation is customary, in the district or regional agreements.[65]

France

Art. 29.   When the workman himself provides and keeps in repair the tools necessary for carrying on his trade, he shall receive an allowance known as the "tool allowance" to cover depreciation of those tools.

The tools must be adequate to enable him to carry out the normal work of his trade and category.

The allowance, which shall vary according to trade, shall be fixed as follows, per month of work: . . .

       Carpenter   500 francs. . . .[66]

---

[63] The Federation of Civil Engineering Contractors, *Handbook, Administrative Year, 1957–1958*, p. 152. For the bricklayer, see, National Joint Council for the Building Industry, *National Working Rules for the Building Industry, Constitutional Amendments—National Working Rule 3E. Tool Allowances*, January 23, 1958.

[64] *Contrat Collectif réglant les conditions de travail pour l'industrie de la charpente, menuiserie et ébénisterie dans le Canton de Genève*, March 29, 1956. The "Liste de L'Outillage Pour Charpentier" shows 27 items to be furnished by the carpenter.

[65] *Bundesrahmentarifvertrag für das Baugewerbe im Gebiet der Bundesrepublik Deutschland vom 6. Juli 1956*, p. 20. In the Bezirkstarifvertrag Norden the allowance for the carpenter is .02 DM. per hour.

[66] *Convention Collective des Ouvriers du Bâtiment et des Travaux Publics du Département de la Haute-Savoie*, pp. 18–19. The agreement for Loire-

Spain

Art. 65. Wear and Tear of Tools. As a general rule the undertakings shall furnish their workmen with the tools they require to perform their work. The normal life of the implements thus provided shall be laid down in the works rules.

When the necessary tools, instead of being furnished by the undertaking, are provided by the workman himself, he shall receive the following amounts as compensation for wear and tear of tools: 3 pesetas per week for tradesmen. . . .[67]

Australia

27 (a) The employer shall provide the following tools when they are required for the work to be performed by the employee:

Dogs and cramps of all descriptions
Bars of all descriptions
Augers of all sizes
Star bits and bits not ordinarily used in a brace
Hammers, except claw hammers
Glue pots and glue brushes
Dowel plates
Trammels
Hand and thumb screws
Spanners
Soldering irons. . . .

30 (b) The employer shall provide on all jobs in towns and cities a suitable and secure waterproof lock-up, solely for the purpose of storing employees' tools.

43 (T) The employer shall insure and keep insured against loss or damage by fire whilst on the employer's premises such tools of the employees as are used by him in the course of his employment. The employee shall, if requested so to do, furnish the employer with a list of his tools so used.[68]

Inférieure in addition to an allowance lists the tools to be supplied by a carpenter as follows: 1 saw, 1 hammer, 1 square, 1 plane, 1 plumb line, 1 level, 1 pair of compasses, 1 tracing iron, 1 ripping chisel.

[67] Chaperon, loc. cit., p. 126.

[68] The Amalgamated Society of Carpenters and Joiners of Australia and R. F. Anderson and Others, Award, 30 January, 1953, Commonwealth Arbitration Reports, Vol. 75, pp. 554–555, 571.

Netherlands

As far as the employees use their own carpentry tools, they shall receive an allowance of 2 cents per hour, with the exception of time spent in traveling and time paid for but not worked.[69]

The rule regarding painters is as follows:

(d) He shall be in possession of serviceable tools and implements, such as putty knives, a glazing knife, a hammer, a chopping knife, a glass cutter, a pocket rule, a dressing brush, and such other tools and implements as may be necessary in accordance with local practice.[70]

STATUS OF THE ACTORS IN THE NATIONAL SYSTEM

The logic of the present analysis is that a comparison of a complex of rules of the work place among national industrial-relations systems will show both the influence of the common technological and market contexts (including their systematic variations) and the distinctive contribution of the power contexts and the status of the actors in their national industrial-relations systems (including their historical development). The attention to a limited number of rules in the first part of this chapter should not leave the impression that there are certain rules (such as travel time and travel expense) in which the technological and market context alone operate and the distinctive national industrial-relations characteristics play no role. Nor is there another group of rules on which the technological and market environment have absolutely no influence but where the features of the power contexts alone are at work. No such sharp differentiation is appropriate even analytically. Each rule is the consequence of the working and interaction of the industrial-relations system as a whole, although the influence of the technological and market contexts is greater on some rules than

[69] *Landelijke Collectieve Arbeidsovereenkomst voor het Bouwbedrijf,* June 10, 1958, Article 6, Appendix A.

[70] *Landelijke Collectieve Arbeidsovereenkomst voor het Schildersbedrijf in Nederland* 1 Febr. 1954–30 April 1955, p. 5.

others. The earlier sections have provided a number of illustrations showing the distinctive contribution of the status of the actors in a national industrial-relations system in shaping the details of rules which are largely forged by the technological and market context. The details of the fund in the Netherlands to compensate for the loss of wages from frost conditions and the circumstances surrounding its origin are illustrative.[71] The second part of this chapter illustrates the way in which national industrial-relations characteristics are relatively more significant to rule-making.

Ideally, the complete collection of rules for each country in the building industry should be surveyed, and this chapter should then review the rules one by one that have not so far been considered. In such a census, the procedures used for disputes settlement, including the role of governmental agencies, the forms in which rules appear (awards, agreements, laws, etc.), social-security programs, the details of hiring arrangements, and the distribution of authority among local, regional, and national rule-making bodies reflect characteristics of the various national industrial-relations systems. These rules peculiarly mirror the relative status of workers and managers (and their organizations) and governmental agencies in a national industrial-relations system. Also some features of the compensation system are influenced by the national systems. For instance, in Yugoslavia the rules provide for possible increases in earnings, or decreases (to 75 percent of the basic wage), according to the distribution of profits or losses by the workers' council. The attempts to make the occupational wage structure conform with a nationwide job-evaluation plan in the Netherlands may be cited as another illustration.

[71] D. H. Nijhof, "Unemployment Due to Frost and the Risk Funds for the Building Trades," *De Sociale Zekerheide Gids*, July–August, 1955. The origin of the fund also reflects the distinctive national system. In 1947 a 6-percent wage increase was not approved by the government Board of Mediators concerned with wage controls. The fund grew out of subsequent three-sided negotiations.

Instead of such a catalogue of rules distinctive to the various national industrial-relations systems, the role of a national system will be explored and illustrated in the remainder of this chapter by examining the three groups of rules which most distinguish the building industry in the United States from the complex of rules developed in other countries. In each case the problems these rules confront are not unknown in other countries. But the magnitude of the problems and the characteristics of the rules developed in the United States stand out as most distinctive. The three groups of rules concern: (1) the definition of jurisdiction and jurisdictional disputes, (2) union security, and (3) the prohibition of piecework.[72] Logically, any country could have been selected and the distinctive characteristics of that national industrial-relations system as reflected in its building rules could have been explored.

Jurisdiction

The jurisdictional dispute is a major problem and feature of the building industry in the United States; an enormous complex of rules is devoted to defining jurisdiction and to procedures for the settlement of these specialized disputes.[73] Such disputes are not unknown in other countries; they appear to be important in Ireland, and have been of some significance in England,[74]

[72] It might also be added that the age limits for apprenticeship tend to be more general in the United States, and apprenticeship is less tied to specific ages. This charactertistic is reflected in the wage structure, as noted in Chapter 5, and is to be attributed largely to a longer period of general education and laws relating to the minimum age for leaving school.

[73] American Federation of Labor Building and Construction Trades Department, *Plan for Settling Jurisdictional Disputes Nationally and Locally, Agreements and Decisions Rendered Affecting the Building Industry* (Green Book), January 1958, and *Procedural Rules and Regulations of the National Joint Board for Settlement of Jurisdictional Disputes Building and Construction Industry*, October 20, 1949, as amended August 28, 1957.

[74] A procedure was established in the National Federation of Building Trades Operatives for demarcation difficulties in 1956. *Minutes of Meeting of the General Council held at the Royal Station Hotel, York on 15th March, 1956*, pp. 6–10.

Denmark, and Sweden, but in no country do they have anywhere near the significance or volume they have in the United States. Why? A theoretical framework of industrial relations should be directly applicable to such a question. It has sometimes been said that these disputes arise largely because of the craft rather than industrial character of building labor organizations. But in Denmark there are a large number of separate craft organizations in the industry, and in the Netherlands there are a number of building unions divided in part by religious and ideological features. Others have attributed the disputes largely to technological change, but many of the most serious disputes in the United States do not involve technical change. It has been customary to treat these disputes solely as conflicts between unions, which is valid for some disputes, but there is a wide variety of types of jurisdictional disputes, many of which are only outwardly in form related to a conflict between unions. The following brief explanation, comprised of four points, highlights the distinctive features of the national industrial-relations system (and its historical development) which largely account for this observed feature of the building rules in the United States.

(1) The strength of the local union in the United States and the direct line of union authority from the national union to the actual site of the work place is a distinctive feature of the national industrial-relations system which has a major role to play in any explanation. The large number of paid union officials at the local level with direct supervision over members at the job site is a feature of the status and relations of workers' organizations in the United States system. "Professionals" are available to appear at job sites to draw fine lines of jurisdiction. National and local union rivalries are expressed at the work place because the machinery and manpower to express them on the job is available. In other countries the line of command may extend from the national to a local or regional branch, but the connection to the job site is much looser, and few full-time professionals are available to police the rules. This factor implies

that some jurisdictional disputes in the United States arise out of the activities of the local business agent, on his own or acting under national instructions. Left to themselves on the job site, the workers would engage in fewer and less severe disputes.

(2) It is an oft-repeated generalization that workers in the United States are less class conscious than workers in Europe, and this more individualistic character is said to be partly responsible for the greater extent of jurisdictional disputes. This view is to be rejected as having any explanatory value; it confuses solidarity of workers in conflicts with managers with solidarity in conflicts of interests among groups of workers; it fails to analyze the position of workers and their organizations in an industrial-relations system along the lines developed in Chapter 4. The fact is that building workers in the United States probably have a higher degree of craft solidarity than elsewhere. The plurality of unions along religious, nationality, or ideological lines at a job site in most European countries tends to reduce craft solidarity significantly. Thus, the relative absence in the United States of religious, nationality, and ideological organizations of workers contributes to a much higher degree of craft solidarity and unity at the job site.

(3) The greater degree of competition among contractors in the United States in a single type of construction, and the keen competition among types or groups of contractors—generals, various specialties and owners—is a major factor creating jurisdictional disputes. There is probably less bid pooling and fewer devices in contract letting to circumscribe competition. There is little tradition handed down from the guilds. Some contractors and their allied unions compete with other contractors and their allied unions. The larger construction market and the greater degrees and types of specialization contribute to the intensity of competition. The greater degree and area of geographical mobility of contractors and workers operates in the same direction. The regulation of jurisdictional conflict and the clear definition of jurisdictional lines are essential to the operation of the bid-

ding system in highly competitive markets; they are as indispensable as the provision for area-wide wage rates determined in advance. The highly competitive characteristics of the product market for building in the United States must be cited as one of the principal determinants of severe jurisdictional conflicts and the rules defining jurisdiction. In a significant sense jurisdiction is a device to circumscribe competition in both the labor movement among unions and in the product market among contractors or between allied groups of contractors and unions.

(4) The historical perspective on the industrial-relations system of the United States would add the significance of the concept of exclusive jurisdiction in the decisive early period of the American Federation of Labor.[75] The struggle between the Knights of Labor and the national unions revealed the unhappy consequences of interunion conflict, and exclusive jurisdiction was developed as a constitutional principle to regulate and to constrain conflicts and rivalries among union organizations in a rapidly changing country and labor scene. This union tradition and the more general principle of majority rule combined in 1926 (Railway Labor Act) and 1935 (Wagner Act) to determine the distinctive feature of exclusive bargaining rights in the national industrial-relations system. The beginnings and the course of evolution of the national system have contributed to the prominence of jurisdictional rules and disputes in the United States.

It should be observed that these four factors are not the type of explanation that has ordinarily been given for the relative prominance of jurisdictional rules and disputes in the building industry of the United States compared with the same industry in other countries. But these are the factors highlighted by the comparative analysis of national industrial-relations systems, and it is submitted that they provide a more useful and

---

[75] John T. Dunlop, "Structural Changes in the American Labor Movement and Industrial Relations System," *Proceedings of the Ninth Annual Meeting, Industrial Relations Research Association*, December 1956, pp. 2–4.

insightful explanation of the comparative concern with jurisdictional rules in the building industry of the United States.

Union Security

Rules designed to define the status of the union organization and the rights to employment of members of a union against both nonmembers of any union and members of rival organizations assume a much larger role in the building industry of the United States than in other countries. However, such explicit rules and practices are not unknown outside the United States as the above quotations on hiring arrangements illustrate (see particularly Geneva, Switzerland). The group of rules in the United States which, taken together, define union security in this industry are the provisions for union recognition and exclusive bargaining rights (typically without benefit of NLRB certification), the recognition of union jurisdiction, and the *de facto* hiring arrangements: historically, the closed shop under which all those hired are required to be union members (if workers are available), or new employees have to join the union if no members are available, and all hiring is done through the union. The following features of the national industrial-relations system, compared to other countries, combine to create the relatively much greater emphasis upon union security.

(1) The strong local unions directly interested in the job site, equipped with full-time personnel, have come to provide a hiring service or labor exchange for contractors. Labor organizations operating only on a national or a regional basis, without direct organizational channels to the job site, are relatively unconcerned with hiring arrangements. The greater mobility of contractors and the lesser isolation of home-town contractors from the competition of foreign or out-of-town contractors creates a demand for the provision of a labor force, preferably of a reliable and standard quality or skill. The greater degree of specialization in building operations requires lists and referrals with specializa-

tions within broad craft groupings. Although no figures are available, it would appear that workers are less attached to particular contractors, or change jobs among contractors more frequently on the average in the industry in the United States than in other countries. Consequently both workers and contractors (and their organizations) have a greater interest in the rationalization of the hiring process.

(2) The absence of division among workers' organizations in the United States based upon religion, nationality, or ideology in the same locality in the building industry permits a sharper cleavage between members of a union and nonmembers. In a country where workers in one craft have worked together on jobs drawn from three different unions for one craft or for the industry as a whole, it is relatively more difficult to control hiring. There can be no exclusive representation, and it may well be difficult to get rival unions of different ideological or confessional persuasions to coordinate activities directed against nonmembers. Under exceptional circumstances such coordination may arise when the employment opportunities of local residents or nationals are threatened by foreigners. This factor no doubt has played a major role in the development of the Geneva "working card" with employment preferences for long-service local residents compared to Italian migratory workers.

(3) The higher degree of competition among contractors in the United States has resulted in a greater interest in control over hiring by the unions in order to preserve standard conditions from nonunion competition. Aggressive wage policies have stimulated the same developments. The control over hiring and the allocation of the work force is an effective means—it may even be indispensable—to see that wage rates and other minimum conditions of employment are being enforced. Where contractors are less inhibited to develop informal bidding and pricing arrangements, less pressure is placed upon the labor market.

(4) The historical perspective on the industrial-relations system of the United States would add that the strong anti-union and "open-shop" tradition of many contractors in the past

served as a stimulant to emphasize union-security rules to a greater extent than in countries in which the forms of opposition were not so vigorous or principled. In some countries, such as Denmark, the traditions of the guild system had not disappeared before modern union and contractor organizations began to emerge. The traditions of organization in such a case contrast sharply with the intense individualism of the nineteenth-century United States. In some regions and fields, such as heavy, high-way, and industrial construction, union status is of relatively recent origin, and in other sectors, primarily housing, substantial nonunion operations continue. The greater emphasis upon union security is related to the long struggle for the organization of contractors and branches of the industry.

The considerable preoccupation with the group of rules defining union security in the United States is seen as a consequence of special features of its national industrial-relations system and the course of its development.

Prohibition of Piecework

One of the agreements cited above contains the following clause which is typical of the rules in the industry in the United States:

> Each Carpenter employed in accordance with the terms of this Agreement shall receive wages based upon the minimum hourly wage rates specified. . . . Any other method of paying Carpenters, such as the use of piecework, bonus systems, or lumping of the work, shall be deemed a violation of this Agreement.[76]

In contrast, piecework, bonus plans, and other incentive methods of wage payment are widely practiced by the building industry of other countries,[77] although the proportion of building opera-

---

[76] *Labor Agreement between Southern California General Contractors and United Brotherhood of Carpenters and Joiners of America*, May 1, 1955, p. 10. The paragraph is entitled "Labor Contracting."

[77] International Federation of Building and Woodworkers, *Minutes of the International Conference on Wage Systems in the Building Industry*, Copenhagen, May 19–20, 1954. There are brief reports on eight countries.

tions on other than a time basis of payment varies considerably. Aside from Eastern European countries, of the countries examined the extent of piecework or similar methods of payment is highest in Scandinavia and lowest in Great Britain and Switzerland. Piece rates or lumping (lump-sum arrangements for performing a designated task) do in fact exist in some branches of the industry in some localities in the United States, particularly in the housing field. But under union conditions, such methods of payment are almost invariably a violation of the agreement. In all of the agreements cited earlier in this chapter, outside of the United States, there is provision for piecework or incentive methods of payment, although the Geneva agreement alone prohibits "piecework and job work" except for clearing land and the digging of ditches related to drainage work (Article 21).[78] In Great Britain the acceptance of piecework on a national basis by the labor organizations, and the provision for piecework in the formal rules of building, dates from the pressures of World War II and the 1947 agreement on incentives.[79]

In the countries studied historically it appears that the trade-union organizations originally opposed piecework and sought to limit compensation to the time method of payment. The simple fact is that the labor organizations were not able to enforce their position. Even in Sweden where incentive methods have been well established for more than half a century, the unions at first opposed piecework. "The leading officials discovered that it was more to the advantage of the workers to accept the principle of piecework."[80] The experience in the Netherlands has been described as follows: "Even in instances where the trade unions have definitely rejected and sought to prevent the principle of piecework payment, they have had to admit that . . .

---

[78] A separate arrangment also apparently applies to parket-flooring layers.
[79] National Joint Council for the Building Industry, *National Working Rules for the Building Industry (as at 26th October, 1956)*, Rule 1 (K), pp. 9, 11.
[80] Knut Johansson, "The Piecework System in the Swedish Building Industry," in International Federation of Building and Woodworkers, *loc. cit.*, p. 2. This is a useful report.

nature has proved to be stronger than theory, and that the workers were nevertheless arranging piecework with their employers." [81] At the outset the formal rules on piecework or payments by result in building, to which labor organizations in most noncommunist countries have been party, seem to have arisen as a consequence of deciding to accept and to regulate what could not be successfully opposed. In great Britain it was the pressure of desperate wartime conditions alone which broke the traditional opposition to incentive payments and brought grudging acceptance of payments by results. One union leader has said that it took the combination of Ernest Bevin and Churchill in wartime to get him to accept incentive payments.[82]

It is not difficult to understand the traditional opposition of union organization to piece rates in building. The hours of work are more difficult to police when individual workers or small groups work on piece or job rates since they may leave early or stay later to complete a task. Accidents may be more likely. There are marked variations in earnings among workers, creating dissension among pieceworkers and demands for wage increases for workers not on piecework. There is a tendency to develop more and more specialization which breaks down a craft and threatens to undermine high standards of workmanship, apprenticeship, and broadly trained skills. The variations in working conditions among jobs and on a single job over time tend to undermine standard conditions and the attempt to place competing contractors on a common footing. Piecework or lumping is often simply a form of subcontracting at less than standard conditions. The wage varies with the bargaining power of individual workers in accordance with short-term conditions of the labor market. The union organization is unable to secure credit for changes in earnings which are frequently the result of direct agreement between contractors and individual workers under

[81] H. Umrath, "Payment by Results in the Building Industry," in International Federation of Building and Woodworkers, *loc. cit.*, p. 1.

[82] There is only spotty enthusiasm for payments by results in the building industry in Great Britain.

piecework. But despite these difficulties individual workers and contractors found mutual advantages in piecework. Individual workers liked the increased earnings and the greater freedom from supervision. Contractors found prices for operations a convenient way to protect a contract bid and to reduce labor costs. In most countries outside the United States, piece rates and incentive methods of wage payment have come to be accepted in varying degrees by the building industries.

But why do the rules in the building industry in the United States uniquely preclude piecework or lumping? A simple answer is that the building unions in the United States have been able to keep out piecework and lumping on any extended scale. The unions, however, have been less strong in the housing field where incentive methods of pay are probably relatively most common in the United States, although seldom formally recognized. (1) The unions have been able to preclude piecework and lumping basically because of strong local unions, with "professional" and full-time staffs, directly oriented toward the job site. This feature of the national industrial-relations system, it has been observed, facilitated control over hiring, which in turn has helped to constrict piecework. (2) Piecework is often designed in part as a substitute for supervision; workers on piecework are said not to need the same amount of supervision except for inspection on quality of workmanship. The greater emphasis on supervision and the larger size of many projects in the United States (outside housing) may be a factor tending to create less interest on the part of contractors in this feature of incentive methods of wage payment in building. (3) The greater degree of mobility of contractors and workers would tend to make the establishment and administration of piece-rate systems in any locality the more difficult. (4) The building industry in the United States has a relatively much smaller proportion of activity in housing where piece rates most frequently have been practiced. The lesser repetitive character of many other operations, which are a relatively larger proportion of the industry, would make the introduction of piecework the more difficult.

The rules against piecework or lumping, just as the rules defining union security and jurisdiction, in the building industry in the United States are significant indicators of distinctive characteristics of the national industrial-relations system. These unique rules are largely the response of the status of the actors at the job site.

SOURCES

United States

Basic Agreement between the Southeast Texas Chapter of the National Electrical Contractors Association and Local Union 716 of the International Brotherhood of Electrical Workers, August 1, 1957.

Labor Agreement between Associated General Contractors of America, San Diego Chapter . . . and A.F. of L. Building and Construction Trades Unions, May 1, 1955.

Labor Agreement between Southern California General Contractors and United Brotherhood of Carpenters and Joiners of America, May 1, 1955.

Great Britain

National Joint Council for the Building Industry, National Working Rules for the Building Industry (as of 26th October, 1956), and supplements.

The Federation of Civil Engineering Contractors, Handbook, Administrative Year, 1957–1958, pp. 111–177.

Civil Engineering Works and Building Works, Joint Demarcation Agreement, July 4, 1934.

National Federation of Building Trades Employers, Application of Incentive Payments to Building Work, June 1949.

National Joint Council for the Building Industry, National Joint Apprenticeship Scheme, National Form of Apprenticeship Agreement, as amended October 2, 1950.

Building and Civil Engineering Holidays Scheme Management Limited, Annual and Public Holidays With Pay in the Building and Civil Engineering Contracting Industries, published January 1958.

National Federation of Building Trades Operatives, General Rules (April 1955).

National Joint Council for the Building Industry, Constitution, Rules and Regulations, as adopted by the Council and the Adherent Bodies, January 1949.

Switzerland

Maçonnerie Travaux Publics et Branches Annexes, Contrat Collectif, réglant les conditions de travail pour l'ensemble de profession dans le Canton de Genève, 1954–1955.
Contrat Collectif réglant les conditions de travail pour l'industrie de la charpente, menuiserie et ébénisterie dans le Canton de Genève, March 29, 1956.

Yugoslavia

Gradevinsko Preduzeće "Rad," Tarifni Pravilnik, za 1957 godinu.

Germany

Bundesrahmentarifvertrag für das Baugewerbe im Gebiet der Bundesrepublik Deutschland vom 6. Juli 1956.
R. Blumensaat, C. Geerling, G. Leber, *Lohnausgleich winterlicher Arbeitsausfälle im Baugewerbe,* Wiesbaden, 1956. The text of the agreements is included.

France

Fédération Nationale du Bâtiment et des Activités Annexes, *Mémento du Chef d'Entreprise, Le Chef D'Entreprise du Bâtiment et des Travaux Publics et Ses Salariés,* Janvier 1955; *Mise á Jour No. 2,* Septembre 1, 1956.
Ouvriers du Bâtiment, Accord National du 21 octobre 1954.
Convention Collective des Ouvriers du Bâtiment et des Travaux Publics de la Loire-Inférieure, 1ᵉʳ février 1956.
Convention Collective des Ouvriers du Bâtiment et des Travaux Publics du Département de la Haute-Savoie, June 6, 1955.
Apprentissage, accord du 15 novembre 1957.

Spain

Carlos M. Fernandez Chaperon, *El Trabajo en la Construcción y Obras Públicas Al Día,* Editorial Goñi, Madrid, 1957; Reglamentación Nacional de Trabajo en las Industrias de la Construcción y Obras Públicas, Ministerio de Trabajo.
Disposición Adicional Redactada Según la Orden de 25 de septiembre de 1951, Boletín Oficial de Estado de 2 octubre del Mismo Año.

Australia

Memorandum of Agreement between The Master Builders Association of New South Wales and The Australian Builders Labourers Federation, July 14, 1955, *Commonwealth Arbitration Reports,* 1955, Vol. 82, pp. 787–797.
The Amalgamated Society of Carpenters and Joiners of Australia and R. F.

Anderson and Others, Award, January 30, 1953, *Commonwealth Arbitration Reports,* Vol. 75, pp. 535–573.

Netherlands

Landelijke Collectieve Arbeidsovereenkomst voor het Schildersbedrijf in Nederland, 1 Febr. 1954—30 April 1955.
Landelijke Collectieve Arbeidsovereenkomst voor het Bouwbedrijf, June 10, 1958.
Stichting Vakopleiding Bouwbedrijf, *Historical Background of the Apprenticeship-System in the Building Industry,* 1957.
International Labor Office, *Netherlands 1, Decree: Employment Relations, Legislative Series,* 1945.

7 · The Yugoslav Industrial
Relations System

THE industrialization process after World War II among the underdeveloped countries is associated with a proliferation of economic and political forms. Between the classical British model and the Soviet apparatus there are emerging new forms of industrial society and new national industrial-relations systems. Nowhere are these developments more distinctive nor inherently interesting than in Yugoslavia. Indeed, the very term "workers' management" appears from both the Western and Soviet points of view to be a contradiction in terms. In western countries the direction of the enterprise is in the hands of managers appointed by private owners or by the government in the case of nationalized industry; in the USSR the managers are in large measure part of the bureaucracy of the state whose objective is the achievement of the production goals established by central authorities. In the Yugoslav system the managing boards and workers' councils elected by the employees of the work place give policy direction to a hired manager selected by competitive bidding and subject to recall. "Workers' self-government under socialism represents that democratic mechanism through the agency of which bureaucracy and bureaucratic tendencies are being overcome in that the direct producers are

264

united with the means of production economically and politically."[1]

The Yugoslav experience is further of particular interest because, at the end of World War II, it adopted a full-fledged Soviet-type system of centralized administrative management of its economy.

> . . . The entire economic life of the country, save agriculture and arts and crafts, where such regulating had been of a somewhat lesser extent, was regulated directly and in detail by the instrumentality of a central plan. The plan decreed what shall be produced, what shall be exported and imported, and the way the goods produced were to be distributed, that is, what portion thereof shall go toward personal consumption and toward consumption by production respectively. The plan not only determined the volume of production, but its assortment. The production costs also were established by plan.[2]

"Decentralization in our country, in fact, is another name for democracy."[3] Since 1950–1952 the economic system has been fundamentally revamped to provide for decentralized decision making by the enterprises and the local communes (local governments), for workers' management through elected workers' councils, and for increasing resort to the free market for economic decisions. Some novel instruments of fiscal and monetary policy and general regulations are used by central authorities to influence the size and direction of new investment, but even these decisions have been increasingly decentralized. The individual enterprises make their own decisions on products, quality, volume of output, prices, wage and salary rates, and the distribution of profits after taxes; they may seek new capital from the investment bank or may import and export within established dif-

[1] Jože Gordičar, "Workers' Self-Government in the Light of Scientific Socialism" *The New Yugoslav Law,* April–December 1957, p. 10.

[2] Jacob Radaković, *Industrial Transformation of Yugoslavia,* Belgrade, Publicity and Publishing Enterprise, 1955, pp. 11–12.

[3] Edvard Kardelj, reprinted in *Supplement, Information Bulletin about Yugoslavia,* Belgrade, Yugoslavija Publishing Enterprise, March 1957.

ferential interest rates and exchange rates. No other country has had this sequence of experience of economic policy.

The Yugoslav experience is of special interest to the field of industrial relations on account of the development since 1950 of workers' councils (*Radnički Saveti*).[4] The organization of workers at the immediate work place and their relations to management organs, to trade unions, to customary governmental agencies, and to the Communist-party apparatus are distinctive features of a national industrial-relations system and instructive for comparative analysis. Organizations at the work place perform a variety of functions in different countries, take a number of forms, and are called by different terms: the *comité d'enterprise* in France, the *commissioni interne* in Italy, joint consultation in Great Britain, or *betriebsrat* in Germany. They have been focal points of the spontaneous uprising of workers from the days of the Paris commune in 1871 to the Hungarian revolt of 1956. They have been widely used to increase worker productivity, as a forum for the discussion of technical and welfare matters with management, and for handling some grievances in some countries. The Yugoslav experience adds quite another sector in the spectrum of organizations of workers at the immediate work place. It also looms as a significant experiment of particular significance to the workers of Eastern Europe.[5]

But Yugoslavia is not simply a rare and unique instance of industrialization; it confronts many of the same basic problems as other countries dedicated to economic development: the restriction of consumption and the maintenance of a high rate of capital formation without impairing the incentives and performance of workers, the relative constriction of agriculture with increasing productivity or yields; the sequence of development among heavy industry, light industry, and social overheads (some

[4] *Congress of Workers' Councils of Yugoslavia, Beograd June 25–27, 1957,* Edition of the Central Council of the Confederation of Trade Unions of Yugoslavia, 1957.

[5] Jan Rosner, "Management by the Workers in Poland," *International Labour Review,* September 1957, pp. 257–277; Milovan Djilas, *The New Class, An Analysis of the Communist System,* London, Thames and Hudson, 1957, p. 94.

regions are relatively more backward); the recruitment, training, and commitment of a labor force including managerial and professional groups, and the structuring of the relations among workers, managers, and the government. The dilemma of rapid industrialization and the rigidity and severity of political and economic controls has not escaped the Yugoslavs. "As every one is aware, it is impossible to pursue a very strained economic policy which demands very great efforts of the whole people and to simultaneously ensure an uninterrupted advance of democracy in the social and political system." [6] These problems common to industrializing countries arise in Yugoslavia with a distinctive set of resources, institutions, and ideology and with the experience of a particular history.

The purpose of the present chapter is to describe and to analyze in short compass the economic development of Yugoslavia and the emergence of a distinctive system of industrial relations with the aid of the tools developed earlier in this volume. This account of the development of one national industrial-relations system also provides an introduction to the general analysis of the relation between economic development and the emergence of national industrial-relations systems and the growth of the body of rules for the emerging industrial work places and work communities. [7]

BACKGROUND

The new state of Serbs, Croats, and Slovenes was created at the end of World War I. [8] Slovenia and Croatia had been parts of the Austro-Hungarian empire. Macedonia was under Turkish

[6] Edvard Kardelj's Address in the Federal People's Assembly, December 7, 1956.

[7] Grateful acknowledgment is made for numerous interviews and visits to plants and to various organizations in Belgrade in December 1957. I also appreciate the opportunity for discussions with Mr. M. C. Wynne-Roberts and Mr. Jan Vanek of the ILO staff. The responsibility for the views here expressed are entirely my own.

[8] The size of the new state was a little larger than Great Britain and Northern Ireland but smaller than the state of Colorado.

rule until 1912, and the independence of Serbia dates from the Berlin Congress of 1878. The intense nationalist rivalries in the interwar years were to result in the paralysis of government and to doom the development of parliamentary government, devoid of deep historical roots.

> To the Serbs it appeared all they now had to do was govern the rest of their compatriots. To the others, it seemed that they had exchanged one form of bondage for another. . . . From the first there was a head-on clash between the Serbian Radicals, under Pashich, who was determined to make the new state a highly centralized "Greater Serbia," and the Croat Peasants, under Radich, who were equally determined to make it a federalized state, and, if possible, a republic.[9]

In January 1929, seven months following the shooting of three Croat Peasant-party deputies on the floor of Skupshtina (parliament) by a Montenegrin, King Alexander abolished the Constitution (Vidovdan, June 28, 1921) and established a royal dictatorship. He sought to eliminate political parties based on "tribal" or religious participation. In his desire to encourage a single common nationalist spirit, he changed the name of the country to Yugoslavia (South Slav) in October 1929. "Police brutality and the arrest of political opponents were standard features of the royal dictatorship."[10] King Alexander was assassinated on a visit to Marseilles, France, in October 1934, and a regency headed by Prince Paul was established for his eleven-year-old son, Peter.

Under pressure from Hitler, the Yugoslav government signed the Axis Pact on March 25, 1941. A *coup d'état* in protest exiled Prince Paul and installed Peter, not yet 18, as king. But on April 6, 1941, Hitler began the bombing of Belgrade without a declaration of war, and in twelve days the Yugoslav army was broken. The Axis powers then proceeded to dismember Yugoslavia.

⁹ Robert Lee Wolff, *The Balkans in Our Times*, Cambridge, Mass., Harvard University Press, 1956, pp. 99, 120.
¹⁰ *Ibid.*, p. 123.

The ensuing four-year period of guerrilla warfare against the Axis powers and of internal civil wars and reprisals is estimated to have cost the lives of 1.7 million Yugoslavs, about 11 percent of the total prewar population. The Germans and the Italians mounted seven offensives to wipe out Yugoslav resistance; the Germans executed masses of hostages for sabotage; Croatian fascists massacred Serbs ("in the whole annals of World War II was surpassed for savagery only by the mass extermination of Polish Jews"); Serbian Chetniks massacred Croats and Moslems and the Chetniks fought the partisans.

It was some time before the Allies came to understand wartime developments in Yugoslavia.[11] "Mihailovich [defense minister in King Peter's government in exile] and his subordinate commanders were either inactive or fighting the partisan forces who were fighting the Germans."[12] The Allies then came to provide supplies and support to Marshall Tito and his partisans.

After World War I the Communist party had won a series of municipal elections in Belgrade and Zagreb, and in the elections of November 1920 for the Skupshtina it won 58 of the 419 seats. In 1921 the party was outlawed; the deputies were deprived of their seats and the Communist press was closed. The Communist organization went underground and remained there until World War II. Josip Broz, whose party name was Walter, became secretary general of the party in 1937. He was a Croat and had been a Zagreb metalworker prior to having been taken prisoner by the Russian armies in World War I.

The partisans welcomed support regardless of creed, nationality, or party. They attracted many to their ranks with the slogan of unity of all Yugoslav nations against the invaders and the traitors. "This slogan provided the only alternative to the fratricidal massacres." This wartime policy was to make a postwar contribution toward the solution of the "nationalist prob-

[11] Fitzroy MacLean, *Eastern Approaches*, London, J. Cape, 1949; Vladimir Dedijer, *Tito*, New York, Simon and Shuster, 1953.
[12] Wolff, *loc. cit.*, p. 213.

lem"[13] which had dominated and frustrated political life in the two decades between the wars. The federal republic is now comprised of six republics—Serbia, Croatia, Slovenia, Bosnia and Hertsegovina, Macedonia, and Montenegro—and two autonomous regions, Voyvodina and Kosovo-Mitohiyan. Matters of language and religion are left to the separate republics and regions in contrast to the single official Serbian language and an Orthodox Church under the monarchy which had aggravated the nationality problems.

The Communist party exercised effective control in the partisan movement and filled the positions of responsibility and leadership. The grim necessities of survival compelled a broad popular base and welcomed support for the Yugoslav cause. In the active war period the Communists were not anxious to emphasize their dominance of the partisans, despite the insignia of a red star on a background of the national flag. It also appears that Stalin was anxious to soft-peddle the role of the Communists, and he was less willing to grant the open support and recognition urged by his Western Allies.

The wartime circumstances provided certain distinctive features to the rise to power of the Communist party in Yugoslavia. These wartime conditions materially affected the status of the party following the hostilities and are essential to an understanding of postwar developments. (1) Its prestige among the mass of the population as a consequence of its wartime record was very high. It had organized and led the fight against the invaders. Its leaders were truly national heroes. (2) Rival political parties and many political leaders were very substantially discredited as "collaborators," or as those who had fled the tough fight. While this was not true of all political leaders by any means, the remaining groups were not large; the old parties were not united, and even together they did not have the standing of the partisans. (3) Marshal Tito and the partisans enjoyed the pres-

[13] Josip Broz (Tito), *Political Report of the Central Committee of the Communist Party of Yugoslavia*, Beograd, 1948.

tige of recognition by the victorious allied powers. (4) The Communist party—through the Anti-Fascist Council of the National Liberation of Yugoslavia (AVNOJ)—had the advantage of a going and operative political organization. (5) The end of the successful war effort found Marshal Tito and his associates in control of military power and the *de facto* government. (6) By the end of hostilities a high proportion (76 percent) of all industrial enterprises were in the hands of the partisans as a consequence of the capture of foreign-owned properties which had earlier been seized by the Nazis, the seizure of enterprises owned by collaborators, or the exigencies of warfare. The nationalization decree of December 5, 1946 on industrial enterprises extended to a minority of private enterprises, a state of affairs created in wartime. (7) The wartime experiences of comrades in arms bound the organization tightly together; the leadership had been proved under the most severe circumstances, and it had established a widespread basis of respect and support throughout the citizenry.

This wartime heritage of Yugoslavia is to be contrasted with those Eastern European countries in which the Communist regime was installed by weight of Soviet military presence and without a comparable basis in the extent of nationalist and popular support. It faced much less opposition than the Communist revolutions in the USSR and in China.

The interim coalition government with Marshal Tito as premier was established with the blessing of the Allies at the end of hostilities; it was soon clear that the remaining prewar political leaders would have little influence. These parties complained of intimidation, harassment by the secret police, and unwarranted arrests. These parties finally refused to submit lists for the first postwar elections, and the AVNOJ lists received 90 percent of the votes in which 90 percent of the electorate voted.

Marshal Tito and his associates proceeded to establish a Communist state with a political and economic organization modeled closely upon that of the Soviet.

But the relations with the Soviet orbit did not develop according to Soviet plans. The war had shown conflicts of interest.[14] Tito is quoted by his official biographer on the war period:

> In fact, the Comintern, at the Kremlin's orders, wanted a resistance movement in Yugoslavia which would serve the interests, not of the people of Yugoslavia, but of Russian great-power policy and its power to bargain with the other great powers. . . . Stalin coolly and systematically prepared to subjugate Yugoslavia as the central point in Southeastern Europe. Not satisfied with having attached six European states with over 80 million inhabitants to the Soviet Union after the war, he reached out for Yugoslavia.[15]

The foundations of a new Yugoslavia independent of the monarchy, established at the second session of AVNOJ in 1943, were steps taken without the advance knowledge of Moscow and met with opposition from Stalin.

In the postwar period Stalin sought to treat the Yugoslavs as other Eastern European countries. Only two of the projected joint-trading companies were established due to the opposition of Belgrade. The Soviets sought to infiltrate sensitive positions in Yugoslavia with agents of the secret police (NKVD) and to split the leadership and the Central Committee of the party. On June 28, 1948, the Information Bureau of Communist Parties, successor to the Cominform, expelled the Yugoslav party and called on Yugoslavs to repudiate their government. There followed an extensive economic blockade by Eastern European countries which severely eliminated projected deliveries of machinery and goods under the first five-year plan, 1947–1951, and required a major readjustment in the plans for economic development. Economic assistance from the West helped to continue a number of the most important basic-development projects and

[14] Jules Moch, *Yugoslavie, Terre D'Expérience*, Monaco, Éditions du Rocher, 1953, pp. 21–42, 301–326.
[15] Vladimir Dedijer, *Tito Speaks, His Self-Portrait and Struggle with Stalin*, London, George Weidenfeld and Nicolson, 1953, pp. 265–266.

to meet the drain occasioned by the ensuing heavy military expenditures. The relations between the Soviets and the Yugoslavs were not normalized until after the death of Stalin, and in 1958 they again became strained over the program adopted by the Yugoslav party.[16]

The simple fact seems to be that in 1948 Yugoslavia did not intend to affront the Soviet Union, but Yugoslavia developed foreign policies without sufficient advance consultation to suit the Soviets and in domestic matters resisted the methods of penetration used on other Eastern European countries. This independence was to be curbed as a lesson to other countries, and there appears little doubt that the Soviets thoroughly expected, by their pressures, to be able to bring the Yugoslav government to a change either through an internal split or through the consequences of united external Eastern European pressures.[17]

ECONOMIC DEVELOPMENT

Although Yugoslavia is a European country, by any conventional test it is to be grouped with the underdeveloped nations. Professor M. K. Bennett's indicators of consumption levels (typically 1934–1938) show Yugoslavia only very slightly above the Philippines and Romania but below Mexico and Brazil.[18] An array of countries by per-capita incomes in 1949 shows Yugoslavia in the $100–$200 group; Cuba and South Africa were in the $200–$300 bracket; the USSR, Israel, and Argentina in the $300–$450 bracket; France, Venezuela, and Norway in the $450–$600 bracket; Canada, Australia, and Sweden were in the

[16] *Draft Programme of the League of Communists of Yugoslavia,* March 1958, Beograd, and *Changes in the Plan of the Programme of the League of Communists of Yugoslavia.*

[17] See the dramatic account of these details, Dedijer, *loc. cit.,* pp. 317–381. Also refer to the useful volume by C. Bobrowski, *La Yougoslavie Socialiste,* Paris, Armand Colim, 1956.

[18] "International Disparities in Consumption Levels," *American Economic Review,* September 1951, p. 648.

$600–$900 bracket, and the United States figure was $1440.[19] The economic development of the country became the major objective of the new regime.

Yugoslavia has the natural-resources base for broad industrialization; she is rich in power resources, metal ores, and other minerals. Only Norway has greater water-power resources in Europe, and Yugoslavia has the advantage of complementary winter and summer supplies. The estimated useful hydroelectric power potential is 66 billion kwh. Production of hydroelectric power in Yugoslavia was .6 billion kwh in 1939 and had increased to 2.9 billion kwh in 1956. (Total power generated, including thermoelectric power, rose from 1.2 billion kwh to 5.0 billion kwh in the same period.) Yugoslav coal resources consist almost entirely of low-quality coal (lignite 19 billion, brown coal 1.8 billion, and bituminous .1 billion tons). Since 1939 brown-coal production has doubled to 8.4 million tons in 1956 and lignite production has increased almost sixfold to 7.4 million tons in 1956, while bituminous-coal output remained relatively unchanged or declined slightly to a level of 1.2 million tons.[20] Crude oil and natural gas are also produced although reserves have not been fully determined.

The nonferrous metal reserves of copper, lead, zinc, antimony, chromium, and mercury constitute the most significant mineral wealth of the country. Yugoslavia is already the leading European producer of copper, lead, and antimony from ores. The favorable location of bauxite to water power has facilitated the development of the aluminum industry, and iron-ore deposits have provided the basis for an iron and steel industry.

[19] United Nations Economic and Social Council, *Volume and Distribution of National Income in Under-Developed Countries,* June 28, 1951, E/2041, Tables 1, 2.

[20] Economic Commission for Europe, *Economic Development Programme of Yugoslavia for 1955 to 1959,* Document drawn up for the ECE Expert Group on the Economic Development of Southern Europe, April 16, 1956; *Statistical Yearbook of the Federal People's Republic of Yugoslavia,* Belgrade, Federal Statistical Office, 1957, and 1957–1958 issues of *Index, Monthly Review of Yugoslavic Economic Statistics.*

The favorable resource base was utilized in prewar years in ways that frequently made Yugoslavia resemble a semicolonial country. "Foreign capital owned 49.5 percent of the total industrial assets; in the extractive industries 78 percent; in metallurgy 91 percent; in the metal-processing industry 55.8 percent; 73.6 percent in chemicals; 61.4 percent in textiles . . . the situation in banking was similar." While there can be no doubt that foreign capital made a significant contribution to the development of the rich extractive industries, the economic development was very partial. Raw materials were exported without processing. Copper was exported as blister copper rather than processed; iron ore was only exported and was not used directly for an iron and steel industry. Some of the mines, the Bor copper mine and the Trepca lead-zinc mines for instance, made extraordinary profits which were not used in the main for further economic development in Yugoslavia. In these respects prewar Yugoslavia could make many of the same complaints against the developed countries which colonial and underdeveloped countries have made with greater support and sympathy recently.[21]

In the period since 1945 there has been very substantial industrial development in Yugoslavia. The 1950 industrial-production index was 172 (1939 equals 100). There followed two years in which the index declined slightly, a consequence of the readjustments made necessary by the Eastern European economic blockade, the increase in military outlays not included in these figures, the first period of decentralization and workers' management, and the poor agricultural harvests as a consequence of unfavorable weather which sharply affected the food-processing and tobacco components. By 1954 the index reached 208, and the figure for 1957 is three times the prewar level. The sectors of greatest expansion relative to prewar have been electrical power (4.3 times), crude petroleum (8.0 times), ferrous metallurgy (3.9 times), metals (4.5 times), chemicals (3.6 times),

[21] For instance, Gunnar Myrdal, *Economic Theory and Under-developed Regions*, London, Gerald Duckworth and Co., 1957.

and new electrical manufacturing. (The military industry is not included in the index of production.)

The volume of industrial employment has also grown sharply. Employment in industry and mining rose from 341 thousand in 1947 (a little higher than the prewar level) to almost 900 thousand in 1957. The total number of people employed outside of agriculture increased from 652,000 in 1946 to 2,171,000 in 1956. Some of the principal employment sectors in mining and manufacturing at the end of 1955 were: coal mining, 83,983; iron and steel, 31,576; nonferrous metallurgy, 38,072; manufacture of metal products, 137,191; building materials, 38,188; wood products, 105,840; textiles, 108,074; leather and footwear, 23,119; food processing, 58,400; and tobacco 22,120. The total of almost 800,000 were employed in 2,745 enterprises, an average of almost 300 per enterprise.

The rapid expansion in industrial output and employment has been achieved by a very high proportion of national product being expended in gross investment. Gross fixed investment, including repairs and maintenance, has averaged steadily approximately 30 percent of gross national product.[22] Expenditures for defense are in addition to this figure out of gross national product and ranged between 18 and 12 percent in the period 1952–1954. It is apparent that consumption expenditures were very severely constricted to divert resources to the major objective of the build-up of industrialization. Investment expenditures in turn were highly concentrated on manufacturing and mining, electrical power, and transport.[23] Agriculture and housing were relatively neglected in the first postwar decade.

The rapid industrial expansion has involved a moderate rise in prices. Producers manufactured prices in the period 1952–1957 increased approximately 8 percent while industrial retail prices rose no more than 3 or 4 percent. Retail agricultural prices,

[22] United Nations, *Economic Survey of Europe in 1955*, Geneva, 1955, Appendix A, Table A:1.
[23] *Ibid.*, Table A:3.

however, rose by more than 50 percent, and rents more than doubled. The cost-of-living index rose by approximately 25 percent in this five-year period.

> In Yugoslavia the authorities have sought in recent years to achieve this restraint [of consumption] by regulating the flow of money incomes rather than by the use of detailed direct controls. Neither the production nor . . . the prices of consumers' goods are centrally determined: both are, in principle, free to move in response to market forces.[24]

During the period of administrative economic management, Yugoslavia established a Soviet-type five-year plan for the period 1947–1951. Thereafter until the end of 1957 only year-to-year programs were adopted. Moreover, the nature of a "plan" was drastically changed as economic decisions were increasingly decentralized; no centralized plans existed for each enterprise. A new five-year plan was adopted in late 1957 for the period 1957–1961; its general outline resembled an Indian rather than a Soviet plan. The plan envisages an 11-percent per-year rise in industrial output, a 9.5-percent per-year rise in gross product, a 9-percent per-year rise in national income, and a 7.4-percent per-year rise in agricultural production. The plan involves both some decline in the proportion of gross national product used for investment (a rise in consumption) and a significant shift within investments to increased relative expenditures on agriculture and on housing. The plan seeks to reduce the dependence upon foreign exchange by increasing the production of certain items (including foodstuffs) which have been imported and to increase the standard of living. ". . . The Plan particularly stresses the . . . rapid reduction of deficits in the balance of payments, as well as a constant and stable increase in the standard of living." [25]

The relatively declining proportion of the population in agri-

[24] *Ibid.*, p. A-3.

[25] Milentije Popović, "FPA Examines the Social Plan of Yugoslavia's Economic Development up to 1961," *Borba*, December 4, 1957. (Joint Translation Service, Summary of Yugoslav Press, No. 2320, p. 28.)

culture is a measure of the extent of industrialization. ". . . the percentage of population employed in agriculture dropped from 76.4 percent in 1931 to 59.9 percent in 1953." The share of agriculture in national income dropped from 50.7 percent in 1938 to 40.7 percent in 1953 at the same time that the share of industry rose from 17.0 percent to 25.8 percent in the same period.[26] "The participation of industry in the national income has increased from about 27 percent in 1939 to 45.6 percent in 1956."[27] The urban population almost doubled compared to prewar figures.

Like many underdeveloped countries, the regional disparities between parts of Yugoslavia have been very large. Macedonia and Montenegro are the least industrially developed republics. Relative industrial labor productivity in 1955 among the six republics is reported as follows as a ratio of the federal average: Serbia 91, Croatia 97, Slovenia 118, Bosnia and Hertsegovina 112, Macedonia 69, and Montenegro 73.[28] The economic development has been directed to improve the relative position of the lesser-developed regions. Gross product in the period 1951–1956 increased 44.7 percent in Macedonia and 58.6 percent in Montenegro compared to a national average of 26.9 percent. The 1957–1961 plan calls for a further increase of 61.3 percent and 107.4 percent respectively compared to a national average of 57.6 percent. The allocation of scarce investment funds in an underdeveloped country between relatively more advanced and relatively more backward areas poses difficult questions of policy. Are the more advanced to be pushed further ahead in order to develop the country as a whole, or what degree of elimination of regional inequalities is required for orderly economic development?

The level of foreign trade in 1952–1954 was about 25 percent above the average of prewar years. Prior to the war Yugoslavia had an excess of exports over imports. In the postwar period Yugoslavia has developed a substantial excess of imports over ex-

[26] Radaković, loc. cit., pp. 52, 22.
[27] Popović, loc. cit., p. 29.
[28] Statistical Yearbook of the Federal People's Republic of Yugoslavia, 1957, p. 190, Table 10-9.

ports as a part of the drive for industrialization. In the period 1948–1954 Yugoslavia received $825 million from abroad which assisted economic development. In 1956 Yugoslavia's export earnings were $321 million while imports were $472 million, a trade deficit of $151 million.[29]

The composition of Yugoslavian trade since the prewar period reflects the industrial transformation. It is in the field of manufactured goods that Yugoslavian exports have risen sharply since prewar days and particularly these exports to nonindustrial countries.[30] The principal products are base metals, chemicals, wood manufactures, and textiles.

The population of Yugoslavia at the end of 1957 was 18.4 million, and the pattern of population movement has followed the cycle normal to developing countries. The crude death rate has fallen from 20.9 per thousand in 1921 to 11.1 in 1956. The birth rate stood at 36.7 in 1921 and has gradually declined to 25.7 per thousand in 1956. The population is increasing consequently at the rate of 1.5 percent per year. "While with 66 inhabitants per one square kilometer in 1953, it belonged to the most sparsely populated countries of Europe; at the same time, with 71 agricultural inhabitants per 100 hectares arable land, Yugoslavia joined the ranks of the European countries with the highest population in agriculture." [31] About 60 percent of the work force (and dependents) are still engaged in agriculture, a figure which indicates the extent to which Yugoslavia is still relatively underdeveloped.

The large backlog of potential industrial workers, largely untrained, is reflected in the figures on unemployment. In 1956 unemployment reached almost 100,000; about seven tenths of this number were reported unskilled and more than one fourth of the total were seeking employment for the first time.[32]

The estimates of increases in industrial labor productivity

[29] GHATT, *International Trade*, 1956, p. 174.
[30] *Ibid.*, p. 264, Tables B, C, and D.
[31] Economic Commission for Europe, *loc. cit.*, p. 2.
[32] *Index*, 1957, 11, p. 49.

show wide variations among industries with an increase of 12.9 percent for all industry in the four-year period 1952–1956, or an average of 3.2 percent per year. The iron and steel group showed an increase of 47 percent for the same period or almost 12 percent per year. In this period, it is to be remembered that industry and mining increased total employment from 615,000 to 845,000, bringing almost 60,000 new employees without prior industrial background into industry each year. This new work force is likely to have affected adversely, at least for a period, the average level of labor productivity.

In the field of agriculture private activity is restricted by a law determining maximum land possession at ten hectares (24.7 acres) since 1953. In 1956 (September 30) 124,576 were engaged in agriculture on state agricultural farms and 98,022 were working in agricultural cooperatives, totaling 222,598. The figure is to be compared with a total active agricultural work force of 5.3 million. Thus, the agricultural sector is overwhelmingly private following the unsuccessful attempt to collectivize agriculture on the Soviet model in 1948–1952.

In addition to agriculture, craft undertakings and workshops are predominately private (198,644 out of 217,352 enterprises in the third quarter of 1954). The private craftsman is defined as the worker whose productive activity is limited to himself, his family, and a maximum of two to four workers, varying among republics.[33] The craft undertakings and workshops include blacksmiths, shoe repairmen, hairdressers, tailors, millers, masons, and the like. Almost all retail trade, however, is in the social or nationalized sector.

WORKERS' MANAGEMENT

The origins and the impetus for workers' management in Yugoslavia are to be sought in a variety of considerations arising

[33] In 1954, there were 255,963 persons employed in the private craft undertakings and workshops while 135,980 persons were employed in these undertakings in the social sector.

from the historical background and economic development sketched in the preceding sections.

First, the experience with centralized administrative planning in the period 1947–1951 was found unsatisfactory in a number of respects although industrial production rose by 72 percent over 1939 by 1950. But large bureaucratic ministries arose in Belgrade to formulate and direct the centralized plans.[34] The limitations have been described by Yugoslavs as follows:

> . . . rigidity of administrative management, suppression of the initiative of the producers, inefficiency, poor development of labor productivity, limited assortment of goods and deterioration in quality, and overexaggeration of the role and position of the state apparatus. . . . The more developed an economy and the higher the technical level of its production, the less does such planning suit it.

The centralization in Belgrade was not entirely compatible with the solution of the "nationalist problem" and the creation of republics. There was no long period of experience with centralized administrative planning in which the more serious limitations could be corrected.[35]

Second, the regime was committed to communism in the sense of nationalization (socialization) of the means of production. In the growing ideological conflict with the Soviets, the Yugoslavs were anxious to appear even more orthodox in Marxian-Lenin terms than the Soviets. The true classless society in the Yugoslav view requires the merging of direct producers with the means of production. Under capitalism a class of capitalists separate the direct producers and the means of production, while in the Soviet state it is the bureaucracy.

> According to the Stalinist conception, then, state ownership under socialism is identical with social ownership. . . . To be sure, all this holds good, but in a formal sense alone. The asser-

[34] Radivoj Uvalic, "The Management of Undertakings by the Workers in Yugoslavia," *International Labour Review*, March 1954, pp. 238–240.
[35] P. J. D. Wiles, "Changing Economic Thought in Poland," *Oxford Economic Papers*, June 1957, p. 197.

tion that the working people under socialism "are the sole masters of the means of production" is a sheer declaration so long as they do not themselves manage those means, so long as they do not themselves decide about the division of the national income. . . .[36]

In the Yugoslav view:

. . . nationalization, even if carried out by governments with socialist trends, may also lead to a bureaucratic administrative socialist system, if their development toward economic democracy and socialism is not insured. For that reason we consider essential the participation of workers in the management of nationalized property and of the means of production. This participation insures social and economic democracy and represents the main barrier to bureaucracy and the domination of the state. The Workers' Councils and the whole system built up on their foundations, are a specific form of struggle against the danger of bureaucracy in socialist economic-social conditions.[37]

In the language of the 1958 program,

. . . the Workers' Councils are neither representatives of the owners nor collective owners of the means of production. They manage the means of production on behalf of the interest of the social community, being stimulated in their work by their own material and moral-political strivings. This is precisely why they are the most suitable socioeconomic instrument of struggle against bureaucracy and against selfish individualism.[38]

The Yugoslavs are thoroughly committed to workers' management as a superior development in socialism and democracy, and since 1950 they have gradually increased the degree of decentralization and the role of the workers' councils and the local communes in the economy. Moreover, they are thoroughly committed ideologically to continue this process. The role of ideology is much greater in Yugoslavia and plays a more independent role

[36] Jože Gordičar, loc. cit., p. 8.
[37] Congress of Workers' Council of Yugoslavia, Beograd 25–27 June, 1957, Edition of the Central Council of the Confederation of Trade Unions of Yugoslavia, 1957, p. 15.
[38] Draft Programme of the League of Communists of Yugoslavia, March 1958, Beograd, Chapter VII, p. 119.

than in British, United States, or Scandinavian socities with their greater pragmatic emphasis. The ideological content of workers' councils is an independent factor in the creation and growth of workers' councils.

Third, every emerging industrial society confronts certain problems concerning the rising group of industrial workers, and the system of workers' management was designed to solve some of these questions. A large number of new industrial workers has to be recruited, trained, committed to industrial work, and made responsive to the necessities of industrial discipline. The workers' management system placed clearly upon the existing workers in a plant a large measure of responsibility in raising new workers to the prescribed standards. As Tito has said: "The problem of rearing and educating of new capable personnel, increasingly demanded by our rapid industrialization, could be solved precisely by giving the factories and enterprises for management to the work collectives, which, as it turned out, achieved in this respect brilliant results." [39]

All industrial societies have been seeking ways to elicit the energies and vitality of its industrial work force. Production committees, workers' councils, schemes for stock ownership, and various wage-incentive plans have been used in Western countries. In Soviet society a combination of wage incentives, honors, and repressive measures have been developed to achieve similar maximum performance. In Yugoslavia

> The direct participation in economic management and in social affairs is undeniably one of the most powerful stimulants of the initiative of the largest number of producers and the other layers of the population.[40]

"It has been proven that no technocratic administrative mechanism (not even the interest of the capitalist himself) can match the conscious activity of the direct producers themselves."

In Western societies there has been considerable discussion

[39] *Congress of Workers' Councils of Yugoslavia*, Beograd 25–27 June, 1957, p. 7.
[40] *Ibid.*, p. 16.

of human relations and communications as a device for improving morale and the performance of the work force by affecting the relations between managers and workers. In this perspective workers' management may be regarded as an arrangement which reduces to a minimum the "directing" or "ordering" content of management and increases to a maximum the need for management by persuasion and salesmanship.[41] The Yugoslavs believe they have "a solution to the conflicts between the management of production and the management of men."

Fourth, every industrial country must determine to whom its industrial managers shall be directly responsible in the first instance. In Soviet society plant managers are responsible to the ministries and other centralized or regional agencies of the state. In Western societies professional managers are responsible to more or less remote stockholders, although some enterprises have directors who are drawn from the senior managerial staff. The Yugoslavs have sought to counteract the remoteness in both systems by making managers responsible to employees directly elected from the work place. In regard to plant operations at least, as contrasted to market developments, such elected workers may be better informed than remote directors or ministry bureaucrats.

In many underdeveloped countries the capitalist class has not been able to inspire the confidence of the emerging industrial workers.[42] These capitalists cannot be compared with the current generation of captains of private enterprise in Western countries. Their interest in quick returns rather than building an enterprise and their lack of social consciousness frequently contributes

[41] Benjamin Ward, "Workers' Management in Yugoslavia," *Journal of Political Economy*, October 1957, pp. 373–386. This article does not seem to me to ask the significant questions about the Yugoslavia experience; it fails to place the Yugoslav experience adequately in the context of economic development (pp. 294–296 below). See, however, the theoretically interesting article by the same author, "The Firm in Illyria: Market Syndicalism," *American Economic Review*, September 1958, pp. 566–589.

[42] See Charles A. Myers, *Labor Problems in the Industrialization of India*, Cambridge, Mass., Harvard University Press, 1958, pp. 93–115.

to the lack of economic development. They are often paternal and dictatorial. The type of private capitalist that characterizes many underdeveloped countries is a poor director or supervisor of professional managers. In the Soviet Union and other Eastern European countries, governmental ministers or bureaucrats have been the alternative to capitalists as the "board of directors." The workers' council as a device of management in Yugoslavia is designed to find an alternative to the capitalist board of directors while escaping the dangers of bureaucratic centralization. It is for this reason that workers' management has attracted widespread attention, particularly in Eastern European countries.

Fifth, every industrial society must also confront the relations between a single plant or enterprise and the rest of the economic system. In the Soviet system these relations are arranged through a single national plan; in the Western societies these relations are organized through the market (product, raw-material, labor, and capital markets) with varying degrees of governmental intervention, primarily of an indirect nature. Workers' management (and the associated checks and balances in the local communes, trade unions, the investment bank, and generalized governmental fiscal and monetary regulations) is designed to introduce the market and competition into increasingly wide areas of decision making previously controlled by administrative and centralized planners. Decisions on prices, output, products, quality, wages, and the disposal of profits are made by the individual enterprise without explicit centralized direction or approval in an economic framework of detailed fiscal and monetary rules. In this sense, since the beginning of workers' management in 1950 the Yugoslavian economy has moved toward a Western-type economy and away from one of the Soviet type.

The workers' management was first formulated by the Basic Law on the Management of Enterprises by Work Collectives of June 27, 1950. In its present form workers' management did not spring full bloom, and the system has frequently been altered in the direction of further decentralization and greater authority to the workers' councils. Further changes were proposed at the first Congress of Workers' Councils held from June 25 to 27, 1957, and additional changes took place at the outset of 1958.[43]

Although workers' councils were established by the Basic Law of June 27, 1950, it was not until early 1952 that detailed centralized administrative planning for individual enterprises was abandoned. In early 1953 workers' councils were given discretion in the distribution of a part of the profits of the enterprise. The councils of producers were provided as secondary elective bodies in local, regional, and national legislatures in which representation, for such groups as industry, agriculture, and arts and crafts, was proportional to economic activity as measured by the value of output. In 1954 the competitive system of bidding for capital investments and operating funds was introduced. Industrial chambers and associations of enterprises were established at the end of 1954. More recently the limitations on the use of profits of the enterprise have been eliminated; provisions for turnover taxes to support local and federal governments, of course, remain. "One of the most important changes envisaged by the proposed bills is certainly the right granted to economic organizations to dispose freely of their income, after having fulfilled their commitments to the community, for the purpose of allocating wages and salaries to their employees and workers or for other purposes." [44]

The Organs of Workers' Management

The main outlines of the system of workers' management may be described as follows. In enterprises with less than thirty, but seven or more employees, the whole staff constitutes the workers' council.[45] In other enterprises members of the workers' council are elected for a one-year term; a two-year term is widely pro-

---

[43] "Work of the Federal People's Assembly," *Borba*, December 12, 1957, Joint Translation Service, Summary of Yugoslav Press, No. 2327, pp. 33–44.
[44] *Ibid.*, p. 39.
[45] No workers' management is provided for enterprises with fewer than seven persons.

posed. In the 1956 elections selecting members of the workers' councils, 88 percent of the workers voted. Membership on workers' councils (*Radnički Saveti*) varies with the size of the work force of the enterprise from fifteen to 120 members, although there were only twenty-one workers' councils with more than 75 members in the whole country, and the average size of workers' councils (in enterprises with more than thirty employees) was twenty members.[46] Three quarters of the members of workers' councils are required to be workers; the other quarter are drawn from clerical, administrative, and professional employees. There is a strong tendency for highly skilled and skilled workers to be more represented on workers' councils; these two categories constituted 71 per cent of councils worker members as compared to a 45 percent distribution within the work force. Only 15 percent of the members of workers' councils are women. Approximately 58 percent of workers' council members are below 36 years of age and 83.5 percent are below 46 years of age. Each workers' council elects a president from among its members, an even higher percentage (85.6) of whom are highly skilled and skilled workers (as compared to 71 percent of the council members and 45 percent of the work force). Members of workers' councils may be re-elected for only one consecutive term. It has been estimated that over one third of all employed workers have served on workers' councils during the first seven-year period.

The members of the workers' councils are nominated on lists drawn up by the trade-union branch or by one tenth of the total number of employees in the enterprise.[47] Of the 124,200 members of workers' councils selected in 1956 in establishments with thirty or more employees, 121,600 (or 97 percent) were selected from the trade-union lists.[48] The candidates receiving the largest num-

[46] Federal Statistical Office, *Workers' Councils and Managing Boards of Economic Enterprises in 1956*, Statistical Bulletin 77, Belgrade, June 1957, Table 1-11.

[47] In plants with over 500 employees, the number of sponsors need only equal the number of positions on the workers' council.

[48] Federal Statistical Office, *loc. cit.*, Table 2-1, p. 22.

ber of votes, regardless of the list from which the votes are counted, are elected. A procedure also exists for voting on the recall of members of workers' councils, and in 1956 in enterprises with more than thirty employees, a total of 998 members of the workers' councils (less than 1 percent) were recalled. The initiative for these recalls was as follows: 18 percent by local communes, 11 percent by directors, 36 percent by organs of self-government, 26 percent by the workers themselves, and 9 percent by political organizations.

The workers' councils have the duty to approve the annual plan for the enterprise which makes provision for output, products, prices, and wages; to receive reports on all facets of the operations of the enterprise; to select the director (through a committee and jointly with the local commune); to approve other senior appointments; to select from among its members the managing board of the enterprise, and to decide upon the distribution of profits remaining to the enterprise.[49] The workers' councils are required to meet at least once each six weeks, although it appears that on the average a meeting was held almost once a month. About 85 percent of the meetings were held outisde of working hours.

The managing boards (*Upravni Odbori*) consist of three to eleven members selected from the workers' councils. Three quarters of the members are required to be workers. Almost 79 percent of the worker members of managing boards were classified as highly skilled or skilled in 1956, and among the nonworker members 23 percent had some university education and an additional 44 percent had secondary-school education. It is apparent

[49] *Ibid.*, Table 1-18, p. 11 and Table 2-32, pp. 41–47. The subjects listed in the statistics as "questions considered" are as follows: "plan of enterprise and statement of accounts, salary and wage-scale regulation, report on work of managing board, plan of investment and reconstructions in enterprise, utilization of resources put at the disposal of the enterprise, production costs, quality and realization; norms, labor productivity and rationalization; labor relations; hygienic and technical protection, labor discipline, social and health insurance, specialized training of workers, distribution of profits, economic crime, problems of the commune, and miscellaneous."

that the workers' councils and the managing boards in turn are a select group of the work force of an enterprise including the more highly skilled and educated groups. The proportion of the members of managing boards below 36 years of age is 53.5 percent, and 82.5 percent are below the age of 46 years. Only 10 percent of the members of managing boards are women. There is also a procedure for the recall of members of the managing boards, and 1.2 percent were recalled in 1956, (476 in plants with thirty or more employees). These recalls were instigated as follows: 15 percent by organs of authority, 14 percent by directors, 40 percent by organs of self-government, 23 percent by the workers, and 8 percent by political organizations. The average enterprise (with over thirty or more employees) had approximately twenty members on the workers' council, and the average size of the managing board (excluding the director) was approximately six.[50] Each managing board averaged approximately seventeen meetings a year,[51] although it is apparent that in a group so small in one enterprise a good deal of informal consultation takes place. Each managing board selects its chairman or president. About 81 percent of these presidents were younger than 46 years and 54.1 percent were younger than 36 years. The highly skilled and skilled group comprised 82.2 percent of these presidents of managing boards while the unskilled only accounted for 6.5 percent and a high proportion of these enterprises were in agriculture.

Prior to 1953 the director of an enterprise was appointed by the relevant ministry. Since then directors are appointed by a commission composed one third of representatives from the workers' council and the balance from the local commune. Directors are selected on the basis of open competition among candidates.[52] The press carries notices of vacancies inviting applications. The following is an example:

[50] *Ibid.*, Table 2-4, pp. 50–51.
[51] *Ibid.*, Table 2-6, p. 65.
[52] *Decree on the Foundation of Enterprises and Establishments*, December 18, 1953, Articles 88–90.

The Workers' Council of the "Kozara" Shoe Factory of Zemun hereby invites applications for the post of factory director. The candidates should hold the degree of Faculty of Law or the Faculty of Economics and they should have at least three years' experience in executive posts in the economy; also eligible are highly skilled leather workers with over ten years' experience in executive posts in the economy. Applications, accompanied by the candidates' *curriculum vitae*, should be submitted, within eight days of the present announcement, to the Commission on Applications and the Appointment of Directors and Executives of Economic Organizations, the People's Committee of the Commune of Zemun.[53]

The compensation of the director and his assistants is determined by the workers' council. Procedures are also established for relieving directors. In 1956 of the 6079 directors of all enterprises, 563 (9.1 percent) were reported relieved of their duties. Only 61 (11 percent) of the group leaving were relieved at their own request; approximately 55 percent were relieved at the instance of organs of authority, 20 percent by organs of self-government, 10 percent by the workers, and 4 percent by political organizations. Almost half the directors are in the age group 36 to 45. The school qualifications of directors show that 21.5 percent were limited to primary school; 46.4 percent had junior-school education; 23.6 percent, secondary-school education, and 8.5 percent, university education.

Although no statistical material is available, it appears that directors tend to hold office for a relatively long period. Certainly, reports of managers staying with an enterprise only a couple of years as is characteristic of Soviet managers [54] are not typical of Yugoslavia. The manager has a longer time horizon. Moreover, only a relatively small proportion of Yugoslav managers are paid on a substantial bonus arrangement; one interview estimate placed the figure at 10 percent of managers. The central administration would probably wish to expand the scope of managerial

---

[53] *Politika,* March 5, 1957.
[54] Joseph S. Berliner, *Factory and Manager in the USSR,* Cambridge, Mass., Harvard University Press, 1947, pp. 47–49.

bonuses, but the salary terms for managers are set by workers' councils. The compensation paid to managers is not generous by either Western or Soviet standards. The salary of the typical director would probably not exceed two to five times the compensation of the average employee in the enterprise. The Yugoslav experience has not ordinarily used very large monetary incentives nor generous perquisites as a major managerial incentive.

The director is responsible for carrying out the plans approved by the workers' council. He organizes the processes of production, hires the work force (except for functional directors and other members of the top staff appointed by the managing board), assigns duties, terminates employment of members of the work force; he is. . . . "the highest disciplinary authority while work is in progress in the economic organization. . . . ;"[55] he has authority to make contracts in the name of the enterprise for purchases and sales. He supervises and administers the operations of the enterprise, and he initiates proposals to the managing board and the workers' council affecting the growth and development of the enterprise. The director has the duty and the right to stay the enforcement of any conclusion of the managing board or workers' council which he regards as contrary to law or government regulations, pending appeal to the appropriate agency. The director is typically assisted by a technical director, a commercial director, a secretary of the enterprise, who may also have personnel functions, and other specialized assistant directors.

In each enterprise the director has authority to impose penalties for breach of discipline which take the form of warnings, "severe public reprimands," or fines up to 5 percent of income for one month.[56] More severe penalties of downgrading or dismissal, on the recommendation of the director, are imposed by the disciplinary committee of the enterprise consisting of a

[55] *Act Respecting Employment Relationships,* Dated 12 December, 1957, *Sluzbeni List,* 25 December, 1957, No. 53, Text 663, Section 264.
[56] *Ibid.,* Section 282.

chairman and one member appointed by the workers' council and a third member appointed by the trade-union organization. There are procedures for appeal from the penalties imposed by the director to the disciplinary committee of the enterprise and in turn to the disciplinary court of the communal people's committee. The statute provides that no disciplinary penalty shall be imposed on a worker before a hearing, that the trade union may defend the worker, and that the hearing before the disciplinary committee be conducted orally and in public.

The workers' council also operates through committees or commissions which may include employees who are not members of the workers' councils. The standing commissions are for production, finance, personnel, health and safety, social standards, and grievances. Special committees are established for *ad hoc* problems. Provision is also made to refer questions on occasion to a referendum of all the workers in the enterprise. In a large trading enterprise, for instance, the managing board and workers' council had approved the proposal of the director to use part of profits to purchase supermarket equipment that had been on exhibit at the Zagreb fair. Some opposition apparently continued to the use of funds for this purpose rather than for wage increases or housing, and at the instigation of the area trade-union branch, which apparently took no position on the issue, a referendum was held, the results of which overwhelmingly supported the purchase of the equipment. Such procedures are only infrequently utilized; in 1956 only 161 such referendums were held.

Brief mention should be made of the workers' universities which are established as a form of extension classes. They provide evening and short-term courses in economics and political subjects. Certain courses are designed particularly for members of workers' councils. The program is designed in part to minimize the advantage of workers and employees with formal education.

In enterprises there are two other organizations which are to be noted—the local branch of the trade union and the League of Communists or the larger Socialist Alliance. The presidents and the secretaries of the trade-union branches in the enterprise are workers or employees. They tend to be younger, on the average, than presidents of the workers' councils and managing boards, and more of them tend to be skilled rather than highly skilled workers.[57] The role of the trade union is to propose lists for the election of workers' councils, to appoint one of three members of the discipline committee of the enterprise,[58] and to take to arbitration any grievance which goes beyond the enterprise, although this is an infrequent occurrence. The president and secretary of the trade-union branch are not ordinarily members of the workers' council. The trade union is also involved in discussions of the wage scale, and the wage scale or tariff requires the approval (and stamps) of the workers' council, the trade union, and the local commune to be operative. But the principal function of the trade union is regarded as one of education and opinion leadership among the workers. The first task listed in the constitution of the Trade Union Federation of Yugoslavia is: "To educate the working class in the spirit of scientific socialism and to work to educate it politically, culturally, and in economic and technical matters." [59] In this respect the trade unions more resemble Soviet unions than Western labor organizations. The local branches of the industrial trade unions seek to get a larger proportion of the employees interested in the enterprise and in workers' council activities; it may initiate meetings of particular departments to discuss the problems of the enterprise, increased productivity, and the achievement of the enterprise's output goals. It seeks to emphasize the interests of workers in one plant in common with those of other workers and the local community. It will emphasize the need for new equipment, com-

[57] Federal Statistical Office, *loc. cit.*, Table 2-25, p. 37.
[58] *Act Respecting Employment Relationships, loc. cit.*, Section 284.
[59] *Second Congress of the Trade Union Federation of Yugoslavia*, Zagreb, October 6–8, 1951, p. 74. Compare, Milovan Djilas, *loc. cit.*, p. 110: "Workers' organizations under the Communist system are really 'company' or 'yellow' organizations of a special kind. The expression 'of a special kind' is used here because the employer is at the same time the government and the exponent of the predominant ideology."

munity housing, and other community social needs in the disbursement of funds.

The Yugoslav Trade Union Confederation in 1954 comprised thirty-three member organizations of national industrial unions and eleven occupational associations representing such groups as teachers and journalists. The 1.6 million members, divided into 16,644 trade-union sections or branches, comprised about 80 percent of all wage and salary earners. There were approximately 400 full-time paid officials including clerical and secretarial employees.

The local unit of the Communist party serves many of the same functions as the unions. It acts as a channel of communication to higher levels in the party organization. The meetings of the local branches of the trade unions and the party are not held during scheduled working hours. It does not appear that the party organization formulates detailed positions on substantive questions and decisions which confront the workers' council or the managing board, although on occasions it may seek to mobilize opinion on a general policy it regards as significant.

Implications of Workers' Management

The system of workers' management has important consequences for the operation of enterprises particularly in view of the underdeveloped character of the country.

1. The role of the manager and his methods are different than those in Western countries or the Soviet Union. He cannot be as autocratic, dictatorial, or paternal as is so frequently the character of private management in underdeveloped countries. He must manage by persuasion and by selling his ideas and proposals to a managing board and workers' council, a group fluctuating each year or two and composed of more skilled workers and technical employees. An able manager who sells his ideas and carefully prepares the ground for a new proposal may come to have even more influence than many Western or Soviet managers. But

the system imposes a more educational approach. Perhaps this is not much different from the practices advocated by the human-relations school of management.

2. In an underdeveloped country managerial talent is in short supply. The managerial boards provide a body to create interest in management, to permit directors to review potential supervisory material, and in general to supplement managerial talents by harnessing the interests, particularly those of the skilled workers, of the enterprise. Scarce managerial talents are supplemented by workers' management.

3. The system confronts a rapidly growing body of industrial workers without previous industrial experience. The workers' management system is designed to facilitate the commitment of this work force and to educate it most rapidly to the industrial system. A period on a workers' council or managing board is an education in the problems of an industrial enterprise. The reasons for rules and regulations and the discipline of the factory are more clearly appreciated. The very large proportion of workers who have served on workers' councils, and the limitations on consecutive re-election, emphasize this educational feature of the system. Thus, in 1956 alone of the 750,000 employed in manufacturing and mining establishments with thirty or more employees, 54,000 were serving on workers' councils (18,000 of this number had served previously), and 15,000 members of workers' councils were also serving on managing boards (3,000 of this number had served previously).

4. One of the major problems of every industrializing country is to contain and to channel the protest and dissatisfaction which inevitably arise. If there is something wrong in the plant, the blame is to be placed largely upon the workers' council, the highest managerial body. The stockholders or the president of the company do not exist. Protest is contained and directed inward to the workers' council. The problems of discipline which are often explosive in an uncommitted work force are largely handled by a special committee of the workers' council.

5. The workers' council provides a forum to bring together, as does the managing board, representatives of all sectors of the enterprise. In particular, it tends to break down the barriers between white-collar and production employees and between production and technical or professional groups.

6. The workers' council provides a means of direct concern with a variety of community problems in the discussion of the distribution of profits. These profits have been invested to some extent in housing, in technical educational facilities, in scholarships, in clinics and medical institutions, and in other social institutions. The conflicts between enterprise and community have been softened by the institutions of workers' management, including their representatives in the council of producers.

7. In a system of nationalized ownership the workers' management provides an alternative to centralized administration of the Soviet type. Some body to which management shall report is essential under widespread nationalization if resort is to be made to the market and to decentralization. Workers' management is an aid to a more open economic system under general nationalization.

THE ENTERPRISE IN THE LARGER YUGOSLAV SYSTEM

The operation of the organs of management within the enterprise—the workers' council, managing board, and the director—need to be placed in the larger context of the institutions and pressures which interact upon the enterprise. The economic context has been increasingly liberalized, and market and competitive forces have come to play a steadily increasing role compared to the centralized administrative planning in effect prior to 1950–1952.

The individual enterprise makes its own decisions on products, output, prices, quality outlets, and wages within certain general regulations, institutional constraints, and market conditions. The principal economic regulations and constraints are as follows. All enterprises pay interest to the Investment Fund directed by the National Bank on the bookkeeping value of fixed capital and working capital according to an established schedule of interest rates. Some few enterprises pay no interest, and rates vary up to 6 percent. Imports and exports take place at a schedule of differentiated exchange rates by product according to whether it is held desirable by the central bank to encourage or to discourage the particular class of transactions. Social-insurance rates are fixed each year. The profits of the enterprise are subject to a tax, percentages of which are used to finance the local commune and for the central government; disposal of the balance is left to the enterprise. A special differential rent tax is also imposed on extractive industries to even out the position among enterprises which deal with ores of different richness.

Until 1953 investments were financed through the federal budget. Since then enterprises secure capital by entering competitive bids to the Investment Fund for both short-term and long-term capital expenditures. The national plan establishes broad categories of projected investment by sectors; the investment bank allocates its funds according to these sectors and makes loans within this allocation on the basis of competitive bids among enterprises. Local communes particularly and the republics may also allocate portions of their revenue to new long-term capital investments and the federal-government budget likewise carries some major developmental projects, particularly those of a social-overhead nature. A new enterprise may be founded by capital supplied by federal, republic, or local governments, by cooperatives, other enterprises, or social organizations as well as by groups of citizens [60] with the approval of the local People's Committee. Provision is also made for the termination of enter-

---

[60] "Where the resources are being provided by the citizens, the last shall have towards the enterprise only the right to have the resources, returned to them, at an interest which may not exceed the interest rate applying to savings deposits." *Decree on the Foundation of Enterprises and Establishments,* December 18, 1953, Article 43.

prises, which have been making persistent losses, by decrees of the People's Committee, or by forced liquidation including the appointment of a liquidation manager.

Enterprises are organized into chambers and associations to promote the interests of individual sectors of the economy, such as hotels and restaurants, building and construction, or enterprises engaged in foreign trade. They may engage in production research and dissemination of information, may represent the enterprises before state organs, and are consulted on drafts of applicable regulations. The chamber is governed by an assembly elected from the workers' councils of the member enterprises which in turn elects a managing board and director. The chambers have "courts of honor" which treat with problems of "good business practices" and "fair competition," although they apparently are not to consider questions of price.

One of the principal constraints upon the enterprise is the local commune. Local government in Yugoslavia is divided into 1479 communes and in turn into 107 districts.[61] The People's Committee is elected by direct vote for a term of three years, and the Council of Producers, for a similar term, is elected in proportion to national income created by industry, commerce, and arts and crafts on the one hand and agriculture on the other.

> Besides the right to found economic organizations, to participate in the appointment of the directors thereof, to grant approval of the wages and salaries schedules, and generally to exercise control over economic organizations, the People's Committee of the Commune was granted practically all the rights of the District People's Committee relative to the management of the basic resources of economic organizations and distribution of total income thereof. . . .[62]

[61] Jovan Dordević, *Local Self-government in the Federal People's Republic of Yugoslavia*, Standing Conference of Towns of Yugoslavia, Belgrade, 1956, p. 96. Also see Edvard Kardelj, "The New Organization of Municipalities and Districts," *The New Yugoslav Law*, July–September 1955.

[62] Dordević, *loc. cit.*, p. 53.

The commune has a continuing interest in the enterprise because the profits of the enterprises constitute a significant proportion of the income of the commune; the level of wages affects these profits and influences the level of wages in other enterprises, particularly for skilled labor; the failure of the enterprise to earn its wage scale requires that the commune guarantee three fourths of these payments; the enterprise creates demands for housing and social services, and some capital expenditures by the enterprise may well mitigate these problems.

The investment bank, the general government regulations particularly affecting fiscal and monetary matters, the chambers and associations, the communes and districts, the trade unions, and the party (although these last two operate directly within the enterprise) are largely external factors shaping the decisions of the enterprise in combination with competition and market forces. These external organs and the market impinge upon the machinery for decision making—the director, the managing board, and the workers' council.

THE OPERATION OF THE YUGOSLAV INDUSTRIAL-RELATIONS SYSTEM

The formal rules of the Yugoslav work place are relatively more explicit than in a country with a long industrial tradition; less is left to custom and practice. The formal rules are incorporated in a series of specific documents applicable to the particular enterprise. Even general regulations are frequently rewritten in minor details and signed by the workers' council. Among the sets of rule books are those setting forth the constitution and bylaws of the workers' council, the bylaws of the managing board, the duties of the director, the rules of discipline, the wage scales or tariffs and incentive norms, the social program—including housing and medical services—of the enterprise, and the social-security program. In United States parlance these rule books are a combination of the applicable statues and regulations, the collective-bargaining agreement, and the working rules of the enterprise.

The wage schedule, typically for a year, is first proposed by the managing board which distributes a draft for comments to all workers fifteen days prior to submission to the workers' council, the People's Committee of the local commune, and the trade union. A joint committee of these three organizations discusses the proposal and all comments, and if agreement is reached in committee, the wage schedule is submitted to the three bodies for formal approval.[63] The wage schedule is then signed by representatives of all three bodies. If no agreement is reached the dispute is necessarily referred to arbitration by two representatives of the trade union, two representatives of the chamber of trade, and an umpire appointed by the government of the republic from lists prepared by the secretary for the affairs of national economy. The decision is final and binding.

In the administration of this wage schedule, as with any other feature of compensation, an employee may lodge a complaint with the director and in turn appeal to the managing board and to the workers' council. Thus, he may object to the rate and classification applied to his work or he may object to a transfer and to the new rate of pay. Each appeal must be decided within eight days, but there is no appeal on such individual grievances outside the enterprise.

If the enterprise does not realize sufficient receipts to cover materials costs, interest on invested capital, land tax, fees to chambers, and other fixed charges, and to pay the prescribed wage scales, then wage payments are reduced (except for apprentices) proportionately to cover these charges. Wages to individual workers are not reduced below 75 percent of the prescribed scale, and this figure is guaranteed by the local commune. The

[63] Under the system in effect before 1952 the state, or state ministries, in cooperation with the trade-union leadership, fixed the wages. Ivan Bozicevic, "The New Wage System," *Second Congress of the Trade Union Federation of Yugoslavia*, Zagreb, October 6–8, 1951, pp. 47–70.

individual workers have a very real and direct interest accordingly in seeing that the enterprise makes a profit.

In the event that the enterprise realizes a profit, then after a payment of a profits tax to the federal and local governments, all the remaining profits (starting in 1958) are available for distribution by the workers' council in ways it selects. ". . . The collective working staff of any enterprise would have the right [under the law effective in 1958] to decide what portion of this profit is to be set aside for the modernization and improvement of production [funds of the enterprise] and how much as supplement to the wages and salaries of the employees." [64] Prior to 1958 only a limited portion of such profits (25 percent under the 1957 plan) were available for distribution as wages and salaries and specified amounts were allocated for premiums, to dwelling-house funds, and to social security. The regular rules of the enterprise on compensation specify whether such wage payments from profits are to be divided proportionately to wage rates or on some other basis. These wage payments averaged 21 percent (an extra 2.5 months) on the average in 1957.

The job classifications in Yugoslavia have been grouped into four broad categories; for production workers they are highly skilled (7), skilled (37), semiskilled (29), and unskilled (27); for office workers they are high category, medium category, lower category, and auxiliary. The figures in parenthesis after each group show the proportion of production workers in manufacturing and mining so classified. [65] The wage differentials of the highly skilled over the unskilled increased from 138.3 percent in 1951 to 209.3 percent in 1956 according to a sample from 101 enterprises. [66] The structure of differentials in average hourly earnings realized during the normal workweek (48 hours) for

[64] *Information Bulletin about Yugoslavia,* Belgrade, Yugoslavija Publishing Enterprise, October 1957, p. 4.

[65] *Statistical Yearbook of the Federal People's Republic of Yugoslavia,* 1957, *loc. cit.,* Table 6-7, p. 114. The data apply to September 30, 1956.

[66] *Congress of Workers' Councils of Yugoslavia, Beograd, 25–27 June, 1957,* p. 22.

the average of 1956 and for June 1957 is shown in the following tabulation:

Average Hourly Earnings, Normal Workweek [67]

	Average 1956 (dinars)	June 1957 (dinars)	Percentage increase
Workers	48.2	53.9	11.8
Highly skilled	72.1	83.5	15.8
Skilled	52.6	59.7	13.5
Semiskilled	44.0	48.4	10.0
Unskilled	39.5	43.0	8.9
Office workers	56.0	65.4	16.8
High category	87.6	104.4	19.2
Medium category	54.9	64.9	18.2
Lower category	43.1	48.6	12.8
Auxiliary	37.6	41.6	10.6

These wage figures do not include the bonuses from profits which are distributed on a three- or sixth-month basis. Total wages for workers including these bonuses increased from a monthly average of 10,090 dinars in 1956 to 11,600 dinars in the first half of 1957, an increase of 15 percent; office employees were increased from 12,780 dinars to 15,590 dinars in the same period, an increase of 22 percent. (The cost-of-living index increased approximately 2 percent from the average of 1956 through 1957.) It appears that in the first half of 1956 wages were supplemented by payments from profits by 6 percent on the average.

The Yugoslav wage structure has shown in recent years an increased differential for highly skilled workers as industrialization has pressed on shortages in these categories and as wage setting has become increasingly decentralized. The authority of the enterprise to expend profits (after taxes) as it deems appropriate may be expected further to increase differentiation in wages among enterprises. The operation of the labor market, in

[67] *Index*, 1957, *loc. cit.*, 11, p. 46.

particular the competition for skilled labor, may be expected to set some limits to dispersion; a new employee, however, is not eligible to participate in profit sharing until after three months of employment. Moreover, the influence of the trade unions, enhanced in 1958, is in the direction of limiting dispersion in wage scales among enterprises.

The disbursement of profits should not be expected to be largely in wage payments under workers' management any more than all profits are disbursed in dividends under private ownership. A variety of influences stress the importance of new equipment and the expansion of the enterprise. The prospects of higher profits and wages exert an influence. The competitive position of the enterprise is often at stake. The manager is likely to stress the need for new equipment and the impact on costs, revenue, and profits. The trade-union branch, as an organ of education, is likely to urge the importance of national policy interests. There are claims for new housing to be financed by the enterprise and alloted to workers of the enterprise; there are claims for medical clinics, scholarships, and social facilities. Despite the added authority, effective in 1958, to disburse profits after taxes as wages and salaries, these competing claims for free funds of the enterprise are not likely to be entirely ignored. It is often to the interests of the director, managing board, and workers' council to increase output and reduce costs in order to increase the profits (after taxes) available for distribution by decision of the workers' council.

The labor problems common to underdeveloped countries, such as increasing labor productivity, reducing turnover, reducing redundant labor in the enterprise, and imposing standards of discipline, under the Yugoslav industrial-relations system are more or less directly subject to influence by the workers, and the performance of the group on these problems directly affects total compensation. Edvard Kardelj states that in 1950 the country had the choice of strengthening the role of the state administration or to rely primarily on economic measures, and chose the second alternative. ". . . We took into account the fact that, under socialism too, the material interest of the working man is the chief motive power of his activity." [68]

The Yugoslav compensation structure has a higher proportion of "fringe benefits," and the basic wage rates constitute a lower proportion of total compensation than in any European country. Thus the nonwage elements of total cost constitute 47 percent of total labor costs in Yugoslavia compared to 42 percent in Italy, 32 percent in France, 27 percent in Germany (Federal Republic), and 11 percent in the United Kingdom.[69] In Yugoslavia wage supplements (social charges) constitute almost as much as the basic wage, including incentive wages. Obligatory social-security [70] contributions constituted 25.6 percent of total labor costs; subsidies for medical care, restaurants, building funds, recreational facilities, and the like amounted to 8.8 percent; hours paid for, but not worked (holidays and vacations), constituted 5.9 percent, and bonuses and gratuities which included the division of profits amounted to 5.6 percent of total labor costs according to this special study.[71]

The Yugoslav industrial-relations system [72] at a given time is to be understood in terms of the relationships among the principal actors—the workers' councils, the managing board, the director, and to a lesser extent the communes, the trade unions,

[68] "Edvard Kardelj's Answers to 'Unita' Correspondent," March 17, 1957, Reprinted in Supplement, Information Bulletin About Yugoslvia, Belgrade, Yugoslavija Publishing Enterprise, March 1957.

[69] "Wages and Related Elements of Labour Cost in European Industry, 1955: A Preliminary Report," International Labour Review, December 1957, Tables I, II, and XI.

[70] "Social Security in Yugoslavia," Bulletin of the International Social Security Association, May–June 1956, pp. 179–237.

[71] Ibid., Table 14, p. 42.

[72] International Labor Office, Report of the Committee on Freedom of Employers' and Workers' Organizations (McNair Report), March 6–10, 1956, Appendix II, pp. 1645–1685.

and the party. The functions performed by these actors and their status and relationships have gradually changed over the period since 1950. The evolving ideology [73] of the party and the objective problems of economic development (which largely constitute the technological and market context) have been the major factors shaping the institutions of the actors and their relationships within the national industrial-relations system.

Among the distinctive characteristics of the Yugoslav industrial-relations system are the group of rules concerned with: (1) the workers' management arrangements for making managerial decisions, establishing new rules, and administering existing rules at the work place, and (2) a wage system which involves profit (and loss) sharing by the workers.

A review of the elaborate compilation of rules for Yugoslav enterprises indicates these two complexes of rules are unique to the Yugoslavian industrial-relations system. Many other rules— such as those examined in coal mining and building construction —reflect the special technological and market characteristics of the particular industries; such rules may have some unique features, but they are broadly similar to rules developed in other countries for the same industries. The nationwide Yugoslav industrial-relations system is distinctive from other national systems, East or West, by virtue of the combination of the system of ideology and the problems of rapid industrialization in a relatively underdeveloped country. The status of its actors has now been defined by the larger Yugoslav society, and a distinctive national industrial-relations system is emerging although considerable evolution is to be expected both in the details of the structure of the system and in the body of rules produced.

The Yugoslavian industrial-relations system confronts all the issues faced by industrial-relations systems generally in economic development as they are set forth in Chapter 8. But a distinctive

---

[73] *Draft Programme of the League of Communists of Yugoslavia*, March 1958, Beograd, and *Changes in the Plan of the Programme of the League of Communists of Yugoslavia*, loc. cit.

contradiction is to be observed: the compatibility of centralized political leadership and decentralized industrial-relations decisions at the work place. The decentralization of wage setting, operating, training, and recruitment decisions to the enterprise, subject to centralized fiscal and monetary controls, necessarily tends in some degree to weaken centralized political dominance. Decentralized economic decision-making tends to decentralize political power.

The next two chapters are concerned with the evolution of industrial-relations systems in the course of economic development more generally.

8 · The Development
of National Industrial
Relations Systems

A<small>N</small> industrial-relations system, it has been repeatedly stated, cannot be understood solely in terms of a structural cross section at one point in time. Comparative statics is not sufficient. Historical perspective and an appreciation of change through time are essential to the theory of industrial relations. The present chapter and the next elaborate systematically the significance of the path of development and its historical course upon the characteristics of national industrial-relations systems and upon the body of rules developed for work places and work communities.

The major characteristics of a national industrial-relations system appear to be established at a relatively early stage in the industrial development of a country, and in the absence of a violent revolution in the larger community, a national industrial-relations system appears to retain these characteristics despite subsequent evolution. It may be said that the dominant features which today characterize the industrial-relations systems of Great Britain, the United States, Scandinavia, Australia, and

New Zealand, for instance, were well established prior to the first World War. There have been some changes in administrative forms and in the accommodation among the actors, but most of the features which today distinguish these separate national systems were evident and widely commented upon a generation ago. In each case developments have come within an established pattern. It would also appear that the distinctive features of industrial-relations systems in India, Israel, the USSR, Yugoslavia, and Chile are even now fairly well established. The early stages of industrial development are decisive to the structuring of a national industrial-relations system.

The formation of a national-industrial relations system in a given country with a specified cultural heritage is not only to be related to the stage of economic development but also to the chronological period of history in which the formation of the system takes place. The characteristics of a national system taking form in the late 1950's may be expected to be quite different from one which congealed in the early 1900's, despite a similarity in the stage of economic development, by virtue of the differences in periods of world history and in the sequence of social changes within a country unrelated to economic development. A national industrial-relations system formulated with labor organizations which are an adjunct to a successful nationalist movement, which has secured independence, may be expected to show some characteristics different from systems in which national independence antedated the union movement or in which the union movement played a minor role in the nationalist movement. The relations between the labor organization and the government or the party of independence, and hence the status of these actors in the emerging industrial-relations system, may be expected to be quite different in these two types of situations.

The three following sections consider in turn the effect of the chronological period, the sequence of social changes, and the process of economic growth upon the development of a national industrial-relations system. The remaining sections of this chapter then examine the major problems or decisions that arise in the emergence of every national industrial-relations system.

The events of history shape an industrial-relations system in important ways, and two countries with similar resources and even similar cultural backgrounds, and at similar stages of economic development, but starting to industrialize at different historical periods, may be expected to develop quite different industrial-relations systems. Different dates of origin must be considered in any comparison of industrial relations systems.

THE PERIOD OF FORMATION OF A SYSTEM

1. *Post-Soviet systems.* National industrial-relations systems established before the Soviet revolution may often show differences from those established after the rise of the USSR. In new noncommunist national industrial-relations systems, the relations of labor organizations to the government may be arranged to seek to insure against capture by the Communists and against subversion. The status of trade-union organizations and their relations to government in Brazil, Egypt, and Greece, for instance, has been substantially shaped in order to prevent the Communists from capturing the government-favored labor organizations. Only noncommunist organizations may be registered or recognized by the government. In other countries, at early stages of development, labor organizations may be effectively suppressed for fear of Communist influence.[1] Among more developed countries with a strong Communist labor movement (outside the Eastern European bloc), the status of competing labor organizations in the industrial-relations system may be organized to cope with the Communist challenge. Thus, the multiple representation in France in the postwar period, and the nonliteral construction of "most representative union" to permit a number of unions, is derived in part from the strong position of Communist unions

---

[1] It is to be recognized, of course, that in some countries this excuse may be a pretense to prohibit all union organizations.

and the desire to encourage the *Force Ouvrière* (F.O.) and *Confédération Française des Travailleurs Chrétiens* (CFTC).[2] Among countries in the Communist bloc, the role of the trade union in treating with workers is largely an instrument of the party.

The central point is that the rise of Communist organizations, nationally and internationally—with a special interest in the capture and direction of labor organizations—has created a new feature to the structuring of an industrial-relations system. In noncommunist countries it has led to, or provided an excuse for, increased governmental surveillance of labor organizations and in Communist countries the use of labor organizations as an instrument of party policy and party education among workers.

2. The ILO. The promulgation of a comprehensive group of conventions and resolutions by the International Labor Organization (ILO) has had a greater effect upon shaping industrial-relations systems at their most sensitive and formative stage in many countries than has ordinarily been recognized, particularly in the United States. The reference is to international instruments (and the International Labor Code) on the rights of organization, freedom of association, collective bargaining, collaboration at the plant level, and the resolutions of industry committees which deal with the status of workers and managers even more than to those documents concerned with minimum economic and social conditions.[3] While one needs always to be on the alert to distinguish actual practice from formal profession, these declarations of workers' rights have had considerable influence in many instances in shaping the formal relations among the actors, particularly among the countries with industrial-relations systems

[2] Adolf Sturmthal, Ed., *Contemporary Collective Bargaining in Seven Countries,* Ithaca, N. Y., Cornell University, 1957, pp. 130–134, 143.

[3] Conventions nos. 29 (Forced Labor), 81 (Labor Inspection), 87 (Freedom of Association and Protection of the Right to Organize), 88 (Employment Service), 98 (Right to Organize and Collective Bargaining Convention). International Labor Conference, *Conventions and Recommendations, 1919–1949,* Geneva, 1949; also see, International Labor Office, *The International Labor Code 1951,* Geneva, 1952, vol. I, pp. 675–715.

taking decisive form in the past ten or twenty years. The drive for economic development and against backwardness often includes the adoption of the forms of modern labor legislation.[4] The appeal to the international instruments in shaping a national industrial-relations system particularly among smaller countries is a relatively new factor.

3. *Government as employer.* Governments have been playing a larger role as employers in many countries where national industrial-relations systems are being established. The government as an employer, directly in public utilities, military establishments, and executive departments or more indirectly in corporations, development projects, and nationalized industries, exerts a greater influence on the formation of the national industrial-relations system than would be the case if government activity were confined to a more limited range of functions. A national industrial-relations system at the formative stages today is more likely to be influenced by government than previously since the government enters the system, not merely as sovereign, but often as the largest single employer of industrial labor. The status accorded to workers, the procedures for disputes settlement, and the quality of personnel practices and human relations may well come to have a significant influence on the emerging national industrial-relations system. The significance of this factor is relatively new in shaping national industrial-relations systems.

4. *Rise of professional management.* The rise of professional management as contrasted to family management is a relative new force on emerging national industrial-relations systems. In newly industrializing countries management is often backward

---

[4] The *Legislative Series* of the ILO provides a very useful compilation of statutes and legislative enactments, but there is no systematic publication of agreements or other forms of achieving the same results on corresponding subjects. Thus, when Germany (F.R.) enacted a statute on workers' councils, the Office carried the text in the *Legislative Series*. When Sweden and Italy established workers' councils by agreement between organizations of workers and managers, the series did not include the text. The form of the rules of an industrial-relations system should not so affect their systematic compilation.

in the handling of workers. It may even be harsh and cruel. "Modern management in India has been slow in changing in response to the protest and challenge presented by the growth of the Indian labor movement, by the partially committed industrial work force, and by evidences of labor indiscipline." [5] But some foreign enterprises have been started in developing countries with modern personnel policies; government development enterprises have used management experts and technical assistance, [6] and some professional management is emerging. There are, of course, great differences among managers in all industrializing countries, as there have always been since the days of Robert Owen. While the picture is very spotty, there is growing interest among managers in the status of workers, in collective relations, in eliminating unrest, and in meeting aspirations of the emerging industrial workers. To the extent that this professional type of management emerges, industrial-relations systems may be expected to be characterized by lesser tensions and protest and more orderly machinery for disputes settlement. Each new labor movement does not have to fight through in the same way the same issues that confronted the early British unions.

There are thus at least four ways in which the formation of an industrial-relations system today may be different from that of an earlier generation, apart from the stage of economic development: the Communist influence in labor organizations, the normative standards for labor-management-government relations symbolized by the International Labor Organization, the larger role of governments as a consequence of being a major employer of industrial labor, and the emergence in some places of a new type of professional management in the handling of workers and their organizations. This is a new atmosphere or setting in which national industrial-relations systems arise as compared to a generation or more ago.

[5] Charles A. Myers, *Labor Problems in the Industrialization of India*, Cambridge, Mass., Harvard University Press, 1958, p. 93.

[6] "ILO Productivity Missions to Underdeveloped Countries," *International Labour Review*, July and August 1957.

THE SEQUENCE OF NATIONAL SOCIAL CHANGES

The sequence of certain major structural changes in a country is significant to shaping the relations among the actors in a national industrial-relations system. There are likely to be significant differences in the status of the actors in the following circumstances: (1) if national independence, including military victory, is secured prior to the rise of a labor movement, or the labor movement is seriously involved in the struggle for independence; (2) if the political status of workers and their organizations is already established when they first appear, or this recognition becomes a major objective of labor organizations and a favor to be disbursed by the leaders of the industrializing drive, and (3) if labor organizations spread gradually with industrial development, or they only later catch up with entrenched and established management. In a sentence, the timing of the national, political, and industrial "revolutions" in a country relative to the rise of the labor movement may be expected to influence the characteristics of the national industrial-relations system.

1. *Labor movements and national independence.* In many countries that have gained national independence in the past several decades labor organizations have played a significant role in the drive for independence. In the unique instance of Israel it may be said that Histadrut was a joint founder of the nation. This relationship between the labor organization and government has created a distinctive industrial-relations system. In India, and to some extent in Ghana, the labor organizations were in large measure an arm of the nationalist movement. In such circumstances, the experience of successful struggle for independence or military victory (refer to the Yugoslav experience) is likely to establish a close and a strong tie between a government or ruling party and a labor movement. In this situation a rival labor organization is not likely to be accorded status. The common experience of the "struggle for independence" may

be expected to give a distinctive coloration to the emerging industrial-relations system as compared to a country where independence (or military victory) were achieved without or prior to the rise of a labor movement.[7] Compare Israel and India in this respect with the Philippines, Turkey, or most South American countries.

The position of managers at the time of independence will also be significant to establishing the relations and statuses among the actors. If managers are primarily foreigners or allied with antinationalist forces, and the labor organizations are a part of the independence movement, the national industrial-relations system may well show the further imprint of this condition.

2. *Status of labor.* In a number of national systems the emerging labor organizations historically had difficulty in establishing their legal position and achieving a status for individual workers; they were bucking a traditional society in addition to seeking recognition and status in the plants from managers. They had to struggle for suffrage, public education, and social legislation. In other national systems the emerging labor organizations found that a social and political revolution had already transformed an old society or that a new and more pliable society was more congenial. When labor organizations have to fight for political and social status, the industrial-relations system may be expected to reflect a greater degree of formal political organization and resort to influence public policy. The experience of France, Italy, and Japan is instructive in this respect as compared to that of the United States. Some countries now beginning to create an industrial work force have apparently still to confront a political or social transformation. Aspects of the experiences of South Africa, Spain, and the Persian Gulf area come readily to

---

[7] In underdeveloped countries nationalist movements play the role of transforming local and regional groups into members of a national society. The centrifugal forces are often very strong. Bert F. Hoselitz, "Nationalism, Economic Development, and Democracy," *Annals of the American Academy of Political and Social Sciences,* May 1956, pp. 1–11.

mind, and their industrial-relations systems are (or are likely to be) characterized by a different relation and a different status among the actors than in systems in which the political and social status of workers and their organizations was early recognized or did not become a major struggle for workers.

3. *Growth pattern of labor organizations.* An industrial-relations system may be expected to be influenced according to whether organization among workers and managers proceeds gradually, more or less in step with the growth of industrialization, or is retarded and then suddenly emerges, transforming large sectors of industry. Such wholesale transformations may also take place following a war or revolution. The postwar reorganizations in the Netherlands, Germany, Yugoslavia, Japan, and Italy are illustrative. When transformation proceeds by such major breakthroughs rather than by more gradual processes, there is likely to be more centralization, and less regional and industrial autonomy, in the industrial-relations systems. There is a lesser number of national labor and management organizations, and they tend to be organized on an industrial and multi-industry basis rather than on a craft or multicraft basis. The role of the government as an actor is enhanced. In one case the industrial-relations system just grows up while in the other it is more deliberately fashioned or refashioned.

The characteristics of a national industrial-relations system, including the status and the relations among the actors, is seen to be influenced by the historical time of its emergence and by the sequence of its national, political, and industrial "revolutions."

THE PROCESS OF ECONOMIC DEVELOPMENT

Every industrializing country, whatever its technical and market context and however early or late its industrialization, establishes a national industrial-relations system. This is ordinarily a gradual process in which the early stages (or those immediately following a war or revolution) are likely to be decisive for the eventual characteristics of the national system. But the process of economic development also molds the emerging system.

In the course of industrialization all the actors in the emerging industrial-relations system gradually undergo changes that affect their status and relations within the system. The principal changes among workers, managers, and governments that directly affect industrial relations are the following.

1. Individual workers who are not committed at the outset to industrial and urban life tend to become a more stable work force with less turnover and absenteeism. There is less attempt to return to agriculture, to the village, and to the extended family; there is more reconciliation with permanent membership in an industrial work force and probably less idealization of escape to the middle class, management, or the professions. A common body of ideas, more or less formalized, comes to be accepted, defining the place of the industrial worker in the new society.

2. Workers' organizations that first emerge tend to be weak, poorly organized, and financed. Gradually they tend to organize a larger proportion of the industrial work force; these organizations have more resources, and they come to be headed by able leaders making a career of labor organizations. These leaders come to exercise wide administrative and executive functions.

3. Managers at the outset are often poorly trained; they do not understand the building of organizations, and personnel and human relations receive almost no attention. Gradually professional managers emerge in privately or publicly owned enterprises, and they tend to become more sensitive to the task of building organizations and of handling workers.

4. The process of industrial development appears to create gradually a larger number, and apparently also a larger proportion, of skilled workers and technicians with considerable responsibility, as well as managerial, administrative, and professional staff. The technology of industries changes, requiring a more highly trained work force.

5. The role of government in the emerging industrial-relations system tends to expand with government becoming both a significant employer (and purchaser) and a regulator and conscious policy maker of the outlines of the system and of the mutual interrelations of workers, managers, and government.

6. At the earliest stages, the tensions and protests of workers against grievances and the new industrial life are more likely to take the form of individual action, the impulse to quit, absenteeism, violence, and the occasionally spontaneous informal group reaction. As industrialization proceeds, more formal procedures arise, and work stoppages or threats of strike and the control of such power become a matter of organizational discipline.

7. In the process of industrialization an expanding web of detailed rules of the work place are established. They constitute a veritable government of the work place which is more or less public government; or a complex of procedural rules arises which receives governmental sanction.

THE DECISIONS OF THE INDUSTRIALIZING ELITE

Each national industrial-relations system, the preceding discussion has argued, is shaped by the particular technological and market context, by the period in history in which industrialization arises, by the sequence of national, social, and political developments, and by the process of economic development. A final decisive influence on the evolution of a national industrial-relations system is the broad strategy of the elite directing the industrialization program of the country. While the end result is industrialization in each case, the policies, methods, and rates of change vary with the program of the leaders of the drive for economic development. These differences in strategy have significant consequences for an emerging national industrial-relations system.

While there is a broad spectrum of strategies, three main types can be distinguished. It must be borne in mind, however, that the rich variety of industrializing societies is not to be arbitrarily ordered into three rigid types. These classifications are an aid to understanding and not a description. They do not directly refer to any particular country in its entirety; the actual experience within a country may illustrate all three types in various proportions. These three strategies are ideal types, and actual experience shows many shades and variants. But these ideal types help to highlight the major forces at work. The three types of industrializing elites (developed in detail elsewhere) [8] may be briefly characterized as follows:

1. *Dynastic-feudal elite* is drawn from the landed or commercial aristocracy; it is oriented toward the past; it cherishes the family, the church, the military, and the national state; industrial progress is no faster than necessary to meet the pressures placed on the elite.

2. *Middle-class elite* is typically drawn from a minority commercial group; it is in conflict to a degree with both the old order and the new industrial workers; it cherishes a release from old restrictions in order to free private initiative; it exalts the market and creates a pluralistic society, and growth is determined by individual incentives.

3. *Revolutionary-intellectual elite* is self-appointed to sweep away the old order and to push industrialization at the fastest possible pace; it relies on an ideology which regards the new industrial society of its design as inevitable; the managerial state is the instrument for creating the industrial order.

Such divergent types of leaders of the industrializing process would be expected to create quite different national industrial-relations systems even in the same environment, period of history, and phase of economic development.

The consequences of these different elites for a national industrial-relations system is most clearly seen by considering ten

[8] *Industrialism and Industrial Man,* unpublished manuscript, Chapter 3. This volume is to constitute a final report of the Inter-University Study of Labor Problems in Economic Development.

of the major questions or issues which confront every architect or analyst of an industrial-relations system. The decisions on these questions frequently are made by countless trials and errors, but they require a certain degree of internal consistency for a system to persist. A national industrial-relations system develops as the directing elite of the larger society confront these common questions and gradually formulate a body of more or less consistent answers in practice.

1. *What are to be the relations of managers to workers?* This question concerns not only attitudes but also policies and arrangements. Where the dynastic-feudal elite directs industrialization, managers regard workers in a highly paternal manner. The worker is treated as dependent upon the leadership and guidance of the manager not only in the plant but likewise in local community affairs. The rules of the work place (see Chapter 9) typically provide for family allowances, housing, and elaborate social security, and managements are expected to provide discretionary assistance in time of acute personal need or family crisis. Management authority is personal and frequently extensive and absolute, but it is tempered by a paternal concern for the welfare of local workers and their families. In the community the government adopts a paternal attitude toward the emerging industrial workers.

Where industrialization is led by the middle-class elite, managers tend to regard the act of employment as little more than a market transaction; managers and workers stand in the relation of buyers to sellers. The manager envisages little, if any, responsibility for the worker or his family in the community outside the work place. The worker is regarded as free and independent. The rules of the work place typically tend to provide for a higher proportion of compensation in the form of wages with fewer allowances and thus greater discretion for the worker in the expenditure of income. Management authority is more qualified and limited by rules of the work place. It is exercised less personally and is more subject to rules and procedures of the work place even when managerial authority is extensive. In the community the government regards the emerging industrial worker as an independent citizen rather than as a ward.

Where the industrialization process is under the control of the revolutionary intellectual, managers see the individual workers as instrumentalities of achieving the assigned share of the national plan. In the plant workers as a group are treated paternally, and the rules of the work place typically provide for extensive social benefits. The system is paternal by its rules but not by the discretion and intervention of the individual manager. Management authority is impersonal through a system of rules imposed from without the plant; it is extensive and absolute. In the community the ruling party regards the emerging industrial workers as uniquely subject to its guidance and leadership.

2. *What are to be the relations of workers to managers?* What attitudes are industrial workers expected by the elite to take toward managers? In a consistent industrial-relations system this question or decision is the converse of the first. The dynastic-feudal case is characterized by the personally dependent worker. The individual worker is expected to look to the paternal manager for guidance in personal economic and social problems; community affairs are not to be his concern. There is no preoccupation with raising the general level of public education.

The middle-class case is characterized by the independent worker. There are extensive resources devoted to free public education designed to raise rapidly the levels of general education, as contrasted to specialized technical training. While the individual worker is required to follow the directions of management in the plant, within a system of rules his personal affairs are his own concern, and in community affairs his vote is the equal of the manager.

The revolutionary-intellectual case is characterized by the dependent worker as a class. The educational system is designed to train specialized skills required by the industrial machine rather than for general education. Industrial workers are to be subject to managerial direction which in turn is an expression of the elite leadership. The personal conditions of individual workers are not the concern of managers, but the system of rules for common problems are paternal. In community affairs the dependent worker is to follow the leadership of the party.

3. *What is the function of workers' organizations?* The dynastic-feudal elite does not in principle encourage workers' organizations. At the plant level any organization frequently supplements and may help to administer the paternal activities of the managers but provides little effective constraint on the decisions of management. At the industry level the organization of workers provides a broad form of minimum regulation which the managers often find congenial to the support of cartels or associations. These standards have little relevance to actual plant conditions, and there is little connection between the plant level and the industry level of workers' organizations. In the society led by the dynastic-feudal elite, political organizations of workers emerge which often have only indirect connections with the plant and industry levels of workers' organizations and which seek to enact narrowly regulatory legislation to offset plant and industry-level weaknesses and division. These political organizations frequently arise to challenge the established elite.

The middle-class elite is more readily reconciled to the principle of workers' organizations and supports the principle of their affirmative public value. At the plant and industry level the organization narrowly regulates management. There is closer coordination and often direct lines of authority in these workers' organizations between the industry and plant level; in some systems this authority extends to a single national center, at least on some questions. The political organization of workers is less concerned with detailed regulation of managements and more preoccupied with community issues. The middle-class elite regards such organized political activity as legitimate, and the workers' political organizations are less dedicated to challenge or to displace the industrializing elite.

The revolutionary-intellectual elite regards organizations of workers at the plant or industry level as its own preserve. The purpose of the workers' organizations is less to constrain managements than to educate, to stimulate production, and to lead the industrial workers on behalf of the ruling elite (party). Independent political organization or activity is precluded except through and under the direction of the party.

4. *How much competition takes place among workers' organizations?* In the traditional society led by the dynastic-feudal elite there are frequently deep social distinctions and religious and party divisions among workers. There tends to be multiple representation at the plant level, as in workers' councils, and at the industry level, as in negotiations for agreements signed by several overlapping workers' organizations. Among these organizations at the plant and industry level, and in political activities, there may be keen rivalry and competition. In the absence of exclusive jurisdiction or representation, the rivalry is limited since it need not end in extinction for one of the competitors. Changing conditions lead to shifts in workers' support, but the existence of the organizations is not endangered. There may also be keen competition between organizations at the plant level and national labor organizations (or labor fronts) over the distribution of functions. Any competition among workers' organizations is lamented; it is tolerated as an unavoided consequence of historical divisions among workers.

In the society led by the middle-class elite there is typically supposed to be one workers' organization for each type of worker by craft or industry. There tends to be severe competition among contending organizations since the triumph of one means the loss of recognition to the rivals among a particular group of workers, at least for a period. A degree of competition among workers' organizations, however, is regarded as an affirmative good to stimulate more responsiveness to the wishes of the workers on the part of organizations. There is relatively little overt competition, however, between organizations over the distribution of functions at the plant and industry levels, although there is internal tension in workers' organizations over the extent of centralization or decentralization of functions.

In the society led by the revolutionary intellectual there is no room for competition between contending workers' organizations at the plant level nor is there any contention over functions to be performed by rival workers' organizations. Since the organization of workers is an instrument of the ruling party to educate and to lead workers, discordant tones serve no purpose and are not tolerated. A degree of tension may arise between plant-level representatives and those higher in the hierarchy. Competition among workers' organizations, however, is seen only as an evil, weakening the regime.

5. *What shall be the structure of the labor movement?* The labor movement under dynastic-feudal-led industrialization tends to build industrial unions to provide minimum regulation on an industrial basis, without a direct line of organizational control at the plant level. The labor organization is constricted on the one hand by plant bodies over which it has little, if any, control and the political organs which seek regulative legislation. The labor union or labor front operates in a relatively narrow corridor between the plant organization and the political party. This corridor helps to shape its structure. There is strong internal confederation control which may be further limited by rival confederations.

The labor movement under the middle-class-led industrialization tends to build a variety of unions: craft, industrial, and general. The range of functions of these organizations is broad, not constricted by other forms of labor organizations. The diversity of structure represents a response to a gradual historical development, to a lesser degree of confederation centralization, and to a greater responsiveness to the preferences of particular sectors and groups of workers. It also reflects an economy with more reliance upon the market mechanism under which the pattern of union growth may have had to conform to market contours to survive. The powers of the confederation often tend to be lesser than in the other ideal types; the principles of decentralization and autonomy are highly regarded values.

The labor movement under the revolutionary-intellectual-led industrialization tends to create a limited number of industrial unions with a high degree of centralization over district and local groups and at the confederation level. This structure also reflects the function of the unions: to serve as the organ of education and communication between the party and the industrial worker and to stimulate industrial output. This narrow range of functions reflects no competition from other organizations of workers but rather a design in which the party and the state in substance fulfill the functions of regulating or constraining managers which is elsewhere performed by labor organizations. This type of organizational structure may be vulnerable to the rise of plant-level labor organization from below.

6. *How shall labor organizations secure their funds?* The operation of a labor organization, as any other, is much influenced by the funds at its disposal and the source of its resources. The industrial-relations system is accordingly affected. In the country led by the dynastic-feudal elite, the labor movement tends to be relatively poorly financed. There are a variety of competitors for support by the workers—the work-level organization, the labor union, and the political party—and their access to workers for funds is not often coordinated. The paternal characteristics of the system are not congenial to large dues payments. The focus of the society around the church, state, and family is not congenial to the financial support of vigorous voluntary associations. The labor organizations do not place a high preference upon building strong financial positions. At times the government may provide some resources in the form of buildings, a subsidy for the performance of labor exchange, or social-insurance services, or in some cases may pay the salaries of leaders who also fill some nominal public function; the elite is concerned in this

way to secure ties to the leadership of the workers' organizations.

In the country led by the middle-class elite, the labor movement tends to be relatively well financed by dues regularly collected from the membership. The labor organizations seek to build strong financial positions, partly to provide more effective services to the members and partly to provide security in case of a struggle with management. The labor organizations typically receive little, if any, support or subsidy from government (save in a few cases related to social services), and financial independence from government is a cherished value. The emphasis upon regulatory functions of the labor movement, in constraining management through establishing and administering rules, operates to create modern administrative organizations which require large-scale budgets.

In the country led by the revolutionary-intellectual elite, labor organizations are relatively well financed by dues assessments levied upon all workers. The organizations are particularly well supplied with buildings appropriate to their status as an arm of the regime. Finances and resources are no problem.

7. *What is to be the source of labor leadership?* Every labor movement confronts, more or less explicitly, the problem of where it shall recruit its leadership. It may be drawn from the ranks or from intellectuals outside the organizations, or it may be imposed from a party or subject to governmental approval. A persistent characteristic of labor leadership affects the operation of the industrial-relations system. The leadership of the labor movement in the dynastic-feudal-led country tends to be drawn relatively more from intellectuals and those ideologically oriented toward political activities. The activities of the labor unions are primarily at the industry and national level, rather than at the plant level, and such interests attract relatively the more intellectually oriented. The emphasis upon social policy and law places a relative premium upon learning. The absence of plant-

level problems decreases the need for leadership more familiar with the actual work processes of plants. An educational system which does not provide a high level of free general education increases the relative advantage of and need for intellectuals in labor organizations. The income of such leaders may not always depend solely upon the labor organization but may be based also upon political activity, legal practice, journalism, and other activities. It should not be inferred that leaders do not rise from the ranks, but the dynastic-feudal arrangements tend to favor the intellectual type for labor leadership.

The leadership of the labor movement in the middle-class-led country tends to be drawn almost exclusively from the ranks of workers. The predominant concern with rules constricting managers and the direct interest in the immediate work place necessarily place a premium upon leadership seasoned in the practical operating problems of enterprises. The more direct organizational tie between plant and industry or confederation levels of workers' organizations creates more of a ladder in which leadership starts at the bottom. Full-time officers arise who regard the labor organization as a career; they are in a sense professionals or bureaucrats of the labor movement.

The leadership of the labor movement in the revolutionary-intellectual-led country tends to be drawn from reliable party leaders many of whom have devoted a career to the work of the party in labor organizations. They are financially secure and are in a sense (with a different type of assignment) professionals or bureaucrats of the labor movement and the party. They are concerned with the administration and implementation of policy and ideology developed by the party.

8. *What attitude shall be adopted toward industrial conflict?* Is conflict to be regarded as only an evil or does it have benefits? Are strikes and lockouts to be permitted or always prohibited? Industrial conflict is abhorrent to the dynastic-feudal elite; it shatters the paternalistic view of manager-worker relations; it involves a moral crisis in which the workers are held to

be ungrateful, stubborn, and rebellious or managers to be insensitive and unjust. In the view of this industrializing elite, it is not so much the loss of production that condemns industrial strife but rather the shattering of the view held of the good industrial soicety. In this sense industrial strife has deeper consequences. Many industrial conflicts take the form of public demonstrations. At times the elite seeks to suppress conflict and demonstrations, particularly if the elite has strong military connections. More frequently it contains the conflict and makes just sufficient concessions to preserve its position.

Industrial conflict is regarded by the middle-class elite as little more than an extension of the market mechanism, a corollary of the freedom to buy and sell labor services. The failure to reach agreement on terms of sale as elsewhere in a market economy results in the withholding of goods or services or a refusal to purchase. Industrial conflict is seldom regarded as affecting the fundamentals of the society. Indeed, a certain amount of conflict has affirmative values: it stimulates private agreement without public intervention; it makes the parties more responsible for bearing the consequences of their decisions. The community is concerned to establish Marquis of Queensberry rules for industrial conflict and to prohibit only those conflicts which threaten health, safety, or national security.

Industrial conflict is repressed as completely as possible by the revolutionary-intellectual elite. Industrial conflict is condemned because it reduces industrial output which the elite is pushing at all costs; the country is held to be unable to afford the luxury of strikes. Industrial conflict would also shatter the view of industrial strife as a prerevolutionary state of affairs; there can be no conflict of interests between managers and workers in the new society. Industrial conflict is seen as a threat to the regime; industrial strife was frequently used by the revolutionary-intellectual elite in its seizure of power from the old regime, and it is regarded as a challenge to the ideology and power of the elite.

9. *How are disputes resolved and who holds the balance of power?* In all countries disputes between managers and workers may not be resolved directly, and there is governmental intervention. But there are differences in the characteristics of this intervention. The dynastic-feudal elite, confronted by industrial disputes, comes to create governmental machinery to compel adjudication of all disputes that might result in industrial conflict. Little attempt is made to strengthen settlement directly between managers and workers, and given other characteristics of the elite, such attempts would not likely be very successful. The decisions of the governmental machinery are substantive rather than procedural, and they tend to cover the full range of employment relations. The proceedings are frequently juridical, and the body of evolving rules is expressed in the legal concepts of the traditional legal system.

The middle-class elite adopts as its first principle the development of machinery between managers and workers to settle all disputes. Every effort is made to stimulate direct settlement. Private mediation and arbitration are extensively developed. When public intervention cannot be avoided, it tends to be procedural and seeks to take as many of the forms of agreement making between the parties as possible. Public opinion comes to play a significant role in major disputes. Governmental machinery is used to settle only a very narrow range of substantive issues of the employment relation, and frequently such machinery is *ad hoc*. Even where settlements take the form of decisions, they are frequently in fact the agreement, or have the consent, of workers and managers. The parties may play a large role in the establishment of the governmental machinery and in the selection of its personnel. The rules developed by government are likely to be expressed in pragmatic terms rather than in traditional legal concepts.

The revolutionary-intellectual elite establishes very much less labor-management machinery to deal with industrial disputes, and even this machinery is used infrequently. The differences of views and interests which result in formal disputes in other countries, including those between different organs of the regime, are typically settled by the party at the level in which the dispute arises or referred to higher levels in the ministries, trade unions, and party apparatus. The decisions of the party are substantive. Any formal decrees or decisions are expressed in the forms of the ruling ideology.

10. *What are to be the fields of interest of university specialists?* The characteristics of these different industrial-relations systems can be further highlighted by reference to the fields of research of university specialists seeking to understand and explain industrial relations. It may appear a little surprising, but the different interests of academic experts seem to be largely a reflection of their type of industrial-relations system. In the society led by the dynastic-feudal elite, law and social policy receive their major attention. The specialists, trained in a law school, have a legal background. Their interests, reflected in their publications, are centered on the concepts which give status to workers and managers and the governmental decrees and decisions which define their relations. It is law and decree rather than fact or analytical concept which occupy the university specialist.

In the system led by the middle-class elite, wages and the labor market are the center of attention. The specialists typically have an economics training. The central interest, reflected in their publications, is the determination of wages by managers and workers' representatives and the consequences for the economic system. The operation of the labor market and the private settlement of disputes are also regarded as key topics of research. It is the actual operation of the institutions, the decisions and analytical models of the economic and industrial-relations system, which are the preoccupation of the university specialist.

In the system led by the revolutionary-intellectual elite, labor productivity is the major topic. The specialists have typically been trained in Marxian economics and the ideology of the elite.

The central interest, reflected in their publications, is to understand the factors affecting labor productivity and to seek ways to increase this productivity. As in other respects, the educational and research system is functionally very directly related to the central objectives of the regime. The measurement of labor productivity and the interpretation of developments affecting workers in terms of the established ideology is the preoccupation of the university specialist.

The table which follows summarizes these ten questions and issues that confront every industrializing elite concerning its national industrial-relations system and the decisions which are to be expected from three idealized types of elites. These questions primarily involved labor organizations and the interrelations of managers, workers, and their organizations and governments. A detailed and specialized treatment of managers is presented elsewhere.[9]

The answers to these questions developed in one country are required to be more or less consistent and interrelated. The answers to one set of questions cannot be established without affecting others. The institutional arrangements must have a degree of inner unity; they constitute ingredients of a system. Thus, the leadership in the labor movement in the country with a middle-class elite must be drawn from the ranks if it is to fulfill detailed plant-level regulative functions; these administrative activities in turn are expensive and require an arrangement to raise a substantial amount of finances. The emphasis by this elite on the market mechanism as a regulator of economic affairs affects the basic functions of management and workers' organizations and has implications for the structure of the labor movement. The same conception influences the attitude toward industrial conflict and machinery for disputes settlement. Internal consistencies and internal dependencies are also to be found in national industrial-relations systems created under the leader-

[9] Frederick H. Harbison and Charles A. Myers, *Management in Industrial Societies*, New York, McGraw-Hill Book Company, 1959.

DECISIONS OF AN INDUSTRIALIZING ELITE ESTABLISHING AN INDUSTRIAL-RELATIONS SYSTEM

Issue	Dynastic-feudal Elite	Middle-class Elite	Revolutionary-intellectual Elite
1. What is the relation of plant managers to workers?	Paternal on a personal basis.	A market transaction.	Paternal according to rules.
How do the elites regard industrial workers?	Paternal wards.	Another citizen.	The special class to be led and guided.
2. What is the relation of workers to plant managers?	Personally dependent industrial worker.	The independent worker.	A class of dependent industrial workers.
3. What is the function of workers' organizations?	Social functions at the plant level; little constraint on management. Provides minimum industry condition to preserve relative market power of managements. Political activity is regulative in details of management and also challenges the elite.	Regulate management at the local and industry level. Independent political activity accepted. Does not challenge the survival of the elite.	Instrument of party to educate, lead workers, and to stimulate production. No political activity except through the party.
4. How much competition shall take place among workers' organizations?	Limited rivalry at the plant level and over the distribution of functions between the local and industry level. No exclusive representation.	Exclusive representation makes for keener competition. Some rivalry between plant and industry levels over allocation of functions.	No rivalry or competition allowed.

DECISIONS OF AN INDUSTRIALIZING ELITE ESTABLISHING AN INDUSTRIAL-RELATIONS SYSTEM (*continued*)

Issue	Dynastic-feudal Elite	Middle-class Elite	Revolutionary-intellectual Elite
5. What shall be the structure of the labor movement?	A relatively large number of industrial unions. A centralized confederation often limited by rival confederations. The unions perform a relatively narrow range of functions.	A variety of structural forms. The confederation is not as centralized as the other types. The unions perform a very broad range of functions.	A few industrial unions. A centralized confederation uninhibited by rivals. The unions perform a very narrow range of functions.
6. How shall labor organizations secure their funds?	Meager resources secured by dues which may not be regularly paid and by some indirect allowances from government. Financial success not highly regarded by labor organizations.	Substantial resources secured by regular dues; regulatory functions require administrative organizations and large budgets.	Substantial resources secured by assessments levied upon all workers; fine buildings; financial resources present no problems.
7. What is the source of labor leadership?	The intellectuals and those ideologically oriented toward political activities. Their income position may be insecure.	The ranks through lower levels of labor organizations. They have an established career.	Reliable party leaders with experience working in labor organizations. They have an established career.
8. What attitudes shall be adopted toward industrial conflict?	Industrial conflict is regarded as a moral challenge to the paternal view of industrial society. Conflicts often take the form of demonstrations.	Industrial conflict is an extension of the market; some conflict has affirmative value; society established rules of conflict.	Industrial conflict is regarded as a challenge to ideology and a threat to the elite. Industrial conflict is repressed.

9. How are disputes settled, and who holds the balance of power?	Government decisions are extensive and substantive. Decisions are expressed in the traditional legal system.	Great effort is made to secure settlement by workers and managers directly. Government intervention is often procedural, and substantive decisions are infrequent. Public opinion plays a major role. The language of decisions is pragmatic.	There is limited formal machinery which is not extensively used. The party determines unresolved issues. Decisions are expressed in terms of the ideology.
10. What are to be the fields of interest of university specialists?	Law and social policy; legal background to study decrees and formal relations.	Wages and the labor market; economic background; facts and analytical models.	Labor productivity; Marxian economic background; statistics and relation to ideology.

ship of the dynastic-feudal and the revolutionary-intellectual elites.

THE CHOICES OF THE UNDERDEVELOPED COUNTRIES

The industrializing elites, and the characteristics of the national industrial-relations system that each tends to create, have been presented as ideal types. No country actually has had precisely an elite with the attributed policies, and no industrial-relations system (apart from the influence of the technical and market context, the dates of its emergence, or the sequence of social changes) has developed an industrial-relations system completely patterned in all respects after such a model. Moreover, in many countries these programs for industrialization today are in competition with each other as are the inherent types of national industrial-relations systems. In many countries, despite dominant characteristics, there is a spectrum of experience drawn from different idealized types, and these divergent arrangements, attitudes, policies, and institutional forms are often in open conflict with each other. In the same country there may be sectors or industries that appear to be under the direction of a dynastic-feudal elite and others under the prototype of the middle-class elite. Other elements in the community may be trying to establish the leadership of the revolutionary intellectual. Contemporary France or Italy particularly well illustrate such disparities.

The idealized types of industrializing elites highlight the main choices confronting the underdeveloped countries now on the march, and the preceding list of questions helps to understand the intense debates under way in many of these countries concerning the national industrial-relations systems being fashioned. These debates not only are taking place among governments, management, and worker representatives in a country, but within governments, management associations, and workers' organizations there are also often sharp differences of views. While a good many hybrids and new combinations of features of an industrial-relations system can be expected, the industrial-relations arrangements of a country require an inner consistency to operate and to persist. Each country must first choose its elite, or more accurately, contending elites struggle to control a country. Under the leadership of the successful elite the decisions of the industrialization process and the building of an industrial-relations system are confronted.

A brief review of the issues in labor-management relations in Ghana provides an application of the formal ideas and illustrates the range of questions and alternatives confronting labor leaders, managements, and governmental agencies as a new national industrial-relations system takes form through debate, pressures, struggles, and conflicts.

The British colonial administrators and private managers had fairly completely established industrial relations on the British pattern (middle-class elite). Even the labor movement was modeled on the British Trade Union Congress (TUC). Labor organizations with a combined membership said to be 100,-000 exist in government employment, mining, building, trade, the docks, railroads, oil distribution, and other sectors. The labor movement became allied with the Convention People's party (CPP) and the nationalist movement, and its economic strength through general strike action was used to further the objectives of national independence. Since independence the top leadership of the labor movement and the government have been considering the appropriateness of the present system of industrial relations. There are few, if any, major domestic employers.[10] In some nationalist thinking the system must be changed solely because of its antecedents; among others there is genuine concern whether the inherited arrangements are most

[10] For a careful assessment of the possibilities of economic development, see W. A. Lewis, *Report on Industrialisation and the Gold Coast,* Accra, Gold Coast, Government Printing Department, 1953.

appropriate to Ghana conditions. "Shall we allow the opportunity we now have of making a new start to pass away or will the labour movement accept the challenge and release our minds from the slavery to the British traditional way of doing things to be able to develop our own African personality and our own African way of organizing workers?" [11] The insistent questions concern the organization of the labor movement, the role of governmental methods of disputes settlement, and the extent of private or public management in a country seeking economic development; there is urgent debate over the form and role of the labor movement, labor-management relations, and government labor policy.

The issues may be highlighted by the changes proposed by John K. Tettegah, general secretary of the Ghana TUC, in the established system of voluntarism patterned after the British.[12] He urges legislation requiring all employers to bargain with a majority union; he favors governmental certification and determination of unfair employer practices. He favors compulsory government determination of all disputes. In his view the government registration of small unions has led to a weak union structure, and he originally favored consolidating all unions into one; a program of consolidating the more than 50 unions into 16 was approved by the TUC. He advocates legislation for compulsory checkoff payable to the TUC with amounts to be paid from the TUC to finance the separate unions. The government makes a contribution to workers' education which is expended largely for salaries of the officers of the Workers' Educational Association, who are also the leading officers of the TUC. Tettegah is a member of the executive committee of CPP and proposes continued close cooperation with this political party, the

[11] John K. Tettegah, "New Charter for Ghana Labour," p. 12, in Trade Union Congress (Ghana), *14th Annual Convention Town Hall, Cape Coast, 25/26th January 1958, Agenda & Reports.*
[12] See the above-cited document for large parts of this program. Also see "Mission to Organise Workers in Ghana," *The Ghana Worker*, February–March 1957, pp. 4–5, 18.

elected government. He seeks £200,000 for a TUC hall. He is deeply concerned with the question of what contribution the labor movement can make to national development, and he was impressed with Histadrut as a model despite the absence in the Ghana labor movement of managerial talent, high-level skills, and access to capital. There are some differences of views on some of these proposals within the Ghana TUC, particularly in regard to the organization of the labor movement.

The Ghana conditions help to highlight very sharply the hard choices which confront the development of an industrial-relations system in an industrializing country, particularly one which is proceeding under the direction of a middle-class elite, with more rather than less governmental direction of economic development. What functions are labor organizations, manage-ments, and governmental agencies to play in the evolving national industrial-relations system? The definition of the role of any one of the three actors necessarily defines the role of the other two. The following brief discussion is cast in terms of the functions of labor organizations in the industrializing countries. The implications for the role of management and the government are not otherwise separately stated.

The role of labor organizations prior to independence tends to be largely a part of the nationalist and independence move-ment. This was clearly the case in India. After a country has passed through the portals of political independence, the dilemma of the function of labor organizations (with a middle-class elite) arises with perplexing urgency. There is, of course, the purpose to "consolidate independence," to "liquidate the evil remains of colonialism," and to push for the more practical ob-jectives, in foreign firms particularly, of training local citizens to replace foreigners in managerial, technical, and highly skilled positions.

1. *Wages vs. Capital Formation.* The issue arises of the con-flicting claims of economic development for the country and im-mediately improved wages and other benefits for workers.

The nationalist labor leaders' dedication to economic development, which requires increased savings, conflicts with the labor organizations' declared purpose and their often promised pie in the sky, to provide immediately improved wages and working conditions.[13] Within some limits, higher wages may increase worker productivity, but this is likely to be a narrow and difficult range of wage policy to find.[14]

2. *Strikes vs. Production.* The nationalist labor leader must choose again on strike policy. Strike action tends to decrease production where successful and may make development investments less attractive to foreign investors, but strike action may be necessary to achieve economic objectives of the labor organization, to build disciplined labor organizations, and to keep interests of the membership.

3. *Grievance Handling vs. Discipline.* Individual workers and small groups in an emerging industrial work force feel they have numerous real or fancied complaints, grievances and frustrations. Industrial managers, be they private or public, are concerned to establish a web of rules including the pace of work and standards of discipline. The nationalist labor leader must choose in some degree between supporting the immediate reactions and grievances of workers or supporting the insistance upon higher standards of discipline, training and production which are vital to economic development.[15]

[13] Simon Kuznets, "Economic Growth and Income Inequality," *American Economic Review*, March 1955, pp. 1–28 and "International Differences in Capital Formation and Financing," in *Capital Formation and Economic Growth*, A Conference of the Universities—National Bureau Committee for Economic Research, Princeton University Press, 1955, pp. 19–106; Alexander Gerschenkron, "Notes on the Rate of Industrial Growth in Italy, 1881–1913," *Journal of Economic History*, December 1955, p. 372.

[14] Harvey Leibenstein, *Economic Backwardness and Economic Growth, Studies in the Theory of Economic Development*, New York, John Wiley and Sons, 1957, pp. 62–76.

[15] Walter Galenson and Harvey Leibenstein, "Investment Criteria, Productivity and Economic Development, *Quarterly Journal of Economics*, August 1955, pp. 343–370.

4. *Organizational Prestige vs. Political Subservience.* The labor movement is often long on political influence and short on economic power. It must consider the price of faithful support and dependence on a political party or government in terms of the benefits of governmental recognition and support in a variety of ways, including exclusive labor rights and discrimination against rival labor organizations and outright financial assistance. The immediate attractiveness of a strong legal position in dealings with employers, members, and rival organizations and financial solvency is to be weighed against the loss in independence of action in dealing with the government.

These basic policy decisions, which are most difficult for a labor movement in a country led by an elite in the spectrum of a democratic middle-class elite, present few difficulties for the labor movement under the revolutionary-intellectual elite. Economic development takes first priority over wage increases; production cannot be interfered with by strikes; labor organizations are to increase labor productivity, and they are always subservient to the party and government. There is a little more of a problem in a country under the dynastic-feudal elite, but in the main wages cannot be raised very much in the face of governmental policies, and strikes are little more than demonstrations. The labor movement cannot secure many concessions from the government or ruling party, although individual leaders or factions may secure benefits in exchange for political support.

It is easy to see why many leaders of industrializing countries and trade-union leaders find the choices posed above to be very hard, and they talk of ways to develop a trade-union movement which will make a more affirmative contribution to the national objective of industrialization. Neither the industrializing elite nor the leaders of labor organizations find congenial the traditional model of the "free trade union" drawn from advanced Western countries. ". . . . The trade union movement has a great part to play and a far wider task to perform than merely the safeguarding of the conditions and wages of its members." [16] The following statement made by an Indian expresses the same view in more detail.[17]

> . . . the role the trade union can most usefully play, may be as follows:
>
> 1. Co-operating with the state or private management to build up the foundations for industrial development;
> 2. Observing the self-imposed wage restraint on all levels;
> 3. Pursuing the members to give up extra-spendthrift habits of the labour class;
> 4. Encouraging small-savings among the classes;
> 5. Increasing the labour productivity through propaganda;
> 6. Settling the differences through the legally instituted machinery based on the principles of conciliation or/and arbitration;
> 7. Co-operating with the state and the Private Sector in maintaining industrial peace during the development period;
> 8. Helping the displaced labour thrown out of employment as a result of rationalisation by inducing them to take training in new skills in the institutions set by the Government or State management;
> 9. Initiating co-operative action in the enforcement of minimum wages;
> 10. Inducing the labour class to effectively participate in social security and provident fund schemes; and
> 11. Sharing in the profits on an acceptable basis which while apportioning a significant percentage of profit to labour will leave sufficient incentive to the management to plough the profits back in the industries they own.

---

[16] Dr. Kwame Nkrumah, prime minister of Ghana, quoted in R. B. Davison, "Labour Relations in Ghana," *The Annals of the American Academy of Political and Social Sciences,* March 1957, p. 139.

[17] Asoka Mehta, "The Role of the Trade Union in Underdeveloped Countries," *Problems of Economic Growth,* Conference under the Auspices of the Congress for Cultural Freedom, Tokyo, April 1–6, 1957, pp. 17–18. Compare this statement with Charles A. Myers, *loc. cit.,* pp. 70–92 and 156–172; Van D. Kennedy, "The Conceptual and Legislative Framework of Labor Relations in India, *Industrial and Labor Relations Review,* July 1958, pp. 487–505; Morris D. Morris, "Labor Discipline, Trade Unions, and the State in India," *Journal of Political Economy,* August 1955, pp. 293–308.

The debate and experimentation over the role of the labor organizations in recently industrializing countries is one of the focal points of the competition among groups for leadership in the process of economic development. It involves the congealing of a national industrial-relations system.

The first four chapters emphasized that an industrial-relations system was to be understood in terms of the technological context, the market or budgetary constraints, and the power relations or status among managers, workers (including their organizations), and the government. But this formulation must be supplemented to emphasize the process of growth and development of a system. (1) The technological and market contexts change with economic development. The status of the actors in an emerging national system of relations among managers and workers (including their organizations) and the government depends, in addition, upon (2) the historical period of formation of the system, (3) the sequence of the national, political, and industrial "revolutions," (4) the process of economic development, and (5) the characteristics and objectives of the elite leading the industrialization process. These five groups of factors are suggested as the analytical tools for the understanding of the evolution of a national industrial-relations system.

9 · Economic Development
and the Rules of
the Work Place

T HE problem of this chapter is the impact of economic development upon the complex of rules developed by an industrial-relations system for the work place and the work community. Is there any consistent way in which industrial growth impinges upon the rules created in a national system? What rules, if any, are likely to reflect systematically the path of economic growth? Can the history of substantive rules of the work place be related more or less uniquely to the course of economic development?

It was observed in Chapters 5 and 6 that many of the rules of a work place are related to specialized characteristics of the particular industrial-relations system. It would require detailed studies of the development of the complex of rules in a number of systems, in the course of industrialization, to test fully the problem posed by this chapter. A series of historical monographs on a comparative basis treating the evolution of rules in particular industries would be invaluable. Within the present limitations, however, attention is confined to the impact of economic development on several large groupings of rules which occur in some form in practically all industrial-relations systems: (1) the recruitment and commitment of a labor force, (2) compensation and wages, and (3) procedures for the settlement of disputes over the application of the existing complex of rules.[1] The problem is whether economic growth affects these rules in any orderly and consistent fashion in different national industrial-relations systems.

The rule-making process itself becomes more explicit and formally constituted in the course of industrialization. At the early stages, the very notion of a rule may be alien, and individual incidents are confronted without regard to their more general implications. The continuing experience of the same work place, the growth in its size, the continuity of the same workers, and the emergence of managerial employees tend to result in customs and traditions which begin to codify past practices. Eventually these may be reduced to writing in general form. Some rules may later emerge which anticipate problems rather than merely state past decisions. The statement of the rule then becomes more formal and elegant, particularly as specialists are developed in rule-making and administration. Thus, the very idea of a rule and a complex of related rules at the work place is itself a part of the process of economic development.

The process of economic growth also appears to bring more and more detailed rules and a larger body of explicit rules. Industrialization proliferates rules. A few rules become many, simple rules become complex, and a small document expands. Changing technology and markets produce new situations; higher compensation takes new forms; organizations of workers and managers develop new interests; a general rule invites loopholes and exceptions. The imagination of ordinary workers and managers, and the talents of their professionals in emerging organizations of growing size, help to create this growing complex of

---

[1] The distinction between disputes over the application of existing rules and disputes over new rules is not made in all industrial-relations systems.

rules. While there are periodic instances of codification and simplification, the dominant tendency is strongly toward a larger complex of rules.

THE RECRUITMENT AND COMMITMENT OF A LABOR FORCE

Every industrial-relations system must recruit workers (including managerial employees), train them, and make temporary and permanent layoffs at the work place. These three activities may constitute a minor or a major problem to managers and workers depending upon technological characteristics and the nature of product and labor-market constraints (see Chapters 2 and 3). The severity of these problems also varies with the fluctuations in the level of activity and the extent of economic development. As all industrial-relations systems develop, some body of rules emerges to govern the recruitment, training, and redundancy of the work force.

Recruitment

The creation of a work force presents no problems to managers unless two conditions obtain, and it is the struggle with such problems that creates a body of rules. When there are plenty of workers available in the required ranges of skill [2] and when workers are identical and can be substituted for each other, there are few problems of recruitment or hiring. Since both these conditions seldom occur for more than a short period, at least under modern technology, a body of rules respecting recruitment sooner or later emerges with industrialization.[3]

A variety of institutions and procedures are used to increase

---

[2] The supply schedule for labor is infinitely elastic. W. A. Lewis, "Economic Development with Unlimited Supplies of Labour," *The Manchester School*, May 1954, pp. 139–191, and "Unlimited Labour: Further Notes," *The Manchester School*, January 1958, pp. 1–31.

[3] Wilbert E. Moore, *Industrialization and Labor, Social Aspects of Economic Development*, Ithaca, N. Y., Cornell University Press, 1951.

the number of workers of the required skills when they are in short supply. Labor contractors have been used to import workers to labor-short countries or regions or to secure the movement of rural workers to cities, often when employment is for a limited period. The contractor may recruit from a large family, a common locality, or an ethnic group. The contractor often performs a variety of functions in addition to selecting and transporting the labor, including the establishment of rules relating to discipline, absenteeism, and compensation. Despite prohibitions, tribal leaders still perform the functions of labor contractors in some areas of Africa, Asia, and the Middle East; the practice was widespread in the past. Historically the recruitment of labor by such means often involved forced labor. "In the French Cameroons labour for the extension of the railway . . . was secured by a system of 'collective contracts' with Chiefs, a procedure which involved a definite form of compulsion. . . ." [4]

The desire of individuals to leave a village or the reserve temporarily in order to earn a sum of money for a specific purpose,[5] or the more advanced interest of individuals or families in more steady employment, or the push away from previous sources of livelihood have been the traditional ways in which an industrial work force has been recruited.

> Various factors operate to impel the African to take up employment outside the reserves—the pressure of land scarcity; the urge towards a higher standard of living; a preference for industrial employment; a craving for the advantages or, at least, the "trappings" of Western civilization; the need to pay taxes or "bride-price"; the desire to purchase trade goods. Few Africans, however, leave their reserves with any intention of cutting themselves off permanently from tribal influences and this consideration— the lack of any *intention* of permanency—must undoubtedly affect the African's whole approach to industrial employment.[6]

[4] H. M. Hailey, *An African Survey* (Rev. Ed.), London, Oxford University Press, 1957, p. 1363.
[5] The term "target workers" has been applied to such entrants to employment.
[6] Colony and Protectorate of Kenya, *Report of the Committee on African Wages*, Nairobi, The Government Printer, 1954, p. 11.

In still more advanced conditions, quickly adopted in many underdeveloped countries, employment exchanges are used to try to influence the flow of a work force. Under conditions of labor shortage, particularly because of location, enterprises may develop social services and housing to attract workers. When an enterprise has been in operation for a longer period, workers may be drawn from previous employees, from those on layoff status, and from children of existing employees. In all of these circumstances, rules are established governing the relations of the prospective worker with both the active agent seeking workers and the management of the work place.

When workers are not fully substitutable for each other, either in the judgment of managers or in their own eyes, then a group of rules arises concerning the choices to be made among types of individuals and groups of workers. Workers may not be interchangeable by virtue that some are more skilled or more productive or more desirable employees for the same job. Some individuals may be willing to work for less compensation than others. There may be differences among whole groups of workers, as among women, children, and men, or among racial, tribal, and ethnic groups, or between expatriates and local residents, or among former or laid-off employees and new workers, or between members of a labor organization and those who are not members. When these individuals or groups of workers are not regarded as interchangeable, a variety of rules (including compensation) tend to arise specifying the relative priorities or preferences in employment. What individual or class of workers shall first be assigned to a job? Which ones shall first be regarded as redundant? As among jobs of different skills (and compensation), what limitations or priorities shall apply other than the qualifications to perform work? In judging individuals for jobs, shall their present qualifications alone be considered or are potential qualities also to be taken into account? Thus, some jobs may be reserved for those of a certain age, sex, color, nationality, residence, or organizational affiliation, or these characteristics may be used as a basis for exclusions from jobs.

The most significant and explosive differentiation (nonsubstitutability) among groups of workers in countries at the early stages of industrialization has to do with race and nationality. The labor forces of different countries have been recruited in different ways, but the following types of situations are to be distinguished. (1) In some cases the manual and clerical work force is entirely domestic but a small group of expatriate managers and staff, who regard themselves as temporary residents, are recruited. This has been the case in British West Africa and the Belgian Congo. (2) In other cases the group of expatriates may be more extensive and include some skilled workers and a large staff, all of whom regard themselves as temporary residents. This case may often be an earlier stage of the first. This situation is illustrated by the Middle East oil operations in their earliest stages. (3) In still other cases the group of "expatriates" of one or more generations may be even more extensive and include the largest proportion of the skilled-labor force; the significant point is that they regard themselves as permanent residents rather than expatriates. The non-Africans in the Union of South Africa and the *colons* in Algeria are of this type.

In each of these cases elaborate rules tend to develop regarding the recruitment and access to skilled-labor and managerial positions; these rules are closely related to others regarding compensation, and there are characteristically two distinct scales of compensation and benefits. The third type of nonsubstitutability involves the largest number of points of potential conflict and involves the most detailed and elaborate set of rules. As in South Africa, stringent rules reinforce mores of segregation designed to confine a group to unskilled jobs and specified areas, and to regulate the movement of such workers through the pass laws. This third type of differentiation in the work force is clearly the most elaborate to manage in the course of industrial development.

In the recruitment of a work force from within underdeveloped countries or regions at early stages of industrialization, two different types of policies are reflected in the rules of the work place. (1) The manual work force is migratory or short term in its employment; it is typically comprised of a high proportion of target workers who leave the village or reserve temporarily for cash income. Typically these workers are alone; they temporarily leave their family connections, narrow or extended, in the village. The work place may provide lodging and even meals, and the wage scale is essentially a "bachelor's wage." Part of the wage may be withheld until the end of the contract period of employment. (2) The manual and clerical work force is more permanent; the object of recruitment is an immediate family rather than one individual. "In its broader sense stabilization involves the emergence of a type of worker who looks primarily if not exclusively to wage-earning for his own support and for that of his family, and is prepared to face the change in his customary mode of life which this demands." [7] The rules of the enterprise may provide family lodging or encourage "home ownership," and the compensation system is geared to the recruitment of an immediate-family unit rather than a "bachelor." These differences in policies of recruitment are necessarily reflected in different rules at the work place. Even within the limitations of the technology of one industry, such as mining, these different policies of labor recruitment have very significant implications for all aspects of the operations of an enterprise. Thus, the rules concerned with the division of work into discrete jobs and occupations, the issue of pensions, the procedures for training and promotion, and the type and standards of supervision are all affected by the basic choice between these recruitment policies.

The recruitment of an industrial labor force in the early stages of economic development is thus associated with the growth of a large body of rules concerned with securing an adequate num-

[7] H. M. Hailey, *loc. cit.*, p. 1387.

ber of workers and with establishing or recognizing certain differentiations among individuals or groups of workers. While this body of rules may be expected to vary with the type of elite leading the industrialization, general economic development may be expected to change these substantive rules. There follows a series of generalizations on the way in which rules of the work place and work community relating to the recruitment of a labor force are affected in the course of economic development.

The Effects of Economic Development

1. There is a tendency for the use of labor contractors to decline as industrialization proceeds, and the use of tribal chiefs or leaders of the extended family for the same purpose tends to disappear. The rise of urban areas, the decline in the degree of control of the tribal leader or labor contractor over his supply, and the high costs of labor turnover are among the immediate factors changing the contractor-hiring system as a recruiting device as economic development proceeds.

2. Early industrial recruitment may involve primary attention upon the single worker—a bachelor, a girl in industries with light work provided there are no cultural bars to women, and historically children. As industrialization proceeds, with longer periods of elementary education and with more stable industrial communities, recruitment is more likely to be based upon an implied commitment to continued employment; wage and employment rules are so geared.

3. Recruitment in the early stages of industrialization, at least by larger enterprises, is likely to involve the enterprise in a wide range of services, such as housing, medical services, canteens, schools, transportation and the like, which may be taken over in some degree by local communities as they become well established. Such services may have been indispensable to recruitment at the start, in the absence of well established facilities, but these activities and associated rules are likely to be

relinquished, at least in part, to more regular governmental machinery.

4. The differentiations among groups of workers that characterize the preindustrial society are likely to be carried over to the early stages of industrialization. These differences are likely to be significant to early recruitment. Priorities in employment may be based on racial and ethnic groups, sex, residence, and family. The industrialization process eventually tends to destroy most of these pre-existing differentiations in employment priorities, and it tends to create a new set of priorities and differentiations of its own, based upon a wide range of occupations and job classifications, nationality, or membership in labor organizations.

5. In former colonial areas the differentiation in employment rights between expatriates and nationals, particularly at managerial and staff levels, gradually tends to disappear and to be reversed; a larger and larger proportion of such positions are reserved for nationals. The programs of substituting nationals in Egypt, Ghana, India, and Iraq, for example, in the public service and in private enterprises has generally proceeded at a very rapid pace in the last five years; in Egypt it is largely completed. By and large these personnel transitions and changes have been made with surprising speed and with a minimum of dislocation for so major a change in the rules of the leadership sector in the work place.

6. The differentiation in employment rights between longtime "expatriate" residents and nationals in the skilled-labor occupations is likely to be the occasion for a continuing bitter struggle as industrialization proceeds. Economic considerations tend to eliminate such differentiation in order to increase the supply of skilled labor, but the political and cultural past desperately resists change. Industrial expansion inherently tends to revise the rules of the work place in the direction of integration.

7. Economic development on the whole tends to increase the

resort to recruitment from within the enterprise. Rules tend to develop favoring promotion from within an organization. Technical changes that might otherwise produce redundancy are increasingly timed to coincide with absorption of these workers elsewhere. The rules of the work community place increased emphasis and incentives upon the stabilization of employment.

Training

When workers are not readily hired to fill a vacancy, or the need cannot readily be met from the existing work force, then a group of rules may be expected to arise concerning training as a part of the procurement of a labor force. Some training may be done at the community or local level, but a work force is seldom available fully adapted to the needs of an enterprise. Hence, rules arise concerning probationary periods, physical examinations, apprenticeship, and a wage schedule with provisions for individual merit reviews, and mention should be made of the fancier indoctrination classes, general-education courses, training within industry programs, supervisory training, job methods, work study, and the like. Rules on discipline are also related to the standards for quality and quantity of work performance and are an integral part of a training program.

At the early stages of industrialization in the contemporary world, there is likely to be a very large gap between the skills and experiences required of workers in the emerging enterprises and those available in the general population of a country. This gap is greatest in the requirements of administrative and managerial skills. There are, of course, exceptions to this proposition to which Israel is the obvious instance of relatively high levels of skill in the population. It is the disparity between the demands for skill and the supply that leads to the importation of labor, particularly in selected skilled manual classifications and in managerial positions. The disparity also leads to intensive training within the enterprise at the early stages of industrialization when the requisite skills are not otherwise being produced in the community. It is another of the anomalous characteristics or "vicious circles" [8] of the early industrialization stage that there is least training in enterprises when it is needed most.

One of the pivotal questions in the procurement of an industrial labor force, for the enterprise or community, concerns the breadth of training or the degree of specialization of workers and technicians. They may be trained to perform only a few operations or a wide range of skills and activities. This decision is very closely related to the speed of development of the industrial work force and the priorities for immediate performance. Rapid industrializing countries tend to adopt a narrow and specialized training program for the work force, and a work force with limited training places greater responsibilities of coordination upon managements.

The training of an industrial labor force in the early stages of economic development is associated with the growth of a body of rules concerned with securing a more satisfactory work force from the perspective of managers. While this body of rules can be expected to vary with the type of elite leading the industrialization, and countries industrializing late may adopt advanced practices, the course of economic development may be expected to change these substantive rules.

Effects of Economic Development

1. Economic development increases the extent of formal training carried on within both the enterprise and the larger community. The technical character of industrial societies and the growth in size of enterprises requires this training.

2. Economic development transfers to the community some of the functions of general education and training developed by

---

[8] Gunnar Myrdal, *Economic Theory and Under-developed Regions*, London, Gerald Duckworth and Co., 1957, p. 11.

larger enterprises during the early stages of procuring a labor force. The rules of the work place come to specify higher and higher standards of general education and training available in the community.

3. In the early stages of economic development the enterprise pays great attention to the training of manual workers. In later stages the significance of supervision and the training of a managerial staff comes increasingly to be recognized; these positions become the center of training and development interests.

Redundancy

The concern with rules regarding temporary or more permanent redundancy implies some degree of development in an industrial-relations system. Managers may come to be concerned with the loss of workers and the costs of training new workers, and workers may be concerned with both insecurity and the issues of equity among different workers when there is to be a reduction in the working force. At the very earliest stages of industrialization few, if any, rules on redundancy seem to arise. There is typically a high turnover with a work force comprised of target workers, migratory groups, supplemental workers in extended families, and many workers only partially committed to industrial life.[9] Where the work force is largely drawn from urban areas, at the early stages of industrial experience for many workers, there may be a good deal of interchange with trading, handicraft, services, and the wide variety of partial employments and self-employed activities which characterize cities in underdeveloped regions.[10] Fluctuations in industrial employment at

[9] "Members of the recently created workers' council complain that the newcomers have no more got used to the rhythm and discipline of factory life than they have become accustomed to the ways of the town." "Poland Revisited," *The Economist*, October 26, 1957, p. 317.

[10] Bert F. Hoselitz, "The City, the Factory, and Economic Growth," *American Economic Review, Proceedings*, May 1955, pp. 166–184.

this stage are likely to be a common experience; no extensive group of rights has been developed in the industrial jobs, and fluctuations in activity are common in the wider community.

In the course of development, however, some of the workers become more committed to an enterprise or to industrial forms of employment; their ties with the larger family system and village are likely to become weaker, and a migratory pattern is broken. These changes may take place in a relatively few years in some cases, but in others they may require several generations. The central point is that sooner or later a group of workers looks forward specifically to return to work with the same enterprise. They feel a special tie to the enterprise. While managements may well have imposed rules on the order of redundancy in order to be rid of the least efficient workers, or those which have proved most troublesome, or those least servile, the workers subsequently come to express, by formal organization or by social pressure, preferences on the vital issues of priority in redundancy.

The rules that are gradually developed take a variety of forms: there is often provision for a minimum period of notice of any layoff; the distinction comes to be made between rules for temporary and permanent severance of the employment relation; hours of work or days of work may be varied, allowing the work force to share available work opportunities; certain probationary or temporary employees may be excluded from the rights created for longer-service workers; in the event of layoffs an explicit priority of rights is often established indicating the order in which different workers are to be laid off; workers in certain nationality, marital status, or sex groups may have to go first; there may develop specific prohibitions or limitations against layoffs, or rules for the payment of a proportion of wages, or the payment of a number of weeks of normal pay in the case of permanent layoffs (severance pay). A variety of rules arise applicable in the community generally; an unemployment-compensation system is such a group of rules.

The problems of laying off industrial workers tend to result in increasingly more detailed and elaborate rules as economic development proceeds. While this body of rules also may be expected to vary with the type of elite leading the industrialization, the course of general economic development changes substantive rules treating this problem.

Effects of Economic Development

1. The growing body of rules seeks to limit narrowly the range of managerial discretion in the order or priorities of layoffs.

2. The rules that are developed seek to make temporary layoffs increasingly expensive and to provide incentives to management to stabilize employment to a greater extent, at least for some categories of workers.

3. The rules increasingly tend to provide special compensation to long-service employees declared permanently redundant.

This section has been concerned with the procurement of a labor force, which is an essential function in every industrial-relations system, and with the associated body of rules to recruit, to train, and to determine redundancy. It might more conventionally be said that industrialization requires the creation of a labor market, or that economic development creates a labor market. But such a statement tends to neglect the elaborate system of rules which is erected in the labor market of any industrial-relations system. Labor markets are arranged in different ways, and it will be seen that different industrializing elites have different strategies for organizing the labor market. In any one country, the labor market may in fact be structured or subject to quite different rules on recruitment, training, and redundancy at different periods in the course of its economic development.

COMPENSATION AND WAGES

The rules of the work place and work community regarding compensation are a central feature of the total complex of rules; they are often related to a variety of other rules since affecting wage costs and workers' income is often an effective method to induce action on the part of managers and workers. As an illustration, seventh-day pay for six days of work in a week (but five days pay for five days work) was probably designed in oil-producing countries of the Middle East to discourage absenteeism, a sort of attendance bonus. The monthly contract in parts of Africa (Kenya) was no doubt designed to attract workers from the reserves for a stated period. The use of high overtime premium rates is often intended to distribute work opportunities and to discourage overtime work, and various elements of compensation are designed to stimulate regularity of employment. Premiums for undesirable or even hazardous working conditions are in part designed to provide an incentive to managements to eliminate or to control these aspects of work operations. Piece-rate methods of wage payment may be designed in part to meet the problems of incentives among workers and often in part to act as a substitute for direct supervision. Thus the full complex of rules on compensation reflect a variety of objectives of managers, workers (and their organizations), and governments; these rules are often an effective instrument, and so compensation provisions are in fact the focal point of a wide variety of problems.

The process of economic development not only creates labor markets, but it also fashions a complex of rules on compensation. While each elite leading an industrialization leaves its distinctive imprint on compensation arrangements (see the last section of the chapter), the general process of economic development has common discernible consequences upon the rules on compensation and wages in all national systems. This section considers the impact of economic development upon some of the major features of compensation.

Payments in Kind

At the early stages of industrialization the proportion of total compensation paid in kind, sometimes called "hidden emoluments," may be substantial. This proportion tends to decline with the growth of the industrial community so that in more developed communities the fraction is very small and may be confined to certain types of medical services and examinations. In very highly developed communities with progressive income taxes, significant payments in kind may return, at least for managerial and staff groups. (The different types of elites place different emphasis upon payments in kind.) In the early stages lodging for single men or housing for some family units, furnished by the enterprise, may be indispensable to recruit a labor supply to isolated localities or from reserves or to offset very serious shortages in housing in expanding urban centers. Thus 35 percent of all private industrial employees in Kenya in July 1953 were housed by their employers.[11] Where housing is furnished only to some employees, a housing allowance typically appears as an additional component in the money wage for workers not provided housing. The rules in the coal-mining industry (see Chapter 5) illustrate this arrangement. In the early stages the furnishing of meals or canteens as a part of compensation is quite common; the provision of food is likely to have a direct effect upon worker productivity where caloric intake is low and where diet is poor and unbalanced.[12] In the Belgian Congo "local regulations

[11] Colony and Protectorate of Kenya, *Report of the Committee on African Wages*, Nairobi, The Government Printer, 1954, Table 6, p. 190. The figure was 95 percent in Thika, 40 percent in Nairobi, and 10 percent in Mombasa. A housing allowance is required in addition to the minimum wage where employers do not furnish housing.

[12] Harvey Liebenstein, "The Theory of Underemployment in Backward Economies," *Journal of Political Economy*, April 1957, pp. 91–103.

now lay down balanced scales of diet and require employers to supply all manual workers and also their dependents with an authorised scale of rations in addition to the cash wage." [13] Payments in kind to Africans employed by Northern Rhodesia copper-mining companies averaged 45 percent in 1949 and 29 percent in 1955 of total earnings in cash and kind.[14] Payments in kind are frequently a carry-over from arrangements practiced for agricultural labor and migratory workers.

As development proceeds the value of payments in kind tends to be incorporated into the money wage, and even when these services are furnished by an enterprise there is often a charge for the services. The rise of communities around a work place and the greater role of local authorities, the heavy capital costs of tying up the funds of an enterprise in housing, the problems of housing with discharged, laid-off, or retired workers, and the diverse preferences of a larger work force are all factors tending to curtail or to eliminate this form of payment in kind. A variety of new forms of allowances or payments in kind may be developed for workers: the provision for medical examinations and clinical work and arrangements for the purchase of the industry's products (when directly used by workers) at less than market prices. But these allowances in kind do not constitute a significant fraction of total compensation.

Effect of Economic Development

The proportion of total compensation paid in kind declines generally as economic development proceeds.

Components of Compensation

The money terms of compensation may be divided into wage rates, which may be set in terms of time or related to a measure

[13] H. M. Hailey, *loc. cit.*, p. 1429.
[14] *Report of the Commission Appointed to Inquire into the Unrest in the Mining Industry in Northern Rhodesia in Recent Months*, Lusaka, The Government Printer, 1956 (The Branigan Report), Table 1, p. 7.

of output or performance, and other components of compensation such as vacations and holidays with pay and a wide range of supplementary-pay practices or fringe benefits. The problem of drawing a sharp line of demarcation between wage rates and other components is not significant for the present purposes.

In the course of economic development the total number of such components tends to grow, although some components, such as family allowances, are characteristic of particular national industrial-relations systems. The proportion of the nonbasic wage components to total compensation [15] varies with the type of industrializing elite. The period of history in which a country embarks on its industrialization has a great deal to do with the extent of nonwage-rate components in the early stages of its economic development. The late starters have from the outset adopted many of the supplemental pay practices of the more advanced countries; the proportion to total compensation is accordingly very high.

It is nonetheless valid that economic growth seems to add additional components to compensation, not merely to increase the amount of existing components. There is a tendency to earmark leisure and compensation for particular purposes or to provide compensation in the event of particular contingencies. Rising incomes may be distributed in a variety of ways; inflation has often added components to compensation; [16] compensation is used to meet a variety of contingencies of industrial society and to curb or to stimulate workers and managers in the face of particular industry problems, for instance, travel time and wet-weather compensation in building construction. A number of the additional components to compensation can be directly related to the role of the government in industrial-relations systems; social-security programs in their full range of components constitute the largest contribution of governments.

[15] "Wages and Related Elements of Labour Cost in European Industry, 1955: A Preliminary Report," *International Labour Review*, December 1957, pp. 558–587.
[16] John T. Dunlop and Melvin Rothbaum, "International Comparisons of Wage Structures," *International Labour Review*, April 1955, pp. 8–10, 19.

Effect of Economic Development

The number of the components of compensation tends to expand in the process of industrial development.

Wage-rate Structure

The wage-rate structure is the complex of time or performance rates applicable to the different individuals or groupings of workers in an enterprise or an industrial-relations system of larger scope. In the early stages of industrial development only personalized wages may exist; the notion of wage rates for job classifications or for a series of explicit tasks may not have been established. Indeed, one of the first effects of industrial growth in an enterprise of some size is to create an explicit wage scale for more or less defined occupations or jobs. A time rate for a job, or a reasonably limited range of such rates, requires a degree of standardization and uniformity within the work force that is grouped together in one job category.

The emergence of an explicit wage scale is accordingly linked to the ordering or structuring of the labor force by skill or performance that was noted in the previous section. A piecework or performance method of payment is compatible with much wider differences in training and skills among members of a work force; it is no accident that because of wide differences within a new and changing work force piecework is prevalent in hired agricultural employment and on plantations. Piecework is predominant in many of the earliest industries to arise in the classical pattern of industrialization, such as textiles, clothing, and shoes.

During the early phases of industrial development, it is well established that the skill differentials in the wage-rate structure tend to be relatively wide.[17] The supply of skilled labor tends to

[17] For instance, International Labor Office, *Problems of Wage Policy in Asian Countries,* Studies and Reports, New Series, No. 43, Geneva, 1956, pp. 24–27; Lloyd G. Reynolds and Cynthia H. Taft, *The Evolution of Wage Structure,* New Haven, Conn., Yale University Press, 1956, pp. 355–360.

be relatively short compared to unskilled workers. The types of skilled jobs required by industrial employment are not found in preindustrial countries and the requisite workers must be created by training or importing. Either method of recruitment results in relatively wide skill differentials. In many parts of Africa and the Middle East the skilled manual jobs will pay three or four times the unskilled rates.[18] The actual skill differentials may be further widened in the early stages by differentials of race.[19] The skilled manual workers may be white and the unskilled black. In such cases some of these wage differentials may not infrequently be as high as ten or twelve times. Not only may European rates be paid the whites but the costs of transportation may be necessary to recruit the skilled labor, and these costs may subsequently be incorporated in the rates.

In the course of economic development skill differentials tend to narrow. As a rough generalization, the skill wage differential among manual workers in enterprises in advanced countries tends to be of the order of magnitude of 25 to 50 percent more than unskilled rates, compared to the 200 to 400 percent or more that skilled manual rates seem to exceed unskilled rates in the early stages of industrialization. The narrowing process is related to the rise of general levels of education and the spread of technical education, the creation of a stable work force in enterprises that can increase the supply of skilled workers by gradual upgrading and training on the job, the emergence of a local supply which reduces the need to import skilled labor incurring the costs of transport and movement, the rise of industrial organizations among workers which may press for more equalization in rates, and inflationary periods in which relatively uniform general wage-rate increases are made on grounds of equity. The elimination or narrowing of other wage differentials will also tend to narrow the gross skill differentials, such as the elimination or reduction of explicit wage categories by race or nationality.

[18] International Labor Office, *Yearbook of Labour Statistics, 1957*, Geneva.
[19] "The Interracial Wage Structure in Certain Parts of Africa," *International Labour Review*, July 1958, pp. 20–55.

The process of creating a labor market tends to eliminate many of the differentiations among workers which are a carry-over from the preindustrial society and which are frequently reflected in wage-rate differentials at the early stages. The assignment of manual jobs by tribe, nationality, or race creates wage differentials which later tend to be eliminated. The assignment of the work force between manual and clerical operations or between mechanical and menial tasks by nationality or tribe are common illustrations. The wage-rate differentials established at the early stages for women and children also tend to show a gradual reduction for comparable operations during the course of economic development. At times the reduction or elimination of such wage-rate differentials directly reflects labor-market developments in the underdeveloped country but more often it reflects the importation of industrial values and specific legislation or international labor conventions from abroad.

Not only does an explicit wage-rate structure emerge in the rules of an enterprise, but a hierarchy of wage rates also emerges among enterprises in the same industry, among industries, and among localities and regions. It does not matter for the present purposes what part of the total interenterprise wage-rate structure of a country is subject to explicit rules and decisions within a national industrial system and which wage-rate relationships are left solely to the workings of the market. In some countries there comes to be a high degree of centralization of wage-rate changes and wage-setting institutions. The arrangements in Australia, New Zealand, the Netherlands, Scandinavia, and Italy are illustrative, although the rule-making processes formally provide for quite different relations among the actors in these national industrial-relations systems. In other countries the interdependence of wage rates among enterprises is reflected more exclusively through the market. In the course of economic development wage rates in an enterprise tend to become relatively more interdependent (whether or not formally recognized in wage-setting machinery) with the wage rates established in other enterprises. The wage rates established within an enterprise can less and less ignore the wage decisions made in other enterprises,[20] although the wage rates established in some groupings of enterprises (contour) are more relevant to an enterprise than all other wage rates set in a country.[21]

The course of economic development tends to narrow inter-enterprise differentials in the wage-rate structure of a country. A grouping of enterprises with common or similar product and labor markets may develop very similar or identical wage rates; this is often seen at an early stage among a group of cotton-textile plants in a single locality or region. The development of the transportation system historically has affected both the movement of products and workers and hence the interdependence of wage rates in different enterprises. The development of a system of roads and the emergence of trucking enterprises very early in the economic development of a country tend to have a significant impact upon the interdependence of the wage-rate structure of a country, particularly for enterprises which are closely competitive in the selling of their products.

The interdependence of wage rates among enterprises in similar product markets, particularly in one locality or region, tends to emerge before the general interdependence among regions. As economic development proceeds further, as levels of employment rise (and underemployment declines), as capital flows more readily among regions (to the south of many countries), the wage rates among localities tend to become more interdependent and pure geographical wage-rate differentials also tend to narrow percentagewise from what they were in the early stages of economic growth.

An industrial wage-rate structure gradually evolves in a country in the process of economic growth as the range of economic

[20] One of the principal functions of the trade unions in Yugoslavia is to be concerned with the emerging wage relationships among enterprises in the same locality and enterprises in the same industrial sector in different localities.

[21] John T. Dunlop, Ed., *The Theory of Wage Determination*, London, Macmillan and Company, 1957, pp. 3–24.

activity expands and new industries arise. The industrial wage structure is characteristically built on top of the rates for hired agricultural labor. In a country with a large population of under-employed agriculture workers, the industrial wage structure may start only slightly above agricultural levels, while in an empty country the industrial wage structure may start at some distance above agricultural rate levels.[22] The industrial wage-rate structure shows a high degree of similarity (rank correlations of industrial average hourly earnings are high) among countries at comparable levels of development. This similarity among countries in the process of economic development is to be explained by the fact that industries use roughly similar technologies among countries which implies roughly similar proportions of workers in occupations or jobs of varying skills (and wage-rate levels). Although the percentage differentials for skill among countries varies, as has been observed, the relative ordering of the wage rates for job classifications in an industry shows a high degree of similarity among countries. Combining a similarity in the proportions of workers at different occupations in an industry with a similarity in ranking of rates for these occupations yields industrial averages of wage rates or earnings that tend to be relatively quite similar among countries in the process of industrializing.[23]

As economic growth proceeds, new industries arise to be slotted into the industrial wage structure, in part determined by the proportions of workers of varying skills, by the requirements for new skills, and by the level of rates that are required to attract workers to an expanding industry. Many of these newer industries tend to be high-wage industries for these reasons. Economic growth thus imparts an upward drift to the average wage in the country by virtue of an increasing proportion of higher wage industries. The course of economic development, however, ap-

[22] W. A. Lewis, *loc. cit.*, pp. 139–191.
[23] There are, of course, differences in the interindustry wage structures arising from some differences in technology, relative factor prices, and labor supplies and the extent to which women and younger persons are utilized, often at lower wage rates.

parently does not appear to have the effect of compressing significantly the industrial wage structure.

Effects of Economic Development

1. The process of economic development creates an explicit wage-rate structure for job classifications or occupations in the enterprise.

2. Economic growth tends to narrow, in percentage terms, wage-rate differentials among types of skill.

3. The industrialization process tends to eliminate or to narrow many wage-rate differentials that arise at the outset of economic development which are a reflection of differentiations (for example, by sex, tribe, nationality, race) among workers significant to preindustrial society. New differentiations arise, characteristic of the industrial society.

4. The process of economic development creates a national wage-rate structure or hierarchy of rates exterior to an enterprise which may in varying degrees be the subject of explicit rules or left largely to the market in different countries.

5. A greater degree of interdependence in the interenterprise wage structure is likely to emerge first among enterprises in the same or closely allied product markets in a locality. Wage-rate differentials among such enterprises tend to narrow, or the wage rates become uniform. Uniformity spreads to enterprises in more distant localities in the same product grouping (contour).

6. The geographical differentials in the wage-rate structure tend to narrow only at a later phase in economic development.

7. The interindustry wage-rate structure among countries in the process of industrializing tends to be similar, and the course of development tends to introduce new industries often at the higher end of the wage-rate structure. There appears to be little systematic narrowing of the industrial structure in the course of economic growth, except as the industrial wage structure is a reflection of changes in the occupational, geographical, and age or sex wage differentials.

Methods of Wage Payment

The relative distribution between time and piece (or incentive) methods of wage payment probably shows little consistent pattern in the course of economic development, although there are marked differences in methods of wage payment among countries [24] and in the policies of industrializing elites. The circumstances which give rise to piece (or incentive) rates at the early stages of industrialization are replaced by others in the course of economic growth. At the outset there are likely to be very wide differences in the quality and performance of members of the work force; moreover, payment-by-time places a heavy burden on supervision which is likely to be in very short supply and relatively expensive. Piece rates have the advantage of paying workers of uneven quality at very different rates (in proportion to their output), and the limited supervision can be concentrated upon the inspection of the quality of output and the rejection of items below quality standards. As capital costs may not be very large, the use of labor of uneven quality under the piece-rate system is not likely to be as expensive as paying a uniform time rate, or seeking to grade workers or to maintain a larger supervisory staff. Moreover, if turnover rates are high and labor plentiful, the enterprise can avoid substantial costs of training involved in time rates and need be less concerned about the possibility of higher earnings resulting in a smaller amount of labor inputs, as is sometimes held to characterize labor in the early stages of economic growth.

As industrialization proceeds and a more stable industrial work force is established, the factors leading to the use of piece (or incentive) rates tend to change. The quality of the work force is more uniform; there is more supervision and its relative price has fallen with the narrowing of skill differentials, and the

[24] International Labor Office, *Payment by Results*, Studies and Reports, New Series, No. 27, Geneva, 1953.

labor supply function in the relevant range is probably not negatively inclined. Piece rates (tonnage rates) are often designed now to stimulate a greater rate of effort among trained workers to get the largest utilization of expensive capital equipment; some workers are on nominal incentives to preserve rate relationships and to prevent complaints arising out of comparisons with other workers on piece or incentive rates; the selling field often leads to commission rates on account of the difficulties of supervision with changing work places and the complex salesman-customer relationship. The process of economic development thus changes the problems and the opportunities for using time or piece (and incentive) methods of wage payment.

SETTLEMENT OF DISPUTES OVER EXISTING RULES

The rules of the work place and the work community regarding disputes over the day-to-day application of rules is the third major group of rules treated in this chapter. These procedures particularly well reflect the characteristics of a national industrial-relations system. In some systems there is relatively integrated machinery for the resolution of disputes (Denmark),[25] while in others there may be no single vertex in the procedures with a variety of autonomous bodies (England),[26] and in still others there may be a number of procedures relatively specialized by type of problems with possible conflicts in jurisdiction among these procedures (France).[27] The present interest is rather the way in which the course of economic development affects the wide variety of rules establishd in industrial-relations systems to resolve the numerous disputes and issues that arise over the

[25] Walter Galenson, *The Danish System of Labor Relations,* Cambridge, Mass., Harvard University Press, 1952, pp. 209–232. The machinery consists of the labor court and a network of industrial arbitration boards.

[26] Allen Flanders and H. A. Clegg, Eds., *The System of Industrial Relations in Great Britain,* Oxford, Basil Blackwell, 1954, pp. 42–127, 252–322.

[27] Val R. Lorwin, *The French Labor Movement,* Cambridge, Mass., Harvard University Press, 1954.

administration of the complex of rules. (Rules which apply to a system but are established and interpreted outside the particular system are beyond the scope of the present discussion.)

The forms of industrial disputes and conflict change in the course of economic development. There is a tendency for conflict at the early stages to involve riots, demonstrations, fights, direct action, and spontaneous outbursts. As organizations of workers develop, the forms of conflict tend to become more disciplined. At the early stages the provocation for conflict as frequently concerns complaints in the community as it does complaints in the immediate work place. Thus, at this stage issues of transportation, housing, return to the village and extended family, racial and religious conflicts within the work force, and protests against racial and nationality characteristics of supervision tend to precipitate conflict. In the course of development there is a sharper division between the work place and the larger community in the issues of industrial conflict.

1. In the course of development of an industrial-relations system rules tend to limit stringently the resort to force of the forms just observed, including the strike and lockout. The established procedures are designed as a substitute for such open conflict. In some systems a place for possible open conflict is deliberately retained and defined while in other systems conflict is entirely prohibited. In the United States, for instance, disputes over such items as production standards may be explicitly excluded from arbitration and left to resolution by possible conflict in some industrial-relations systems. There also tend to develop detailed procedures to treat with violations of the rules against the use of force and other violations of the rules of the work place, and there are likely to be specified penalties established which may be invoked within the industrial-relations system.

2. In the earliest stages of industrialization, the development of dispute-settling machinery frequently tends to utilize the pre-existing tribal and family system among the work force. The

following account of the Northern Rhodesian copper mines shows the sequence of development:

> As esult of the recommendations by the Foster Commission the s em of consultation between the mine managements and Afric i tribal elders, established at some of the mines prior to 1940, was developed in 1942 and 1943 into a general system of Tribal Representatives. In 1943 "Boss Boys' Committees" were formed at individual mines. The Tribal Representative system continued to deal with domestic matters, living conditions, etc., exclusive of industrial matters, until it was terminated in 1953. In 1947 and 1948, from the "Boss Boys' Committees" were evolved "Works Committees" representative of African workers in all departments, and during the year 1948 those committees were finally replaced by four African Mineworkers' Unions established at the four major mines with the assistance of a Labour Officer with trade union experience. In May, 1949, these four separate Unions were amalgamated to form the Northern Rhodesia African Mineworkers' Trade Union. . . .[28]

In the later phases of development of an industrial-relations system, procedures for handling disputes over existing rules create neutrals who have final authority to decide certain disputes questions. The emergence of neutrals is often a necessary corollary to the limitations on conflict. Systems differ widely depending on whether such neutrals are the appointees of workers' organizations and managers or selected by government, and different systems illustrate a variety of combinations of interests in these selections. Systems also differ in the extent to which decisions or judgments of neutrals (alone or as the deciding vote in a body with representatives of workers' organizations and managers) are in fact characteristically agreements or mediated solutions to disputes between representatives of the partisans and the extent to which decisions are in fact exclusively litigated judgments.

[28] *Report of the Commission Appointed to Inquire into the Unrest in the Mining Industry in Northern Rhodesia in Recent Months*, Lusaka, The Government Printer, 1956, pp. 13–14.

3. In larger industrial-relations systems provision for specialists or professionals tends to develop in the rules of the work place and in the processing of disputes in the machinery. The rules tend to provide that all disputes must be channelled on each side through these specialists. It is to the interest of each partisan to be concerned about the sequence in which cases are presented to establish a principle, and weak cases may be settled or withdrawn to avoid an adverse precedent on a vital question. Continuing machinery compels attention on each side to strategy which transcends the concern with individual disputes.

4. In the course of development of industrial-relations systems that are above some minimum size, the tendency is for the neutrals to become continuing or permanent, subject to some term of office, rather than limited to a single dispute. The technical nature of the disputes in many industries, the specialists among the workers' organizations and managers, the resort to precedents, and the example of judicial tenure (where governments make the appointments) tend to encourage a degree of stability in the neutral.[29]

5. An industrial-relations system tends to develop a constantly expanding body of precedents in the settlement of disputes over existing rules. These are normally in written form. But the way in which precedents are used and the weight attached to them shows a wide spectrum among systems. Thus, systems differ depending upon whether or not decisions are accompanied by elaborate opinions and explanations. They differ in the extent to which procedures are formal, in the extent to which precedents are regarded as binding on future disputes and in the degree to which argument, evaluation, and the decision on each new dispute are considered in the framework of precedent.

These major characteristics of machinery for the settlement of disputes over existing rules provide a useful check list for a comparison of different arrangements for disputes settlement among

---

[29] The railway boards of adjustment in the United States are an exception. There are also significant exceptions in Great Britain.

both national industrial-relations systems and among different industrial-relations systems within one country. Attention to these points not only traces the evolution of the dispute-settling machinery, but they also reflect the distinctive features of the particular machinery. These are the major features to examine in seeking to understand the dispute-settling machinery in operation.

THE INDUSTRIALIZING ELITES AND RULES OF THE WORK PLACE

The preceding sections have been directed to the problem of the impact of economic development upon the rules for work places and work communities. The discussion concentrated on three broad groups of rules central to every industrial relations system: (1) the recruitment and commitment of a labor force, (2) compensation and wages, and (3) machinery for the settlement of disputes over existing rules. It was suggested that different types of industrializing elites might be expected to develop rules that differed in some respects. The preceding chapter distinguished three ideal types of industrializing elites: the dynastic-feudal, the middle-class, and the revolutionary-intellectual elites. This final section, summarized in the table on pages 377–379, indicates the way in which the body of rules, necessarily created in the process of industrialization, is distinctively fashioned by each of the industrializing elites. Each elite adopts policies and strategies with respect to the organization of the labor market, wage policy, and dispute settlement which are different in some significant respects.

Recruitment and Commitment of a Labor Force

Each of the industrializing elites tends to approach the development of a labor market with somewhat different interests, objectives, and methods. The dynastic-feudal elite is anxious to preserve as much as possible of the pre-existing social and family arrangements and the differentiations among groups of potential workers. The middle class has no particular attachment or animus toward the pre-existing arrangements among potential workers, but they advocate changes brought about by the working of a labor market structured by the middle class in which movements of workers are ordered by the choices of individual workers registered in the market against the demands of employers. The revolutionary intellectuals seek rapidly to sweep away the pre-existing differentiations; agricultural policy is designed to separate potential workers from the land leaving them to go to the cities, and strong indirect pressures and even enforced direction is used to secure the rapid creation and allocation of the industrial labor force.

1. *Labor contractors.* The dynastic-feudal elite tends to preserve for the longest period the labor contractor and family or tribal arrangements used to recruit a labor force. This elite tends to emphasize the recruitment of primary families rather than single individuals; its paternal characteristics are apt to stress housing and community services. The middle-class elite uses labor contractors in some restricted circumstances such as for some casual labor, but much more reliance is placed upon the labor market in recruiting a work force. There is no particular interest in family recruitment, and enterprises will seek the labor supply (men, women, or children) available at the lowest price, consonant with minimum standards established in the community. Housing and community services are established by enterprises only to the minimum extent necessary to recruit labor in the rare case when such services have not been furnished by the market. The revolutionary-intellectual elite uses the machinery of the party and state rather than labor contractors or pre-existing tribal or family arrangements to recruit and to channel an industrial labor supply. It places less reliance upon the labor market than does the middle-class elite. There is more paternalistic interest

in housing and community services than in the middle-class elite typically, on the pragmatic grounds that a minimum of such facilities is essential to the rapid build-up of an industrial labor supply; but it has less concern with housing and family than evidenced by the dynastic-feudal elite.

2. *Training.* The dynastic-feudal elite is least concerned with the development of formal training arrangements either in the enterprise or the community. The slower pace of industrialization and the objective of minimum dislocation of the established order leads to minimal training for workers. The training that does take place is in the traditional apprenticeship patterns. Formal technical and professional training for the small elite receives more emphasis. The middle-class elite develops formal training programs in the enterprise primarily in response to immediate market pressures from labor shortages; in the absence of such incentives few programs for workers are established, and the enterprises seek a labor supply of the requisite skill from the labor market. The community develops broad programs of general, technical, and professional education available to workers and their children as to all citizens. The revolutionary-intellectual elite, concerned with achieving the most rapid possible pace of industrialization, recognizes from the outset the necessity for a program of intensive and narrow specialization in training both in enterprises and in the community.

3. *Layoff policies.* In the system led by the dynastic-feudal elite rules tend to develop which severely restrict the temporary or permanent layoff of workers. Layoffs tend to violate the paternal character of the system; they complicate housing arrangements, and they are at variance with the presumptions behind recruitment. The middle-class elite regards temporary and permanent layoffs as normal and necessary features of the operation of the labor market. While some rules are developed to constrain and cushion the impact of layoffs, few attempts are made to prevent layoffs outright. The primary concern is to develop rules which establish the priorities and relative rights of individual

workers in jobs. The revolutionary-intellectual elite places strictures on layoffs which lie between the other two elites. The short-term fluctuations in employment are reduced by the normal adjustment of the total work force to the planned level of output.

Wage Policies

Each industrializing elite tends to develop compensation and wage policies which are consonant with their arrangement of the labor market and wider strategy of the industrialization process.

Payments in kind. The dynastic-feudal elite is most likely to adopt payments in kind and to retain them longer than either of the two elites. Payments in kind are well regarded in themselves. The middle-class elite would regard such payments as temporary and exceptional departures from a market economy, while the revolutionary-intellectual elite is more inclined to use these methods of compensation when essential to the direct allocation of the labor force.

4. *Fringe benefits.* The dynastic-feudal elite tends to multiply particularly the components of compensation and to put particular emphasis upon family allowances, social-security benefits, and the like, so that basic wage rates constitute a relatively smaller proportion of total compensation. In the system of the middle-class elite there is a tendency to pay a much larger fraction of total compensation in basic wage rates and to look to individual workers to allocate income among competing uses rather than to predetermine such allocation. There is relatively little interest in family allowances. The separate components of compensation that arise are frequently designed to regulate management or meet specialized industry problems rather than to increase income. The compensation system serves a significant regulatory function of enterprise management. The revolutionary-intellectual elite tends to develop a relatively larger number of components of compensation than the middle-class elite, and

these are frequently designed to affect the direction and supply of workers rather than to circumscribe management.

5. *Wage-rate differentials.* The dynastic-feudal elite tends to establish much lower wage-rate differentials for skill than in the case of the other two elites. The dynastic-feudal elite does not need such wide differentials to recruit skilled labor with a relatively slower rate of industrialization. The wage structure of the country as a whole is less highly interdependent, and product-market competition is a much less active factor influencing relative wage rates and the allocation of the labor force. In the economy of the middle-class elite, all wage-rate differentials are relatively more interdependent and more responsive to labor- and product-market competitive conditions. Skill differentials tend to be determined in the same way. The revolutionary-intellectual elite establishes relatively wide skill differentials to help to attract the large amount of skilled labor needed in a short period of time. The wage structure, as the price structure, on the whole plays a less immediate and short-run role in the allocation of resources. The wage-rate structure is less responsive to changes in product prices, and accordingly it is less interdependent than in the middle-class elite economy.

6. *Incentive payments.* The dynastic-feudal elite tends to use piece rate and incentive methods of wage payments least frequently, while the revolutionary intellectuals, in their drive for production, seek to use them as universally as possible. In the system led by the middle-class elite piece rates tend to be used only moderately.

The Settlement of Disputes

The procedures established by the industrializing elites for the settlement of disputes over existing rules also tend to show some characteristic differences. The dynastic-feudal elite establishes industrial-relations systems which leave no role for conflict.

The neutrals are government representatives, and the parties have little direct role in their selection or in shaping directly the decisions. The proceedings tend to be formal, and decisions are seldom a form of agreement. The neutrals tend to be lawyers, and great weight is attached to formal precedents. The middle class establishes industrial-relations systems which deliberately leave some room for conflict on some types of disputes in the event of failure to achieve an earlier agreement. The parties play a large role in the selection of neutrals whether or not they are appointed by governments. The proceedings tend to be more informal, and decisions are frequently mediated and constitute real agreement between the parties. Neutrals need not be lawyers. Precedents are more flexibly used. The revolutionary intellectuals establish industrial-relations systems which provide no room for conflict. The neutrals are government appointed, and procedures tend to be formal. Neutrals are likely to be trained as lawyers. Any mediation of the dispute is likely to involve the roles of party and governmental agencies rather than the managers and workers' organizations, although some of the same individuals may be involved.

Groups of Rules	Dynastic-feudal Elite	Middle-class Elite	Revolutionary-intellectual Elite
1. *Procurement of a labor force*			
(a) Recruitment	Preserves for the longest period labor contractors and family or tribal recruitment. Housing and community services regarded as desirable. Family rather than individual recruitment.	Very restricted use of labor contractors; primary reliance on labor market to recruit workers. Housing and community services only rarely established by enterprises. Individual or family recruitment.	Agricultural policy designed to release labor; party and state apparatus directs flow of workers by pronouncements and at times by forced orders. Housing and community services used where regarded as pragmatically essential.
(b) Training	Least concerned with training in enterprise or community. Traditional apprenticeship pattern. Technical and professional training for elite.	Training in enterprise varies with the shortage of workers. Community develops broad programs of technical and professional training with all citizens eligible. Broad training.	Elaborate training programs in enterprises and in the community required by rapid industrialization from backward levels. Narrow, specialized, and rapid training. Technical and professional education provided for large groups selected by elite.
(c) Redundancy	Severe restrictions on layoffs developed in rules.	Layoffs a normal condition of employment. Rules cushion layoffs and assign priorities in remaining employment opportunities.	Short-term fluctuations in employment reduced by concern to attain production plans; short-term fluctuations in markets are of little significance to employment.

Groups of Rules	Dynastic-feudal Elite	Middle-class Elite	Revolutionary-intellectual Elite
2. *Compensation and wages*			
(a) Payments in kind	Most likely to adopt payments in kind and to retain them longest.	Payments in kind regarded as undesirable and temporary departure from the market.	Some use of payments in kind when essential to direct the labor supply.
(b) Components of compensation	Components of compensation other than basic wages the largest proportion of total money compensation. High family allowances and high social-security payments.	Basic wages relatively much larger proportion of total money compensation. Against family allowances. Moderate social-security payments. Components of compensation often designed to regulate managements or meet specific industry problems.	Components to compensation other than basic wages are relatively large. Moderate family allowances and high social-security payments. The components of compensation are directed to control the work force rather than regulate managements.
(c) Wage-rate structure	Wage rates not highly interdependent. Relatively low skill differentials.	Highly interdependent wage-rate structure. Skill differentials sensitive to labor market and typically moderate.	Wage-rate structure not highly interdependent. Skill differentials relatively large.
(d) Piece rates	Few piece rates.	Moderate number of piece rates.	Extensive use of piece rates.

| 3. *Procedures for settlement of disputes over existing rules* | There is no room for conflict. Neutrals are government representatives. Parties have little voice in their selection. Formal proceedings. Decisions are seldom a form of agreement. | Some disputes may be left to agreement-making and possible conflict. Neutrals need not be government representatives nor lawyers. Parties have large voice in their selection. Informal proceedings. Decisions are often a form of agreement. | There is no room for conflict. Neutrals are government representatives. Formal proceedings. Decisions are seldom a form of agreement between managers and workers' organizations in these roles although the same individuals may play a role as representative of party. |

10 · General Theory
of Industrial Relations

THIS volume seeks to present a new way of thinking about
industrial-relations experience. It develops a systematic body
of ideas for arranging and interpreting the known facts of worker-
manager-government interactions; it also provides a set of concepts fitted together that require the collection of new facts, presented in new categories. The rules of the work place and work
community become the general focus of inquiry to be explained
by theoretical analysis.

The analytical framework formulated and illustrated in the
preceding chapters would release industrial-relations discussion
from the preoccupation, if not the obsession, with labor peace
and warfare. Industrial strife is a surface symptom of more fundamental characteristics of rule making and administration in a
given industrial relations context. This body of ideas is also designed to shift industrial-relations perspective from collective
bargaining, as it first developed in Great Britain and as it is
known in the United States, to the full spectrum of contemporary
industrial relations.[1] A general theory of industrial relations is
proposed, not alone to encompass countries with diverse eco-

[1] Clark Kerr, Frederick H. Harbison, John T. Dunlop and Charles A.
Myers, "The Labour Problem in Economic Development," *International
Labour Review*, March 1955, pp. 3–15.

nomic and political forms, but also to relate experience in component sectors to a country as a whole.

The central concept is that of an *industrial-relations system*. The idea is derived in part from the intuition of practitioners and from the growing number of titles written by careful observers of countrywide industrial-relations practices that use the term "system" without explicit or rigorous definition. These insights suggested that the notion of an industrial-relations system might be a fruitful starting point for more systematic work.[2] Moreover, the analogy of the constructive use of "system" in economics comes readily to mind. While a glance at the world of affairs may belie resort to an idea that denotes order and an inner rationality, economics has developed a rigorous analytical discipline, applicable to a variety of political forms, which highlights the interdependence of activity within a system, the response of the output of the system to exterior changes and features of long-term development from within a system.

There are, of course, serious pitfalls to the direct transfer of concepts from one field of intellectual activity to another, although the danger is probably the more serious the greater the distance of transfer across fields. Each theoretical edifice for a new discipline must be designed afresh if it is to meet the tests of consistency, style and, most of all, usefulness. Formalism rather than functional design is no less sterile in intellectual model building than in using bricks and mortar.

It is important to be clear about the relations between the study of industrial relations and other social sciences, particularly about its relation to economics. In the United States and Great Britain the study of industrial relations is, in large part, an offshoot of economics, although other fields have made some contributions. In France it appears as if the industrial sociologists have been most concerned with developing the field. In many other countries it is largely the preserve of lawyers. In all coun-

[2] Joyce Cary, *Art and Reality*, Cambridge, England, University Press, 1958, pp. 1, 96.

tries it has been a crossroads where various specialties have converged. The present purpose has been to present a distinctive analytical apparatus for the study of the industrial-relations aspects of behavior in industrial society.

An industrial-relations system is a subsystem of the social system. It is on the same logical plane as an economic system. Both abstract from many significant aspects of human behavior, and both select a limited number of aspects of behavior for rigorous inquiry. Each takes certain data as given, and each seeks to explain limited features of behavior in terms of a small number of variables within its system.[3] But the two systems are not identical, and the disciplines of economic theory and industrial relations have different major problems and analytical subject matter.

Some parameters that are given in economic theory are variables in industrial relations. The rules on workmen's inspectors in coal mining or apprenticeship in building, to select two examples from Chapters 5 and 6, are treated in economics as data or as given from outside the economic system; they are not to be explained. These rules have the same status in economics as technical (engineering) conditions of production. For industrial relations these particular rules are rather variables to be explained by the operation of the industrial-relations system.

There are other parameters treated as given in industrial relations that are variables in economic theory. The level of economic activity and the rate of economic growth, for example, are treated in the main as given for industrial relations but are variables to be explained in economic theory. Other parameters such as technical (engineering) conditions are treated as given for both disciplines. Still other parameters, notably the setting of rules of compensation and the operation of labor markets, are to be explained within both systems.

The economic system and the industrial-relations system are thus partially overlapping, and the disciplines of economics and

[3] J. Tinbergen, *On the Theory of Economic Policy*, 2d Ed., Amsterdam, North-Holland Publishing Company, 1955, pp. 1–26.

industrial relations are closely related although they select different variables and givens from industrial society. Economics centers its attention on the national product (output) and its variation over time, and industrial relations centers its attention on the rules of the system and their variations over time. The national product has certain common-sense meaning, but it is only to be fully understood in terms of the operation of the economic system as a whole. The web of rules likewise conveys a common-sense meaning, but it also is to be understood in terms of the operation of the industrial relations system in its entirety.

An industrial-relations system is comprised of three groups of actors—workers and their organizations, managers and their organizations, and governmental agencies concerned with the work place and work community. These groups interact within a specified environment comprised of three interrelated contexts: the technology, the market or budgetary constraints and the power relations in the larger community and the derived status of the actors. An industrial-relations system creates an ideology or a commonly shared body of ideas and beliefs regarding the interaction and roles of the actors which helps to bind the system together.

Some rules are more or less directly related to the technological and market context of the system, and other rules are associated more uniquely with the power status of the actors in the larger society. Thus, in coal mining similar rules across countries with diverse economic and political systems were observed relating to workmen's safety inspectors, concessionary coal, housing for miners, wet conditions or high temperatures, the measurement of the working day for underground miners, tools and protective clothing, rights in jobs, and some aspects of compensation, particularly the occupational structure (see Chapter 5). In building, rules that are similar across countries were observed relating to travel compensation, unfavorable weather, apprenticeship, the protection of standard conditions, layoffs and hirings, tools and some aspects of compensation, particularly the area rate (see

Chapter 6). The common elements in these rules across countries were attributed largely to the common characteristics of the technological and market or budgetary contexts. It was recognized that in some cases the explicit international borrowing of rules may have arisen from the migration of workers, managers, and engineering enterprises. But even in these cases the industrial relations climate in the importing country would have to be congenial for the transplanted rule to take root and flourish.

Even within the group of rules attributed largely to the technological and market or budgetary contexts, numerous illustrations were observed of the influence of the national social systems. Thus, the distribution of concesisonary coal in accordance with size of family in France and Germany and equally among households in the United States and Great Britain is a reflection of national industrial-relations characteristics in a rule largely oriented toward a common technological and market context. Or the rules relating to travel time and travel expense all draw the distinction between job sites within communting distance and job sites which require a change in living quarters, but the distances which workers are expected to travel, the means of transport, and a variety of other features of these rules reflect national industrial-relations characteristics. The three-kilometer zone in Geneva and the bicycle allowance in the Netherlands are illustrative. Thus, almost any rule involves the subtle weaving together of technological and market influences and the special characteristics of the national industrial relations system. The context is a whole.

The brief survey of some major rules in coal mining and building provides numerous instances of rules which primarily reflect the status of the actors in the national industrial-relations systems. The diverse rules defining the status of labor organizations in their relations to members, workers' councils, rival union organizations, managements, and governmental agencies are illustrative. The pluralistic arrangements as to organizations of workers in the French coal mines as compared to compulsory union membership in New Zealand are indicative of the role of the national industrial-relations systems in the rules of particular work places. The rules relating to methods of settling disputes and extending rules from one group of enterprises throughout a coal industry are of the same order. In the building industry, the rules in the United States relating to jurisdiction, union security, and hiring arrangements, the prohibition of piece or incentive methods of wage payment, and the absence of age differentiation in the wage structure were attributed to the distinctive features of the national industrial-relations system rather than to the technological and market characteristics of building.

The context of an industrial-relations system is not alone significant to its substantive rules but also to the internal organization of the hierarchies of workers, managers, and specialized governmental agencies. The formal organizations, the actual internal operations of all three actors and their interaction are sensitive to the variety of technologies and markets or budgets created by industrial society. The status of the actors will likewise affect the forms and the operations of the separate hierarchies. Consider, for instance, the differences in the internal organization of industrial-relations systems in large industrial plants, in the mobile work places of transportation, and in the shifting sites of construction, and further consider the differences in the internal organization of each in the USSR, the United States, Spain, and Yugoslavia. The scope of the organization of each actor, the specialization of functions, the resort to specialized personnel in rule-making, the degree of centralization in policy making and administration, the matching of corresponding levels of contact in the several hierarchies, the channels of internal communication within each hierarchy, indeed, the whole setup of the actors to produce and to administer rules is responsive to the context of the industrial-relations system.

The concept of an industrial-relations system is deliberately variable in scope; it may be used to characterize an immediate work place, an enterprise, a sector, or a country as a whole. The grouping cannot be arbitrary or capricious; the work places and the actors, at varying levels, that are grouped together must reflect a considerable degree of cohesiveness and formal or informal interdependence. Although the scope of an industrial-relations system is variable, according to the problem at hand, the formal structure of the system and its internal logic is unchanged. The scope of the hierarchies of the actors, their prescribed relations, the actual technology, and markets or budgets and the rules which they establish are different. But the logic of a system does not alter with its scope.

The comparative analysis of industrial relations among sectors within a country is facilitated by use of the notion of a system in the same way that comparisons are made among countries. As the scope of a system is narrowed within a country from a large sector to an industry or to an enterprise, the context naturally changes. The status of the actors is particularly affected. Rule-making by the actors at the plant level in the engineering industry in Great Britain or the basic steel industry in the United States is, within relatively narrow limits, prescribed by rules established by the national actors for these sectors. The status of the local actors and their degrees of freedom is prescribed at these plant levels in the analogous way that the status of the actors in a national system is defined by its larger community, the full social system.

An industrial-relations system, within a country, is a device to integrate the study of wage rates and other forms of compensation with industrial-relations experience. One of the major difficulties with the present state of discussions of wage determination is that wages tend either to be completely isolated from industrial relations, as in formal economic theory, or they are treated as a vague response to organized pressures in industrial-relations discussions.

Wage rates and other forms of compensation are here treated as another group of rules of the work place, on the same plane as rules respecting physical working conditions or discharge and layoffs. This procedure has the merit of showing how the forms of the rules on compensation, such as travel pay in building, and underground allowances in some coal-producing countries, are directly related to other rules. Wage rules and other rules are not two separate boxes; there is a single highly interrelated body of rules in an industrial-relations system. The actors are frequently concerned with the internal consistency and the internal interdependence among the rules. It is well known that there are substitutions in bargaining, in national industrial-relations systems with collective bargaining, between wage rules and other rules. The rules on wages are related to other rules on the development of a labor force, as was observed for industrializing countries in Chapter 9. The concepts here developed help to break down an artificial barrier between wage rules and all other rules.

The scope of an industrial relations system within a country is directly related to the problems of wage determination. In another connection the idea has been developed of a *wage contour* as a wage-setting unit.[4] The wage contour consists of a grouping of enterprises with uniquely interdependent wage rates and other forms of compensation. Thus, the group of plants in the basic-steel industry in the United States or the engineering sector in Great Britain constitutes a wage contour. The scope of a wage contour can be identified with an industrial-relations system. The study of wage setting and the formation of other rules normally make use of a common grouping of enterprises, although the precise scope of enterprises may vary with some rules.

An industrial-relations system can be used as a tool of analysis as in comparative statics to explore the relationship between changes in elements of the system and changes in rules. A significant change in technology, in the market or budgetary context, in the status of the actors (reflected into the industrial-relations system from the larger community), or in the ideology of the sys-

[4] John T. Dunlop, "The Task of Contemporary Wage Theory," in *New Concepts in Wage Determination*, George W. Taylor and Frank C. Pierson, Eds., New York, McGraw Hill Book Company, 1957, pp. 131–134.

tem may be expected to change one or more rules. There is a significant place in the discipline of industrial relations for deductive propositions, checked by empirical testing, relating specified changes in the system to specific changes in the rules. The following illustrations, drawn from Chapters 5 to 7, may better convey this judgment.

The rules in coal mining regarding the measurement of the work day, portal-to-portal, and the rules in countries with hot mining temperatures are to be directly related to the deepening of mines or the lengthening of drifts. The postwar changes in the market position of coal, as compared to conditions in the two decades between the wars, vitally affected the rules prescribing the level of wage rates compared to other industries. A shift from family management to professional management may be expected to create a more explicit body of rules. The change in the ideology of the Yugoslav system in the period 1950–1952 was an independent factor having influence on the complex of rules defining the status of the actors.

An industrial-relations system implies an inner unity and consistency, and a significant change in one facet of the context or the ideology may be expected to displace an old equilibrium (in the comparative statics sense) and to create new positions within the system and new rules.

The concept of an industrial relations system is used most fruitfully as a tool of analysis when a specific system is examined in its historical context, and changes in the system are studied through time. While comparative statics is likely to be fruitful in analyzing the consequences of changes in technology and market or budgetary constraints upon a group of rules, the status of the actors and the unifying ideology or commonly shared beliefs particularly need to be understood historically. (1) The status of the actors in a national industrial relations system is likely to be significantly influenced by the period in world history in which the system was first congealed, or drastically reconstructed following a revolution or a war. (2) The status of workers, managers and governmental agencies in a national system is much affected by the sequence in which the larger community secures independence, starts its industrialization drive and recasts traditional or preindustrial political forms. (3) The status of the actors alters systematically in the course of economic development and varies according to whether the industrializing leaders conform to the ideal types of the dynastic-feudal, the middle class or the revolutionary-intellectual elites (see Chapter 8).

The main outlines of a national industrial-relations system emerge at a relatively early stage in economic development. The power context is set early and is much influenced by the industrializing elite. While a national industrial-relations system, and particularly the status of the actors, gradually evolves in a variety of ways with the industrialization process, the main structure and relations of a system congeal early, unless transformed by revolution or the dislocations of war in the larger community. Accordingly the present generation is extremely sensitive in the formation of industrial-relations systems in the large number of countries recently embarked on the road to the industrial society.

The whole complex of rules of the work place and work community is altered through changes in a national industrial-relations system during the course of economic development. The rules relating to the procurement of a labor force, compensation and wages and the settlement of disputes were examined in Chapter 9 and were related to the industrializing process and to the type of elite directing the transformation to modern industry.

Index